REVOLUTION AND FOREIGN POLICY: THE CASE OF SOUTH YEMEN 1967–1987

This book is a study of the foreign policy of South Yemen, the most radical of Arab states, from the time of its independence from Britain in 1967 until 1987. It covers relations with the west, including the USA, and with the USSR and China, and also highlights South Yemen's conflicts with its neighbours, North Yemen, Saudi Arabia and Oman. The author provides a detailed analysis of the foreign relations of one of the USSR's closest allies in the third world and shows how conflicts within the country relate to changes in foreign policy.

South Yemen has traditionally not been an easy country for analysts to study, both because it is so secretive and because the revolutionary regime still arouses such strong passions. Professor Halliday is, however, one of the few since 1967 who has been able to visit the country to collect material and has carried out one of the most thorough investigations yet into the foreign policy of any state in the Arab world.

Revolution and Foreign Policy: the Case of South Yemen 1967–1987

Cambridge Middle East Library aims to bring together outstanding scholarly work on the political, social and economic history, politics, sociology and economics of the Middle East and North Africa in the nineteenth and twentieth centuries. While primarily focussing on monographs by younger scholars based on original research, the series will also incorporate broader surveys and in-depth treatments by more established scholars.

Revolution and Foreign Policy
The Case of South Yemen 1967–1987

FRED HALLIDAY

The right of the University of Cambridge to print and sell all manner of books was granted by Henry VIII in 1534. The University has printed and published continuously since 1584.

CAMBRIDGE UNIVERSITY PRESS

CAMBRIDGE

NEW YORK PORT CHESTER MELBOURNE SYDNEY

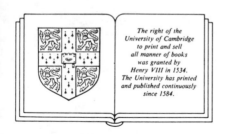

Published by the Press Syndicate of the University of Cambridge
The Pitt Building, Trumpington Street, Cambridge CB2 1RP
40 West 20th Street, New York, NY 10011, USA
10 Stamford Road, Oakleigh, Melbourne 3166, Australia

First published 1990

Printed in Great Britain at The University Press, Cambridge

British Library cataloguing in publication data

Halliday, Fred, *1946–*
Revolution and foreign policy: the case of South
Yemen 1967–1987. – (Cambridge Middle East library; 21).
1. (People's Democratic Republic) Yemen. Foreign
relations, 1967–1987
I. Title
327.53'35

Library of Congress cataloguing in publication data

Halliday, Fred.
Revolution and foreign policy : the case of South Yemen 1967–1987
/ Fred Halliday
p. cm. – (Cambridge Middle East library)
Bibliography.
Includes index.
ISBN 0-521-32856-X
1. Yemen (People's Democratic Republic) – Foreign relations.
I. Title. II. Series.
DS247.A28H35 1989 89-583 CIP
327.53'35—dc 19

ISBN 0 521 32856 X

SE

Contents

Acknowledgements

Research on this book can be said to have begun nearly two decades ago, when I first visited South Yemen in early 1970. At that time the revolutionary regime had been in power for little over two years, the left-wing leadership that emerged from the 'Corrective Move' of June 1969 had been in office less than six months. Aden presented itself as the centre of a revolutionary movement that encompassed North Yemen, Oman and, across the Red Sea, Eritrea, and it is to a considerable extent the origins and subsequent development of that internationalist commitment that I have tried to analyse in this book.

I was fortunate in 1970, and again in 1973, to visit the guerrilla-held areas of Oman, and to discuss at length with the leadership of that movement the role which South Yemen was playing in the Arabian Peninsula. During my stay in Aden in 1977, I was able to meet a wide range of government and party officials, including Foreign Minister Muṭiyyaᶜ, and representatives of opposition movements from North Yemen, Saudi Arabia, Bahrain, Oman, Iraq, Egypt, Palestine, Sudan, Iran and the various regions of Ethiopia. Representatives of a number of countries allied to the PDRY, including Cuba and Ethiopia, were especially helpful in discussing their relations with Aden. Later, in Ethiopia in 1977, in Iran in 1979, and in North Yemen in 1984, it became possible for me to assess, from the vantage-point of these countries that had themselves passed through a revolutionary phase, the contribution of South Yemen to the upheavals of the 1960s and beyond. On visits to Washington in the late 1970s and early 1980s, and on visits to Moscow in 1982, 1984, and 1987. I was able to gather background information on how the great powers regarded events in South Arabia.

In 1970 and on subsequent visits to Aden, and in many conversations conducted elsewhere in the ensuing years, I have benefited greatly from the time and assistance provided by many people, Yemenis and other, concerned with the political and international position of the PDRY. While a conclusive list would be impossible, I would like to record here my thanks to the following people who, over this period, have helped me in this work. Neither before nor after independence has the nationalist and socialist movement in South Yemen been characterised by strategic unity, or by the ability to resolve conflicts in a democratic and responsible manner: the result is that many of those with whom I have spoken during their periods in office have subsequently left power, or lost their lives, as a result of factional disputes. While it is not the role of outsiders to adjudicate in quarrels the full content of which it is difficult for them to assess, I have tried, where relevant, to discuss in the following pages why on the available evidence it would appear that such conflicts erupted. I can only hope that this account, necessarily preliminary, is as honest, accurate and explanatory as is practicable.

Here I would like to record, without distinction of faction or result, my thanks to all those Yemenis who have helped me in my research: Muḥsin al-ʿAyni, Muḥammad ʿAkkūsh, ʿAbd Allāh al-Ashtal, Saʿīd al-ʿAttār, Fayṣal al-ʿAṭṭās, Muḥammad Hādī ʿAwwaḍ, ʿAbd Allāh Bādhīb, ʿAbd al-Razzāḳ Bādhīb, ʿAbd Allāh al-Bār, Ḥasan Bāʿūm, ʿAlī al-Bīḍ, ʿAbd al-ʿAzīz al-Dālī, Saʿīd Djināhī, ʿAbd al-ʿAzīz ʿAbd al-Ghanī, Muḥammad ʿAlī Haytham, Khālid Harīrī, ʿAbd al-Karīm al-Īryānī, ʿAbd al-Fattāḥ Ismāʿīl, ʿAbd al-Malik Ismāʿīl, ʿUmar al-Djāwī, ʿAbd Allāh al-Khāmrī, Saʿīd Khubbārā, Ḥusayn Ḳumāṭa, Thurya Manḳūsh, Muḥammad Midḥī, ʿAlī Nāṣir Muḥammad, Sālim Sāliḥ Muḥammad, ʿAishā Muḥsin, Faḍl Muḥsin, ʿAlī Asʿad Muthanna, Muḥammad Hazā Muḥammad, ʿAbd Allāh Muhayrīz, Muḥammad Sāliḥ Muṭiyyaʿ, Sultān Nādjī, Hādī Aḥmad Nāṣir, Faḍl Salāmī, ʿAbd Allāh al-Sallāl, ʿAlī al-Sayyādī, Nadjīb al-Shamīrī, Sulṭan ʿAhmad ʿUmar, Aḥmad ʿUshaysh, ʿAbd al-ʿAzīz ʿAbd al-Walī, ʿAīda Yāfaʿī, Anis Ḥasan Yaḥyā.

Of the many non-Yemenis who have assisted me, I would like to mention: James Akins, John Duke Anthony, Michael Arrietti, Jacques Audebert, Patrick Bannerman, Robin Bidwell, Gregori Bondarevsky, Ursula Braun, Norman Cigar, Christopher Clapham, Jacques Couland, Claudio Cordone, Stephen Day, Anoushiravan Ehteshami, Ruth First, Patrick Gilkes, Alain Gresh, Jean Gueyras, Muḥammad Salmān Ḥasan, Denis Healey, Fārūk Muḥammad Ibrāhīm, Hakan Johanssen, Mark Katz, David Korn, Joseph Kostiner, Helen Lackner, Eskil Lundberg, Arthur Marshall, Sāʿīd Masʿūd, Katrina Moberg, Dev Murarka, Ḥusayn Mūsā, Vitali Naumkin, Roger Owen, Vasili Ozoling, Stephen Page, Marc Pellas, Robert Pelletreau, John Peterson, Roderick Pitty, William Quandt, Eric Rouleau, Osman Sāliḥ Ṣabbiḥ, Reinhard Schlagintweit, Lord Shackleton, Gary Sick, Joe Stork, Yūsīf Tāhir, Fawwāz Tarabulsī, John Townsend, Jean-Pierre Viennot, Matthias Weiter, Manfred Wenner.

I have a special debt of gratitude to my wife, Maxine Molyneux, with whom I have observed and discussed the events of South Yemen over many years. Her encouragement, guidance and tolerance have been indispensable to the completion of this work.

Abbreviations

CDSP	*Current Digest of the Soviet Press*
CMEA	Council for Mutual Economic Assistance
CPSU	Communist Party of the Soviet Union
DLF	Dhofar Liberation Front
ELF	Eritrean Liberation Front
EPLF	Eritrean People's Liberation Front
EPRP	Ethiopian Poeple's Revolutionary Party
FCO	Foreign and Commonwealth Office
FE	BBC, Summary of World Broadcasts, Part III, The Far East
FLOSY	Front for the Liberation of Occupied South Yemen
FRG	Federal Republic of Germany
GCC	Gulf Cooperation Council
GDR	German Democratic Republic
KSA	Kingdom of Saudi Arabia
MAN	Movement of Arab Nationalists
ME	BBC, Summary of World Broadcasts, Part IV, The Middle East
NDF	National Democratic Front in the Yemen Arab Republic
NF	National Front (of South Yemen)
NLF	National Liberation Front (of South Yemen)
PDFLP	People's Democratic Front for the Liberation of Palestine
PDRY	People's Democratic Republic of Yemen
PDP	People's Democratic Party (in Saudi Arabia)
PDU	People's Democratic Union (of South Yemen)
PFLO	People's Front for the Liberation of Oman
PFLOAG	People's Front for the Liberation of Oman and the Occupied Arab Gulf (1968–71); People's Front for the Liberation of Oman and the Arab Gulf (1971–4)
PFLP	People's Front for the Liberation of Palestine
PLO	Palestine Liberation Organisation
PMAC	Provisional Military Administrative Council
PONF	Political Organisation, the National Front (of South Yemen)

PR	*Peking/Beijing Review*
PRC	People's Republic of China
PRF	People's Revolutionary Forces
PRSY	People's Republic of South(ern) Yemen
PVP	People's Vanguard Party
RAF	Rote Armee Fraktion
RDP	Revolutionary Democratic Party
SAA	South Arabian Army
SADR	Sahrawi Arab Democratic Republic
SAF	Sultan's Armed Forces
SOAF	Sultan of Oman's Air Force
SPC	Supreme People's Council
SPD	Sozialistische Partei Deutschlands
SU	BBC, Summary of World Broadcasts, Part I, The Soviet Union and Eastern Europe
SWB	*see* ME
TFAI	Territoire Francaise des Afars et des Issas (later Jibuti)
UNDP	United Nations Development Project
UPONF	United Political Organisation, the National Front
YAR	Yemen Arab Republic
YPUP	Yemeni People's Unity Party
YSP	Yemeni Socialist Party

Note on nomenclature

The area referred to in this study as 'South Yemen' has been known in English by several names in the twentieth century. In the colonial period it was conventionally known as 'Aden' or 'Aden and the Protectorates', as well as by the broader geographic name 'South Arabia', and, after 1959, as the Federation of South Arabia. The official title of the state was, from 1967 to 1970, the People's Republic of South (or Southern) Yemen, and, from 1970 onwards, the People's Democratic Republic of Yemen. The terms 'Southern Yemen' and 'South Yemen' are geographic ones that came into Arabic usage in the latter part of the 1950s and into English usage after independence. In this work, the term 'South Yemen' is used, irrespective of historical period, to cover the geographic area, and the 'People's Democratic Republic of Yemen' is used to denote the post-independence state, except where the term People's Republic of South Yemen is specifically appropriate.

The political organisation now ruling South Yemen has undergone several changes of title since its establishment in 1963. It was known from 1963 to 1967 as the 'National Liberation Front of Occupied South Yemen', from 1967 to 1972 as the 'National Front', from 1972 to 1975 as the 'Political Organisation, the National Front', from 1975 to 1978 as the 'United Political Organisation, the National Front', and, from 1978 onwards, as the 'Yemeni Socialist Party'. I have tried to use whichever term is appropriate for the period under discussion, but for the post-1967 years have used the terms 'ruling organisation' and 'ruling party' interchangeably, even where, prior to 1978, no party in the formal sense yet existed.

Note on transliteration

The system of transliteration from Arabic used here is based on that of the *Encyclopaedia of Islam*. However, where names of places or individuals are conventionally rendered into English in other forms, these have been retained (e.g. Aden, Bahrain, Imam, Nasser, Saudi Arabia, Yemen).

Outline chronology

1839	British occupation of Aden
1950s	Formation of the Federation of South Arabia. Growing nationalist opposition in Aden
1962 SEPTEMBER	Revolution in North Yemen, proclamation of the Yemeni Arab Republic; inclusion of Aden in the Federation
1963 JUNE	Founding of the National Liberation Front of Occupied South Yemen (NLF)
OCTOBER	NLF begins guerrilla resistance in Radfan mountains
1964–1967	NLF and rival Front for the Liberation of South Yemen (FLOSY) challenge British plan for handover to rulers of Federation, growing NLF–FLOSY conflict
1965 JUNE	First Congress of NLF, Proclamation of National Charter
1967 JUNE	British begin withdrawal from hinterland
SEPTEMBER–NOVEMBER	NLF defeats FLOSY in Aden and hinterland
30 NOVEMBER	Independence of South Yemen: Britain hands over to NLF; Ḳaḥṭān al-Shaʿabī President of People's Republic of South Yemen (PRSY)
1968 MARCH	Fourth Congress of NF; 'left' ousted by President al-Shaʿabī
JUNE	Dhofar Liberation Front becomes People's Front for the Liberation of the Occupied Arab Gulf (PFLOAG)
1969 22 JUNE	'Corrective Move': al-Shaʿabī ousted by NF 'left'; Sālim Rubiyyaʿ ʿAlī becomes President

24 OCTOBER	Breaking of diplomatic relations with USA
NOVEMBER	Nationalisation of most foreign property
1970 NOVEMBER	Proclamation of the People's Democratic Republic of Yemen (PDRY)
1972 MAY	Fifth Congress of NF; proclamation of Political Organisation of the NF (PONF)
JULY	Sālim Rubiyyaᶜ ᶜAlī organises 'Seven Glorious Days' mobilisation
SEPTEMBER–OCTOBER	First war between YAR and PDRY; Cairo and Tripoli agreements on unity
1974 JULY	PFLOAG becomes People's Front for the Liberation of Oman (PFLO)
1975 OCTOBER	Unification Congress: PONF fuses with PDP and PVP to form United Political Organisation (UPONF)
1976 MARCH	Establishment of diplomatic relations between PDRY and Saudi Arabia; unofficial ceasefire on PDRY-Omani frontier
1977 JULY onwards	Somali-Ethiopian war, PDRY sends troops to fight with Ethiopia
1978 JUNE	Crisis in Aden: Sālim Rubiyyaᶜ killed in coup attempt; Arab states break relations with PDRY. Relaunching of guerilla war in the YAR, with PDRY backing
OCTOBER	Founding Congress of Yemeni Socialist Party (YSP); ᶜAbd al Fattāḥ Ismāᶜīl becomes President
1979 FEBRUARY–MARCH	Second YAR-PDRY war; Kuwait Agreement on unity
NOVEMBER	Twenty Year Treaty of Friendship and Co-operation betwen PDRY and USSR
1980 APRIL	ᶜAbd al Fattāḥ Ismāᶜīl resigns as President, replaced by ᶜAlī Nāṣir Muḥammad
OCTOBER	'Extraordinary' (Second) Congress of YSP
1982 MAY	Agreement between YAR and PDRY on ending guerrilla war in YAR, intensified discussions on unity
OCTOBER	PDRY-Oman agreement on establishing diplomatic relations
1985 OCTOBER	Third Congress of YSP, growing conflict within leadership

1986	13 JANUARY	Two-week civil war, thousands killed, ʿAlī Nāṣir Muḥammad loses Presidency; Abū Bakr al-ʿAṭṭās President, ʿAlī al-Bīḍ General Secretary
1987	FEBRUARY	Al-Bīḍ meets with Gorbachev in Moscow
	JUNE	Special YSP 'Conference', condemns 'left' and 'right' deviations
	NOVEMBER	Celebration of twenty years of South Yemen's independence.

Introduction: the foreign relations of South Yemen

This study is intended to be a contribution to three distinct areas of investigation – the modern history of the Arabian Peninsula, the foreign policies of Third World states, and the international consequences of revolutions. Each is an area on which a substantial amount has been written in recent years, and it is hoped that the analysis in detail of twenty years of South Yemen's foreign policy will contribute to this literature, to a better understanding of this part of the Middle East, and to more documented study of some of the broader, comparative issues involved.

The literature on the Arabian Peninsula, and on the Yemens in particular, has expanded greatly since I first began working on this area in the late 1960s. There is now an international community of people writing on this region to whose labours I owe a special debt of thanks, both for the research which they have published, and for the encouragement which the very existence of a wider community of scholars provides.[1] While part of the Arab world, the two Yemens have distinctive characteristics and recent histories that make the analysis of their policies challenging and rewarding. Among these are the relation of social upheaval to foreign relations, especially important in regard to the two Yemens; the tense relations between oil-producing monarchies and the, until very recently, oil-less republics; and the specific impact on the Peninsula of regional issues – not only the Arab–Israeli dispute, but also those of the Horn of Africa and of the Persian Gulf. The second theme, the comparative study of foreign policies of Third World states has also greatly expanded in the past decade, as it has become possible to assess the first years of post-independence decision-making and policy implementation in a range of Third World countries. It is the great strength of this literature that while not seeing Third World states as unique, it does identify a range of specific problems and trends evident in their foreign policies.[2] This is particularly so with regard to regime security, economic development, and nation formation, all issues central to the evolution of South Yemen's foreign policy.

The third dimension of this study is that of the comparative analysis of how revolutionary states conduct their foreign policies. For all that is individual to such states, certain underlying questions recur: the commitment to supporting like-minded movements in other, often neighbouring, states and the difficulties such a commitment encounters; the effects upon foreign policy of factional divisions within the revolutionary states and, conversely, the impact of external forces upon the politics and economic structure of the state; the search for strategic allies, to guarantee the survival of the revolutionary state, and the issues of autonomy and consultation which such alliances pose; the manner in which, over a longer time span, the revolutionary state balances its desire to maintain beneficial relations with other states, including quite conservative ones, and the commitment to supporting change on an international scale. The common-sense assumption is that revolutionary states begin with an internationalist commitment to promoting change and then, over time, accept the constraints of the international system and the permanence of other, initially contested, political regimes: but this oversimplifies the question, not least because such a transition may cause considerable tension within the revolutionary state itself. How states manage, and justify, such transitions is itself an important part of a comparative study, as is the manner in which former counter-revolutionary opponents handle their accommodation. The passage of time may also pose another problem, namely the emergence in the same region of other revolutionary states with whom relations may not be of the easiest.

Rather than attempting to establish a comprehensive, empirical record, the analysis aims, within the constraints of the available information and space, to elicit some themes in South Yemeni foreign policy that are both significant in themselves and of broader, comparative interest. It is this selective approach which has guided the choice and ordering of the different chapters. Chapters 1 and 2 establish the domestic context of South Yemen's foreign relations and the broad lines of foreign policy determination. They chart the transfer of power from Britain, the determination of the regime's foreign policy in the years after independence by successive governments and congresses, and the impact of factional conflicts on foreign policy. The four chapters that follow each focus upon a major theme in South Yemen's foreign policy. These chapters analyse both the reasons for this policy being a central one and the manner in which policy on this issue has developed.

Chapter 3 discusses South Yemen's policy towards political and economic ties with the west. While all transitions from colonial rule to independence involve an element of discontinuity, the degree of discontinuity, even rupture, attendant upon decolonisation in South Yemen was greater than in many other post-1945 instances. The question arises of to what point such a radical or revolutionary decolonisation was taken, not only internally but also internationally, and what the costs of this kind of decolonisation were. This issue is posed with especial force in regard to two aspects of South Yemen's foreign policy: its diplomatic relations with the west, and its ties to western economies, upon which its prosperity had hitherto relied.[3]

The second theme in South Yemen's foreign policy to be analysed is the claim that the PDRY was only part of a divided country, a 'greater' Yemen encompassing the two states of North and South Yemen, as well as, on occasion, parts of Saudi Arabia. This comprises the material of Chapter 4. The problem of national unity has arisen in many other parts of the contemporary world. This has been the case in Germany and Korea where two distinct states have come into existence since 1945. It has also been so in, among other places, Mongolia, China, Bengal, Somalia, and Ireland: in these cases independent and distinct states have claimed that part of their national territory remains under the control of another state. In many of these, 'unity' and territorial claims persist even where realisation of 'unity' seems remote.[4] It is not necessary to believe that unity of the two Yemeni states was feasible to see that the issue of 'unity', and of the conflictual but persistently intimate relations between the two states, was an important factor in South Yemen's foreign policy, not least because here the issue of national unity intersected with that of promoting change in another state. The history of policy on Yemeni 'unity' provides an example of interaction between two states of similar national but divergent social characters that is pertinent to some of the other instances.

South Yemen's foreign relations with neighbouring states are of interest for a further reason, namely the intention which they embodied of encouraging revolution in other states of the region apart from North Yemen. This topic forms the subject-matter of chapter 5. As much as any state in this century that has issued from a revolution, South Yemen sought to conduct its foreign relations at two, often contradictory, levels – that of inter-governmental relations with other states, and that of relations with revolutionary forces within other states, ones that were seeking to overthrow the existing governments. This commitment to opposition groups was true of South Yemen's relations towards all three of its land neighbours – Saudi Arabia and Oman as well as North Yemen – and towards other, more remote states in the region – Ethiopia, Iran and Israel. Despite its lack of many of the resources that make for a strong or resilient foreign policy, South Yemen persisted for many years in such support to radical groups beyond its frontiers. Chapter 5 seeks to chart the extent of this support, to analyse the factors maintaining it, and to see under what conditions it abated.[5]

Chapter 6 analyses the quest for allies, how this orientation in favour of revolution in the region was accompanied by the development of a multifaceted relationship with the USSR, the state which from the late 1960s was the main supporter of South Yemen in the international arena. While this alliance with the USSR was more far-reaching than that of any other Middle Eastern state with Moscow during this period,[6] in a comparative Third World perspective South Yemen's record was not so exceptional. The PDRY was one of over a dozen Third World non-communist countries that developed close relations with the Soviet Union in the post-war years. South Yemen therefore provides a case study of such relations: of the impact of Soviet policies upon an already radicalised Third World state, of the manner in which the relationship developed, of the problems that arose, of the constraints involved on both sides in such an alliance, and of what factors sustained it. Relations with China, subordinate to those with the USSR but nonetheless continuous, are also discussed in this chapter.

These four factors – renegotiated relations with the west, the viccissitudes of the Yemeni unity question, the pursuit of a revolutionary foreign policy in the region, and the pattern of ties to the communist bloc – indicate dimensions in which PDRY sought to conduct its foreign policy and in which, beyond its particular Middle Eastern interest, the foreign policy of South Yemen may repay closer and more systematic examination.

There are, however, two substantive objections which a proposal of this kind may occasion. The one is that there is as yet insufficient empirical material available upon which to base a study of South Yemen's foreign policy. The country has been independent for only two decades, and the events which are being described and analysed may therefore be too recent to permit of serious study. Moreover, South Yemen has conducted its foreign policy amidst conditions that are unfavourable to academic investigation: its decision-making bodies are secretive, its press is confined to endorsing official policies, foreign policy has already become an issue of too much dispute within the ruling party to permit of accurate discussion inside the country, and there is little independent access to much of the material relevant to a study of its foreign policy. Secondly, it can be argued that, as a state, South Yemen is too insignificant to merit analysis of its foreign policy: a country of less than two million people, amongst the poorest in the world, with little economic, political or military weight in international affairs, and geographically on the margin of the Middle East, in only the more limited senses might the PDRY be said to have a foreign policy at all, if by this is meant the capacity to influence other states or autonomously to determine its relations with the rest of the world.

Both of these objections pose valid questions. There is much that we do not know about South Yemen's foreign relations and which, given the reticence of its government, the factionalism of its leaders, and the probable lack of written documentation on many issues, we shall, in all likelihood, never know. No-one who tries to follow developments in South Yemen can be unaware of the gap between the two available discourses – the official language of socialist theory and class categories, and the unofficial, spoken discourse of personalities and tribal affiliation. Yet the temptation to reject either must be resisted, since both have an effect. In the context of world affairs as a whole, South Yemen is certainly one of the weaker states, without even the power or influence of many of the other countries in the Middle East. Yet these two constraints do not entail that investigation of South Yemen's foreign relations is impossible, or without justification. In addition they need to be offset against the ways in which the topic is of interest both as a study of an Arab state's foreign policy and in a comparative dimension.

The sources used in the following study fall into three categories.[7] There are, in the first place, official statements of the South Yemen state and ruling organisation. Texts of South Yemen policy can be found printed in reports of party congresses and in the South Yemen press, in the BBC's transcripts of radio broadcasts, and in special, often occasional, publications issued in Aden and by embassies abroad. Complementing these are official materials from other interested parties – governments, international organisations, non-governmental groups – with whom South Yemen has had relations and/or been in conflict. Secondly, there are publications of an unofficial kind containing relevant information on the PDRY – newspapers, journals, books and compilations of specialist data. Whilst frequently inaccurate and unreliable, these nonetheless perform an important function in outlining the course of events and of policy: they can be used with appropriate caution. Thirdly, there are my own first-hand observations of South Yemeni foreign policy based on four research visits to the country – in 1970, 1973, 1977 and 1984 – and on numerous interviews, on and off the record, conducted with South Yemeni officials since 1969.[8] These interviews have themselves been accompanied by discussions with officials of many other states and organisations that have been in dealings with South Yemen over the same period. Amongst those whom I have interviewed are officials of Britain, the Federal Republic of Germany, the German Democratic Republic, the USA, Cuba, the USSR, China, Israel, Egypt, Algeria, Iraq, Saudi Arabia, North Yemen, Iran, Somalia, and Ethiopia, as well as representatives of several guerrilla groups supported, at one point or another, by South Yemen. Taken together these three categories of material provide a definite, albeit limited, basis for establishing and analysing the record of South Yemen's foreign policy in the period under discussion.

The argument of insignificance is equally debatable. No state is so powerful that it can operate without constraint, internal and external, and impose its influence beyond its frontiers as it might like. No state is so weak that it cannot be said to have a foreign policy, in the sense of being able in some measure to determine its external relations – be they political, economic, military or cultural – and to have some impact upon those of others. The arguments of insignificance might exclude study of the foreign relations of many states in the world, and overstate the degree to which a meaningful foreign policy can only be conducted by states with a measure of power that was above a certain supposedly definable level. It might, above all, underplay the extent to which smaller states can indeed play a role of some influence in international affairs, autonomous of, if not independent from, the stronger powers of the region and world in which they find themselves.

While placing greatest emphasis upon relations between states, this study does, at appropriate points, go beyond the confines of state-to-state relations, predominant as these have been in the course of South Yemen's foreign relations. There are four respects, at least, in which the analysis of state relations is here supplemented by additional considerations. In the first place, a part of South Yemen's relationship with the outside world involved not states but international organisations: the UN, the IMF, the Arab League, the CMEA, the Non-Aligned Movement, the Islamic Conference Organisation. South Yemen sought to play a part in these and to receive support from their membership. Secondly, South Yemen devoted considerable attention and, at times, resources to relations with non-governmental organisations, most evidently guerrilla groups seeking to overthrow established governments in different countries of the area. The most obvious cases of these were guerrilla movements in Oman, North Yemen, and Eritrea, and among the Palestinian resistance. Thirdly, as a country of exiguous material resources and one historically reliant for much of its prosperity upon foreign economic contacts, South Yemen had to pay particular attention to its economic links with other countries, whether through trade, aid or investment, or through the remittances of its emigrants. This salience of economic relations was important in its own right and as a factor shaping more general foreign policy decisions. Finally, as in the analysis of other countries, the study of South Yemeni foreign policy necessitates examination of the domestic forces shaping that policy and of the institutions and constitutional stipulations affecting it. Analysis of the internal context of foreign policy determination involves both the internal arrangements made for foreign policy to be conducted, and the manner in which South Yemen's foreign policy intersected with the course, orientations and conflicts of international politics. The impact of factionalism on foreign policy is characteristic of revolutions in general: that of the PDRY has been no exception.

The premiss of what follows is that there was something distinctive and significant about the foreign policy pursued by South Yemen after independence. It was distinctive because of the internal changes preceding and accompanying the execution of this foreign policy, changes that merit the term 'revolutionary'; as a result of these, the country's foreign policy differed from that of other states in the region with more continuous and traditional internal arrangements. It was significant in that it shows how, with all the limitations upon it, even a small and economically weak state such as South Yemen could nevertheless pursue a foreign policy that was to some degree of its own choosing. There was certainly much that was rhetoric and not capable of realisation, and there were commitments to change that were, over time, reduced and then terminated. But this was itself an interesting process, of the shifting reconciliation of programme and reality. It can be fruitfully examined in smaller states as it can in large.

This study covers what is a discrete, but ultimately unresolved, period in South Yemeni foreign policy. The public commitment to revolutionary change in two neighbouring states, North Yemen and Oman, was modified in 1982 by agreements with the government of these two countries, and a phase of apparent calm ensued: but this interlude was threatened by the crisis of January 1986 in South Yemen, the external consequences of which remain obscure. This partial reconciliation of 1982 apparently marked the end of a phase of upheaval in the South Arabian region that had begun twenty years before, with the North Yemeni revolution of 1962, and which had included the conflict in South Yemen in which the National Front had come to power.[9] But the 1986 crisis destabilised the regime internally and threatened to reopen conflict with North Yemen and other Arab states. The longer-run direction of South Yemen's foreign policy must, therefore, await the passage of more years, until the consequences of the 1986 crisis become clearer. It is nonetheless possible, on the basis of the record as so far available, to establish in some degree the initial contours of this unusual, twenty-year-long experience of post-independence diplomacy.

1 Development of foreign policy: through the first decade

A revolutionary decolonisation

On 30 November 1967 British rule in South Arabia ended, and a new independent state, the People's Republic of South Yemen, came into existence. The termination of British authority had been preceded by negotiations between the United Kingdom and the guerrilla group that now assumed power, the National Liberation Front, and, at the moment of independence, Britain recognised the new state and offered it some economic aid. Nevertheless, the transition from colonial rule to independence in South Arabia was, by the norms of decolonisation in most British colonies, an exceptional one.[1] It had been preceded by a four-year period of guerrilla war against British rule and that of the British-supported Federation of South Arabia, as well as by fighting between the rival nationalist groups, the NLF and FLOSY. It had culminated in a revolutionary uprising against the established rulers of the hinterland. Public contact between the Front and the UK authorities had begun only three weeks before independence itself.[2]

In condensed form, it can be said that four major factors had contributed to this outcome in the South Arabian arena. First, following the British occupation of Aden in 1839, the colonial power had, during the late nineteenth and twentieth centuries, established control of a fragmented territory and created a new administrative entity, South Arabia. It had later sought to establish there a unified governmental structure, the Federation of South Arabia.[3] The tensions involved in building this state, and the several changes in British policy, had occasioned uncertainty and considerable opposition amongst the local population. The British decision of 1966 to withdraw entirely both reflected and encouraged this opposition.[4] Secondly, in the post-1945 period, there had been substantial economic expansion in the port of Aden, the capital of South Arabia, during which a trades union movement of nationalist affiliation had emerged.[5] Meanwhile, in the countryside, both emigration and the gradual intrusion of money relations were in some measure undermining the traditional loyalty of the population to their rulers, Sultans, Amirs and Sheikhs.[6] The political tensions of the 1960s were in part a response to such social and economic change. Thirdly, from the 1950s onwards, the rise of Arab nationalism, epitomised in Nasser's Egypt, exercised a strong influence over the population of South Arabia and its political organisations.[7] Fourthly, the revolution of September 1962 in North Yemen, in which the Imam was overthrown and a Republic proclaimed, provided a new and proximate focus for nationalists in what they saw as 'South Yemen'. From 1962 to 1970 civil war raged in the North, and the nationalists in South Arabia quickly became involved in support of the Republic, as Britain and some of its associate rulers in the South did in support of the Republic's opponents in the North.[8] In 1963 a guerrilla group, the National Liberation Front of Occupied South Yemen, usually known in English as the NLF, was created with North Yemeni and Egyptian assistance.[9] The combination of these four factors – colonial policy and its changes, socio-economic development, the growth of Arab nationalism, and the 1962 revolution in North Yemen – led to a situation in 1967 whereby Britain was compelled to hand over authority to a recently established guerrilla force that it had until just prior to independence been seeking to defeat.

The independence negotiations

A British commitment to the independence of South Arabia had been made first in 1964, when a decision to withdraw in 1968 was announced, and then, in 1966, in an announcement that Britain would not only withdraw but also evacuate the base by January 1968: from February 1966 onwards, therefore, British policy was that the UK intended to hand over power to the Federal government and would do what it could to ensure that the Federation remained in existence until independence.[10] In 1966 and 1967 this support involved a security guarantee, not only against guerrilla forces inside South Arabia itself, but also against a feared invasion of South Arabia by the Egyptian forces still present in the Yemen Arab Republic (YAR). By the early months of 1967, some British officials recognised that any viable post-independence government would have to include representatives of the guerrillas, and in May 1967 British representatives began to appeal for talks with the NLF and FLOSY.[11] The first, secret and inconclusive contacts between London and the NLF took place at that time. On 19 June 1967 the British High Commissioner, Sir Humphrey Trevelyan, announced that he was lifting the ban on the NLF imposed in 1965. He appealed to the opposition political parties for open discussions with a view to forming a caretaker government.[12] The NLF, however, refused at this point to enter into negotiations with the British authorities. In May they had laid down three conditions before this could happen: the evacuation of British forces, the liquidation of the 'colonialist presence' and the rule of 'reactionary Sultans', and surrender of authority to the NLF.[13] In June these had still not been met.

At this point, British policy continued to be one of supporting the Federal government while seeking to broaden its base. In a statement in the House of Commons on 19 June 1967 the Foreign and Colonial Secretary, George Brown, outlined British policy in the following terms: independence would be on 9 January 1968; for six months after that date a strong naval force, including an aircraft carrier, would operate in South Arabian waters; a force of V-bombers would be stationed on the RAF base on the Omani island of Masira for the same period or as long as the South Arabian government wanted; and, in addition to the £50 million in civilian and military aid promised over the three years after independence, an additional £10 million in military support costs would be provided.[14] This announcement was followed by a reading of the Aden, Perim and Kuria Muria Islands Bill in the House of Commons, an enabling act that relinquished British sovereignty over those parts of South Arabia under direct British rule.[15] In the course of the debate on this Bill, Mr Brown also stated that he favoured the internationalisation of the Red Sea island of Perim and its transfer to some kind of UN control.[16]

The June 1967 commitment to backing the future independent government with military force reflected a shift from the 1966 position, which had precluded such a commitment. But the assumptions upon which this new British policy was formulated were soon undermined. On the one hand, the defeat of Egypt by Israel in the June 1967 war led to the process by which Egypt agreed to withdraw its forces from North Yemen, and so removed the British and Saudi fear of an Egyptian takeover in the South. In August 1967 Nasser committed himself at the Khartoum conference of Arab states to withdraw his forces by December. They had in fact left by the end of October. On the other hand, the NLF had continued to refuse negotiations with Britain and as British forces withdrew in the sumer of 1967 it pressed on with its seizure of power in the hinterland. Attempts by the UN to meet with Federal ministers and arrange a compromise were attacked by the NLF. A statement on 8 August stated: 'We have no alternative but to strike harder blows at the enemy until Britain actually recognises the revolution and negotiates with it directly for the surrender of power.[17] On 2 September NLF Secretary-General Ḳaḥṭān al-Shaᶜabī gave a press conference in the town of Zindjibār, east of Aden. He stated that the Federal government had collapsed and he demanded the immediate withdrawal of British troops. He added: 'We are not against the South Arabian Army, so long as the army is not against us.'[18] The High Commissioner then made a statement on 5 September that the Federal government could no longer expect to replace British rule. He recognised the 'nationalistic forces' as representatives of the people and called on them to negotiate with him.[19]

Yet despite these developments it took another two months for official and meaningful contact between the NLF and the British authorities to be established. The intervening period was taken up by the NLF in consolidating its position in the hinterland and in defeating the forces of its rival FLOSY, as well as in resisting pressure from the Egyptians and the UN to form a coalition with FLOSY.[20] It was also necessary for the Labour government in London, to a degree influenced by pro-FLOSY sentiments, to accept the NLF.

The final round of policy-making on the British withdrawal began on 2 November with a statement from George Brown in the House of Commons.[21] He announced that the date for withdrawal had been brought forward to the latter half of November 1967, that all British forces would be withdrawn by the end of that month, and that in the light of the Egyptian withdrawal from North Yemen it was no longer necessary to station V-bombers on Masira. He also announced that the offer of financial support made in his 19 June statement would be left 'for decision rather later, when the future may be clearer'. The proposal of internationalising Perim had not found support at the UN; the island would therefore remain part of the new state. On 6 November, when the NLF had inflicted a decisive defeat on FLOSY in fighting in Aden, the South Arabian Army (SAA) declared its support for the NLF and its officers asked the British authorities to negotiate with the NLF.[22] In talks with the British authorities between 7 and 10 November, SAA officers told the British authorities that they supported the NLF. A statement in the Sheikh Othman district of Aden by NLF leader Ṣayf al-Ḍāliʿī on 8 November claimed full NLF control of the whole country, and said that this constituted a formal request to Britain to negotiate with it.[23] But it was only on 11 November that the NLF took the initiative of sending a telegram to George Brown stating their claim to be the legitimate authority in South Arabia and asking him to negotiate on the transition of independence. The British High Commissioner had, apparently, wanted to contact the NLF but he had been overruled by officials in London, who insisted that the guerrillas had to come to them.[24] The British authorities had, therefore, no formal contact with the NLF until but a few days before South Arabia became independent. Yet once the NLF approach of 11 November was made, it was possible for the UK government to enter into the independence negotiations. In a statement on 14 November George Brown announced that negotiations with the NLF would now take place, and that South Arabia would become independent on 30 November.[25]

Negotiations were held in Geneva from 21 to 29 November.[26] Because of the NLF's previous refusal to negotiate with FLOSY under UN auspices, the UN authorities in Geneva declined to provide facilities for the negotiations and they had to be held in the local branch of the Young Women's Christian Association. The NLF delegation included Ḳaḥṭān al-Shaʿabī, Fayṣal ʿAbd al-Laṭīf al-Shaʿabī, Ṣayf al-Ḍāliʿī, ʿAlī ʿAntar, ʿAlī al-Bīḍ, ʿAbd al-Fattāḥ Ismāʿīl and Muḥammad Aḥmad al-Bīshī. According to one British source:

> It was evident at the Geneva conference that they had prepared very carefully for the moment when they would take power. They were well-documented on all the issues and greatly surprised the British delegates, who expected them to be revolutionary fighters rather than politicians, by their grasp of the issues at stake. Lord Shackleton himself thought they were men of high calibre.[27]

Yet only Ḳaḥṭān al-Shaʿabī, the oldest of the NLF leaders, was personally known to the British authorities, from his days as an agricultural engineer in Lahej. The others were young men from the hinterland and North Yemen, who had remained underground during the guerrilla campaigns. The British delegation, on the other hand, included several experienced and well-known experts on South Arabia. It was headed by Lord Shackleton, the FCO Minister who had been handling South Arabian affairs, Sir Humphrey Trevelyan, the High Commissioner in Aden, Sir Harold Beeley, the former ambassador to Cairo, John McCarthy, former Counsellor to the High Commission in Aden and now Head of the Aden Department of the Foreign Office, John Wilton, Deputy High Commissioner in Aden, Tony Rushford, legal counsellor to the Commonwealth office, and Oliver Miles, Private Secretary to the High Commissioner, who did much of the translation between Arabic and English.[28]

The main requests of the NLF were: that they be recognised as the government of South Arabia; that Britain provide aid at twice the level offered in June to the Federation; and that the islands attached to South Arabia under British rule remain as part of the new republic. The British requests were that there be an 'orderly' handover, that the new republic should observe 'previous external obligations', by which was meant that it should not interfere in the internal affairs of other Peninsular states, that it should continue to serve two public debts incurred by the Aden government and the Federation, and that it agree to pay public service pensions incurred during colonial rule. As Lord Shackleton later put it: '*We* were hoping to get a sensible settlement . . . It was in *their* interests to get us out.'[29]

Some issues were settled without great difficulty. The British agreed to recognise the NLF, and to exchange diplomatic relations at ambassadorial levels. The NLF agreed upon an 'orderly' handover, and attacks upon British personnel had ceased by the end of the first week in November. The prospect of a fighting departure by Britain was thereby removed. The NLF also accepted the two inherited debts, the Aden government one more rapidly than that of the Federation. The issue of 'respecting previous external obligations' was not dwelt upon at length but, according to one British delegate, the leader of the NLF delegation, Ḳaḥṭān al-Sha'abī, stated: 'We won't make trouble for anyone, not even the Sultan', an apparent reference to the Sultan of Oman.[30]

Disagreement centred on three other questions: the Kuria Muria Islands, the amount of British aid and the issue of pensions. The British agreed that Perim and Kamaran should be part of the new republic: the local inhabitants had opted for adhesion to the republic. The NLF insisted that since the Kuria Muria Islands had been officially attached to Aden colony they too should be part of the new state. But the British argued that this had only been a temporary arrangement. The few dozen inhabitants had, it was claimed, opted for the Sultan of Oman, and the islands off the southern coast of Oman would accordingly be returned to him. At Geneva, the NLF claimed that the British were going to hand the Kuria Murias over to the Sultan of Oman, and the British did not tell them that this had already taken place. A Privy Council decision ratifying the transfer was postponed. By mutual agreement, no mention of them was made in the communiqué. George Brown announced on 30 November that, under a Treaty signed on 15 November, the islands were being retroceded to the Sultan on that day. The NLF protested but made no practical attempt to control them.

The issue of aid was even more controversial. The British view was that the June 1967 offer had been made to the Federation government and that it included sums disbursed between that date and the date of independence. There was also strong pressure on the British government within the UK not to give aid to the NLF because of the latter's killing of British soldiers, and in particular because of the slaying of twenty-three British soldiers in Crater on 20 June by pro-NLF SAA forces.[31] The financial difficulties of the British government in the latter part of 1967, following upon the closure of the Suez Canal in June and the devaluation of sterling by early November, added to this argument for stringency and made it easier for the British representatives to resist an aid commitment that was already unpopular at home on political grounds.[32] For its part, the NLF had political objections to its paying public service pensions. The conventional British position on pensions was that post-independence governments became liable for all those citizens of their countries who were liable, or who would become liable, for pensions as a result of service with the colonial government in the territory concerned. The NLF objected to this, both on the grounds of the expense involved and because of the ideological implications of committing themselves to paying the pensions of people against whom they had spent four years fighting.[33]

Such was the disagreement on these three questions that at one point it appeared that no overall agreement between the two sides could be reached. In Geneva, Lord Shackleton felt that such obstacles had been encountered that he flew back to London to discuss matters with the British government. In Aden, the colonial authorities sent home all the British civil servants still working with the Federation and the Aden government, as well as most of those scheduled to serve in the new British embassy. In the end, on 29 November, a joint text was agreed upon entitled *Memorandum of Agreed Points Relating to Independence for South Arabia (The People's Republic of Southern Yemen)*.[34] This stated that independence would be on 30 November, and that on that day the People's Republic of South Yemen would be established by the NLF, whom the text recognised as 'representatives of the peoples of the territory of the Republic'. The two parties agreed to exchange diplomatic recognition at ambassadorial levels, and the UK offered to sponsor the PRSY's application to the UN. All pre-existing treaties and agreements between the UK and 'other governments, rulers or any authorities of the various parts of the territory of the PSRY' would lapse on 30 November, but all laws in force before independence would continue afterwards, unless they were inconsistent with the arrangements established by the Republic. Point 16 stated that the issue of public service and pensions would be discussed at an early date after independence, as would that of public debt.

A Financial Note, in three points, elaborated on the vexed issue of aid. The two sides agreed to continue negotiations on civilian and military aid and, in the meantime, the British agreed to provide £12 million for six months beginning on 1 December, this being more or less the amount promised to the Federation. It was 'noted' that the NLF requested that this be paid in a lump sum as soon as possible. But it was also 'noted' in the third point that this offer was made 'on the assumption that the Government of the People's Republic of Southern Yemen would continue to discharge certain existing financial commitments mentioned during negotiations'. This presumably related both to pensions and to the debts of the former Aden and Federal governments.

With the negotiations completed, it only remained for the British to complete their withdrawal from their last redoubts in Aden, and for the NLF delegation to return home to participate in the independence celebrations.[35] The NLF was now in control of nearly the whole of the country and was functioning as the effective government. The British were able to point to some positive aspects of this final settlement: the final withdrawal had taken place forty days earlier than the 9 January date announced by George Brown in June, and the final pullout took place in an 'orderly' manner. Despite fears in the UK that Britain might abandon the country to anarchy, the Geneva negotiations had produced a government that Britain could hand over to and which appeared to have the ability to administer the country. As the High Commissioner later wrote: 'We were lucky in at last finding someone to whom we might be able to hand over in peace.'[36] The judgement of the High Commissioner, Trevelyan, summed up the British position:

> So we left without glory but without disaster . . . Nor was it humiliation. For our withdrawal was the result not of military or political pressure but our decision, right or wrong, to leave, and if we failed to hand over our colony in the manner which we should have wished, it was principally because the South Arabians were unable to produce in time a responsible political party having the support of the majority of the people and prepared to negotiate a more civilised approach to independence . . . All we could say at the time was that it might have been much worse. And, in the end, another little independent Arab country came into being, desperately poor and probably destined to go through periods of violence and revolt. The mark of the British on it was light and will soon have disappeared save for the great barracks, the airport, the disused churches and a few half-obliterated signs to the NAAFI or the sergeants' mess. Our period of occupation did the country little permanent good, for all the selfless work of many devoted Englishmen and so many good intentions. Whatever the rights or wrongs of the way we left, whatever was to come after us, the time for us to be there was over. And if we were to go, it was better not to linger on.[37]

By the standards of other British withdrawals, that from South Arabia was certainly exceptional. No British representatives attended the independence celebrations, the new state in common with all other Arab countries ruled by Britain made no gesture of joining the Commonwealth. Trevelyan's premonition about the superficial impact of British rule was given immediate confirmation: the Queen Elizabeth Hospital in Khormaksar was renamed the Republic Hospital; a monument to the martyrs of the revolution was erected in the garden in Tawahi where once Queen Victoria had gazed from her plinth. Few states had been granted independence by Britain amidst conditions of such ill-will, and in the whole history of British colonial rule only one other case of withdrawal was marked by such a degree of conflict between Britain and the local representatives, namely that from the United Colonies in 1783. Trevelyan was accurate in saying that the decision to withdraw had not been forced on Britain by the NLF: the date for independence had been fixed in

1964, the decision to abandon the base had been taken in 1966, before the NLF emerged as the predominant force. But one factor in accelerating both those decisions was the perception on Britain's part that governing or maintaining a position in South Arabia would become increasingly costly because of the opposition of local forces, whether that cost was measured in terms of loss of life, security expenditures, or diplomatic complications.[38]

Moreover, if the decision to withdraw was not itself the result of NLF activity, the political conditions under which it occurred were, and it was over these conditions that the last two years of conflict had raged. For Britain had hoped to leave behind a government that would be favourable to the interests of the west. These were not primarily economic: the importance of Aden as a port was declining, and this process was greatly accelerated by the closure of the Suez Canal some five months before independence as a result of the June 1967 war. Rather, the interests of Britain and its allies lay in the regional context of the Arabian Peninsula and the Persian Gulf as a whole. A contested withdrawal and a defeat of Britain's local allies would, it was believed, unsettle rulers in the Persian Gulf. This was evident from the fact that King Feisal of Saudi Arabia tried in May 1967 to have Britain postpone its withdrawal.[39] It was already realised that a hostile state in South Arabia, particularly if it later became allied with the USSR and assisted rebels elsewhere in the Peninsula, might constitute some threat to the interests of the west. It was to prevent these two eventualities that Britain sought to ensure a transition to rule by the Federal government. It was in the failure to guarantee the political conditions that would have ensured such a handover that the failure of British policy consisted, as did the victory of the NLF.

The triumph of the NLF was at one level a result not of the impact of external factors upon South Arabia, but of the opposite – the failure of external factors to maintain the influence which they had and to bring about the kind of post-independence regime they desired. Britain had intended to hand over power to the Federation, a coalition of Adeni politicians and hinterland rulers. In the last few months of British rule, when the Federation was no longer credible, the authorities had hoped to encourage some coalition of other forces to emerge – combining the Federal rulers, FLOSY and the NLF, or, from September onwards, merely a coalition of the last two.[40] All these policies had failed and, in the end, the British government agreed to hand over power to, to recognise, and to extend some aid to a single force, the one that had been opposing Britain most intransigently since 1963. The argument has been made, both by some Arab and by British writers, that in some way Britain encouraged the NLF or favoured it in the final period: it was advanced by Arab rivals of the NLF in 1967 to discredit their opponents, and it is used by critics of the British withdrawal as a way of emphasising what is seen as a loss of political nerve on London's part.[41] On the basis of evidence so far available, the British government had no understanding with the NLF until November 1967. The decision to recognise it as the successor government was taken not out of political preference but in the light of the practical consideration that it was the NLF which exercised power in all regions of the country not remaining under British rule.[42]

If British hopes were confounded by the victory of the NLF, so were those of another external power, the Egyptians. Egypt had played an important part in stimulating the nationalist movement in Aden in the 1950s, and in bringing the NLF into being in early 1963. The fact of Egypt's presence in North Yemen and its military commitment both to the YAR and to the guerrillas in the South was of immense importance for the NLF.[43] The fear of a straightforward conventional military advance by Egypt's forces into South Yemen once Britain withdrew was a factor in shaping British policy, right up to the June 1967 statement by George Brown guaranteeing naval and air support to the independent state after the then scheduled independence date of January 1968.[44] But, in the end, the Egyptians were unable to maintain their influence in the South Arabian arena either. The withdrawal of their troops from the YAR in the latter part of 1967 removed their main instrument of influence, and the main threat they posed to the South. The *coup* in Sanaʿa of 5 November 1967, that ousted President Sallāl, marked the end of the Egyptians' control of events in the YAR at the very time that their ally FLOSY was being defeated in the South. But even before that withdrawal the growth of conflict between the NLF and the Egyptian authorities had created tensions that meant that any South Arabian government run by the NLF would, in some degree, be independent of Egyptian intentions. The NLF therefore triumphed at the expense of the two major external powers in the region, and came to power in the vacuum created by their simultaneous withdrawal in the latter part of 1967.

The National Front and foreign policy

At the moment of independence the NLF, henceforward known as the National Front or NF, was faced with an economic crisis at home, and with unsatisfactory and inconclusive negotiations on aid with Britain; but it was not entirely without guidelines as to the foreign policy it would later pursue. For in the four years since its establishment the Front had evolved a set of policies that were either practised by it, in its capacity as a guerrilla organisation, or which were proclaimed as intentions to be implemented once it came to power. These were most clearly laid out in the National Charter of June 1965. In the first place, the Front was committed to substantial changes in the local economy: land reform, which would expropriate many of the former rulers,[45] nationalisation of foreign-owned components of the Adeni economy, and an ending of the free port status upon which Aden had relied since the middle of the nineteenth century.[46] While these were measures to be implemented in the domestic economy, they nonetheless entailed alterations in the relations that South Yemen had with the outside world. The NF also came to power with two particular external commitments. Once concerned North Yemen. In its 1965 charter the NF had proclaimed itself to be the Front for the liberation of the 'Yemeni South', and throughout its campaign it had insisted on the belief that Yemen was one country.[47] In his press conference of 8 November in Sheikh Othman, Ṣayf al-Ḍāliʿī had stated: 'We have always made it clear that we believe all these areas – the Yemen Arab Republic and the areas which have been under British control – are all Yemen and that Yemeni unity should be maintained.'[48] At the time that the PSRY acquired independence, the YAR was going through a period of turmoil attendant upon the withdrawal of Egyptian troops, and royalist tribesmen, supported by Saudi Arabia, were besieging the YAR capital, Sanaʿa.[49] The NF's commitment to Yemeni unity was therefore construed by the Front as a commitment to support for the YAR, to the government and the political forces in the North fighting the royalist tribes in defence of the Republic proclaimed in 1962. It involved not just a commitment to eventual unification of the two countries, but to support by the NLF for the more radical forces in the North.[50] Ever since the days of the Imam, the question of unity between North and South had been made conditional by many in South Yemen upon the emergence of a regime in the North which they favoured. During the period from 1963 to 1967 it had been the YAR which had provided backing to the guerrillas fighting the British, i.e. which had implemented its commitment to unity and sought to bring a comparable regime into power in the South. But from November 1967 onward the process was reversed: now it was the government in the South which sought to back like-minded forces in the North in order to clear the way for a later unity.

The second commitment which the NF brought over from the pre-independence period was its membership of the pan-Arab grouping known as the Movement of Arab Nationalists.[51] Although this movement had ceased to exist as a coherent organisation in 1967, the different groups that comprised the MAN remained in contact with each other, and the

NF, even after independence, remained under the intellectual influence of the MAN's Palestinian and Lebanese founders. The events of 1967 had, if anything, strengthened the distinctive political outlook of the MAN left: on the one hand, the 'petty-bourgeois' character of Egypt had, it was argued, been revealed by the defeat in the June 1967 war; on the other, the triumph of the radical MAN in Aden had demonstrated the possibilities of victory through guerrilla struggle.[52] Now that it was in power the NF felt itself able to maintain relations with other factions of the MAN. These included: the MAN branch in North Yemen, which had been in conflict with Egypt since 1964;[53] the MAN branch in the Sultanate of Oman, where since 1965 guerrillas had been fighting in the Dhofar province of the Sultanate, bordering the PRSY; and the radical groupings that emerged within the Palestinian movement after the June 1967 war, the People's Front for the Liberation of Palestine, led by George Ḥabbash and founded in December 1967, and the People's Democratic Front for the Liberation of Palestine, led by Nāyyif Ḥawātma and established as a distinct group in February 1969. Ḥabbash and Ḥawātma had been among the founders of the MAN, and had been involved in Yemeni affairs, of both North and South, prior to independence.[54] The radical wing of the NF drew intellectual inspiration from them, and support for other members of the MAN was to remain an important part of the Front's programme for years to come.

This association with the MAN had, inevitably, a double implication. On the one hand, it gave the NF a set of commitments to causes elsewhere in the Arab world, and most evidently to the guerrillas of the Palestinian resistance. But it at the same time drew the Front into the factional disputes that were dividing the Palestinians at that time, which was one of particularly bitter conflict between the ex-MAN groups, led by Ḥabbash and Ḥawātma, and the PLO and Al-Fatḥ. As a result, independent South Yemen was for several years committed to supporting the Palestinians in general, while having strained relations with the main force within the Palestinian resistance movement, Al-Fatḥ. It was only in November 1974, when the Arab League officially recognised the PLO as the sole legitimate representative of the Palestinians, that the PDRY agreed to do likewise.[55] ʿArafāt, the PLO leader, visited Aden only in 1977.

In general, foreign and domestic policy were closely interrelated in the post-independence period. The course of South Yemeni foreign policy was to a considerable extent affected by the course of politics within the country, by the evolution of the policies of ruling organisation and state, and by the conflicts within the leadership that continued throughout the first decade and a half. At the same time, internal political processes were themselves continuously influenced by foreign factors – by the economic pressures bearing upon the Republic, by the international conflicts in which the PSRY became embroiled, and by the relationships established between external powers and specific factions within the ruling organisation itself. Even when such ties did not exist, they were widely alleged to do so. Moreover, the transformations of front, state, economy and society were, despite the acquisition of independence, to a considerable degree guided by foreign models, especially by Soviet ideas of 'socialist orientation'. Despite the apparent desire of the country's leadership to make South Yemen politically independent and economically more self-sufficient, it therefore remained open to a variety of external influences, and to pressures to which the government was forced to respond with the limited resources available to it.

The post-1967 history of the ruling organisation in South Yemen is of the gradual evolution of a radical Arab nationalist grouping into a more formally structured party modelled on the ruling parties of the USSR and eastern Europe. This history can be analysed at two levels: the formal level of party congresses, official declarations, and personnel changes, and the informal, unofficial, level of muffled inner-party conflicts, sudden depositions of leaders, and unanticipated revisions of policy. Neither level of analysis is in itself sufficient. Formal development masks important events and tensions within the organisation. The informal history has to be matched by attention to the congresses and other official events that establish the development or confirmation of the organisation's policy and set the stage for each further, informal, conflict that follows. Both levels have a foreign policy dimension: the congresses of the front and party established what the guidelines of foreign policy were to be, and foreign policy issues played an important part in the conflicts within the front and party that constituted the informal level.

At the moment of independence the NF was a loosely organised grouping of a few thousand members. Founded in 1963, its general guidelines had been given in the National Charter of the First Congress of June 1965, and had been modified in the Jibla and Khamir Congresses, the Second and Third, of 1966.[56] Throughout much of 1967 the more radical faction of the Front had been calling for a Fourth Congress, to fix the policies the Front would pursue after independence.[57] But this had been resisted by Ḳaḥṭān al-Shaʿabī and his associates. Thus, as it assumed power, the NF had apparently defeated its main rivals within South Yemen, but it was itself divided by a continuation of that conflict that had been developing between Ḳaḥṭān and his more radical opponents in the 'secondary leadership' of the Front.[58]

The first official statement on foreign policy by the new government was made by President al-Shaʿabī when he returned to Aden from

Geneva.[59] He said that the Front would pursue a policy based on 'positive neutralism', and that it would protect foreign nationals and communities within the Republic. The latter had been a major concern of the UK during the Geneva negotiations. The broad lines of the future policy were also specified: consultations with North Yemen aimed at furthering 'natural Yemen unity', support for 'the liberation of Palestine' and 'the liberation of Arab lands still under foreign rule', an implicit reference to the British-protected states of the Persian Gulf. In mentioning the Geneva talks with Britain, al-Shaᶜabī said that the NF had rejected the suggestion that a British mission be appointed to the South Yemeni armed forces, and he referred to 'attempts to put aside a part of our country', by which he presumably meant the Kuria Muria Islands and Perim. One of Ḳaḥṭān al-Shaᶜabī's first acts upon assuming office as President was to appoint a governor for Perim, Kamaran and the Kuria Muria Islands, and in his address to the UN General Assembly the new Foreign Minister, Ṣayf al-Ḍāliᶜī, repeated that the Kuria Muria Islands were an 'integral part' of the new state.[60]

With the end of British rule and of the Federal government, South Yemen ceased to have an operating consitutional system, and one of the NF's first actions upon taking office was to appoint its own leadership or General Command as the legislature until a constitution had been drafted.[61] The National Front would henceforward be the ruling body in the new one-party system. The affairs of Front and state were, for the time being at least, merged. The determination of foreign policy, as well as regulation of the conflicts attendant upon it, were therefore to be the responsibility of the leading bodies of the Front.

The Fourth Congress of the Front was finally held on 2–8 March 1968 in Zindjibār, and attended by 167 delegates.[62] At this Congress, the general dispute between the two main wings of the Front came into the open. The Programme of National Democratic Popular Liberation, drafted by ᶜAbd al-Fattāḥ Ismāᶜīl, Minister of Culture, National Guidance and Yemeni Unity Affairs in the first post-independence government, argued for a 'national democratic revolution'.[63] In this regime, power would be vested in the workers, peasants, soldiers and revolutionary intellectuals. It called for the establishment of a Supreme People's Council, drawn from a nationwide network of local popular councils, to act as the legislative authority in the country, and for the construction of a people's militia of between 100,000 and 150,000 members. The policy advocated by this Programme in South Yemen was frequently contrasted with what were termed the 'petty-bourgeois' policies of other Arab countries – Egypt, Algeria, Syria and Iraq were all mentioned by name.[64] It also called for a series of economic measures to enable the 'national democratic revolution' to continue – nationalisation of foreign banks and foreign trade, and the ending of Aden's free port status except for tourism and goods in transit. Only in this way could South Yemen avoid the fate of other Third World countries which had gone from colonialism to neo-colonialism. The proposal to establish a popular militia was placed in the context of the overall conflict in the Arabian Peninsula:

The presence of counter-revolutionary forces surrounding our country, combined with the ferocity of the counter-revolution in the Arabian Peninsula, where the oil fields are located, prevents our country from remaining as a revolutionary democratic island in the middle of a reactionary imperialist sea. In addition there is the viciousness of the counter-revolution in the Arabian Peninsula because of oil resources. The mass arming of supporters of the revolution constitutes the only means of ensuring the security of the revolution and defeating the counter-revolution within and on our frontiers. It is in this way that our country will be able to play an effective role in the propagation of the revolutionary fire throughout the Arabian Peninsula without fearing the hostile reactions of the imperialist-reactionary coalition which will find itself facing a people that is armed, fighting with deeds and not words, inch by inch to defend its land, its factories and its revolutionary democracy.[65]

A Political Declaration issued by the General Command of forty-one members elected at the Fourth Congress outlined the foreign policy of the new regime in terms reflecting the apparent victory of the left.[66] It began by analysing the contemporary international context, as one of the conflict between capitalism and colonialism on one side, and socialism and the national liberation movement on the other. It stated that 'The existence and growth of the socialist camp constituted a firm ground, a rear support to the liberation movements to enable them to steer towards socialism in favour of the oppressed masses.'[67] But, while it did mention the USSR by name, it also mentioned China; it did not fully espouse the Soviet viewpoint, and the final resolutions asserted the need for 'interaction and opening to all socialist experiences and regimes in the world'.[68] In analysing the Arab world the Political Declaration attributed the Israeli victory of June 1967 to the 'lack within the national liberation movement of its vanguard revolutionary instrument, the non-existence of a clear progressive social consciousness, and the non-participation of the broad toiling masses'.[69] The Declaration went on to stress that the revolution in South Yemen would only be completed with the victory of revolution in North Yemen and the realisation of Yemeni unity. The final resolutions adopted by the Congress on 8 March restated the general approach of the Declaration, and gave a list of six foreign policy positions: support for the revolution in North Yemen and for Yemeni unity, extension of support to the liberation movements against imperialism and reaction in the Arabian Gulf and Peninsula, support for the Palestinian resistance, support for anti-imperialist movements in the Third World, solidarity with the socialist regimes, and condemnation of imperialism and colonialism, particularly in South Africa and Vietnam.[70]

The dispute between the two NF factions involved both domestic and foreign policy: al-Shaʿabī and his supporters wanted a more cautious policy on both fronts, and they disliked the criticism of such countries as Egypt and the emphasis upon the revolutionary groups elsewhere in the Peninsula, as much as they opposed the call for a purge of the armed forces and a radical land reform.[71] Soon after the Fourth Congress matters came to a head over the armed forces. On 20 March, following the arrest by the army of some leading members of the left, al-Shaʿabī, while criticising the army's actions, was able to dismiss most of the left-wing representatives from the government and the party leadership.[72]

Ḳaḥṭān al-Shaʿabī was now apparently in a stronger position within the NF and he successfully defeated attempts by the forces of the left to stage armed uprisings in the hinterland in May 1968.[73] But in June 1969 he was forced to resign after a clash with the Minister of the Interior, Muḥammad ʿAlī Ḥaytham. He dismissed Ḥaytham on 16 June 1969, but Ḥaytham had built up good connections in the armed forces and, in alliance with Muḥammad Ṣālih ʿAwlaḳī, the Minister of Defence, and with the regrouped forces of the left, organised a bloodless *coup* on 22 June 1969, in which the President and his supporters were removed from government and replaced by a coalition of the left and other opponents of Ḳaḥṭān al-Shaʿabī.[74] A five-man Presidential Council was appointed, consisting of the new President, Sālim Rubiyyaʿ ʿAlī, the Defence Minister, Muḥammad Ṣāliḥ ʿAwlaḳī, ʿAbd al-Fattāḥ Ismāʿīl, ʿAlī Aḥmad ʿAntar and Ḥaytham, now Prime Minister.[75] The new government adopted a more radical line in foreign policy: while it committed itself to building ties to Arab countries, headed by Egypt, it also stressed its support for the Palestinians and for the PFLOAG, fighting in Oman.[76] Most significantly, perhaps, the new government committed itself to improving relations with the 'socialist' countries, and in particular with the USSR: this would, it was stated, be a 'guiding principle' of the new government's foreign policy.[77]

Once in power again, the new leadership of the NF proceeded to implement some of their plans. In July West Germany broke off relations after Aden recognised the GDR. Relations with the USA were broken in October.[78] Foreign banks and insurance companies were nationalised in November 1969.[79] In 1970 a new land reform law was passed, and in November 1970 a constitution was introduced.[80] The latter changed the name of the country to the People's Democratic Republic of Yemen and under it legislative power was to be transferred to a Supreme People's Council. However, although it was initially stated that this body would be elected, it was, when established in August 1971, a Provisional Supreme People's Council, a body of 101 members, all of whom were nominated.[81] The evolution of the Front continued, parallel with these economic and constitutional changes. In December 1969, when the Presidential Council was reduced from five to three members (Sālim Rubiyyaᶜ ᶜAlī, Muḥammad ᶜAlī Ḥaytham, ᶜAbd al-Fattāḥ Ismāᶜīl), the government was reorganised to include representatives of two other political groupings, the pro-Soviet People's Democratic Union (PDU) and a local Baᶜthist faction, the People's Vanguard Party (PVP): the secretary-general of the former, ᶜAbd Allāh Bādhīb, became Minister of Education, the secretary-general of the latter, Anīs Ḥassan Yaḥyā, Minister of Economy.[82] This broadening of the government was interpreted by some as signalling a desire for better relations with, respectively, the USSR and Syria, erstwhile patrons of those factions, but it was at least equally motivated by a desire to promote greater collaboration between opposition tendencies in the YAR, and to encourage the formation of a single party there. In 1970 a small affiliate of the PDU, the Shabība or Youth Organisation, merged with the NF.[83] A further change in the composition of the government occurred in August 1971, when, after a conflict between Prime Minister Muḥammad ᶜAlī Ḥaytham and the leaders of the left-wing faction, Ḥaytham resigned and went into exile. A new three-person Presidential Council, of Sālim Rubiyyaᶜ ᶜAlī, ᶜAbd al-Fattāḥ Ismāᶜīl and the new Prime Minister, ᶜAlī Nāṣir Muḥammad, was then created.[84]

The incorporation of the two smaller allied parties into the government, and the removal of the uncertain allies with whom Ḳaḥṭān al-Shaᶜabī had been linked in June 1969, then prepared the way for the Fifth Congress at which 171 delegates met in Madīnat al-Shaᶜab, outside Aden, on 2–6 March 1972.[85] This Congress marked an important step in the reorganisation of the Front away from its Arab nationalist, MAN, form to one of a more orthodox pro-Soviet kind. Thus the name of the organisation was now no longer what it had been in the immediate post-independence period, the National Front, but the Political Organisation, the National Front (*Al-Tanẓīm Al-Siyyāsī, Al-Djabḥa Al-Ḳawmiyya*), the concept Political Organisation suggesting a transitional phase between the loose Front and a future centralised Party. A new set of internal statutes were adopted, incorporating Soviet norms, and stressing the primacy of 'democratic centralism'.[86] The old system of leadership by a General Command (*Ḳiyyāda ᶜĀma*) was now replaced by a Central Committee and a Politburo (*Maktab Siyyāsī*). In one sense, this Fifth

Congress took the decisions of the Fourth further, in deciding on the immediate establishment of a Popular Militia and of Popular Defence Committees (*Lidjān al-Difā al-Shaᶜabiyya*), the latter being designed to combine educational and social welfare functions at the neighbourhood level with security duties. But, in another respect, the Fifth Congress introduced an element of caution: it adopted a more moderate tone, avoiding the attacks on the 'petty bourgeoisie' in the Arab world, and stressing the limits of what could be achieved in the 'national democratic' phase of the revolution.[87]

The Congress Programme repeated the NF's general support for Yemeni unity, and the bonds between the revolutions of 26 September and 14 October, but it made no specific recommendations on how this was to be achieved.[88] In chapter 7 of the Political Programme adopted by the Congress, some foreign policy guidelines were clarified. After hailing the contemporary era as that of the 'victory of socialist revolution', the report analysed the 'international revolutionary movement' as consisting of three parts: the socialist camp, the international workers' movement, and the movement of Arab and international liberation.[89] It called for a common struggle in the Arab world against colonialism, neo-colonialism, Arab reaction, and Zionism, and against foreign bases and monopolies. In specifying policy for the Arab world the Programme pledged support for: (1) 'the revolutionary armed struggle in the occupied Arab Gulf' under the leadership of the People's Front for the Liberation of Oman and the Arab Gulf; (2) 'The national liberation movement in the Arabian Peninsula against imperialist military bases and the control of the monopolies, and for the liquidation of the royalist agent Saudi regime'; (3) the Palestine resistance movement; (4) 'liberationist' (*taḥarruriyya*) Arab countries in their struggle against Zionism and world imperialism; (5) national and democratic 'detachments' in their struggle against reactionary Arab regimes and for the establishment of national democratic regimes.[90] It also called for the setting up of 'an Arab progressive democratic front' (*djabḥa ᶜarabiyya taḳaddumiyya dīmuḳrāṭiyya*) to unify the common struggle against imperialism, Zionism and Arab reaction.[91]

In the listing of tasks on the international level the Programme then went on to identify the major tasks of the Political Organisation on the international, i.e. non-Arab, plane, stressing that the Yemeni revolution was part of the world-wide national liberation movement. It mentioned in particular: (1) support for the people of Indo-China; (2) support for the Korean struggle against American occupation of the south and for national unity; (3) support for the peoples of Latin America and, in particular, Cuba; (4) condemnation of the 'racist policy' of governments in Africa.[92] A third section of the chapter on foreign policy discussed relations with the socialist countries. It began by stating that the unity of the socialist camp was a necessity not only because of the need to build socialism, but also to support the workers' and national liberation movements.[93] The Programme appealed for the unity of the socialist countries because, it said, the imperialists could exploit divisions within the socialist camp; and it called for the development of relations between Yemen and the socialist countries 'without exception'.[94]

Certain features of this Programme are of particular interest. On issues relating to the Arabian Peninsula, the Programme adopted a markedly radical note, backing the guerrillas in Oman, calling for the overthrow of the Saudi monarchy, and denouncing, though not by name, the smaller states in the Gulf for their ties with 'imperialism'.[95] As far as Saudi Arabia was concerned, this was a more explicit commitment than that of the Fourth Congress. On the other hand, the Programme laid great stress on the need for unity among the 'progressive forces' in the Arab world – it appealed for unity in the 'Arabian Gulf', stressed the need for Palestinian unity, and proposed the establishment of a common Arab front. Neither the Fifth nor the Fourth Congress mentioned the PLO by name. The Programme avoided attacks on the 'petty-bourgeois' Arab governments denounced at the Fourth Congress, and it made no mention of Ethiopia, a country where South Yemen was supporting Eritrean guerrillas even as it had diplomatic relations with Haile Selassie. A mention of 'self-determination for national minorities' in the section on the Arab world could have been seen as relating to Eritrea, but it might also have related to the Kurds in Iraq.[96] The sections on the 'socialist camp' were studied in their caution. The theoretical terms used in the report were very much those of Soviet theory. But no mention was made in the Programme of either the USSR (mentioned in the Fourth Congress documents) or China. Of the communist countries only Vietnam, Korea and Cuba received mention, and this was under the section dealing with *international* relations, not the 'socialist camp'. The call for the unity of the 'camp', and the stress on South Yemen's desire to have relations with all socialist countries 'without exception' could be taken as an appeal to China and the USSR if not to unite, then at least not to force the PDRY to side with one overtly against the other.

Although the Fifth Congress was held after the removal of both Ḳaḥṭān al-Sha<u>sh</u>ʿabī and Muḥammad ʿAlī Ḥay<u>th</u>am, it did not mark the termination of factional disputes within the Front. Rather, as after the Fourth Congress, the apparently decisive convening of a Congress to settle disagreements within the Front was the occasion for a further outbreak of factionalism within the leadership that affected the conduct of foreign policy, as it did that of domestic. This time the division was within the left itself, with a faction under the Secretary-General, ᶜAbd al-Fattāḥ Ismāᶜīl, opposed to that under the President, Sālim Rubiyyaᶜ ᶜAlī. This conflict involved three kinds of broad issue – party, economy, and foreign affairs. ᶜAbd al-Fattāḥ favoured the construction of a 'democratic centralist' party on the Soviet model, and he wanted the PDRY to align itself clearly with the USSR. He was also the advocate of a much more orderly, formalised conduct of economic affairs by state bodies. Sālim Rubiyyaᶜ relied much more on personal contacts, and appointments, both in party and state matters, and he stressed the revolutionary potential of the 'masses' more than the construction of the 'vanguard party'.[97] In October 1970 he had begun to organise a process of 'tremors' (*intifāḍāt*) or uprisings by peasants as a means of implementing land reform.[98] While not opposed in foreign policy to the alliance with the USSR, he also wanted to maintain good relations with other countervailing countries – China and, later, Saudi Arabia and those of the west.

The conflict between the two groups became evident soon after the Fifth Congress when in July 1972 Sālim Rubiyyaᶜ ᶜAlī launched a week of mass demonstrations in Aden known as the 'Seven Glorious Days', with workers and peasants brought into the town and being marched through the streets campaigning against 'bureaucracy' and for lower wages.[99] Apparently influenced by the Cultural Revolution in China, this event was also a means by which the President could use his popular following against the officials in place in the Front and government offices. It constituted a clear alternative to the procedures of the Fifth Congress. Yet, although it persisted, this conflict was for some time contained, and it appeared as if the transformation of the NF was continuing without major opposition. In the mid-1970s, a somewhat more cautious policy towards the monarchies of the Arabian Peninsula became evident: Aden's relations with the Amirates improved; the guerrillas in Dhofar abandoned their claim to represent the whole of the monarchical 'Arab Gulf', and instead confined themselves at their July 1974 Congress to being the People's Front for the Liberation of Oman.[100] In early 1976, with the defeat of the Oman guerrillas, a *de facto* ceasefire came into operation on the Oman–PDRY border.[101] Relations with North Yemen also improved, and Sālim Rubiyyaᶜ ᶜAlī developed a good personal relationship with the reforming North Yemeni President, Ibrāhīm al-Hamdī, who came to power in a *coup* in June 1974. In March 1976, after more than six years of hostilities, the PDRY and Saudi Arabia established diplomatic relations.

Parallel to this evolution of policy in the Peninsula, the evolution of the Front was taken a step further in 1975 with the establishment of the United Political Organisation, the National Front (UPONF)[102] – *al-Tanẓīm al-Siyyāsī al-Mawḥid al-Djabḥa al-Ḳawmiyya*. Following an agreement between the Central Committees of the three parties on 5 February, the Sixth Congress of the PONF had met in March 1975, the Second Congress of the PDU in July, and the Third Congress of the PVP in August to ratify the unification agreement. The Unification Congress, held on 11–13 October in Aden, completed a process that had been in train since the incorporation into the government of members of the two smaller parties, the PDU and the Baʿthists, in December 1969, by merging the PONF with these two organisations. This Congress was considered necessary as a prelude to the conversion of the PONF into a new party, but it also occasioned a reaffirmation of those foreign policy orientations which the 1969 alliance at government level had embodied, vis-à-vis the USSR and North Yemen.

The foreign policy resolutions of the Unification Congress followed, in their main points, the lines laid down at the Fifth Congress three years earlier. There was a slight shift in the characterisation of 'our contemporary epoch' with which the section began, the 1975 Congress describing it as the era of the 'transition of peoples from capitalism to socialism' whereas the 1972 one had characterised the epoch as one of 'socialist revolution': the new formulation appeared to allow implicitly for peaceful non-revolutionary transitions to socialism.[103] Yemeni unity was again endorsed but the Congress now called for the establishment of a Unified Yemeni Vanguard Party, i.e. one in both the YAR and the PDRY.[104] While the specific stipulations followed the same general themes and order, there were also some modifications. Point 1 supported the PFLO, thus limiting the guerrilla struggle to Oman, and excluding the Amirates and other smaller states. It added the need to fight 'Iranian intervention'; substantial Iranian intervention into Oman had taken place in 1973, after the last Congress.[105] Point 2, which had in 1972 called for the overthrow of the Saudi monarch, now confined itself to supporting 'the national liberation movement in the Arabian Peninsula against imperialist military bases and the control of the monopolies'.[106] Point 3 supported the Palestinian resistance, but in addition to repeating the call for unity it specified for the first time that this should be within the framework of the PLO. It repeated its general call for the support of the 'liberationist' states confronting Israel, and for the constitution of 'an Arab Progressive and Democratic Front'. The section on international politics contained no new elements, but repeated the lines of the Fifth Congress: support for Vietnam, Cuba and North Korea, for the movement against nuclear weapons, and for the international workers' movement.[107] Similarly, the section on the 'socialist camp' repeated the statement that it was 'the revolutionary ally' of the PDRY; but it made no specific mention of the USSR and it appealed for unity of all components of the camp in the face of 'imperialism'.[108]

The Yemeni Socialist Party

The Unification Congress and the initiatives in the Arabian Peninsula appeared to indicate that a more careful new foreign policy was emerging – consolidation of relations with the USSR without wholly alienating China on the one side, reduction of tensions with conservative neighbours on the other. But, as external relations appeared to be entering a calmer phase, a conflict was developing within the PDRY which was to culminate in the events of June 1978, when President Sālim Rubiyyaᶜ ᶜAlī was executed. As the campaign developed to construct *Ḥizb Min Tīrāz Dj̲adīd*, the Arabic version of Lenin's call for a 'Party of the New Type', so Sālim Rubiyyaᶜ ᶜAlī sought to resist this new organisation by constructing his own network of appointees.[109] He resisted the growth of the centralised planning apparatus begun under the Three Year Plan of 1971–4, but taken much further with the first Five Year Plan of 1974–9, and he used his personal funds and his contacts to appoint 'radical' but often inexperienced personnel to important positions.[110] He also sought to ensure that he maintained persons loyal to him in the army. Yet, while the gradual establishment of more orderly structures of the party and state did meet with his opposition, foreign policy pressures also combined to lessen his room for manoeuvre: relations with Saudi Arabia deteriorated again in late 1977, with the crises in the Horn of Africa and in North Yemen.[111]

On 26 June 1978 President Sālim Rubiyyaᶜ ᶜAlī attempted to stage a *coup*.[112] After several hours of fighting, he was defeated. The President and two of his closer associates, ᶜAli Sālim Laᶜwar, Secretary of the Presidential Office, and Dj̲āᶜam Ṣāliḥ , NLF Secretary in the Third Governorate and a leader of the peasants' movement, were executed on the same day.[113] Some hundreds of other people were also killed or wounded, and a significant minority of the Front leadership was removed from office: two members of the Politburo and eight out of some seventy members of the Central Committee.[114] Four out of six party secretaries in the Governorates were dismissed, an index of the President's influence in the UPONF outside the party offices of Aden itself. As a result of the June 1978 crisis the top organs and personnel of the state were altered. A new five-person Presidential Council was set up and ᶜAlī Nāṣir Muḥammad, Prime Minister since 1969, was appointed President *ad interim*.[115] Then, at a meeting of a newly elected Supreme People's Council on 27 December, Abd al-Fattāḥ Ismāᶜīl became head of state, while ᶜAlī Nāṣir remained as Prime Minister. The Presidential Council, established in 1969 after the 'Corrective Move' and later used by Sālim Rubiyyaᶜ as an instrument of influence, was abolished in favour of a Presidium of the SPC and, with ᶜAbd al-Fattāḥ both President and Secretary-General, the organs of state were integrated even more closely with the party.[116] A revised constitution, introduced in October 1978, had prepared the way for these changes.[117]

Foreign policy played a part, but by no means an exclusive one, in the crisis surrounding the fall of Sālim Rubiyyaᶜ ᶜAlī. The former President had to some degree, it seems, opposed the orientation of foreign relations that developed in the 1970s: on available evidence he was not 'pro-western' but his position was more a matter of wanting to maintain a diversity of relations – with the President of North Yemen, al-Hamdī, and with Saudi Arabia – rather than of his opposing close ties with the USSR or the PDRY's new regional ally, Ethiopia. Sālim Rubiyyaᶜ ᶜAlī, however, suffered from the deterioration of the situation in the Red Sea area following the development of the Somali–Ethiopian war in the latter part of 1977 and the assassination of al-Hamdī in October 1977: these developments deprived him of his ally in the North and led to a cessation of the Saudi connection which he had wanted to use to maintain foreign policy flexibility. Sālim Rubiyyaᶜ also favoured maintenance of some relations with Egypt: he valued the latter's help in the establishment of contact with Saudi Arabia and was cautious about the anti-Egyptian Steadfastness Front. He was not, however, willing to accept the policies of his opponents and in his speech on the tenth anniversary of independence, in November 1977, he did not mention the USSR by name.[118] Sālim Rubiyyaᶜ ᶜAlī's *coup* attempt on 26 June had been preceded two days earlier by the death of the then North Yemeni President, Aḥmad Ḥuṣayn al-Ghashmī, and it is widely believed that the bomb that killed al-Ghashmī had been sent by Sālim Rubiyyaᶜ as a means of detonating a crisis in the North in which forces more sympathetic to him could once again come to power. While it can never be established with certainty what his motives or involvement were, it seems that Sālim Rubiyyaᶜ ᶜAlī, with a reduced room for manoeuvre at home, may have sought as a last resort to provoke a crisis in the North that might provide him with an opportunity to hit his domestic opponents.[119]

The fall of Sālim Rubiyyaᶜ ᶜAlī also had important foreign policy consequences. Many Arab states asserted that the events of 26 June had been organised or encouraged by the USSR and Cuba.[120] China also adopted a more hostile position than hitherto to the PDRY.[121] In the list of cases where Soviet policy had, it was argued by western commentators, been aggressive in the latter part of the 1970s, South Yemen came to have a place alongside Angola, Ethiopia, Cambodia and Afghanistan.[122] Henry Kissinger talked of a 'communist *coup*' as having occurred in June 1978.[123] Saudi Arabia encouraged the PDRY's suspension from the Arab League.[124] North Yemen broke of diplomatic relations after al-Ghashmī's death. An American diplomatic mission in Saudi Arabia on its way to both Yemens to discuss relations turned back, and attempts to encourage talks between Washington and Aden, in train for some time, then ceased.[125] At home, the fall of Sālim Rubiyyaᶜ ᶜAlī marked the end of the conflict that had been dividing party and state for some years and so opened the way for the final transformation of the Front, NF, through the PONF and UPONF, into the Yemeni Socialist Party. Sālim Rubiyyaᶜ was denounced in official statements for his erratic activities at home and was also accused of having had links with 'imperialist' governments, an apparent attempt to blame him for the US mission that had been en route to Aden.[126] In fact, the policy of opening talks with the US in 1978 was one that had been generally accepted: the Aden government later repeated its invitations to the US to send a mission, albeit without success.[127]

The organisational completion of this restructuring came when the First Congress of the Yemeni Party was held in Aden on 11–13 October 1978.[128] This marked the apparent consolidation of the process under way since the early 1970s and now made easier by the fall of Sālim Rubiyyaᶜ ᶜAlī and the purge of his supporters that had followed. The Political Programme of the YSP Congress covered many of the same points as those of the preceding NF Congresses, but in a number of significant respects it marked a shift in emphasis. In the first place, the Programme more than ever stressed the relationship with the USSR, both in praising the October revolution and the role of the Soviet Union in defeating fascism, and in calling for strengthening of relations with the 'socialist regimes and, in the first instance, with the Soviet Union'.[129] The USSR had not been mentioned since the Fourth Congress of 1968 and this tribute was now phrased in more specific terms than a decade earlier, as well as omitting as it did any reference to China. The Programme repeated Soviet positions in its call for 'peaceful coexistence' between countries of different socialist systems, a cautious note rather remote from the revolutionary appeals of the Fourth and Fifth Congresses.[130] It also underlined the need to learn from the experience of the 'socialist bloc' in party building and ideological work. This learning was, it was stated, needed to wage the struggle within the YSP itself against what it terms 'splittist attempts', 'rightist and "leftist" revisionist tendencies' and 'ideological deformation'.[131] Such phrases appeared to mean that the example of the CPSU, in ideological line and organisational practice, could be applied to the struggle against groups such as those of Sālim Rubiyyaᶜ ᶜAlī and Ḳaḥṭān al-Shaᶜabī. There were a number of separate points at which the leading role of the USSR in the 'socialist bloc' was explicitly mentioned.[132] The call for the unity of the socialist countries, and the assertion of the right of the PDRY to have relations with all socialist countries without exception, reiterated in all previous Congresses, were no longer present. Instead, the Programme gave particular emphasis to a policy of 'strengthening our relations of solidarity with the world socialist order',[133] a periphrasis for stronger relations with the USSR, and of the need to 'learn from the experience' of the socialist states in all spheres.

In outlining specific policy guidelines for the Arab world, two major modifications of positions adopted at previous Congresses can be noted. First, the struggle in the Arabian Peninsula is played down, by comparison with previous Congresses: it now comes *after* discussion of the Palestinian issue; and, whereas previously the guerrilla organisation in Dhofar was mentioned by name, and in the YSP Secretary-General's Political Report the PFLO is given support, the Programme talks only of the '*peoples*' of the Arabian Gulf and the Arabian Peninsula and their national movement.[134] Neither Oman, nor Saudi Arabia, nor any other Peninsula state are mentioned. On the other hand, the issue of Palestine is given much greater prominence and is placed at the head of the list of Arab world causes supported.[135] Stress is laid on the need for Palestinian unity, yet in a return to the general stance characteristic of the Fourth and Fifth Congresses the PLO is not mentioned by name. This is not, however, necessarily an indication of a return to the general radical positions of those two post-independence Congresses on the Palestine issue, since the sections on Palestine also adopt a clear limiting of what YSP demands – Israeli withdrawal from the occupied territories and the establishment of an independent Palestinian state. While no recognition is given to Israel's right to exist, there is no call for the liquidation of Israel, or for the establishment of a single 'secular and democratic' Palestine as the PLO charter demanded. Israel is mentioned by name, being described as 'the political incarnation' (*tadjsīd siyyāsī*) of Zionism.[136]

In addition to what it lays down as YSP policy, the Programme of the October 1978 Congress is significant in certain other respects. As on previous occasions, it makes no mention of what had by then become a major factor in the PDRY's foreign policy, namely the emergence of an allied regime in Ethiopia. The earlier reference to rights for ethnic minorities in the Arab world, perhaps a veiled reference to Eritrea, is no longer present, but there is no (even implicit) recognition of the Ethiopian revolution, a rather significant development on the other side of the Red Sea, in which the PDRY had become involved. The issue of Yemeni unity is certainly mentioned, but it is treated in far less specific terms than might be expected, given its overall place in the PDRY's foreign policy and the intense conflict then raging in the YAR between the allies of Aden and the YAR government.[137] No particular analysis or policy guidelines are provided in the individual chapters, and it is only in the most general terms that the aim of a 'United Democratic Yemen' (*al-yaman al-dīmuḳrātī al-mawḥid*), bringing together the revolutions of 26 September and 14 October, is evoked.[138] An overall impression is that the specifically regional and Arab issues, with the exception of Palestine, are played down in favour of stress on the YSP's participation in the international communist movement. In particular, the October 1978 Founding Congress appears to have been intended to confirm the consolidation of relations between the PDRY and the USSR, and the YSP and the CPSU, and so to complete that process of transformation which went back to the inter-NLF conflicts of the pre-independence period. However, far from completing a process of transformation and introducing a new more stable political process in South Yemen, the October 1978 Congress was to be a prelude to new uncertainties and conflicts. Many of the characteristics of the earlier, 'pre-scientific', phases of the National Front were to re-emerge within the structures of the party of the new type.

2 The Yemeni Socialist Party: 'normalisation' and factional conflict

The presidencies of ʿAbd al-Fattāḥ Ismāʿīl and ʿAlī Nāṣir Muḥammad

The defeat of Sālim Rubiyyaʿ ʿAlī and the establishment of the YSP seemed, at first sight, to introduce a new, more stable, phase in the post-independence evolution of South Yemen. With the transformation of the NLF into a centralised 'scientific' socialist party, on the Soviet model, and the resolution of the main division within the leadership itself, the transformation begun in the early 1970s appeared to be complete. South Yemen faced the second decade of independence with a clear leadership strategy, and a more structured and comprehensive relationship with its main ally, the USSR. These prospects were, however, to be subject to severe strain in the years ahead. While the overall alliance with the USSR survived, as did the YSP regime itself, the pressures of regional issues, intersecting with continued factionalism in Aden, were to subject the relationship with Moscow to considerable strain, and to place the future of the whole regime in jeopardy.

At first, this process of strengthening USSR–PDRY links seemed to be continuing successfully in the period after the YSP Congress. In June 1979 the PDRY acquired observer status with Comecon and in September 1979 Soviet Premier Kosygin visited Aden.[1] In October President ʿAbd al-Fattāḥ Ismāʿīl visited Moscow and signed a Twenty-Year Treaty of Friendship and Co-operation with the USSR, as well as new agreements on economic and technical co-operation and on CPSU–YSP relations. Yet divisions inside the PDRY government and the YSP continued and within a year of the Founding Congress tensions had again come into the open. At a meeting of the Supreme People's Council on 11 August 1979 the reassignment of five top ministers and Politburo members was ratified: one, the Interior Minister Ṣāliḥ Muṣliḥ Ḳāsim, was later, in October 1980, reappointed to an influential post, but the four others were all demoted or sent into exile. These were Foreign Minister Muḥammad Ṣāliḥ Muṭiyya, Minister of State Security Muḥammad Saʿīd ʿAbd Allāh, Industry and Planning Minister ʿAbd al-ʿAzīz ʿAbd al-Walī, and Fisheries Minister Muḥammad Sālim ʿAkkūsh.[3] These four included three of the nine members of the Politburo. Both Muṭiyyaʿ and ʿAkkūsh were believed to be critical of the Soviet Union in some respects: during his period as Minister of Fisheries, Akkūsh had openly criticised Soviet fishing practices off the PDRY coast. Their dismissal could be seen as in part an attempt to remove individuals who might create difficulties for the new relationship with Moscow. But Muḥammad Saʿīd ʿAbd Allāh and ʿAbd al-ʿAzīz ʿAbd al-Walī were reportedly sympathetic to the USSR and close to ʿAbd al-Fattāḥ Ismāʿīl: their fall seemed to represent a threat to him, both because of their pro-Soviet sympathies and because they were, like the President, from North Yemen. There had been a growth of hostility to the North Yemeni influence in PDRY after the death of Sālim Rubiyyaʿ ʿAlī, a Southerner, and this issue became intertwined with that of the close relations with the USSR: the result was that both issues were used against the President and his associates.[4]

In 1980 President ʿAbd al-Fattāḥ Ismāʿīl himself left office. In April, after a meeting of the Central Committee, he resigned from his positions as President and Secretary-General of the YSP and went into exile in Moscow. The official reason given was ill-health, but the real grounds were believed to involve two other questions: his administrative abilities and the degree of his reliance on the USSR.[5] A theoretician, ʿAbd al-Fattāḥ Ismāʿīl lacked competence in economic matters, as he lacked the personal appeal which had marked Sālim Rubiyyaʿ ʿAlī. He was widely known as '*al-fakīh*', literally the person learned in Islamic jurisprudence, a term applied favourably in Iran to Ayatollah Khomeini but here denoting distance from practical matters. ʿAbd al-Fattāḥ's unpopularity was also linked to the issue of relations with the USSR; he had apparently argued that once the YSP placed itself firmly on a pro-Soviet orientation then greater economic aid would be forthcoming. The inability of ʿAbd al-Fattāḥ Ismāʿīl to provide that economic improvement which he had hoped would follow from the clear pro-Soviet policies of the Founding Congress thereby provided a situation in which a majority of the Central Committee voted for his departure.

His place as President and Secretary-General was taken by ʿAlī Nāṣir Muḥammad: an Extraordinary YSP Congress in October 1980 confirmed this change. The Resolutions of this Congress indicated that there had been no change in the YSP's general orientation. They reaffirmed that the USSR was the 'vanguard' of the socialist countries and the 'firm support' of the Arab countries.[6] They condemned the Camp David agreement signed by Israel, Egypt and the USA in the previous year, and singled out Syria and Ethiopia as two countries to which the PDRY pledged support. In discussing the Gulf the Resolutions condemned the installation of

American bases in Oman, but did not mention the PFLO by name.[7] The section on the YAR praised the 'democratic discussion between the leaderships of the two parts of the homeland'. While it called for the creation of a 'free, democratic, united and prosperous homeland', it also indicated that there were intermediate steps of 'joint work' and 'brotherly co-operation' which could precede this.[8]

ʿAlī Nāṣir sought to maintain relations with the USSR, but at the same time to improve those with Arab countries and to build alliances with the more radical states in the region. In 1981 the PDRY signed a Tripartite Treaty with Libya and Ethiopia, while it maintained a Rejection Front, first set up in 1977, with Libya, Syria, Algeria and the PLO.[9] Slowly, relations with North Yemen improved and in early 1982 the completion of a draft constitution for a united state was announced: in May the PDRY ended military support for the NDF guerrillas in the North. Later in the year diplomatic relations were established with Oman, thus marking the end of the commitment to revolution in the 'Arabian Gulf' which had been so central in the early years. Relations with Saudia Arabia also thawed again. As a result of the more moderate image of the new leadership, aid from Arab countries increased, and the economic situation within the PDRY eased considerably.

Yet that bonding of internal factional disputes and foreign policy that had characterised so much of South Yemen's post-independence history continued even after the accession of ʿAlī Nāṣir to power. In January 1981 a YSP Politburo member, ʿAlī al-Bīḍ, was dismissed from the Central Committee and from his post as Minister of Local Government: while one reason given was that he had committed a moral offence, his dismissal was also believed to be connected with his opposition to improved relations with Saudi Arabia.[10] In February 1981, it was reported that the former Foreign Minister and later Party Secretary for External Relations, Muḥammad Ṣāliḥ Muṭiyyaʿ, had been imprisoned and executed.[11] While no official announcement was ever made, Muṭiyyaʿ was accused of illegal dealings with Saudi Arabia, during a visit by President ʿAlī Nāṣir Muḥammad to the Kingdom in June 1980. Unofficially, Mutiyyaʿ was accused of having made an unauthorised, secret visit to the house of Amir Turki, a senior Saudi intelligence official: others suggested that any such contacts would have been made with full Politburo agreement. In the summer of 1982 there was a further conflict, involving a meeting in eastern Europe of three pro-Soviet personalities now in exile there: ʿAbd al-Fattāḥ Ismāʿīl, who was officially 'studying' in Moscow, ʿAbd al-ʿAzīz ʿAbd al-Walī, who was 'studying' in East Germany, and Muḥammad Saʿīd ʿAbd Allāh, who was Ambassador to Hungary. Although press reports talked of their having prepared a pro-Soviet *coup* the precise purpose of their meeting is not known.[12] But, following the meeting,

Muḥammad Saᶜīd ᶜAbd Allāh was recalled to Aden, where he was imprisoned for a time and then released. ᶜAbd al-ᶜAzīz ᶜAbd al-Walī remained in the GDR, and died there in May 1983. ᶜAbd al-Fattāḥ Ismāᶜīl remained in Moscow, but without as full an endorsement from the USSR as he had initially enjoyed, upon his arrival there in 1980.[13]

The conflicts of policy and personality that had characterised the YSP leadership even after the fall of Sālim Rubiyyaᶜ ᶜAlī in 1978 were not, in the end, to be contained by the apparently stabilising resolutions of the early 1980s. As in some other Third World revolutionary regimes, most notably Afghanistan, the dynamic of factionalism seemed to reproduce itself, however dire the consequences of such indulgence by the leadership might be, for themselves and the people they were supposed to lead. International issues, in the specific sense of disputes over the conduct of foreign policy, were not at the centre of the growing crisis within the YSP: but the policy conflict that did underlie the 1986 explosion involved, in part, a dispute about the place of the PDRY in the international arena, and, as after June 1978, the winning faction was to make accusations about its defeated opponents concerning alleged contacts with conservative forces abroad.

ᶜAlī Nāṣir was, for some time, able to consolidate his position and remove from influence those within the leadership who opposed him. In 1983–4, he was in a strong enough position to release those who had been imprisoned in 1978 because of their association with Sālim Rubiyyaᶜ and to allow back the most prominent exiles: Muhammad Saᶜīd ᶜAbd Allāh, who was appointed Minister of Housing in April 1984, and ᶜAbd al-Fattāḥ Ismāᶜīl, who was given an initially nominal organisational position, Secretary of the General Directorate in the YSP Secretariat, in February 1985, and who returned to Aden in the following month. ᶜAlī Nāṣir's economic policies brought considerable prosperity to the country, in the form of greater supplies of consumer goods and a more relaxed attitude to traders and farmers. The USSR for its part gave general endorsement to his approach: some muted hints about the overall direction of the PDRY's socio-economic development were voiced prior to 1986, but these were as much concerned to deflate the revolutionary claims of the YSP as to signal anxiety about rightist trends. Overall, the Soviet view was that ᶜAlī Nāṣir provided the best guarantee of stability within the PDRY.

Implicit reservations apart, there were no signs of substantial strain in the cornerstone of PDRY foreign policy, the relationship with the USSR, and Soviet commentators, official and semi-official, explicitly endorsed the internal and international policies of the YSP.[14] The development of Moscow's own relations with Gulf states, leading to the establishment of diplomatic relations with the Amirates and with Oman in 1985, was, if anything, parallel to and supportive of Aden's own shift in foreign policy. The confidence of the YSP in Soviet support was also evident in its ability to improve relations with China which, while never reaching breaking point, had deteriorated in the late 1970s, and which significantly improved in 1983: the fact that in January 1986, when the intra-YSP crisis broke out, the Prime Minister and Deputy Prime Minister were en route to Beijing for an official visit, the second at that level in three years, was an index of an overall improvement in PRC–PDRY relations. By contrast, relations with the west showed little substantive change: while trade with western European countries developed, there was no progress in the re-establishment of relations with the USA, a step which, despite some pretentions of concern, neither Aden nor Washington appeared interested in taking.

A comparable process of broadening and consolidation was evident in regional policy. While no breakthroughs in foreign policy occurred, relations with former enemies continued to be formally correct: visits were exchanged with Saudi Arabia, and negotiations continued, albeit in a protracted and inconclusive way, with the YAR and Oman. With one formerly conservative foe in the region, namely Sudan, there was a definite improvement: immediately following the overthrow of President Nimeiri in April 1985, broadcasts by an anti-YSP radio station based in Khartoum, which had been operating since 1981, ceased, and in December 1985 PDRY Foreign Minister al-Dālī visited Sudan to revitalise relations between the two states that had been frozen since the late 1970s – as a result of the Horn of Africa crisis of 1977–8, the Camp David negotiations of 1978–9, in which Sudan supported Egypt, and the Libyan–Ethiopian–South Yemeni agreement of 1981.[15] If anything the main development of the 1983–4 period was a marked worsening of relations with Libya: this was in part because Libya opposed Aden's ending of support for the guerrillas in the YAR and in part because of divergences between Aden and Tripoli over the Palestinian resistance movement, where Aden enjoined unity under PLO leader Yāsir ʿArafāt, while Libya backed the anti-ʿArafāt forces of Abū Mūsā and Abū Ṣāliḥ who, with Syrian support, provoked a split in 1983. The result of this was that in early 1984 Libyan aid to the PDRY was stopped and Libya, while not breaking diplomatic relations, later closed its embassy in Aden, allegedly on financial grounds. The PDRY developed friendly relations with Iran, and when the January 1986 crisis broke Aden was about to play host to President Ali Khameneʾi of Iran. Friction continued over the role of pro-Iraqi Baʿthists in North and South Yemen, and in 1985 eleven South Yemenis accused of being Iraqi Baʿthist supporters were put on trial in Aden for espionage: but despite this Aden also improved relations with Iraq, which had been at their lowest level in 1980, when Baghdad had championed the anti-YSP exiles, and Aden insisted, in contrast to Tehran, that there should be an immediate end to the Iran–Iraq war. The PDRY was associated with, but not a full member of, the front of Arab states comprising Syria and Libya that did side openly with Tehran. Overall, the international pressures on Aden diminished in the early 1980s. In contrast to the situation in the latter half of the 1970s, when considerable hostile attention had been paid to developments in the Yemens and the Horn of Africa, the Arab world, and the Peninsula in particular, was now preoccupied with other issues: the Iran–Iraq war, Lebanon and the divisions with the Palestinian movement. The PDRY seemed to have won low-key acceptance and to have entered a calmer period, when energies would be devoted to internal development. In 1982 the twenty years of conflict, within and between South Arabian states, that had begun with the 1962 revolution in North Yemen, appeared to have come to an end.[16]

However, beneath the surface, conflict within the PDRY continued, as evident in the post-1980 leadership changes. At the 9th Plenary Session of the YSP Central Committee, held in early May 1984, it is believed that some criticisms of ʿAlī Nāṣir were made concerning, in particular, his monopoly of the top offices of party and state. At the same time, ʿAlī ʿAntar and others appear to have called for the return, and reintegration into the YSP leadership, of ʿAbd al-Fattāḥ Ismāʿīl. From early 1985 onwards, signs of tension within the PDRY began to re-appear. In February 1985, prior to the actual return of ʿAbd al-Fattāḥ there were a number of changes in the leadership of the PDRY and the YSP: ʿAlī Nāṣir, who had been Prime Minister since replacing Muḥammad ʿAlī Ḥaytham in 1971, resigned his position and was replaced by Ḥaydar Abū Bakr al-ʿAṭṭās, an Egyptian-educated electrical engineer, who had since 1977 been Minister of Communications. ʿAlī Nāṣir thereby lost the monopoly on the top three positions of power (President, Prime Minister, Secretary General of the YSP) which he had maintained since the fall of ʿAbd al-Fattāḥ in 1980. At the same time, membership of the Politburo and Central Committee that had been elected at the 1980 'Extraordinary' Congress was expanded to include al-ʿAṭṭās, and ʿAlī Shāʾiʿ Hādī, both of whom were later to emerge, in different ways, as opponents of ʿAlī Nāṣir.[17] It was at this time too that ʿAbd al-Fattāḥ Ismāʿīl, although not readmitted to the Politburo, was given his new position in the YSP Secretariat.

Despite these changes and organisational compromises, divisions within the leadership continued to sharpen, and in May 1985 there were reports of troops being placed on alert and of an attempted *coup* by elements believed to be opposed to ʿAlī Nāṣir and in support of the former

Defense Minister ʿAlī ʿAntar.[18] In an emblematic but significant move which appeared to be designed to strengthen ʿAlī Nāṣir's position, the forthcoming YSP Congress was now proclaimed to be the 'Third'. It was technically the 'Second' in that the 1980 Congress, which removed ʿAbd al-Fattāḥ and his supporters, had been hitherto categorised as 'Exceptional', i.e. supernumerary: but the 'Exceptional' 1980 Congress was now to be restrospectively legitimated as the 'Second'. This 'Third' Congress was scheduled to take place in October, and the selection in June 1985 of delegates and of members of the Central Committee and Politburo occasioned considerable conflict within the YSP. ʿAlī Nāṣir now faced opposition from a group focussed around ʿAbd al-Fattāḥ, Muḥammad Sāʿīd ʿAbd Allāh, ʿAlī ʿAntar and Sāliḥ Muṣliḥ. Supporters of the latter seem to have won an unexpected number of seats in the scheduled Congress, and open conflict was staved off only by a series of last-minute compromises. It is believed that the Soviet Ambassador, Vladislav Zhukov, was active in arranging for a compromise solution, but there were reports in the months preceding the Congress of each side arming its supporters. It was perhaps significant of uncertainties surrounding the Congress that, while foreign parties sent messages of congratulation to the Congress, no foreign delegations actually attended its proceedings, an unusual omission in such cases. South Yemeni readers can hardly have failed to note the curious photograph of the Congress audience that appeared in the official paper *14th Oktobr* accompanying ʿAlī Nāṣir's report as Secretary-General: the front row, conventionally reserved for the Politburo, was almost empty, with only three leading officials – Sālim Sāliḥ, ʿAlī al-Bīḍ and Ḥaydar al-ʿAṭṭās – pictured as present in the hall.

The end result was that, while the YSP Congress was being held, from 11–13 October 1985, positions in the new governing organs were allocated by an apparently calculated division of predominance: ʿAlī Nāṣir Muḥammad's supporters had a majority in the Central Committee, while his opponents had a majority in the Politburo. The new Politburo comprised fifteen members, whose affiliation, on the basis of subsequent developments, can be identified as follows:

(i) for the President, 6: ʿAlī Nāṣir Muḥammad, Abū Bakr ʿAbd al-Razzāḳ Bādhīb, ʿAbd al-Ghanī ʿAbd al-Ḳādir, Anīs Ḥasan Yaḥyā, ʿAlī ʿAbd al-Razzāḳ Bādhīb, Aḥmad Muṣāʾid Ḥusayn.

(ii) independent, 2: Ḥaydar ʿAbu Bakr al-ʿAṭṭās, ʿAbd al-ʿAziz al-Dālī.

(iii) opposed, 7: ʿAlī ʿAntar, Sāliḥ Munaṣṣir al-Siyyalī, Sāliḥ Muṣliḥ Ḳāsim, Sālim Sāliḥ Muḥammad, ʿAlī Shāʾīʿ Hādī, ʿAbd al-Fattāḥ Ismāʿīl, ʿAlī Sālim al-Bīḍ.[19]

A sixteenth candidate and member of the Politburo, ʿAbd Allāh al-

Khāmrī, was also, on later evidence, not part of ʿAlī Nāṣir's group. The power of the President's opponents amongst the voting members of the Politburo was further enhanced by the unpublicised but continued presence of representatives of the North Yemeni opposition on the Politbuto. While not able to vote, and themselves divided over the YSP leadership issue, these North Yemeni cadres were, in the main, also opposed to ʿAlī Nāṣir.

All in all, this outcome of the third YSP Congress was unstable: major issues of personnel allocation and policy were left for resolution after the Congress. It was not that the documents of the Third YSP Congress proclaimed, or hinted at, any significant changes in foreign or domestic policy, and on international issues in particular the decisions and policies were very much in the mould of the 1978 and 1980 Congresses.[20] There was an overall statement of earliest positions, and the USSR and Cuba were singled out for special praise. Support was expressed for the unity of the Palestinian movement and for the nationalist forces in Lebanon. One new element was an outspoken attack by ʿAlī Nāṣir on the Muslim Brotherhood and the use made of Islam by 'reactionary' forces outside the PDRY. Indications were that this was particularly strong in the Hadramaut, and was being encouraged by the inflow of remittances from Saudi Arabia. At the same time, while condemning this trend, ʿAlī Nāṣir warned against 'leftist' and 'chauvinist' responses to it. There did appear to be unanimity on major policy issues. Rather, as so often in such situations of one party monopoly of power, the real tensions were developing beneath the surface, and were to emerge, later, in a form all the more explosive because of the inability of the formal, and supposedly democratic, organs and congresses of the party to give controlled and legitimate expression to them.

The crisis of January 1986

The particular issue around which tension grew after the Congress was that of leadership posts in the government and the YSP. In February 1985 ʿAlī Nāṣir had conceded to pressure and resigned one of the three top posts he had held: as already noted, the position of Prime Minister was then taken by Ḥaydar Abū Bakr al-ʿAṭṭās: in no sense was he a political counterweight to ʿAlī Nāṣir, since, while to some extent autonomous of the President, al-ʿAṭṭās was not one of the historic leaders of the YSP. Following the October Congress, pressure mounted within the Politburo for additional changes in the personnel holding key posts in the YSP Secretariat, an institution which, as in the USSR, often served as the central policy-making body and directed the work of the formally more important Ministries. The critics of ʿAlī Nāṣir wanted ʿAbd al-Fattāḥ to become Secretary for Ideological Affairs and Sālim Sāliḥ Muḥammad, a former Foreign Minister, to become Secretary for External Relations. Most importantly of all, however, they wanted ʿAlī Nāṣir to give up his post of YSP General Secretary. According to later accounts, the meetings of the top leadership in the weeks following the Congress were tense and inconclusive, and ʿAlī Nāṣir's opponents later accused him of ignoring decisions that had gone against him. He, for his part, was to accuse his critics of trying to stage a *putsch* within the YSP.

In January 1986 the conflict within the leadership broke into armed conflict in Aden and parts of the hinterland. In a sanguinary fortnight beginning on 13 January, thousands of party members and members of the armed forces and militia were killed: the official figure was 4,330, but other observers put the figure considerably higher. Many millions of dollars worth of damage was done to buildings and economic installations in Aden, the figure being put some months later by the new President at $120 million, and by other observers at over $140 million, equivalent to a fifth of all foreign aid received since independence.[21] Of even greater economic moment was, however, the fact that the crisis within the country dealt a serious blow to the confidence of the emigrant communities in the regime and precipitated a sharp fall in remittances, which were already reduced because of falling revenues in the oil-producing states. The economic consequences of a loss of morale on the part of the population as a whole, and of a severely fragmented administrative apparatus, were unquantifiable but immense. As a result of this intense, if short-lived, civil war, ʿAlī Nāṣir and thousands of his supporters fled into exile, in the YAR and in Ethiopia. Of the fifteen Politburo members elected in October 1985 the six associated with the President escaped into exile. Soon afterwards, however, a new leadership emerged, composed both of people who had apparently been neutral in the dispute and of opponents of ʿAlī Nāṣir. Many of the leading opponents of the former President were slain in the fighting, including four Politburo members killed by ʿAlī Nāṣir's supporters on the first day: ʿAbd al-Fattāḥ Ismāʿīl, ʿAlī ʿAntar, Sāliḥ Muṣliḥ, ʿAlī Shāʾīʿ Hādī. But ʿAlī al-Bīḍ survived to become Secretary General of the YSP, as did two other members of the Politburo known to have been strongly opposed to the President, Sāliḥ Munaṣṣir al-Siyyalī, and Sālim Sāliḥ Muḥammad, and the two independents who were out of the country on 13 January, al-ʿAṭṭās and al-Dālī. These five members of the Politburo remaining in power in Aden were supplemented on 6 February by the addition of four new full members and two additional candidates: the Politburo now included Muḥammad Saʿīd ʿAbd Allāh, the Minister of State Security Saʿīd Sāliḥ Sālim, Faḍl

Muḥsin ʿAbd Allāh, a former Minister of Finance and now a secretary to the Central Committee, and the new Prime Minister, Yasīn Saʿīd Nuʿmān, an Egyptian-educated economist who had been Minister of Fisheries and Deputy Prime Minister and who had been elected to the YSP Central Committee only a year beforehand. Muḥammad Ḥaydarah Maṣdūs, the new governor of Abyan, the region from which ʿAlī Nāṣir came, was appointed as a candidate member, along with Sāliḥ ʿUbayd Aḥmad, the Minister of Defense.[22] Of the neutrals, Ḥaydar Abū Bakr al-ʿAṭṭās now became President, while the Foreign Minister, Dr ʿAbd al-ʿAziz al-Dālī, remained in his position. But many of the country's top diplomats were either dismissed, or resigned in support of ʿAlī Nāṣir, during the following months. A major haemorrhage of the top personnel of state and party occurred, in addition to the overall destruction and loss of life involved. The lists of top officials expelled from the YSP and the Supreme People's Council contained the names of dozens of important officials, as did, equally, the lists of the dozens of YSP personnel slain in the January fighting.[23] Perhaps the most important change of all was not in who joined the Politburo or was expelled, but rather the appointment, initially as a member of the Central Committee and as new Chief of Staff, of Colonel Hayt͟ham Ḳāsim Ṭāhir, the tank commander whose opposition to ʿAlī Nāṣir had done so much to turn the tide of the fighting in the first few days. He, and the military apparatus he led, were to emerge in the months ahead as major actors on the South Yemeni political scene, an importance symbolised in the latter part of 1987 by his nomination as a candidate member of the Politburo itself.

Following the January 1986 crisis the YSP leadership was gradually able to reconstitute itself, bringing together committed political opponents of ʿAlī Nāṣir, such as ʿAlī al-Bīḍ and Muḥammad Saʿīd ʿAbd Allāh, and figures who had been in a more neutral position prior to the crisis, such as al-ʿAṭṭās. There were evident tensions between these two groups, not least on how to treat prisoners associated with ʿAlī Nāṣir, and those who been ousted early in ʿAlī Nāṣir's period can hardly have found it easy to work with those, such as al-Siyyalī, who had for a long time collaborated with the former President. But the fragility of the new regime alone must have acted to ensure, at least temporary, coherence.

In effect, the nine-man Politburo formed in early February 1986 acted as the directing group within the country, but it was noticeable to many observers that the power of the YSP had been to a considerable extent consolidated thanks to the emergence in a stronger position of the institution that had held out against ʿAlī Nāṣir, the army. In November 1986 new elections were held for the Supreme People's Council and these definitively removed from its ranks those who were accused or suspected of support for ʿAlī Nāṣir. In June 1987 a new YSP leadership was confirmed by a General Party Conference, the term 'Conference' signifying, as in the USSR a year later, an extraordinary gathering designed to reconstruct the Party, rather than a regular policy-making 'Congress'. This Conference reappointed the existing Politburo, although al-Dālī was to be dropped in the following September, and appointed a new Central Committee: twenty-four members of the 1985 Central Committee were removed, in addition to the six Politburo members already dismissed in February 1986. The June 1987 General Party Conference introduced no new directions in foreign policy, and was fulsome in its praise of the USSR: but it was accompanied by indications on the part of the YSP leadership that a more critical and open style would be introduced into its operations.[24] Whether this was in fact to occur, or whether such declarations were merely designed to acknowledge the 'international significance' of the new Soviet policy of *glasnost* remained to be seen. The past record of the YSP, and the precarious situation in which it now found itself, hardly suggested that a serious democratisation of the regime was about to occur.

Causes of conflict: a tentative assessment

Initially, both sides claimed that the other had begun the fighting on 13 January, and there is evidence that, in the manoeuvring of the previous few months, both factions had indeed mobilised support in their respective strongholds within the armed forces. The nervousness occasioned by fears of an Israeli strike against Aden, following the seizure of the *Achille Lauro* passenger ship by armed Palestinians in October, may have served to heighten tension between the factions and ʿAlī Nāṣir's public declarations in early January that PLO forces were *not* stationed on PDRY-controlled islands at the mouth of the Red Sea would indicate that this fear was widespread. In the weeks before 13 January opponents of ʿAlī Nāṣir had made a number of statements that were interpreted by the President as threats to his person or his position, in addition to their unreported attempts to weaken his influence at YSP leadership meetings. It would be difficult to claim with any confidence that the President's opponents had *not* contemplated using force against him. But, in the light of the evidence subsequently available, there seems to be no reasonable doubt that, whatever his opponents may have been intending to do at some later date, the events of 13 January were precipitated by ʿAlī Nāṣir Muḥammad himself: in an attempt to rid himself of his opponents within the YSP leadership, the President organised a secret plan to murder tens of top officials in a single day. Aden Radio indeed announced on 13 January that four top officials had been executed for treason –

ʿAbd al-Fattāḥ, ʿAlī al-Bīḍ, ʿAlī Shāʿīʾ and ʿAlī ʿAntar. The plan seems to have been for persons loyal to ʿAlī Nāṣir to surprise the President's opponents at meetings scheduled for different parts of Aden on the morning of 13 January, and for the President then to claim there had been an attempt on his life. The plan partly succeeded, and several YSP leaders were murdered in the Politburo meeting room on the morning of the 13th. But some escaped, and they were able to rally support within the party and armed forces. While ʿAlī Nāṣir's supporters brought in militia from outside Aden, much of the regular armed forces, angered by the murder of top officials, especially those from Radfan and al-Dālī, where the post-1967 army had recruited heavily, opposed the President. Although ʿAlī ʿAntar himself was killed at the start of the fighting, his investment in placing recruits from his native area of al-Dhālīʿ in the tank corps paid off, and gave ʿAlī Nāṣir's opponents an important source of strength in the ensuing battles.

After several days of fighting, it was the coalition of opponents that came out on top. Prime Minister al-ʿAṭṭās and Foreign Minister al-Dālī were in India at the time, on their way to a visit to China, and it would seem that they were unaware of the conspiracy brewing. But on 17 January they flew to Moscow and after negotiations with the Soviet leadership agreed to form part of an alternative government. ʿAlī Nāṣir had come close to victory in his factional dispute, but in the end he failed, at the cost of a terrible blood-letting and enormous damage to the country. The remark attributed to Fidel Castro when he met ʿAlī al-Bīḍ a few weeks later at the 27th Congress of the Soviet Communist Party summarised what many allies of the PDRY were thinking: 'When', he reportedly said, 'are you people going to stop killing each other?'

As with earlier factional disputes in South Yemen, it is only partly possible to reconstruct the causes of the January 1986 crisis. Rivalries of personality certainly played a part, and ʿAlī Nāṣir appears to have been unwilling to share power with other historic YSP leaders. Some indication of the underlying course of development during ʿAlī Nāṣir's Presidency can be gained by examining the fate of those nine leaders who comprised the 1978 Politburo. Seven (out of a total of nine) members of the 1978 Politburo were formerly members of the NLF, and of these ʿAlī Nāṣir in time stood alone against the other six in the years that followed. His opponents were later to claim that he had killed three YSP leaders, two of them 1978 Politburo members, who had died in the early 1980s: Muḥammad Sāliḥ Muṭiyyaʿ, executed in 1981, while ʿAlī ʿAntar was in India; ʿAbd al-ʿAzīz ʿAbd al-Walī, who had earlier been said to have died in the GDR of natural causes in March 1983; and Huṣayn Ḳumāṭa, the militia chief, whose death in prison had been ascribed to suicide. While the latter two accusations are debatable, especially so in the case of ʿAbd al-ʿAzīz ʿAbd al-Walī, the charge that ʿAlī Nāṣir had Muṭiyyaʿ killed in prison, without judicial proceedings or Politburo authorisation, appears justified. All four of the other 1978 YSP Politburo members from the NLF were set against ʿAlī Nāṣir in the 1986 crisis, two being killed (ʿAbd al-Fattāḥ and Sāliḥ Muṣliḥ) and two forming part of the new post-crisis leadership (al-Bīḍ, Muḥammad Saʿīd ʿAbd Allāh).

At the same time, the explosive conflict over positions in the Party Secretariat involved not just personality, but also the question of who would have their hands on the levers of power. The record of ʿAlī Nāṣir's period in power, from 1980 to 1986, suggests that he was trying to consolidate his own position by using minority factions within the YSP to reduce the power of the historic NLF leaders. Thus he relied on the supporters of Sālim Rubiyyaʿ ʿAlī who he had released from prison and on the two smaller groups that had formally merged into UPONF in 1975, the PDU and the PVP. This is suggested by the fact that the only members of the 1978 Politburo to remain loyal to ʿAlī Nāṣir were the PDU and PVP representatives: in statements following the crisis ʿAlī Nāṣir was, for his part, to claim that his opponents within the YSP had broken the February 1975 agreement under which the NLF merged with these two smaller groupings. In addition to reliance on the PDU and the PVP, ʿAlī Nāṣir also bolstered his position by promoting previously marginal ex-NLF officials into key positions: two of these, Muḥammad ʿAlī Aḥmad, Governor of Abyan Province, and Aḥmad Muṣāʿīd, Minister of State Security and promoted to the Politburo in February 1985, are believed to have played an important role in urging the President on to attack his opponents. One dimension of the factional dispute was, therefore, a struggle for power, that of ʿAlī Nāṣir and his various allies competing against the remaining 'historic' leadership of the YSP that had emerged from the earlier Movement of Arab Nationalists and the NLF.

Much was said at the time about the influence of 'tribal' factors: while PDRY leaders denied with indignation the relevance of these, there can be little doubt that loyalties and animosities of a tribal and regional kind had played a part in the development of the crisis and did so in the fighting itself. Soviet writers had no hesitation in adducing this as one factor, even as PDRY leaders branded such explanations as 'unscientific'.[25] As in other countries of the Peninsula, tribe and regional identity was not just a relict of nomadic or peasant society, but was a form of association that permeated new state systems, affecting employment and patronage patterns in the post-1967 regime as it had that of the Federal apparatus, and especially the army, before 1967.[26] The officer corps of the Federal Army had been drawn disproportionately from what was later the Third

Governorate, comprising the former Sultanates of Aulaqi, Dathina and Abyan and, while many of these military personnel had been maintained in the post-revolutionary state, there had since independence been a broader recruitment policy from Radfan, Yafaʿi and Dhālih. People from these areas had coalesced, in alliance with people from the YAR, against those from Dathina and Aulaqi. In many cases these links were not tribal in a straightforward sense but encompassed regional groupings broader than the traditional tribe. Such affiliations did not *on their own* provide an explanation of political factionalism in the PDRY, but a striking degree of correlation could be observed: thus ʿAlī Nāṣir, a Dathini, relied on the former supporters of Sālim Rubiyyaʿ ʿAlī, himself from the Third Governorate, and on those of the Aulaqi Aḥmad Muṣʿid and the Audhali Muḥammad ʿAlī Aḥmad, the Governor of the Third Governorate in January 1986. The opponents of ʿAlī Nāṣir were drawn from Dhālih (ʿAlī ʿAntar, Sāliḥ Muṣliḥ), Yafai (Sālim Sāliḥ Muḥammad, Faḍl Muḥsin), and from the YAR (ʿAbd al-Fattāḥ Ismāʿīl, Muḥammad Saʿīd ʿAbd Allāh). Two other regional and mainly non-tribal groupings were on the sidelines, but fell, to a considerable extent, into one or other position: those of Adeni origin, represented in the PDU and PVP, sided with ʿAlī Nāṣir, while Hadramis tended to oppose the former President (al-Bīḍ, al-ʿAṭṭās, al-Siyyalī).

That tribal affiliation was not a sufficient explanation is evident from the shifts in alliances over the post-1967 period: if such loyalties had been the sole determinant, then it would be hard to explain the fact that ʿAlī Nāṣir had opposed Sālim Rubiyyaʿ ʿAlī in 1978, despite the fact that they both came from the same region, or that Sālim Sāliḥ had remained in a regime that had killed his relative Mutiyyaʿ. The limited explanatory power of tribe or region is also shown by the fact that comparable intra-revolutionary disputes have broken out in societies that do not have a tribal or comparable regional component – from China to Grenada. But such links can do much to account for the positions of individuals, and, perhaps more importantly, for the way in which different sections of the state apparatus, especially the army, reacted in crises. If official PDRY policy after the January crisis was to dismiss any mention of tribal and regional factors as 'unscientific' and mischievous, such affiliations were known to every Yemeni, and were something that the Russians, like the British before them, were well, and at times resignedly, aware of in the functioning and malfunctioning of the South Yemeni state.

Beyond these factors, however, there were differences on policy, and in particular over the question of how far to liberalise the economy and orientate it for increased consumption. Ever since the March 1968 NLF Congress ʿAbd al-Fattāh Ismāʿīl had always been on guard against what he saw as 'petty-bourgeois' tendencies in the Yemeni revolution and, on his return from exile in the USSR in March 1985, he based his criticism of ʿAlī Nāṣir on this question. He and his associates claimed that in removing rivals from within the YSP leadership ʿAlī Nāṣir had, with the help of money from the west and the conservative oil states, formed an alliance with the technocrats of Aden and with the remnants of the Adeni bourgeoisie. The result was corruption in party and state, and unwarranted concessions to foreign businesses and governments. While these differences were muted at the time of the January crisis, the post-ʿAlī Nāṣir leadership was later to spell them out in its critique of his 'right opportunist' policies. Thus in a statement of support to the new leadership issued by YSP members at Aden University in late January 1986 reference was made to the economic policies of ʿAlī Nāṣir: 'These disgraceful practices have struck at the national economy, resulted in parasitism in the public and co-operative sector, and opened the internal market for the allurement of capitalist consumer goods which spoil the strugglers' spirit and conflict with our economic and political policy. This has all been accompanied by the spread of social ills – bribery, favouritism, mediation at the government's various organisations, and the misappropriation of public property: at the same time blocking the duties of security, unionist, and accountancy organisations and hampering their role in protecting public properties from misappropriation and misuse'.[27] In a major assessment of the crisis issued by the Central Committee in the following September the same themes were raised:

[t]here is . . . an emerging bureaucratic and bourgeois layer which has allied itself with the parasitic layers in society. It is given vocal support by the opportunist rightist current.

Corruption has also spread into some parts of the government machinery as a result of certain administrative leaders taking part in brokerage and making personal gains in dealings with foreign capitalist companies who are implementing a number of projects relating to development plans, as well as with trading companies in the capitalist countries with which commercial relations are increasing.

The gravity of those phenomena has been compounded by the weakness of ideological and political action within the ranks of the state borders and the non-application of a revolutionary class policy in the context of dealing with cadres, instead of which the criteria of balance and personal relations were applied. This afforded technocratic elements the opportunity of domination over important positions in the state apparatus.

These themes, centred on a condemnation of the 'right opportunist' line of ʿAlī Nāṣir, were resumed and presented at greater length in the 'Critical-Analytical' document submitted to the YSP membership for discussion prior to the June 1987 Conference.[28]

Overall, it can be said that this issue, of economic policy and the relations between political and social processes within the PDRY and external factors, was a central one in the YSP indictment of ʿAlī Nāṣir: to this were added the other charges of a more specifically political character – his alleged violation of norms of party control, his links with disgraced members of the regime, and his, unspecified, ties to 'counter-revolutionary' forces external to the PDRY.[29] The latter involved generic and unsubstantiated claims that he had been supported by 'counter-revolutionary' elements outside the country:[30] the 'Critical-Analytical' document submitted in mid-1987 charged ʿAlī Nāṣir with being unduly influenced by his relations with western commercial interests. The charge that he had political ties to the west appears factitious, but there may have been more truth in the claim that lax control of contracts and projects inside the PDRY had led to undesirable consequences. The case of the governor of Abyan, Muḥammad ʿAlī Aḥmad, who invested funds received from a construction contract in bowling alleys rather than in housing the poor, may illustrate this concern. There is not adequate evidence on the basis of which to assess how just this critique of ʿAlī Nāṣir was, or how realistic the, presumably more revolutionary, alternatives of ʿAbd al-Fattāḥ and his supporters were. Suffice it to say that whatever policies its leadership pursued, the PDRY was in a difficult economic situation: before 1986 the economic climate had worsened as a result of rising debt repayment rates, falling remittances, and persistent low productivity. Difficult choices were there for any leadership, which could not be resolved by resort to an idealised more egalitarian system, or by branding all attempts to manage the PDRY's place in the world economy as 'petty bourgeois'. In this context, it is worth recording that, for all its denunciation of 'right deviationism', the post-ʿAlī Nāṣir leadership pursued economic policies apparently similar to those pursued by the previous President.

Such an examination of the internal causes of the 1986 conflict makes it more possible to address the question of how far foreign policy issues and the influence of other states played a part in the January crisis and in its outcome. At first sight, there was remarkably little indication that this had been the case. All outside states, not least the USSR, seem to have been taken by surprise by the events of 13 January. The USSR had certainly encouraged the return of ʿAbd al-Fattāḥ Ismāʿīl, but the Soviet expectation seems to have been that his return would consolidate the unity of the YSP (see below, chapter 6) and Soviet diplomatic and party advice throughout 1985 was in favour of reconciliation and unity within the YSP. The Russians seriously miscalculated what the results of ʿAbd Fattāḥ's return would be; this is not the same as saying that they realised what could happen. On 13 January itself, the Soviet news agencies at first repeated ʿAlī Nāṣir's claim about the execution of four Politburo members, and only on the fourth day did it begin to report that the situation was confused and uncertain. The pattern of Soviet diplomatic activity during the crisis bears this out. The two aims of Soviet policy were to assist the emergence of a stable successor government, and to prevent outside powers from taking advantage of the situation inside the PDRY. There were some reports of other external elements in the conflict but these are unsubstantiated and, even if true, would appear to be marginal: thus some western diplomats reported unidentified planes, said to be Omani jets, as having participated in the fighting around Aden airport, and the new leadership was to claim that ʿAlī Nāṣir included amongst his supporters criminals and right-wing exiles who had returned from Saudi Arabia, possibly with KSA support and with US money. Some western reports, including statements by William Casey, Director of the CIA, subsequently claimed that Soviet military personnel had played a role in the later stages of the fighting, but this too was an unsubstantiated charge.

This apparent insulation of the crisis was compounded by the emphasis of the new YSP leadership upon continuity in their foreign policy, and by the efforts they made to reassure Peninsula states, and particularly Oman, of their good will. Although the opponents of ʿAlī Nāṣir had, in broad terms, been associated in the 1970s with a more militant foreign policy in the Peninsula, it does not seem that this issue was one that acquired prominence in the pre-January factional disputes. Moreover, the new regime at once proclaimed continuity in foreign policy, and despatched messages and envoys to the countries of the Peninsula, beginning, in early February, with a mission to Oman. The continuity at the Foreign Ministry, where al-Dālī remained as Foreign Minister, and the promotion of al-ʿAṭṭās and Nuʿmān, two moderates with good contacts in the GCC countries, seemed to confirm this. If anything PDRY foreign policy in the following months showed a tilt towards a more centrist Arab position, moving towards some reconciliation with Egypt and refusing to adopt Iranian positions on the Gulf war. There was no sign after January of a more militant position on Oman or the YAR, or of any revival of support for the NDF or PFLO. The former was divided by the YSP crisis and a significant proportion of its leaders and members supported ʿAlī Nāṣir: another faction under Djayr Allāh ʿUmar, secretary of the cadre party within the NDF, supported the new regime. If Aden did give some hints that the NDF still remained able to rekindle guerrilla war in the North, at least through a revival of clandestine radio broadcasts, this was more a means of encouraging the YAR not to back ʿAlī Nāṣir in any attempt to recapture power than a declaration of a reversal of policy. As for relations with the USSR, these two were marked by continuity, with both sides stressing the need to consolidate and develop previous commitments.

The official post-crisis view on the role of foreign policy in the conflict was laid out on the 'Critical-Analytical' document submitted to YSP members as part of the pre-Conference discussions in June 1987. The majority of this text was devoted to internal issues, and 'left' and 'right' deviations were identified. In the field of foreign relations, the 'left' had, it was said, failed to find an appropriate balance between national and internationalist interests, and had engaged in 'adventurist' initiatives that had harmed the Party's policy of peaceful coexistence. As for the 'right deviationist' current, i.e. that of ʿAlī Nāṣir, it was accused of having undermined relations with the USSR and other socialist countries, and of seeking to replace economic ties with the USSR by relations with the advanced capitalist countries. The 'right' was accused of an unacceptable interpretation of the policy of peaceful coexistence, and of having sought to subject the Foreign Ministry to control by the President himself. The 'right' had also, it was claimed, used its influence in the field of international relations to mislead friendly parties and states about the nature of the differences within the YSP (an apparent reference to Ethiopia and to Arab Communist Parties). This constituted, therefore, a clear statement that the foreign policy of ʿAlī Nāṣir Muḥammad was to be criticised, but not that any specific element in it would be changed. Foreign issues were deployed to augment the critique of ʿAlī Nāṣir, but there was to be no fundamental shift from the policy he had pursued.

This apparent insulation of the YSP leadership crisis was deceptive, however, for the events of January 1986 had, for three main reasons, important connections with the PDRY's international stance. First, the core reason for the crisis was a dispute within the YSP leadership about the overall direction of the South Yemeni revolution, and of how to preserve that revolution in a Peninsula of oil-rich and conservative states. It reflected the difficulties faced by the YSP in balancing the commitment to socialist orientation with economic relations with other Peninsula states, and the expectations about consumer goods and commercial liberalisation which proximity to the oil states had created. In this sense, the January crisis was about the same issue that had so divided many other Third World revolutionary states, including China, of how to integrate themselves to a degree with the world market without, in so doing, losing their distinctiveness and overall strategic direction. In South Yemen as in so many other revolutionary states, the leadership discovered that the 'middle road' had its own special dangers.[32] Secondly, while the USSR played no instigatory role in the crisis, it did act energetically once the crisis had begun to protect its investment in the PDRY and to encourage a transition to a stable, post-crisis regime: this was evident in Soviet mediation attempts during the fighting, in the rapid resupply of military and economic equipment in February and March, and in the subsequent greater assertion of Soviet control over party and state apparatuses in the PDRY. The model of restabilisation and assertion seen elsewhere in situations where local party personnel lost control of a situation – be it in Afghanistan or the Central Asian Republics of the USSR – was repeated, in milder but equally firm fashion, in the PDRY.[33]

Thirdly, while the January crisis led to no direct clashes with neighbouring states, it did disrupt the peaceful and increasingly close ties between Aden and some of its neighbours. Relations with Ethiopia and the YAR were affected because of the presence there of tens of thousands of ʿAlī Nāṣir supporters whom Sanʿāʾ and Addis Abbaba refused to hand over. In the case of Ethiopia there was, well after the crisis, recognition of ʿAlī Nāṣir as the legitimate leader of the PDRY, a commitment in clear and unique divergence from that of the USSR. In August 1986 there was an additional crisis concerning relations with Jibuti, when PDRY planes forced down an Air Jubuti flight on its way from Sanʿāʾ, in the mistaken belief that high-ranking ʿAlī Nāṣir associates were on board. Other states in the region realised that the great internal debilitation of the South Yemeni state might provide an opportunity for new pressure on the PDRY, something in which some officials in the USA at least were keen to encourage them. One further area in which the PDRY's international relations were negatively affected was in dealing with other radical parties in the region. If the NDF from North Yemen was split, the majority of the Arab communist parties were alienated from the new YSP leadership. The 1987 Conference announced that fraternal delegations from around the socialist bloc, including Afghanistan, Vietnam, Ethiopia and Cuba, were present but there was no mention of any Arab communist party attending.

Although no military consequences followed immediately, the 1986 crisis did introduce a period of much greater tension and uncertainty in the PDRY's relations with the region. The end of the twenty years of war in the South Arabian arena which came in 1982 did not, therefore, mark the termination of upheaval within the PDRY: rather, the very terms of the early 1980s settlement themselves provoked conflicts within the YSP and within South Yemeni society as a whole that were to lead, in January 1986, to another bloody explosion of factionalism, on a scale and with a destructive import never seen before. The January 1986 crisis placed in jeopardy the whole future of the South Yemeni regime, and opened a period of uncertainty in its relations with neighbouring states.[34]

This debilitation of the regime was all the more significant because the international climate in which the PDRY found itself in the late 1980s was in several respects less favourable than that which had prevailed earlier. The fall in oil prices affected both the prospects of Arab state aid to the PDRY and the level of remittances from migrants. While the relative decline in tension in the Horn was helpful, the growing crisis in the Gulf made it more difficult for Aden to straddle the Iranian–Iraqi gap. On what was, for the PDRY, the most important regional front, that of relations with the YAR, the balance of advantage had been shifting significantly in the North's favour, well before the 1986 crisis broke out. Of long-run but as yet incalculable import was, of course, the change in overall policy in the USSR. The more vigorous search by the USSR for resolution of Third World crises, on the one hand, and the enjoining of more sober and open politics within Soviet allies on the other, meant that the YSP leadership emerged from the 1986 crisis to find itself in a much less certain world. In common with other Soviet allies in the Third World, the YSP cannot have been fully confident that the *perestroika* being advocated by Moscow was entirely appropriate to its own position, and must also have been alarmed that the more open criticism and assessment evident within the USSR would be applied to it. If, despite its conflicts with neighbours and its own internal divisions, the South Yemeni revolutionary regime had been able to remain in power for the first two decades after independence, and if its main external supporter remained committed to it, the third decade nonetheless promised not a little uncertainty and not a few difficult decisions.

The making of foreign policy

If in all political systems domestic factors and divisions within the leadership play a role in the making of foreign policy, this is especially so in revolutionary regimes. Indeed, there could be a special branch of foreign policy analysis, the study of how foreign policy is made, concerned with revolutionary regimes alone. Four general factors account for this. First, revolutionary regimes are engaged in substantial transformations of their own societies, and these processes, however framed in domestic terms, have inevitable international repercussions, in terms of the supports the transforming states need and the reactions of states and social groups outside. Secondly, revolutionary regimes are prone to extremes of factional conflict, and, whether or not international issues play an initiatory role in these conflicts, they inevitably affect the making of foreign policy and the ability of such regimes to pursue international goals in a consistent manner. Thirdly, as a result of such factional disputes, the victors in any round of conflict draw on whatever resources and arguments they can to discredit their defeated opponents: thus the accusations about foreign policy levelled against Sālim Rubiyyaᶜ ᶜAlī and ᶜAlī Nāṣir Muḥammad after their defeats may or may not have been accurate, but they served an internal, factional purpose. Finally, and perhaps most importantly, the legitimacy of the regime at home rests in some measure on the international goals it pursues – on the allies it acquires, and the political forces it assists. All of these foreign policy considerations, whilst by no means unique to the PDRY, were evident in the formulation of its foreign policy in the post-1967 period.

The disputes within the Yemeni state had many causes. They involved personal, tribal and domestic policy issues distinct from foreign policy; but it is noteworthy that at each major change in the post-1967 history of the PDRY and of its ruling institution issues of foreign policy did play a role. The evolution of the ruling organisation, from NLF to YSP, was marked at each stage by an intersection of internal and external forces, as was that of the YSP after 1978. If this was in some measure due to the factionalism within the Front, it was also due to the forces acting on it from without. The process of restructuring the Front itself was to a considerable degree one marked by the influence of the Soviet Union, and by a series of agreements on co-operation between the NF and the CPSU.[35] Since 1972 Soviet instructors had been teaching at the High School for Party Studies and Soviet advisers were present in the rest of the state apparatus. Yet this increase in Soviet influence was offset by other tendencies which either opposed or sought to modify the alignment of state and party with the USSR – by the resistances of Ḳaḥṭān al-Shaᶜabī and Sālim Rubiyyaᶜ ᶜAlī, both of whom ultimately lost their positions as President, by the more diffuse, critical climate within the YSP which brought about the fall of ᶜAbd al-Fattāḥ Ismāᶜīl in 1980, and by the factional momentum that exploded in January 1986. The vicissitudes of events in neighbouring states, especially the YAR and Oman, also had an impact on the PDRY, in enlarging and then reducing its room for manoeuvre, and its search for allies.

Yet this intersection of foreign and domestic issues also points to another central feature of the process of policy determination, namely the centrality of the ruling organisation in foreign policy making. The reason why foreign policy disputes were reflected in party conflicts was that it was in the latter that power remained concentrated: the NF had taken power in the latter half of 1967 and, through its various transformations, it remained the ruling institution in South Yemen, with all bodies of the state, civilian and military, subordinated to it. As the Internal Statute of the UPONF stated in 1975, the Central Committee of the Front 'appoints its representatives to the supreme bodies of state and economy, and approves the nomination of its representatives as Candidates of the Supreme People's Council'.[36] There was a duality of power – of the formal and the informal – but this split was sited in the Front itself.

This dominance of the Front was evident in the manner by which foreign policy was actually implemented. The official leading decision-making body in the country was always the Front leadership or the Congress: it was from here, not from the periodic meetings of the Supreme People's Council, that the guidelines on foreign policy emanated. Moreover, the everyday determination and conduct of foreign policy reflected the domination of the party. Some influential ministerial positions were given to people who were not leading NF personalities – either junior officials, but with technical qualifications, or members of the PDU and PVP, or non-party officials. This was not so in foreign policy, where the first six foreign ministers between 1967 and 1979 were all senior Front personalities, with the ability to take and enforce decisions within the NLF as a whole. Ṣayf al-Ḍāliʿī (November 1967 to February 1969)[37] was a leader of the NLF in the pre-independence period. Fayṣal ʿAbd al-Laṭīf al-Shaʿabī (February to June 1969)[38] was the cousin of the President, Prime Minister from April to June and the leading theoretician of the NF moderates. ʿAlī al-Bīḍ (June 1969 to January 1971)[39] had been a major guerrilla leader in Aden and the first Minister of Defence. Muḥammad ʿAlī Ḥaytham (January to August 1971)[40] was simultaneously Prime Minister and had been Minister of the Interior under Ḳaḥṭan al-Shaʿabī. Muḥammad Ṣāliḥ ʿAwlaḳī (August 1971 to May 1973)[41] was a military commander before independence and the Minister of Defence who, through his contacts with the officer corps, helped the left to come back to power in June 1969. Muḥammad Ṣāliḥ Muṭiyyaʿ (May 1973 to August 1979)[42] was a former military commander in Aden and Minister of the Interior. Later appointees were a little less prominent. Sālim Ṣāliḥ Muḥammad (August 1979 to August 1982),[43] Muṭiyyaʿ's cousin, had been Party Secretary in charge of external relations, ʿAbd al-ʿAzīz al-Dālī (appointed September 1982)[44] was a former Minister of Health. Thus for almost the first twelve years, up to late 1979, the Foreign Ministry was in the hands of a senior member of the NF. All six were members of the top body of the organisation (General Command to 1972, thereafter Politburo). Only from 1979 was the Foreign Ministry assigned to persons with previously less prominent careers in the Front, and who did not already have membership in the Politburo. Yet even then the practice of conferring the Foreign Ministry upon a technician or older professional, a Chicherin or Maisky, was not followed, since both Sālim Ṣāliḥ and al-Dālī were long-established members of the NF, who later became Politburo members.

Despite the importance of the Foreign Ministers, however, the conduct of foreign policy was never confined solely to them. For at least two other sections of the ruling apparatus came to play a significant role in the formulation and implementation of foreign policy, and so to be elements in the conflicts that revolved around foreign policy, and as a result of changes within it. One alternative centre was the Central Committee of the Front/Party itself, with its Section for External Relations and its Secretary. According to the 1975 Statutes of the Party, the Central Committee was charged with conducting relations 'with communist, socialist and workers' parties, and with progressive movements'.[45] This body grew in importance from 1972 onwards, as the PONF itself came more and more to act as a Soviet-style ruling party. As the Statutes indicated, the External Relations Section was, in the first instance, designed for relations with other parties – ruling parties in the countries of the eastern bloc, and communist and left-wing parties in the Arab world and elsewhere which had relations with Aden. It was also responsible for dealing with the international organisations of the communist movement – the World Peace Council, the World Federation of Democratic Youth, the International Union of Students and several others. Since the Arab world had its comparable organisations, the Secretary also took responsibility for dealing with them. In common with other communist and left-wing countries, a considerable amount of attention, time and money was devoted to the activities of relations with such bodies involving conferences, seminars, visiting delegations, exchange of messages, congratulations on anniversaries and related 'solidarity' activities.

A third centre of foreign policy conduct was the Presidency. Both Constitutions, of 1970 and 1978, gave the President the task of 'representing' the state externally, while they assigned to the Council of Ministers the task of 'proposing the broad outlines of foreign policy'.[46] Moreover, as chief executive, the President was involved in discussions on and the carrying out of foreign policy decisions. But the Presidential role also reflected the particular place which certain issues had in South Yemeni foreign policy, both because of their intrinsic importance and because of the absence of conventional diplomatic channels for dealing with them. One was North Yemen, the other the Palestinian resistance. Although North Yemen was a separate state, it had no conventional diplomatic relations with South Yemen: neither state accepted the legitimacy of the distinction between them, and there were no embassies in each other's capital. Rather, relations were conducted bilaterally, between the Presidents of each country, and the appropriate delegates and sub-committees attached to the Presidencies.[47] The most frequent publicised form of contact between the two countries was by means of the message, verbal or written, conveyed by a personal envoy of one President to the other. Considerable importance attached, therefore, not only to the individual wishes of each President, but also on the state of personal relations between the two heads of state. The collaborations of al-Ḥamdī and Sālim Rubiyyaᶜ ᶜAlī (1974–7) or of ᶜAlī Nāṣir Muḥammad and ᶜAlī ᶜAbd Allāh Ṣāliḥ (1980–6) therefore represented significant foreign policy developments. Relations with the Palestinian resistance were also centred in the Presidency, and the various Palestinian groups had missions in Aden, for both diplomatic and military assistance purposes. After initially cool PLO–South Yemeni relations, the PLO established a diplomatic mission in Aden; its representative, Abbas Zakī, was accredited as an ambassador and had become, by 1977, the doyen of the diplomatic corps.[48] In the case of both North Yemen and the Palestinians, the President derived political benefit from being seen as the person who represented South Yemen in dealings on what were two important and domestically sensitive foreign policy issues.

The ruling party was also responsible for dealings with another kind of foreign organisation, namely the guerrillas whom the PDRY aided. The two most important of these were those operating in North Yemen and Oman. The former included parts of the MAN, and the process of unification in the South was explicitly seen as encouraging a process of convergence in the North, first into one single North Yemeni party, a unified party as in the South, and then, at some later stage, to the creation of the single Yemeni party envisaged by later Congresses. Some Northern officials served in the Southern party, and several leading officials in the South were by origin from the North.[49] Given the fact that the PDRY claimed from 1970 to be the state of the whole Yemen, this claim to a pan-Yemeni party identity was therefore central to the whole policy of the PDRY towards the North. The creation in 1976 of the NDF and in 1979 of the cadre party, the YPUP, within the NDF, based on MAN elements, was very much an extension of organisational developments in the South. The Omani guerrillas were, similarly, a former MAN branch, and were also strongly supported for many years by the South Yemeni party: only in November 1982 were the PFLO's radio facilities in Aden ended.[50] However, Omani representatives did not sit on the NF–YSP Politburo, as NDF cadres did.

The President's special position in foreign relations was, however, confirmed by a quite different tendency, namely his position in dealings with some foreign governments. Some of the latter, and in particular the oil-producing Arab states, seemed to view and conduct state-to-state relations in predominantly personal terms. They believed in dealing with individuals they trusted, and in giving aid to that individual rather than to a government or ministry in the recipient state.[51] In the case of Saudi Arabia, this meant that after Sālim Rubiyyaᶜ ᶜAlī's visit to Riyadh in 1977 some Saudi gifts were given directly to the President.[52] This may have encouraged Saudi Arabia to believe that it had greater influence over the PDRY government as a whole than it was warranted to believe, and it may also have encouraged Sālim Rubiyyaᶜ ᶜAlī to imagine that he could use Saudi aid to consolidate his own domestic position by using Saudi donations. A similar mistake, of undue reliance on one individual, may have been made by the USSR in the period 1978–1980, when ᶜAbd al-Fattāḥ Ismāᶜīl was President. Yet in both cases the apparent monopoly by the President of dealings with another state from which aid was expected was followed by an adverse reaction within the PDRY.

Beyond the course of internal political development and factional conflict, there were other major influences upon the course of foreign policy-making. The independence won by South Yemen in 1967 and the accompanying revolution initiated a course of political and economic development within that country very different from that which had previously existed there. The government committed itself to establishing state control of domestic politics and of the economy, and, under the policy of 'anti-imperialism', to preventing foreign states, individuals and economic forces opposed to these changes from exerting influence upon the country. Given the revolutionary origins of the leadership and their willingness to maintain the urban economy at levels of austerity in contrast to pre-independence days and in increasing contrast with the other states of the peninsula, it was possible for the PDRY to pursue this radically different path in the post-independence years. Yet the ability of the leadership to implement and sustain such a course was also limited in a number of important respects and these limits compelled it to modify or compensate for its programme as the years went by.

In the first place, the leading party was itself impeded in what it could define as policy. Divisions within its membership persisted from the pre-independence period right through to the late 1980s: of the two dozen or so leading personalities of the early 1970s only five were left in positions of influence by 1982,[53] and only one, ᶜAlī al-Bīḍ, after January 1986. The political leadership also lacked the education or experience to conduct the transformation of the country, and was to some extent forced to rely on technical experts from inside the country, or from abroad, to formulate and implement its policies. Secondly, while the Front leadership did not submit its decisions to the population for assent, it could not simply ignore the wishes of the population on all major issues. If this was true of such political issues as Yemeni unity or Palestine, it was even more so in the matter of living standards. The urban population remembered the prosperity of the British days; the population as a whole was aware of the increased wealth of the oil states, and of the consumer goods which this made available. Coupled to the widespread pressure for emigration, in order to earn higher wages in the oil states, was the desire for higher standards at home and for more consumer goods. From the late 1970s onwards the demonstration effect of Saudi Arabia and Kuwait, even of North Yemen, induced the government to go some way to meet expectations, to open relations with the states of the Arabian Peninsula and to lessen restrictions on migration and domestic business.[54] A third internal limit was the meagre economic base of the country: the PDRY had a small population, of under two million, but even that was too large for the country's agricultural resources to meet. A combination of a limited area of cultivable land, low productivity, bad administration and natural disasters kept agricultural output down.[55] Despite hopes of finding oil or other minerals, no major source of primary product exports was found up to 1984, and the oil discovered then was limited in quantity. A foreign investment law was passed in October 1981, but it had no noticeable results. And, although the port revived somewhat in the mid-1970s, it could never regain its former prosperity because of changes in the international economy that would have affected Aden whatever the political regime in power there. Throughout the post-1967 period the PDRY ran a deficit in foreign trade, and by the early 1980s it had imports at over $700 million and exports (excluding re-exports) of around $30 million: the gap was filled by remittances, at up to $450 million, and aid at around $170 million per year.

These internal limitations were compounded by the external situation in which PDRY found itself and by the policies which it sought to pursue. By posing as the champion of revolution in the region, it placed itself at odds with the neighbouring states and with much of the Arab world. This led to a series of wars and border clashes and to a constant preoccupation with security. While military expenditures remained low – at around 25 per cent of the total budget compared to over 40 per cent in the days of the Federation[56] – the concern with security necessitated South Yemen finding an ally for military aid, training and strategic guarantees. It soon did so, in the USSR. The requirements of the post-independence PDRY, however, went further than military needs, since the crisis of the economy and the development aims of the new government necessitated that it find economic assistance from abroad: Russia, China and the GDR were willing to provide some aid, but increasing amounts were also acquired from international agencies and from the Arab states. At the end of 1982 total foreign debt stood at $817 million of which 48 per cent was owed to the USSR and eastern Europe.[57] Even apart from state-to-state aid, the economy of South Yemen relied on external funds from migrants for the balance of payments and this reliance on workers' remittances was double-edged: if it provided foreign currency that could be used as the state wished, it forced it to pay more attention to the wishes of the emigrant population, and it also deprived the country of up to a third of its able-bodied men.[58] In addition, the remittances created a reliance that could not be sustained: the oil states would not employ such numbers of Yemeni men for ever, since their own expenditures would fall, and as they aged the migrants' ability to earn would decline. This latter trend forced the PDRY government to make a choice – to accept a drop in foreign currency earnings, or to permit more men to emigrate to reproduce the emigrant labour force.

There was a further factor that led the PDRY leadership to establish new links with the external world, namely its pursuit of models according to which to reorganise policy, society and economy. The divisions within the PDRY leadership and the NF's lack of government experience meant that in the initial period a variety of goals and models were proposed for the post-independence course. These ranged from adaptations of radical Arab states' policies – as in Egypt, Syria or Algeria – to proposals for implementing Soviet or Chinese strategies. In the end, it was the Soviet model that was to prevail, both because of the growth of the special foreign policy alliance with the USSR and because the Soviet model accorded in certain respects with the requirements felt by the leadership to be present in South Yemen. This was evident in the political institutions of the country – in the YSP and the legislative system – in the economic development around the five-year plan, and in social policy, on such matters as education, women and the press. It was not a matter of simply reproducing the model applied in the USSR so much as adopting that modified version of the Soviet model developed by Soviet theorists and administrators for third world countries classified as 'states of socialist orientation'.[59] One result of the January 1986 crisis was to reinforce the hold of Soviet advisers on the South Yemeni state.

Ultimately, and most importantly, the PDRY's post-independence course in foreign policy relied upon developments in the region surrounding it – on the attitude of existing governments, and on the fate of the revolutionary movements to which the PDRY oriented itself. Events in North Yemen, Saudi Arabia, Oman and the Horn of Africa had a bearing on the foreign policy of the new Republic and on its ability to find allies in a conflictual environment. The search for an independent political and economic path had, therefore, to be balanced by these other preoccupations, which produced new constraints upon the country, and limited its opportunities. Distinct as they were from the constraints of colonial rule, they were nonetheless major factors in South Yemen's development from 1967 onwards.

3 The advanced capitalist countries

At the moment of independence in November 1967 South Yemen was granted diplomatic recognition by the major industrialised countries of the west – Britain, the USA, France, West Germany and Japan. Its entry into the UN on 14 December 1967 was unopposed and was welcomed by, among others, the representatives of the UK and the USA.[1] In October 1969 it joined the International Monetary Fund and the World Bank. Yet from the beginning, its relations with the OECD states had an ambivalent character: while South Yemen continued to conduct the majority of its trade with these countries, and to maintain diplomatic relations with most of them, it was in sustained conflict with them on political issues. This was not so much due to the legacy of the pre-independence years: though some issues of conflict with Britain inherited from this period remained, they gradually subsided and were not prominent features of South Yemen's post-1967 foreign policy. Nor was it due to conflicts over developments internal to South Yemen itself – the country remained, as it had been before independence, of limited intrinsic interest to the developed countries of the west: there were few disputes over investment, citizens of these countries, or the political character of the regime. Most criticism of developments *within* the PDRY came from Amnesty International, the independent human rights organisation, which was repeatedly critical of judicial and prison procedures in South Yemen.[2] Conflict with western states centred, rather, on issues of another character, namely those pertaining to the international role of South Yemen, in particular its policies in the region of the Red Sea and Arabian Peninsula, and to the manner in which South Arabia as a whole was involved in the east–west conflict.

It was, above all, South Yemen's support for the rebellion in neighbouring states and the development of its military alliance with the USSR that antagonised the west. It was the west's support for conservative regimes in the region and the development of an enhanced western military presence on land and sea that constituted the main point of grievance in Aden. In this sense there *was* a certain continuity with the pre-independence period: the conflict between the conservative and radical forces had been in train in the Peninsula since the overthrow of the Imam in North Yemen in September 1962, and was to continue to take a military form right through to the signing of the PDRY–Oman recognition agreement in 1982. The independence of South Yemen therefore represented a major punctuation, a point of transition, but not a beginning or an end, in this twenty-year South Arabian conflict between local insurgents and external powers. At the same time, east and west had been in conflict in the Arabian Peninsula and its flanking waters for some time before 1967: the Soviet presence in Egypt, Iraq and North Yemen had been seen as threatening to the west, just as the western presence in Saudia Arabia, Iran and the British protected states of the Peninsula had been seen as unwelcome by the USSR.

What the independence of the PDRY did was to introduce a new chapter in this drawn-out conflict, by transferring South Yemen from one side of the east–west conflict to the other, and by linking this transfer to the increased support for rebel movements in Oman and North Yemen that now came from the PDRY. Coming as this transition did in conjunction with two other major developments, the defeat of Egypt in 1967 by Israel and its withdrawal from North Yemen soon afterwards on the one hand, and the January 1968 British decision to withdraw from the Persian Gulf by 1971 on the other, the independence of South Yemen therefore formed part of a reorganisation of the terms of the east–west conflict as they were posed in the west Asian arena as a whole. While the British and Egyptian withdrawals removed one major factor of conflict, on the western side of the Arabian Peninsula, they coincided with the emergence of a new and major element of uncertainty on the eastern side, the Gulf: in the late 1960s the centre of western strategic concern therefore shifted from Red Sea to Persian Gulf. But if the major protagonist of the radical movement in Arabia, Egypt, was thereby removed and found no comparable replacement, the departure of Britain, Egypt's opponent, *was* compensated for by the growth in influence of other powers that had till then played a secondary role in determining the affairs of Arabia, namely Iran and the United States. Thus, while the pattern of east–west conflict in Arabia had, up to 1967, been dominated by the Egyptian–British clash in the south-west corner of the Peninsula, the post-1967 independent regime in Aden now found itself increasingly confronting not Britain but the major power that replaced it in Arabia, namely the USA.

In the years immediately after independence, South Yemen's relations with the industrialised western countries consequently developed in a controversial manner. Aid talks with Britain were terminated in May

1968. Relations with West Germany were suspended, by the latter, in July 1969, and broken with the USA, by Aden, in October 1969. All foreign-owned businesses in the Republic, with the exception of the BP refinery and the Cable and Wireless facility, were nationalised in November 1969. But by the early 1970s a different note had entered into South Yemen's policy. While maintaining its militant stand on issues in the Arabian Peninsula and the Third World generally, and while consolidating its relations with the socialist countries, particularly the USSR, the PDRY sought simultaneously to work towards improving those with the west. This process of consolidation was reflected in the Fifth Congress of 1972. Then, according to Foreign Minister Muṭiyyaᶜ, the NF 'took the decision to diversify our relations, to co-operate with all western countries which were prepared to respect our sovereignty and which were disposed to contribute to the economic development of our country.'[3]

For the PDRY, the motives behind this revised policy were evident. First, having established state control of the economy, it no longer needed to lay as much stress as before on the campaign *against* foreign capital and new laws on foreign investment were later introduced. Conversely, as development plans were initiated from 1971 onwards, the PDRY experienced a shortage of foreign aid and technical assistance. The reluctance up to 1975 of Arab states to provide aid and the limits on that offered by the socialist countries reinforced the sense that aid from the west was worthwhile. South Yemen continued to conduct around half of its trade with the industrialised western countries (see table 1) and its economic experts realised that the country could benefit both from the financing and from the expertise of these developed economies. Calculations of diplomatic balance may also have played some role: while Aden's foreign policy was clearly directed against these western powers, the PDRY leaders could see that a complete rupture, in the manner of China or North Korea, would be politically as well as economically harmful.[4] They also believed, as many other Arab and socialist states did, that a degree of 'inter-imperialist contradiction' existed, between Americans and Europeans, particularly France, as well as between America and Japan, from which smaller states of the Third World could benefit.[5] A general policy of seeking improved relations with these states simultaneously involved a belief in the possibilities of such a differentiation.

From the perspective of the developed western states, however, the attractions of improved relations with the PDRY were more limited. Some diplomatic contact was obviously beneficial, as the UK calculated. Two western European governments France and Sweden, did provide some limited economic aid. But there were major reasons why such

Table 1. *PDRY imports from industrialised capitalist countries: 1985 (in US $m.)*

	Imports
World total	762.00
Industrial countries of which	351.34
Australia	70.11
France	35.49
Germany	23.83
Italy	24.58
Japan	43.47
Netherlands	39.95
UK	49.86
USA	10.01

Source: IMF *Direction of Trade Statistics*, 1986.

relations were, from the point of view of the western states, restricted. First, the PDRY was a small and poor country: there were few benefits to be gained from improved political or trading relations with it. Secondly, the PDRY remained committed to a course of revolution in Arabia, a 'rejectionist' stance on the Arab–Israeli question, and alliance with the USSR, all policies that alarmed the west, particularly as the issue of Arabian oil grew in importance during the 1970s. Thirdly, the PDRY was in conflict with more powerful states in the region, in particular Saudi Arabia and Iran, and western states did not want to take initiatives vis-à-vis Aden that would antagonise these countries. Fourthly, unlike Egypt and Somalia, the PDRY seemed unwilling to modify its foreign policy in return for substantial aid, Arab or western. South Yemen's interest in improved relations with the west was not therefore reciprocated to the extent Aden desired, or, at least, not on the conditions Aden was willing to accept. While growing commercial ties with the west were to be an issue of disagreement in the 1986 conflict, foreign businesses were not interested in investing in the PDRY, with the exception of joint ventures in fishing and oil exploration.

Relations with the United Kingdom: commerce and suspicion

The period immediately following the accession of the PRSY to independence in November 1967 was one of continued tension between Britain and its former Arabian colony. Fearful of attacks upon its embassy staff and upon British nationals still in Aden, the UK maintained a commando force on an aircraft carrier near South Yemen for some time after independence.[6] The PRSY authorities continued, on their side, to denounce the British retrocession of the Kuria Muria Islands to Oman, and the new Foreign Minister drew attention to this when he spoke at the UN following the PRSY's admission to the United Nations on 14 December 1967.[7]

It was not these concerns, however, which led to the first disagreements between the UK and PRSY. There was no outbreak of violence against British nationals in Aden and there was nothing in practice that Aden could do about the Kuria Muria Islands. However, in keeping with its hostility to the years of British rule and to those who co-operated with it, and perhaps in part to impress upon the population that a new era had begun, the PRSY authorities began in early 1968 to organise a series of trials of former Federation officials accused of collaboration with Britain.[8] Those present in court were sentenced to long prison sentences, while those sentenced *in absentia* were condemned to death. They included former members of the Federal Supreme Council, the assembly of the Federation, and both Adeni and Protectorate political leaders. Among the specific charges were inciting tribalism in the armed forces in collaboration with Britain, preparing political projects in collaboration with British advisers, and conspiring with the British to bomb guerrilla forces. They were condemned as 'colonialist stooges' and 'rubber stamps, mercenaries and collusionists'. In British eyes, such measures were hostile acts.[9]

These trials were accompanied by a dispute over British military experts serving with the PRSY armed forces. At the independence negotiations in Geneva, the NLF had rejected a British suggestion that a training mission be attached to the Republic's armed forces, something the UK had offered to the earlier Federation.[10] But the Federal army had received supplies of new British equipment in the last months before independence, including coastal patrol boats and an air force of twenty-four planes. To service and fly these, a total of twenty-eight British personnel remained with the new armed forces: eighteen with the air force, seven with the navy, and three with the army.[11] In early 1968, tension grew on the PRSY's borders with the YAR and Saudi Arabia, and the British government delivered a warning to the Aden authorities, demanding that British nationals not be employed in actions outside the PRSY's territory.[12] The response of the PRSY government on 27 February 1968 was to dismiss all the British experts on service with the PRSY's forces and expel them from the country.[13] Official British sources let it be known that they were happy with the result, since they wished to be no longer involved in assisting the PRSY government.[14] Presumably, the radical intent of the new government was now clear and proven. The PRSY government, for its part, had just sent a military mission to the

USSR and it may already have received a commitment of some alternative aid. According to the Minister of Defence, ʿAlī Sālim al-Bīḍ, who dismissed the British personnel, 'They were more in contact with the British Embassy than with the Defence Ministry. We therefore had to get rid of them since they formed a government within a government and posed a constant threat to us.' He referred to the British note about use of personnel outside the PRSY's frontiers as 'a provocation, meddling with our independence, and interference in our internal affairs'.[15] A subsequent Foreign Ministry statement declared that

> it was within the rights of the Government of the People's Republic of Southern Yemen to order those Britons working in the armed forces . . . to carry out any operations against any state committing an act of aggression against the People's Republic of Southern Yemen.[16]

The next issue that arose between Britain and South Yemen was the matter of the financial aid which had been left inconclusive at Geneva. There, the British had promised £12 million for the first six months after independence and had agreed to discuss further aid with the PRSY at a later date. In April 1968 a delegation headed by Sir Richard Beaumont, the British Ambassador in Cairo and former Head of the Foreign Office's Arabian Department, arrived in Aden, but on 10 May the talks ceased without the two sides reaching agreement.[17] The British government's offer of £1.8 million was not acceptable to the PRSY, and was thereby rejected. The South Yemeni request was for £60 million, and the PRSY also declared that it would not meet the other payments which the British government argued should be paid by it: these were the pensions for former employees of the colonial power and compensation for the Britons dismissed in February.[18] The British response to this was to deduct these payments from the £12 million initially promised at Geneva, and so reduce the net amount that had been negotiated as a compromise there. No definite figures are available from either the British or PRSY sides on the net amount actually paid by Britain after independence; the figure is the more difficult to arrive at because some of the items, such as planes, included by Britain in the £12 million, were capital goods already in the pipeline at the time of independence and were not, by the PRSY's calculations, part of post-independence aid. As one British official later put it, there were 'conflicting philosophies of what was meant' by the £12 million.[19] Unofficial British estimates of the net amount finally paid after independence range from as high of £3.25 million to a low of £250,000. The PRSY argued in May that £5.4 million was still outstanding. Whatever the precise amount, however, all British aid to the PRSY had ceased by the summer of 1968; in a further mark of disassociation, at the end of August the PRSY broke the line between sterling and the Yemeni Dinar.[20]

A statement by the British Minister of Overseas Development, Reg Prentice, on 12 May 1969, confirmed that the UK had 'no plans to resume' aid negotiations with the PRSY. According to Prentice the question of pensions 'is one which would have to be considered if there were a resumption of aid'.[21] In retrospect, while each put the blame on the other, it would seem that both sides had calculated that it was not worth continuing such talks. On the British side, any hopes initially entertained after 30 November 1967 that the NF would become more accommodating to British intentions in the Peninsula as a whole must have been dissipated by the spring of 1968, and even though Ḳaḥṭān al-Shaᶜabī had expelled the NF left from the government this apparently was not sufficient to allay British anxieties or those of the UK's allies. On the PRSY side, the calculation seems to have been made that the aid offered was not only far short of what the Aden government regarded itself entitled to as 'compensation' from the British government for the years of colonial rule, but also that the aid would entail a South Yemeni commitment to continue paying the pensions and debt incurred from the Federation.[22] As Lord Shackleton, the British Minister involved, later stated, the British offer 'was scarcely adequate to meet the requirements of debt or pensions'.[23] On purely economic grounds, the British offer was therefore of questionable value to Aden. In more general political terms, moreover, the advantages to the PRSY of repudiating the British connection, both domestically and internationally, may have been deemed greater than the benefit of the aid itself.

Within one year, therefore, of the British departure from Aden, the substantive links still remaining between the United Kingdom and the colony it had ruled for over a century had been broken. With the departure of Sir Richard Beaumont's mission in May 1968, meaningful meetings between British and South Yemeni government officials all but ceased. In February 1970 the diplomatic staff of the British embassy in Aden was reduced from seventeen to eleven. In 1978 the then Labour government declined to cancel South Yemen's debts and in 1979 the Foreign Secretary, David Owen, stated that he had 'no plans' to meet his South Yemeni counterpart.[24] This lack of high-level contact appears to have lasted until 1982, when the Foreign Minister ᶜAbd al-ᶜAzīz al-Dālī was received at the Foreign Office in London by the Minister of State responsible for the Middle East, Douglas Hurd.[25] South Yemen, usually still referred to in Britain as 'Aden', thereby came to occupy an insignificant part in British foreign policy, and in the British public's memory of empire.

For its part, South Yemen became preoccupied with other issues, and with other enemies, and the protracted campaign for independence seemed to loom no larger in the state's account of its origins than the struggle against the Royalists in the North, against the monarchs of the Peninsula, or against factional enemies within the Front. In the official calendar 22 June 1969, the anniversary of the ousting of Ḳaḥṭān al-Shaʿabī, became as important a date as 30 November, independence day. The USA soon replaced Britain as the major international foe.

Yet, on both sides there were issues that persisted in reminding the respective governments of the situation prior to November 1967. On the British side, there was the sensitive issue of colonial pensions. The South Yemenis had been particularly decisive in doing so, but they were not the only post-colonial state to challenge the British policy according to which pensions were a responsibility of the successor state. After Aden repudiated responsibility, a lobby in favour of former British employees in South Arabia formed in the UK, and supporters of pensioners in other overseas colonies formed an Overseas Service Association to change government policy.[26] As a result, the British government in March 1970 introduced temporary measures, paying what were seen as loans to former civil servants in South Yemen whose pensions were not being paid by the Aden government.[27] But the UK refused to see the loans as substitutes for the pensions themselves, since they wished to maintain the legal position that it was the successor states who were liable, and the 1970 loans also excluded former military personnel. The figure so committed for the financial year 1970–1 was £430,000.[28] Pressure then arose in the British Parliament in favour of Britain formally taking responsibility for the South Arabian and other pensions, and extending these to military personnel, and in 1973 the Overseas Pensions Bill was introduced, under which Britain did take responsibility for pensions and undertook to obtain repayment of the amount from the foreign governments. This bill, however, still covered only civilian employees and there was considerable resistance when an attempt was made by a group of Lords previously associated with South Arabia to extend this bill to covering former members of the Federal army and other military bodies.[29] Some of the latter were stated to have participated in the killing of British troops during the Crater uprising of June 1967. In the end the bill covered only civilian employees, but the British government agreed to pay money as loans to about 300 former military employees from South Yemen, at an annual cost of initially £100,000–£200,000, rising later to, on average, £1 million per year.[30]

On the South Yemeni side, the NF government remained committed to the 'struggle' against the 'vestiges' of British colonialism inside South Yemen and, while waging many other political campaigns, continued to pay some attention to this issue. Political statements and analyses reminded the population of the history of resistance to British rule and the date of 14 October 1963, the official beginning of the NLF's guerrilla campaign in the mountains of Radfan, continued to be celebrated. 14 October was also the name of the only daily paper. Speaking at the tenth anniversary of independence in November 1977, President Sālim Rubiyyaᶜ ᶜAlī described 14 October 1963 as

> a reply in deeds to the presence of colonialism and to the system of Sultanic rule, and to all the submissive practices associated with them. The 14th October was the correct path which enabled our people to force colonialism to evict our country. The language of revolutionary armed struggle was the main language through which our people addressed the colonial invaders.[31]

The colonial past was evoked in Law no. 17 of 1970 which created the Ministry of the Interior: this described one of the functions of the Ministry as 'enthusiastic support of all measures taken or being taken to eliminate the residues of the British colonialist and Sultanic regime and its agents'.[32] Yet these statements, even when denouncing the British role in the past, had two meanings: one an attack on the British policies of the past, the other a use of this attack and of the NLF's guerrilla resistance in order to discredit other forces in the South Yemeni arena – the Sultans and Sheikhs associated with Britain in the Federation, and FLOSY and other forces to whom 14 October was also a challenge. Thus, even when the years of struggle against Britain were evoked, this had an internal intra-Yemeni political function as much as an external foreign policy one.

Indeed, once the disputes of the 1967–8 period were over relations with Britain continued at a relatively low level. Both countries maintained embassies in the other's capital, although throughout much of the 1970s there were no ambassadors resident in either country. While South Yemeni Foreign Ministers and other officials frequently passed through London on their way across the Atlantic – to the UN or other destinations – they did not usually meet British representatives. Yet trade continued at substantial levels, with Britain accounting for between 6 and 12 per cent of South Yemen's imports during the 1970s and 1980s, more or less equal to the pre-1967 proportion.[33] Moreover, despite calls for 'liquidating' the residues of British colonialism, the major British assets in the PDRY were not immediately nationalised: BP owned the refinery till 1977, and continued to run it under a service contract thereafter, and the Cable and Wireless station was not nationalised until 1978.[34] While compensation for some of the firms nationalised in 1969 was not agreed upon, the issue of nationalised property did not constitute a major issue of disagreement between the PRSY and the UK.

Ties were also maintained in two other areas. One was education. While the independent South Yemeni state gradually reorganised its curricula and course content under the influence of Egyptian and later East German models, some links from the pre-independence period were maintained. A number of students were still sent to the UK for post-graduate work: the Minister of Trade, Muḥammad Midḥī, had studied in Britain after independence, and one of ʿAlī Nāṣir's closest advisers, Aḥmad Ḳutayb, had studied at Birmingham University in 1975.[35] The Technical Institute at Maʿala, founded in 1951 to train technicians for the port and related facilities, continued as late as 1977 to set its courses and examinations according to the British GCE system, and to have its examination papers marked in English.[36] The other area of continued contact was through emigration. No accurate figures on the number of Yemeni migrants in Britain are available, but it would seem that several thousand people from both North and South had settled in the UK by the early 1960s when British legislation prevented further flows.[37] Many Yemenis believed that the real reason for the blocking of migration in 1962 was the British fear of Yemenis radicalised by the September 1962 revolution in the North visiting the UK. But the 1962 Nationality Bill was for all colonial citizens and, although some Yemenis living in the UK did face difficulties during the last years of British rule in Aden because of fund-raising for the NLF and FLOSY, this was never a major issue.

After independence, the migrants continued to work in the UK and to return home for visits once every few years. By 1975 the PDRY authorities had established a branch in the UK of the General Union of Yemeni Workers, the comprehensive trades union operating at home. Its roughly 1,800 members organised literacy and political education classes, collected money to send home for particular development projects, and participated in political activities in the UK relevant to them, such as demonstrations on Palestine or marches against racial discrimination.[38] The numerical decline of the community, more than a decade after independence, was not a result of political factors, but of the recession in the light engineering industry of the British Midlands and North where these migrants were particularly concentrated. This led many to return home, or to seek work in the oil-producing states.

The course of UK–PDRY relations after 1967 was, however, dominated by a quite distinct issue which arose not from the past, but from the emergence of a new situation, this time in the Persian Gulf. For if the NLF had, in its view, defeated 'British colonialism' in South Yemen, the Front, now that it was in power, saw itself as encouraging an analogous resistance in those areas of the Arabian Peninsula still considered by it to be under British influence, in what was termed 'the occupied Arab Gulf'. At the time of independence in 1967 this comprised three kinds of entity:

Kuwait, an independent state since 1961, but backed by a British guarantee against Iraq; Bahrain, Qatar and the Trucial Oman states, all under British Protection, in a manner analogous to the hinterlands of South Arabia before 1967; and the Sultanate of Muscat and Oman, a formally independent state which was under considerable British influence and which was, in most important practical respects, another British Protectorate. Although at the Geneva negotiations Ḳaḥṭān al-Shaʿabī had, according to British sources, committed himself not to support resistance in other states in the Peninsula, including, explicitly, the Sultanate, the policy of the PRSY was from the beginning one of opposition, verbal and material, to Britain's presence in the Peninsula and to the arrangements made for British withdrawal when this came in 1971. The commitment to combatting 'colonialism' and 'imperialist bases' was stated quite clearly in the documents of the Fourth, Fifth and Unification Congresses and, albeit in a toned-down form, in the documents of the YSP Founding Congress of 1978.[39]

This conflict between UK and South Yemeni policies had effects in two arenas. One was Oman itself, where, from 1967 until 1975, there was a substantial guerrilla movement in the Sultanate's Dhofar province, adjoining South Yemen. As analysed below in chapter 4, Aden provided logistical support, financial aid, arms, training facilities and radio facilities to the guerrillas. South Yemen's regular forces took up position on the frontier and on a number of occasions were involved in direct clashes with Omani forces. Since Britain was bound to Oman by a defence treaty and since British officers, both seconded and contract, served with the Sultan's armed forces, Britain was therefore directly involved in military conflict with South Yemen long after independence. Although cross-border military movement ended more or less in 1976 and the British withdrew from their last base in Oman in 1977, border tensions continued until 1981, as the British support for the Omanis was maintained, albeit at lower levels. PDRY condemnations of Britain's role in Oman continued until 1981.[40] Only with the signing of the South Yemen–Oman agreement of 1982 was this major issue of dispute between the PDRY and the UK in some degree resolved. Some British contract officers were, reportedly, involved in the isolated border flareup of October 1987, but this was without longer-run consequences.

The other issue of dispute related to 'the occupied Arab Gulf' concerned the British withdrawal from the Gulf Protectorates in 1971. When the announcement of Britain's intention to withdraw was made in January 1968, British policy was to encourage the entities under Protection – Bahrain, Qatar, the seven Trucial States – to form a single federation. Previous British experiences in encouraging federations under such conditions had not been successful – in the West Indies, Central Africa and South-east Asia – but in the case of the Persian Gulf the UK's endeavours met with some greater success. Bahrain and Qatar chose to become independent as separate states, but the seven Trucial Oman states did agree to form the United Arab Amirates. The example of what had happened in Aden weighed on both sides. The British and some local rulers feared a repetition of the South Arabian scenario, with a British announcement of intended withdrawal precipitating a political upheaval. It would seem that the radical forces in the Peninsula expected something similar, especialy given the success of the guerrillas already established in Dhofar.[41] In this context, the PSRY's policy was one of hostility to the British plan, since they regarded it as illegitimate for power to be handed at independence to potentates who appeared to them to be as traditional and pro-western as the leaders of the South Arabian Federation had been.[42] In the South Yemeni media, criticism of Britain ran high to the end of 1971.[43] The PDRY also believe that there was 'British connivance' in the Iranian seizure of three Gulf islands in November 1971,[44] although Aden stopped short of breaking diplomatic relations with Britain on this issue, as Iraq did. It was only later, in the 1970s, that the PDRY achieved some accommodation with these smaller Persian Gulf states and, thereby, with the UK on this issue.

In the early 1980s PDRY–UK relations appeared to have reached a stable, if rather low altitude, plateau. South Yemeni imports from the UK ran at, on average, $60 million a year, a little lower than those from Australia and Japan, but well above other western European competitors. The number of British construction and consultancy firms involved in development projects appeared to indicate that Aden, political problems notwithstanding, was keen to develop economic ties. At the same time, there was no indication from London that it was prepared to initiate any aid programme. UK assistance amounted to one or two scholarships, at £17,000 each, for Yemenis to study in the UK, and, from 1984, £78,000 for two English language teachers in Aden. A comparable policy, restricting aid to scholarships, was pursued towards Nicaragua after 1979. Of the total sum classified as UK aid to the PDRY the overwhelming majority (£854,000 out of £970,000) was for pensions, although between 1979 and 1983 food and disaster relief was also provided on a modest scale. The political obstacles to any aid programme remained: not even the non-governmental aid agencies based in Britain had programmes in the PDRY, and South Yemen was one of around twenty states that these agencies were enjoined by the FCO not to assist. It would, moreover, have been surprising had the UK sought to spend money on assisting the development of a state which it was also, as was revealed later in Washington, conspiring with the CIA to undermine. The 1986 crisis did lead to a momentary increase in the UK interest in South Yemen, not least because the Royal Yacht *Britannia* was by chance near Aden, on its way to New Zealand, and helped to evacuate hundreds of British and other nationals. The FCO took advantage of this to express hopes of improved relations: but there was little, in retrospect, to show for this, and during 1986 and 1987 the PDRY voiced criticism of British policy in a number of contexts, British aid to the guerrillas in Afghanistan and British naval deployments in the Gulf being two cases in point.

Overall, the PDRY did not break diplomatic relations with Britain as it did with the USA, despite the much higher level of direct conflict between London and Aden. Britain for its part did not follow the example of West Germany in suspending relations, even if it did leave the post of ambassador empty from 1970 to 1980. General FCO policy was not to break diplomatic relations with states except in extreme cases, and the embassy in Aden, although cut off from most forms of contact with the surrounding society, served, it was argued by British officials, two low-key functions: as a means of exerting some influence on the Aden government and as a means of communication, the latter being enhanced by the fact that after October 1969 the UK represented the USA in Aden as well. Aden also served as a useful information-gathering post and Britain was known to share her expertise on the country with Washington. Since in the early 1970s no Arabian Peninsula state apart from Kuwait had diplomatic representation in Aden either, it was believed by the UK that its small embassy there was, however isolated, in some degree useful, even if it was a markedly reduced remnant of what had, but a few years before, been one of Britain's largest official presences overseas.

For the first few decades after independence, UK–PDRY relations were therefore at a restricted level mainly for the reasons that impaired relations between South Yemen and the developed western states as a whole. One reason was the conflict between UK and South Yemeni policies in the Arabian Peninsula, a tension that was a continuation not just of the immediate pre-independence dispute in South Yemen but of that internationalised conflict that had begun with the fall of the Imam in North Yemen in 1962. A second factor was Britain's concern not to antagonise or alarm other states in the region, which were themselves hostile to South Yemen and with which Britain had degrees of alliance. Oman was one district case, but of equal importance were Saudi Arabia and Iran. As one British official put it in an interview in 1981: 'One could not maintain more than a correct relationship with South Yemen given our relations with other states in the area.'[45] If these two factors were the most important, there were, however, two further considerations that weighed upon British policy-makers. One was a specific Anglo-Yemeni issue – the weight of history: the fact that South Yemen had been the site of an unusually bitter conflict between British forces and the local population before independence and that there was therefore reluctance in London to offering substantial aid to the new Republic. As Aden saw it, British conduct in the months after independence, both in occasioning the February 1968 dispute over the contract officers and in precipitating the breakdown in the May 1968 negotiations on aid, was at least in part designed to break whatever remaining links the PRSY had inherited from the Federation.[46] But British policy towards South Yemen was also influenced by that obvious negative fact evident to all the western states, that the PDRY was a small and poor state unable to offer any major economic benefit to Britain, whatever the political regime. South Yemen could not be an Algeria or Iraq – a significant trading partner despite disagreement on political issues. It did not therefore make sense to prejudice relations with Arabian oil-producers in favour of what remained, under independence as under British rule, an impoverished country.

Secondary actors: France and West Germany

France had, historically, little influence or presence in the Arabian Peninsula, although in the 1970s it sought to gain access to markets there, military and civilian, at the expense of other more established competitors. However, France did have a colony at the mouth of the Red Sea, opposite South Yemen, at Jibuti, officially entitled, until it became independent in 1977, the *Territoire Française des Afars et Issas*.[47] Aden had an interest in this colony: it was a rival port, a substantial minority of Yemenis lived there, as merchants and labourers, and, with the departure of Britain in 1967, the TFAI constituted the only permanent western military presence in the Red Sea area.[48] Yet, throughout the independence period, Aden maintained a cautious posture on the issue of Jibuti. The PDRY did not direct at the French presence in the TFAI anything comparable to the criticism directed at the British presence and later that of the Americans in the Persian Gulf.[49] Indeed, while aid was given to the Eritrean guerrillas and while some Jibuti opponents of France were for a time resident in Aden,[50] the official National Front and government policy on the Horn of Africa as a whole was one of caution and silence.

After the initial establishment of diplomatic relations between France and the PDRY in 1967, Aden indeed tried to develop closer relations with France and some low-level aid was later promised.[51] An incident in March 1972, when PDRY artillery on the island of Perim bombarded a French warship that had entered South Yemeni territorial waters, did not lead to a deterioration in relations.[52] The French decision, announced in

1976, to give independence to the TFAI involved a shift in political power within the colony, away from the Afars to the Issas. The latter were of Somali origin and the PDRY was at that time allied to Somalia; French policy did not arouse the hostility with which South Yemen had regarded the transition to independence in the British Protectorates of the Gulf in 1971. Moreover, while many had feared that the conflict developing between Ethiopia and Somalia would affect Jibuti as it neared independence and that one or other would invade, the opposite happened: while Ethiopia and Somalia went to war in the latter part of 1977 with each other, both accepted the independence and neutrality of Jibuti, and this acceptance by the states of the Horn seemed to guide the PDRY in the same direction. The result was that neither the manner of the French granting of independence nor the French decision to maintain a garrison of some 3,000 men there after independence was criticised by Aden.

This policy was enunciated during a visit of the South Yemeni Foreign Minister, Muḥammad Ṣāliḥ Muṭiyyaᶜ, to Paris on 8–10 December 1976, where he met high-ranking members of the French government, including President Giscard d'Estaing: this was the most important visit by a PDRY leader to western Europe in the whole post-1967 period. Muṭiyyaᶜ stated that Aden wished to preserve 'security, stability and peace' in the region and that it supported the French policy in the TFAI.[53] In March 1977 the Taʾiz Summit of North Yemen, South Yemen, Sudan and Somalia also endorsed French policy. The PDRY was at times critical of French policy elsewhere in the Indian Ocean. One particular case was French support for the separation of Mayotte from the Comoro Islands in 1976, and a pro-French *coup* in the latter in 1978. The PDRY also criticised French participation in the multi-national Sinai peace-keeping force.[54] But PDRY attitudes to France were in general characterised by considerations of a positive kind, namely the fact that France was the major western state with which Aden had the best relations. Seeking for an alternative to Britain, Aden developed relations with France, as well as using its delegation at UNESCO, based in Paris, to promote cultural and educational programmes.[55] According to Muṭiyyaᶜ, France constituted the PDRY's 'window on the whole of western Europe'.[56] Two bomb attacks on the PDRY embassy in Paris, in 1981 and 1983, were blamed on French right-wing elements, and did not visibly effect Aden–Paris relations. France was the only major western country to engage in some aid to South Yemen's economic development programmes. From the later 1970s onwards a number of French *co-opérants*, volunteer teachers and doctors, worked in South Yemen on limited-term contracts, and, although France was not a major source of South Yemen's imports, it provided economic assistance through a limited loan programme, which was used to develop infrastructural projects.[57] A French company, Frantel, built the major international hotel in Aden, and ran it until it was seriously damaged in the 1986 fighting.

The PDRY's relations with the German Federal Republic were in contrast to those with France, and more analogous to those with the UK, despite the lack of a pre-independence link between the two countries. This was because, as in dealings with the UK, West German and South Yemen foreign policies clashed directly, on the issues of Bonn's German policy and on 'terrorism', and because within the FRG relations with South Yemen became an issue of public debate. Diplomatic relations between the FRG and the PRSY were established after the latter became independent, but soon came up against the then prevailing FRG policy of the Hallstein Doctrine. According to this, the FRG would not have diplomatic relations with a state that had recognised the German Democratic Republic. One of the first acts of the PRSY government after the 'Corrective Move' was to establish relations with East Germany, and on 2 July 1969 the FRG announced that its relations with South Yemen had been suspended.[58] The Hallstein Doctrine was abandoned, however, with the development of Brandt's *Ostpolitik* in the early 1970s, and in September 1974 full diplomatic relations between the two states were re-established. The PDRY did not maintain an embassy in Bonn, conducting relations with the FRG from its Paris embassy. The FRG maintained an embassy in Aden, but the ambassador himself was resident in Sanaʿa and made periodic visits to Aden.[59]

The re-establishment of diplomatic relations between Aden and Bonn in 1974 did not however open the door to better relations, and the vicissitudes of Germany's politics continued to affect Aden's dealings with Bonn. Trade between the two countries was considerable, with South Yemen's imports running at an annual average of YD 2.0 million in the years 1969–77, compared to an average of imports from the GDR of YD 0.7 million, or a third of the FRG figure, for the same period.[60] The PDRY government was also interested, however, in receiving aid from West Germany and here the situation proved to be much more complicated. In 1968 the FRG had agreed in principle to provide the PDRY with aid totalling DM 10 million, but this had not been granted because of South Yemen's refusal to sign what was known as the 'Berlin Clause'. The FRG maintained that West Berlin was part of the Federal Republic and that all treaties or agreements signed with it should also apply to West Berlin. Aid to Third World countries was made conditional upon acceptance of this clause which stated:

Dieser Vertrag (oder: Abkommen) gilt auch für das Land Berlin, sofern nicht die Regierung der Bundesrepublik Deutschland gegenüber der Regierung . . .

innerhalb von drei Monaten nach Inkrafttreten des Vertrags (oder: Abkommens) eine gegenteilige Erklärung abgibt.[61]

The position of the USSR and of the GDR was that West Berlin was not part of the FRG, and its allies endorsed this position. The PRSY, although it did not at the time have relations with the GDR, refused in 1968 to sign the Berlin Clause.

With the re-establishment of diplomatic relations in 1974 the FRG offer of aid was repeated, but in March 1975 a new incident occurred to trouble relations between the two states. A group of terrorists from the *Rote Armee Fraktion*, or Baader-Meinhof Group, kidnapped a West Berlin politician, Peter Lorenz, on the eve of elections in that city and released him only after payment of a ransom and permission to fly out of West Germany to another country. The RAF members were given four or five possible countries to fly to, but none of the latter accepted until the West German Interior Minister, a member of the SPD government, Dieter Genscher, flew to Aden and persuaded the PDRY authorities to receive them.[62] The Aden government understood that the FRG was, in return, to provide the PDRY with the economic aid promised, and allowed the plane to land. However, as the date for the Berlin elections came nearer, with Lorenz the leading candidate for the Christian Democrats, the Bonn government made a formal application to South Yemen for the extradition of the RAF members. The West German press also put pressure on the SPD authorities by arguing that South Yemen was 'harbouring terrorists'; as a result, no aid was provided, apart from some emergency food aid and some pumps for the Aden water supply, totalling DM 3.2 million.[63] There is no evidence that the PDRY had agreed in the negotiations with Genscher to extradite the terrorists at a later date, and the official PDRY position was that Bonn had double-crossed it.[64] But, under the pressure of domestic politics, the SPD government later stated that there *was* such a commitment to extradition and declined to honour what had been a commitment on its part to supply the aid.

In 1976 a new agreement was, in principle, reached between the FRG and the PDRY, and the latter agreed to sign the Berlin Clause.[65] But, because of continued criticism inside the FRG about the failure of South Yemen to extradite the RAF members, no agreement was actually signed. In 1977 the FRG agreed that, for the year 1978, DM 14 million would be provided but soon afterwards a further incident in relations between the two countries arose when another Lufthansa jet was hijacked by the RAF in an attempt to get the release of leaders imprisoned in Germany. Mindful of what had occurred in 1975, the PDRY refused the plane to land at Aden and even tried to block the runway with tanks. The pilot

Schumann did, nonetheless, bring the plane down on land next to the runway, but he was then shot by the hijackers and his body dumped on the runway, after which the plane then flew on to Mogadishu.[66] Far from winning support in West Germany, however, by its refusal to give refuge to the plane and its statement that it wanted nothing to do with 'terrorists', the PDRY government only aroused further criticism. A series of subsequent revelations by West German and other 'terrorists', who stated that they had been trained in the PDRY, added to this hostility within West German public opinion.[67]

By 1978 it was evident that Aden was no longer willing to sign the Berlin Clause, as it had earlier indicated; however, the SPD government in Bonn still believed it could overcome these internal difficulties, and a body of official German opinion favoured the use of German aid precisely in order to counter the influence of the GDR.[68] In general, West German aid was distributed widely on a 'watering-can principle' to over eighty countries, and only states such as Vietnam and Cuba were excluded. Since 1971 a compromise version of the Berlin Clause had been elaborated, which some countries who refused to sign the standard clause were allowed to endorse. This stated: 'Entsprechend dem Viermächte-Abkommen von 3.09.1971 wird dieses Abkommen in Übereinstimmung mit den festgelegten Verfahren auf Berlin (West) ausgedehnt.'[69] But it was only countries where the FRG interest in outbidding the GDR was obvious that were permitted to sign this second clause – examples of these being Iraq and Syria. Given the hostility to the PDRY in West Germany and the limited economic and strategic attractions of South Yemen, the Bonn government would not allow the PDRY to sign this second version of the Berlin clause, and the PDRY's role in supporting Ethiopia during the Horn of Africa crisis of 1977–8 was cited as a further reason for withholding FRG aid. Somalia, with whom Ethiopia was at war, had allowed the Lufthansa jet hijacked in October 1977 to land and had permitted West German soldiers to storm the plane and release the passengers. It was rewarded with FRG aid, and even some arms. In 1980 a further obstacle to FRG aid to the PDRY arose when the Christian Democratic opposition argued against giving aid to governments which had supported the USSR in UN votes on Afghanistan.[70]

While the amount offered was small by comparison to the aid committed to the YAR (DM 45 million in 1981 as against DM14 million for the PDRY), political difficulties in Bonn prevented the commitment from being realised. Even under the Presidency of ᶜAbd al-Fattāḥ Ismāᶜīl the PDRY had re-affirmed its interest in aid from the FRG, but the precarious position of the SPD government facing re-election, and then the victory of the CDU/CSU in the March 1983 elections, meant that an aid commitment first made fifteen years earlier had still not been implemented in 1983. It was a curious development that the FRG, which had no political presence in Arabia, should have had such complex relations with the PDRY and that it was in West Germany, more than any other western country, that the issue of relations with Aden should have become an issue of domestic political debate.

Aden and Washington: causes of a rupture

As outlined above, the independence of South Yemen in 1967 coincided with an important shift in the overall strategic situation in the west Asian region, and in the Peninsula and Persian Gulf in particular. For the British withdrawal from Aden in November 1967 and the subsequent withdrawal from the Gulf in 1971 opened the way for the USA to play a much more important and direct role in the affairs of the Arabian Peninsula. US oil companies had long been present in Saudi Arabia and Bahrain, and the USA's strategic relationship with Saudi Arabia, initiated during World War II and confirmed by the Eisenhower Doctrine of 1957, had been further confirmed by Washington's support for Riyaḍh during the Yemeni civil war to offset the Egyptian presence in North Yemen that followed the fall of the Imam. In contrast to Britain, the USA had at the beginning recognised the Republic in Sanaʿa, but as civil war continued and Saudi Arabia came to see itself as more and more threatened by the Egyptian presence in the YAR, the USA downplayed its relations with Sanaʿa and the YAR broke them in 1967. The British withdrawal from the Gulf, however, as much against the USA's wishes as had been that from South Yemen, led to increased US interest in the Persian Gulf and to the evolution of a new, more forward, US strategy. Under this, Washington assumed strategic responsibility for the region as a whole, and became a major arms supplier not only to traditional clients, but also to what had till then been British-dominated states.[71]

This evolution in western policy had as a consequence the fact that for much of the post-independence period it was the USA and not the UK against whom South Yemen's foreign policy was primarily directed. While Britain remained the dominant power in Oman until at least the mid-1970s, the USA was the main partner of the major regional powers affecting South Yemen – Saudi Arabia to the north, Iran in the Gulf, and Ethiopia across the waters of the Red Sea. As the importance of Gulf oil to the USA increased in the 1970s, so the PDRY and the USA had further reason to oppose each other's initiatives. From 1972 onwards, when US–YAR diplomatic relations were established, the USA therefore came to play a role in North Yemen, as it did increasingly in Oman, especially from 1977 onwards.

The two states therefore opposed each other in Peninsula affairs; and, despite the limited range of the PDRY's foreign policy impact, there were at least three other areas where the two states' approaches were in evident contradiction. One was the Arab–Israeli issue: the Rogers Plan of 1970 and the range of US initiatives from the Kissinger shuttle of 1974 onwards, through Camp David in 1978 and the Reagan initiative in 1982, were all opposed by South Yemen. The PDRY formed part of the bloc most critical of the USA, and in 1977 joined the Front of Steadfastness and Rejection set up to oppose the Egyptian initiatives towards Israel.[72] A second area of disagreement was the Indian Ocean which had since 1968 become an area of US–Soviet rivalry and where the PDRY repeatedly sought to rally opposition to US naval and air deployments.[73] The third region was the Horn of Africa: there, prior to 1974, the PDRY supported the Eritrean guerrillas and Somalia, both rivals of the pro-American Ethiopian monarchy, and after 1974 Aden increasingly supported the revolutionary military regime in Addis Ababa that was in conflict, and for a time at war, with a now pro-American Somalia. Consequently, while the issues varied, South Yemeni–US relations were almost continuously hostile throughout the post-1967 period.[74]

Prior to South Yemen's independence trade between the two countries had been slight – 0.4 per cent of the South Arabian total in 1966 – but the USA had for many years maintained a consulate in Aden, and on 7 December 1967 the two countries exchanged diplomatic recognition.[75] There were those in the State Department who believed that the NLF's anti-Egyptian orientation might provide a basis for US containment of Egypt,[76] but within a short time relations between the two countries became acrimonious. One issue was the PRSY belief, first voiced in July 1968, that the USA was arming forces that were active from the YAR and Saudi Arabia against the Republic, and which were trying to overthrow the new regime.[77] A second issue was economic aid: both before and after his eviction of the left, Ḳaḥṭān al-Sh̲aʿabī and his ministers had asked the USA for economic aid to offset the grave problems caused by the British withdrawal and the closure of the Suez Canal. Yet throughout 1968 and 1969 they made no progress with these requests, despite some support from within the Johnson administration.[78] A third factor concerned an incident during the crisis of 20 March 1968 when a group of army personnel, angered by the radicalism of the Fourth Congress, arrested some left-wing leaders and apparently tried to stage a kind of *coup*. Ḳaḥṭān Sh̲aʿabī quashed this attempt, but a US military attaché, Dale Perry, was stopped by police while driving his car during the curfew. He stated that he had made an innocent mistake, but the PRSY authorities claimed he had been conspiring with the rebellious military.[79] Since the 20 March *coup* attempt objectively helped President al-Sh̲aʿbī to consolidate his power, the left-wing NLF opposition claimed that the move against them at that time had been carried out with the support of the USA. Militants in the rural areas even went so far as to allege that 'US imperialism' had taken power in Aden.[80]

When the 'Corrective Move' of June 1969 occurred, criticism of the USA increased and on 24 October 1969 South Yemen broke off diplomatic relations with the USA and ordered the staff to leave within twenty-four hours. The official reason given was that the USA was assisting Israel by allowing citizens with dual US–Israeli nationality to fight in the Israeli army: the moment of diplomatic breaking came after an Israeli military incursion in Lebanon, and the Aden statement spoke of 'the hostile attitude adopted by the US government towards Arab causes and above all the just cause of the Palestinian people'.[81] US officials were later to blame the incident on an inexperienced US press attaché in the Tel Aviv Embassy, who naively disclosed the figures for US nationals serving in the Israeli armed forces. But it could well have been that the issue of soldiers with dual nationality was more a pretext for the PSRY to do something it had wanted to do anyway, namely align itself with the other radical Arab states, who had broken relations at the time of the June 1967 war. Thus Algeria, Egypt, Iraq, the Sudan, Syria and the YAR had broken diplomatic relations in 1967, and the PRSY's establishment of ties with Washington so soon afterwards may have placed it in an anomalous position with the other radical states. The problem was, however, that having broken relations South Yemen found it much more difficult to re-establish them, in informal or formal terms. Two of the others were oil-producing states where, despite political disagreements, the USA had an economic incentive to maintain trade. Thus Algeria continued to trade substantially with the USA, as an alternative to France, during the period of diplomatic break, and re-established full relations some years later. Iraq followed a US interest section to operate in Baghdad as an embassy and traded substantially with the USA. Syria became involved in diplomacy around the Arab–Israeli issue and re-established relations in June 1974.[82] Egypt and Sudan under new leaders became strong allies of the USA in the 1970s, and North Yemen, after allowing a US interests section to operate within the Italian embassy from 1970, re-established diplomatic relations in 1972.[83] The PDRY, however, which had broken relations to align itself with these countries, now found itself without major assets: it had little economic attraction, it was not a major actor in the diplomatic arena, and it pursued policies that antagonised Washington and its more influential regional allies.

The change in orientation towards the industrialised west following the Fifth Congress of 1972 did not, therefore, lead to a successful rebuilding of links with Washington. Rather, both sides continued to see each other as threatening the other's interests: in late 1973 and 1974 US anxiety about the PDRY was at its height, because of the October war, and because Oman was playing up the South Yemeni threat in order to acquire US anti-tank weapons. Addressing the House of Representatives subcommittee on the Near East and South Asia in June 1973, the Assistant Secretary of State for Near Eastern and South Asian Affairs, Joseph Sisco, had drawn attention to what he saw as the security threats posed to US allies in the region.

> Mr. Chairman, as the states of the gulf and the peninsula have taken on more responsibilities for their economic destiny, they, too, have become increasingly aware of the threats they see to their security and of the need to improve their defensive capacity. These concerns have intensified as a result of the conflict between South and North Yemen last September, the continuing insurrection in Oman's Dhofar Province which has its base of support in South Yemen, and the arrest in recent months in the United Arab Emirates, Bahrain, and Oman of a number of members of the subversive South Yemeni-supported Popular Front for the Liberation of Oman and the Arab Gulf (PFLOAG), the increasing supply of Soviet arms, equipment, and technicians to South Yemen and to Iraq, the March 20 border skirmish between Iraq and Kuwait, and the March 22 attack by South Yemeni aircraft on a Saudi border outpost . . .
>
> Saudi concerns have been stimulated by the growing supply of Soviet arms into South Yemen and Iraq. In South Yemen the Soviets have stepped up their deliveries of sophisticated weapons and aircraft.
>
> The Saudis view the radical regime in Aden as representing a threat (a) to North Yemen, which is practically defenseless and which depends largely on Saudi Arabia for help in maintaining its security and (b) Oman because South Yemen continues to provide the base for the Communist-led insurgency into Oman's western province of Dhofar, and (c) Saudi Arabia itself, which last March was hit by South Yemen Migs at a Saudi border post.[84]

A number of US observers did point out that the actual capabilities of the PDRY were rather low, and for this reason they opposed the Administration's invoking of the PDRY as a reason for the large sale of US arms to Saudi Arabia and Iran. As the Chairman of the Subcommittee wrote:

> The Soviet-backed threats to Iran and Saudi Arabia supposedly emanating from South Yemen and Iraq may be real, but they are small and potential. You do not need a sledge hammer to crack a nut. Since 1965, our sales of arms and services to Iran and Saudi Arabia are roughly six times estimates of Soviet activity in the Persian Gulf area.[85]

Such reservations did not prevail: neither US arms sales policy to the region, nor official attitudes to South Yemen, were altered.

During the October 1973 war, when South Yemen co-operated with Egypt in blockading Bab al-Mandeb, the mouth of the Red Sea, for some weeks, the USA sent an aircraft carrier, the *Hancock*, to the sea off South

Yemen, together with a task force;[86] a group of ships, including an aircraft carrier, was maintained in the area until April 1974. No actual incidents were reported, but the PDRY authorities did denounce the US naval presence in the Indian Ocean and say that this force violated the Republic's territorial waters around the island of Socotra.[87] US sources speak of it as having been used as 'a visible demonstration of US presence and interest'.[88] Such a 'demonstration' could have included deterring a continuation or repetition of the Bab al-Mandeb blockade. This US naval deployment nearer the coast of South Yemen came soon after the opening of the US base on the Indian Ocean atoll of Diego Garcia: leased by Britain to the USA for fifty years in December 1966, Diego Garcia provided the USA with naval and air facilities from its operational beginning in March 1973.[89] These two events, the opening of Diego Garcia base and the 1973 war, marked the beginning of a more forward naval strategy by the USA in the western Indian Ocean that was to be developed further in the years to come,[90] and was seen as menacing by the PDRY.

In early 1974 the PDRY took an initiative in inviting to Aden a Republican Congressman, Representative Paul Findley of Illinois.[91] The official reason for the visit in January 1974 was Findley's desire to secure the release of a constituent of his, a US teacher who had been arrested for photographing Aden harbour during a transit visit some years earlier. The constituent was released and flew home with Findley. But the PDRY authorities used the occasion of the first official US visitor since 1969 to press their case. Findley came with letters to himself from Secretary of State Henry Kissinger and Assistant Secretary of State for Near Eastern and South Asian Affairs, Alfred Atherton. Kissinger's letter confined itself to stressing that the USA was 'working actively to achieve a just and durable peace in the Middle East'.[92] Atherton went further and laid out the USA's position on diplomatic relations:

> Basically, we do not feel that the existence of differences in national ideologies or political structure, or divergent views on many international issues should necessarily pose an obstacle to our having diplomatic relations with a given country. . . . As a matter of policy, we are prepared to reestablish diplomatic relations with countries which have broken relations with us when such countries wish to do so.[93]

In Aden, Findley talked with Foreign Minister Muṭiyyaᶜ who said that the PDRY wished for diplomatic relations with the USA. But there were conditions: the USA must first cease supporting forces opposing the PDRY from Saudi Arabia and North Yemen. According to Finley,

> He talked at length about diplomatic relations. He said it was necessary to view the question in context of the whole Arab world. The reason for severance was the

Israeli attack on the Beirut airport. Without US support, he said, the attack could not have occurred. Nor could the Israeli occupation of Arab lands and denial of Palestinian rights to their lands. He said Palestinians are not against the Jews. Instead, they want only a democratic Palestine state where they can live where each will have the same full rights as others.

Muti' repeated the charge that in 1968 a US military attache had a hand in resisting an attempted change in the Aden government. This led to a feeling of the people against America. Regarding border fighting, he said he believed camps were organized with the support of the US. 'We have information and proof that the American embassy in Sanaʿa supports the subversive acts against Democratic Yemen . . . Still, we are not against diplomatic relations with the US. We favour diplomatic relations with all governments which respect our sovereignty.'

He said Saudi Arabia gives support and encouragement to all ex-sultans and ex-sheiks. 'Why should Saudi want US equipment except for use against the Republic?'

'While the past is not good,' he said, 'the present looks better. We are looking ahead. We have diplomatic ties with Britain. We hope the US changes its attitude.'

He said economic, trade and cultural relations would help towards establishing diplomatic relations in the future . . .

Before any kind of diplomatic representation can be established, he cautioned, the US must first cease support of anti-revolutionary movements. 'Our people are fully mobilized against such US policies, and it is not easy or possible to change their attitudes quickly. A beginning can occur when the US stops giving any kind of assistance for subversions and starts promoting economic relations.'[94]

Later, in a meeting with President Sālim Rubiyyaʿ ʿAlī, Findley was told:

Now, the belief is held by the people of my country that all suffering, all damage caused by subversives is the work of the US government. There is much hostility to the US government. They believe all subversive acts are due to US support of subversion. All military equipment we capture is US equipment, and this makes the people feel the US is behind the attack.[95]

Findley's visit did not lead to any noticeable improvement in US–PDRY relations, although clashes along the Saudi–PDRY and Oman–PDRY frontiers ceased when Riyadh and Aden established diplomatic relations in 1976: if anything, bilateral US–PDRY relations deteriorated further, because other issues came to concern both sides. The South Yemenis were concerned about the now greater US naval presence in the Indian Ocean and the decision taken after the October 1973 war to expand greatly the facilities on Diego Garcia.[96] Criticism of the USA was at the same time occasioned by developments within the PDRY when in 1974–5 a group of employees of the US firm ITT were put on trial, accused of espionage, and some were given long prison sentences.[97] Aden was also concerned by the emergence of what US officials termed a 'trilateral relationship' in North Yemen, where the USA initiated in 1975 a plan to re-equip the YAR army with Saudi funds. In justification of this policy, a Congressional committee report of 1977 stressed the PDRY threat to the YAR, and the presence of Soviet, Cuban and East German advisers in South Yemen. According to the report, 'PDRY's superiority in numbers of troops is enhanced by an extensive array of Soviet armor, artillery, aircraft, and other weapons. To offset this impressive PDRY capability a modernized YAR armed force is deemed essential.'[98] The PDRY blamed the USA for the Iranian military presence in Oman, and when the USA began using the base on the Omani island of Masira after the British departure in 1977 this too provoked criticism in Aden.[99] The other regional issues already mentioned now began to loom larger in PDRY foreign policy: first, the shift by Egypt of allegiance to the USA from the USSR and the evolution of an active US mediating role in the Arab–Israeli dispute, and, secondly, the growing crisis in the Horn of Africa that culminated in the Ethiopian–Somali war of 1977–8.[100]

The advent of the Carter administration in January 1977 had, at first, appeared to offer some hope of improved relations between Aden and Washington. The PDRY was not a significant object of the new administration's interest and it was noteworthy that in a major speech in June 1977, outlining US willingness to displace the USSR in six left-wing Third World countries, including Somalia, Algeria and Cuba, the President did not include the PDRY.[101] In September 1977, however, in part due to the continued lobbying of Representative Findley and in part as a result of Saudi suggestions to Washington, US Secretary of State Cyrus Vance did meet with Foreign Minister Muṭiyyaᶜ at the United Nations and it was agreed that the USA would send a mission to Aden to discuss the question of having talks on re-establishing diplomatic relations. In January 1978 Findley made a second trip to Aden: he again met Sālim Rubiyyaᶜ ᶜAlī and conveyed good wishes to Carter. It is worth noting, however, that in the words attributed to him by Findley, Salīm Rubiyyaᶜ did not actually say that he wanted to re-establish *diplomatic* relations.[102] A US mission set off in June 1978, under the leadership of Joseph Twinam, the Director of Arabian Peninsula Affairs in the State Department, but it had travelled no further than Jidda in Saudi Arabia when the crisis in both Yemens broke out, and President Sālim Rubiyyaᶜ ᶜAlī was killed. The Twinam mission then returned home, and the USA refused to resume the mission, although Aden repeated its invitation to the USA to send a delegation to discuss holding talks.[103] Indeed, Washington let it be known a few weeks later that it was not interested in pursuing talks. According to one report, 'The State Department has concluded that Southern Yemen, which has only about 1.5 million people, does not pose a real threat to anyone and hence is not worth larger concern.'[104] The official view was that the USA 'cannot hope now to normalize relations with a country at odds not only with other Western powers but also with its Arab neighbors'.[105]

A number of developments appear to have led to this hardening of the US position towards the PRDY. One was the US claim that the USSR and Cuba had provoked the crisis in Aden. Another was the much more critical Saudi attitude following the June 1978 crisis: Saudi Arabia led a move to suspend the PDRY's relationship with the Arab League, and the reference to the PDRY being 'at odds' with Arab neighbours indicates that this was a factor in American thinking. (US officials were later to imply that they only agreed to the Twinam mission in the first place to gratify Saudi Arabia). The subsequent second North–South Yemen war of February 1979 can only have increased Saudi and US apprehension about the course of events in the South. A second factor in discouraging US initiative was the South Yemeni role in the Horn of Africa: although PDRY military participation in the Ethiopian–Somali war preceded the Twinam mission, it must certainly have been a major preoccupation of the State department at this time, as it was of Saudi Arabia, and the continuation of tension in the Horn was therefore an aggravation in both Aden–Washington and Aden–Riyadh relations.[106]

With the growing deterioration of US–Soviet relations as a whole from 1978 onwards, there was little prospect of improvement in the PDRY's relations with Washington. Yet some more attention was paid to the PDRY in the US political debate. For events in this Arabian state now came to symbolise the kind of threat which the USA reportedly faced in the Third World, and the June 1978 crisis was widely construed by US politicians and writers as a 'Soviet *coup*', comparable to the Soviet invasion of Afghanistan of 1979 or the Cuban intervention in Angola of 1975.[107] The change in Washington attitudes to the Third World, which began in the latter part of 1978, then combined with a particular Yemeni crisis, the war of February 1979, to produce the most significant conflict yet in US–PDRY relations. As a development of the 'trilateral' policy begun in 1975, the USA had been planning from the summer of 1978 to sell up to $400 million worth of military equipment to North Yemen. This provision would normally have involved Congressional approval, but when fighting between North and South Yemen broke out in February 1979 US officials used this as a means of highlighting the 'Soviet threat' in the Third World. On 7 March 1979 President Carter himself signed an executive order, Presidential Determination 79–6, waiving the normal Congressional approval for such arms sales.[108] The weapons were to be sent directly to the YAR as a token of US resolve. Carter is believed to have seen the inter-Yemeni war as the opportunity to take a stand after what was seen as his weakness during the Iranian revolution. Some US officials later argued that Washington exaggerated the crisis in order to appear to make a publicised stand against the USSR and reassure both Saudi and US domestic opinion, but the result was that, for a few weeks in early 1979, US policy saw itself as 'drawing the line' against communism on the border of the PDRY. US officials exaggerated the *Soviet* role, but there was a *South Yemeni* threat to the YAR.[109] In addition to the decision to supply arms to the YAR on an emergency basis, the USA at this time also despatched a naval task force, including an aircraft carrier, the *Constellation*, to the Red Sea region. As during the 1973 Arab–Israeli war, this US force was never actually used in fighting, and it was not anticipated in Washington that action would be needed. But its purpose was clearly intended to deter any possible South Yemeni advance into the North, should the opportunity for this on the ground arise.[110] The phrase 'vaguely menacing' summed up the intent. In the end, the US attempt to consolidate a new position in the YAR by the arms supplies of March 1979 was a failure. The YAR authorities resented the manner in which Saudi Arabia sought to control the supplies, and some months later it was the USSR which supplied Sanaᶜa with most of its new equipment. But the February-March 1979 crisis did make it all the more difficult for there to be an improvement in US–PDRY relations, or to relaunch the Twinam mission. Separate from these public moves, and undisclosed at the time, the CIA had begun to organise a sabotage campaign inside the PDRY that was to be launched in 1981.[111]

The US evaluation of the war itself was clear enough:

> The current fighting, which began on February 23, is more serious than past incidents. It is clearly a coordinated campaign with the apparent intention of seizing and occupying North Yemeni territory and destablizing the North Yemen government.
>
> The timing of the attack may have been related to South Yemen's desire to exploit its current superiority in equipment before our announced military assistance reaches and is integrated into the North Yemen Armed Forces.[112]

A US evaluation later in the year spelt out what Washington believed to be the underlying cause of the war:

> US intelligence . . . provided the basis of the belief that the PDRY attacks, if pressed, could succeed in gaining radical control over the southern parts of the YAR or toppling the government in Sana.
>
> Thus, the invasion seemed, at the time of the waiver, to present a threat not only to the YAR but also to the Peninsula as a whole.[113]

The issue of the North–South war in February-March 1979 was, however, compounded by the emergence of another question that further complicated US–PDRY relations at the end of the 1970s, namely the issue of 'terrorism'. While this had long been a matter of dispute in PDRY–West German relations, and while generic charges against the PDRY had been made in the US press and Congress, it was only in the latter part of the Carter administration that, under pressure from Congress, this matter became central to US foreign policy and legislation.

In correspondence between the State Department and Senator Jacob Javits of New York released in May 1977, the PDRY was named by the US government along with Iraq, Libya and Somalia as having aided terrorism in recent years. According to the report: 'There is some public evidence that the People's Democratic Republic of Yemen has on occasion allowed its territory to be used as a sanctuary for terrorists.'[114] Under the 1979 Export Administration Act controls were introduced on the sale of equipment with potential military use to countries on the terrorism list and, when, in that year, the South Yemenis tried to purchase a Boeing jet for their national airline, al-Yamda, this was blocked by the US government.[115] A report issued by the CIA's National Assessment Center in June 1981 repeated the US position:

> The government of the People's Democratic Republic of Yemen provides camps and other training facilities for a number of international terrorist groups. The PFLP maintains a major training camp there, and members of many different terrorist groups have all benefited from the PFLP training facilities.[116]

The issue of a country being accused of favouring 'terrorism' did not, however, directly relate to that of diplomatic relations: the USA did, until 1981, maintain diplomatic relations with Libya, and re-established relations with Algeria and Syria from 1974 and with Iraq from 1983. In hearings on the March 1979 Presidential waiver for arms to the YAR, Deputy Assistant Secretary of State William Crawford was pressed by Congressman Findley on why the US did not send a diplomatic mission to Aden. His explanation is worth quoting at length as it gives a good overall picture of US thinking.

> MR. FINDLEY. Up to now, up to this decision on the part of the administration, I think, our Government has been perceived as weak, as unsure, as vacillating in this part of the world. I hope that this is the beginning of a new policy, not just a spasm that will soon be forgotten and replaced by other signs of weakness.
>
> We have been through a period of reversals, Iran, Afghanistan, Ethiopia, and South Yemen. As Mr. Twinam especially knows, for 5 years now I have been urging the administration – that includes the Republican administration before the Democratic administration – to recognize the vital importance of the Yemens, and especially South Yemen, and to get a diplomatic mission down there.

I happen to be in a position to report directly, with authority, that the South Yemeni Government, throughout this 5-year period, extended the hand of friendship, seeking a better relationship with the Western World, and especially the United States. This was ignored month after month by our Government, and now we are kind of reaping the results.

My question is, are we seeking to establish a mission in Aden at this point, recognizing the importance of the geography, the importance of having a listening post, the importance of having a point of hopefully some influence?

MR. CRAWFORD. Congressman, I am deeply and gratefully aware of your interest in South Yemen, I have followed with admiration your long and ultimately successful efforts to free one of your own constituents from a very bad situation in Aden, and I am full of admiration.

The answer to your question is, we are not currently seeking to.

MR. FINDLEY. Can you explain why not? One would think we would want to be there with a diplomatic mission, today more than any other time, when the fighting is underway.

MR. CRAWFORD. I think the immediate answer is, our friends simply would not understand nor, I think, would the American people understand.

We all support the principle of universality in diplomatic relationships. President Carter is particularly strong on this point as, I think, you know. But it is easier to apply the principle of universality with some governments than others. The government in Aden, unfortunately – and this newest incursion into North Yemen is an example – makes it rather more difficult, as does its support of terrorism.

MR. FINDLEY. But, Mr. Ambassador, all of us recall that terrible pair of incidents 1 year ago when the President of North Yemen was executed – on the eve of Mr. Twinam's arrival in Aden to hopefully set up a diplomatic mission. And yet, in the wake of that execution, the new government sent word to our Government that the door was open. Mr. Twinam was still welcome to come down. To the best of my knowledge, even today, our mission would be welcome in Aden to take up the question of a diplomatic mission.

MR. CRAWFORD. On the principle of the matter we are entirely in accord with you, but we must judge not only by the words that we hear from Aden, but by its deeds; and its current pattern of deeds and its previous pattern of deeds make it very difficult to respond in the positive way.

MR. FINDLEY. But, can we not influence deeds better if we have diplomats present in the capital of the offending country?

MR. CRAWFORD. As a general matter I would agree with you. In terms of the situation in which foreign diplomats find themselves in Aden, the capital of the PDRY, I am doubtful, frankly. The experience of our allies, the West Germans, the British, and so on who are physically present, who have relations there shows that they have very curtailed freedom of movement; strong efforts are made to force the diplomatic colony to live in a single, very secluded area where it will not have access. I am myself convinced that any efforts to have the kind of free access that American diplomats like to all strata of society and have a free discourse that might influence the policies of the South Yemeni Government in exactly the direction you indicate would result in the most stringent surveillance and hampering the movements of our diplomats.

MR. FINDLEY. I am sure of that. The diplomatic movement would be hampered, but I would think a little movement would be better than nothing at all.

I want to express my deep concern over what I believe to be the policy of our Government of letting other states in the region have what amounts to a veto over our decisions to establish missions. I believe that was true in the case of Aden, and I think it is most unfortunate for us, as a world power – undignified for us to let other states veto a decision we might take on establishing a mission in an important region.

MR. CRAWFORD. I would quite agee with you if that were the case. I said, it is important that we take into account the points of our close friends in the area. I would agree our actions, if we see it as being in our own interest, should not be subject to a veto. It is a fact that the policy positions of the Aden Government make it very difficult to be responsive in this kind of situation, much as we would wish.[117]

Although a more flexible policy in general was evident in Aden when ᶜAlī Nāṣir became President in April 1980, with the advent of the Reagan administration, the prospects for improved relations with the PDRY receded further. The US view in 1981 was that there was no signal from the PDRY of interest in relations with the USA, and that a US response would be conditional 'on a more moderate approach on the South Yemeni side'.[118] Issues such as the maintainance of 'terrorist camps' and continued publicity for the PFLO were, according to one official, obstacles to improved relations. Other factors were the Soviet Union's 'unrestricted access to whatever facilities exist in South Yemen', and 'worrisome border activities' on the frontier with the YAR.[119] Robert Pelletreau, a leading State Department Arabist interviewed in 1982 repeated these views, arguing that the USA had no interest in resuming relations with the PDRY. 'To resume relations just to disagree on everything does not seem to be a very profitable course just now,' he stated. Pelletreau added that the Saudi Arabians were 'not urging us' to resume, a factor which he said was 'a consideration' in the formulation of US policy.[120] In the US media and Congress more generally, generic hostility to the PDRY continued. One influential columnist, Joseph Kraft, argued that the USA should pursue a 'spoiler strategy' of putting economic pressure on Soviet allies in the Third World, giving as an example South Yemen.[121] Another conservative strategist talked of what he termed 'the Cuba–Yemen–Oman' connection, a theme repeated by Reagan in 1980 campaign speeches in Miami.[122] In the initial days of the Reagan administration, White House officials even talked of making a Soviet withdrawal of military forces from South Yemen a test of Soviet good intentions and interest in improved relations.[123] Yet, despite this hostile climate, the Reagan administration did make some slight accommodation when in March 1982 it eased restrictions on the export of civilian aircraft to South Yemen and Syria, provided these states committed themselves not to use them for military purposes.[124] The fact remained, however, that in the early 1980s, the PDRY had no relations with the USA, while all the other Arab states who had broken in 1967 had to some degree restored them. The PDRY, along with Angola, Iran, Libya, Albania, Vietnam, Cambodia and North Korea, was one of the only eight states in the world which neither had a US embassy nor a US diplomatic mission operating in some other guise. For the many thousands of Yemeni migrant workers in New York, Detroit and California, the only consular support they had was via the PDRY mission at the UN.

From the PDRY side, the late 1970s and early 1980s had also seen new problems arising, albeit ones quite different from those experienced by the USA. The US intervention in the 1979 inter-Yemeni war was not a decisive consideration, since the US arms programme went awry, and the two Yemeni states proceeded to conduct their relations bi-laterally via the series of unity talks. What worried Aden far more than the emergency supplies to the YAR was the increased US presence in another neighbouring state, Oman. A covert US intelligence presence in Oman dated from 1971 but after acquiring the right to land at Masira island in 1977, the USA gradually increased its overt military presence there, especially after the establishment of the Rapid Deployment Force in 1980.[125] Facilities at Masira and Muscat were used by the USA, but so too were the desert airstrip at Thamrit, in Dhofar, fifty miles from the PDRY frontier, and the Dhofari port of Raysut. US equipment was positioned there, and on several occasions from 1981 onwards US troops participated in manoeuvres in Oman which were criticised by the PDRY.[126] At the same time, official publicity in the USA reported desert war games in which attacks on states similar to the PDRY were simulated.[127] To counter these developments, the PDRY conducted a widespread diplomatic campaign. It signed the agreement with Oman in October 1982, in the hope that this might lessen the room for conflicts in which the USA could intervene, and, in the following December, there were demonstrations and official statements denouncing the US manoeuvres in Oman and Somalia.[128] Domestic anxiety about the USA was heightened by a publicised court case in 1982 in which thirteen people were convicted of trying to blow up oil storage installations in Aden after receiving training from the CIA in Saudi Arabia; of these ten were subsequently executed.[129] As was later revealed, this covert operation had originated as a US response to the 1979 inter-Yemeni war, and involved the collaboration of British experts. To this was added PDRY criticism of the US role in the Arab–Israeli dispute, during and after the June 1982 Israeli invasion of Lebanon.

Both states therefore regarded the other as a threat to its security interests. US officials, from former Secretaries of State Kissinger and Haig onwards, presented the PDRY as a 'threat' to Saudi Arabia, and to both Oman and the YAR. US officials also stressed the role of the USSR in the PDRY, and there was in 1978 and 1979 considerable speculation about whether Cuban forces based in South Yemen would participate in conflicts in the Arabian Peninsula, perhaps repeating their roles in Angola and Ethiopia.[130] Both the Carter and Reagan administrations emphasised the need to show commitment to the USA's major allies in the region, and this necessitated confrontation with the PDRY. Both administrations also derived domestic benefit by conducting the campaign against 'terrorism' in which the PDRY was one, if not the most important, object of criticism. Washington therefore had no motive to re-establish relations with the PDRY, a state regarded as both too resolutely hostile and too insignificant to merit US approaches.

On its side, the PDRY felt that the USA was also a threat, its menaces ranging from support for the exiles operating in Saudi Arabia in the 1960s and early 1970s through to the arming of Oman and Saudia Arabia in the late 1970s and early 1980s and military manoeuvres in the region.[131] Aden clearly gave priority to maintaining its militant stand on regional issues, and to emphasising the US threat to its own population. Moreover, while it gave indications, as in discussions with Congressman Findley, that it wanted to have diplomatic relations with the USA, it is questionable how far this desire ever went, from 1974 onwards. The official PDRY position was that the resumption of diplomatic relations was conditional on a change in US policy; but as one issue receded, namely arming the exiles, others came to the fore, and in particular the US role in Oman. In private PDRY officials were sceptical of the benefits of having a US embassy in Aden: 'What would they do except make trouble and spy on us?' was how one senior PDRY diplomat summed it up in 1982. In the late 1970s and 1980s the disunity within the PDRY leadership made it even less likely that any initiative would be taken. The issue of diplomatic relations was therefore a function of a much wider conflict between these two states that reflected a set of tensions that pervaded the Middle East and the world.

Washington and the 1986 crisis

The failure of the 1978 initiatives, and the more overt incorporation of south-west Arabia and the Horn into east–west rivalry that developed in the latter part of the 1970s, paralysed US–PDRY relations. The Carter

Administration had already decided not to pursue dialogue with Aden any further, before the outbreak of the second inter-Yemeni war in February 1979. This latter event was portrayed in Washington as an east–west issue, and used to demonstrate American resolve: its real significance may, perhaps, be gauged from the fact that, while it was much highlighted at the time, the US response and the background to the crisis are not even mentioned in the memoirs which Carter himself, and his National Security Adviser Brzezinski, were later to publish. The Yemens, even more than other Third World conflicts, were of sympatomatic rather than intrinsic significance.

It was perhaps, indicative of the low importance of the PDRY in US policy towards the Middle East that the advent of the Reagan Administration, in January 1981 did little to alter this. Despite the odd critical reference to the PDRY in statements by US leaders, such as the first Secretary of State, Al Haig, who suggested that Soviet 'good behaviour' in the PDRY was a condition for improved east–west relations, this Soviet ally in the Third World invited little of the ire and pressure visited upon others, such as Nicaragua and Libya, and the only overt new sign of hostility was the opening in April 1981 of *The Voice of the Free Sons of South Yemen*, a clandestine opposition radio operating from Khartoum, with Egptian backing and, it can be assumed, some CIA support as well. The covert operation by the CIA that was uncovered in 1981–2 had been organised by the outgoing Carter, Administration, and its failure, in March 1982, led the new CIA Director, William Casey, to withdraw a second team of Yemeni saboteurs, as well as to tighten up the CIA's ability 'plausibly to deny' activities in which it was involved.[132] If, as South Yemeni leaders were later to aver, this sabotage campaign was linked to a broader plan by Egypt, the YAR and Saudi Arabia to overthrow the Aden regime, the reason for such a campaign, namely support for the guerrillas in the YAR, ceased to apply after the May 1982 accord between the two Yemens. In other respects, US hostility to the PDRY, if anything, decreased. Thus in 1983 Aden was permitted to import a Boeing plane for its civilian airline, despite the fact that such exports were forbidden to countries seen as supporting 'terrorism', and in January 1985 State Department officials were quoted as encouraging US investment in the PDRY as a way of countering Soviet influence.[133] In a speech attacking 'terrorist' states in July 1985 President Reagan omitted the PDRY together with Syria from a list of those countries allegedly backing such activities, despite the fact that both countries remained on the State Department's official list.[134] Some Washington observers were later to suggest that the omission of the PDRY was deliberate, exempting Aden to meet Boeing's desire to sell a plane to Aden.

These were small improvements, however, and there was no significant shift in the impasse that had continued ever since 1969, with the brief and slight improvement of 1977–8. This impasse in US–PDRY relations was re-affirmed through the January 1986 crisis. All the evidence suggests that the USA was as taken by surprise by this as were other states, and US reaction was initially reserved. US officials told reporters that their information on the crisis was 'outdated and based largely on analysis of previously known data'. As one official put it: 'We have interests in South Yemen, but no friends.' According to the same report, 'whatever the outcome, there is no thought in Washington of gains for the West'.[135] While the more serious US press reported as extensively as available information permitted on the crisis ('Leninism Amock' was the title of one *New York Times* editorial), it was only on 23 January, ten days after the crisis began, that the State Department made a formal statement: this was one directed at the USSR, and in it the USA 'expressed the hope' that Moscow would not 'intervene' in the war.[136] The State Department alleged that there were indications of a Soviet involvement on the side of ᶜAlī Nāṣir's opponents, something the Russians denied: the 23 January statement was, it would seem, designed both to lessen the degree of any Soviet involvement in restabilising the situation and to score a point against the Russians, by casting them as interfering in the South Yemeni crisis.

This statement apart, however, it is noticeable that the US short-term response to the January 1986 crisis in Aden was less than it had been to earlier Yemeni crises – those of June 1978 or February 1979. There was at first little of the propaganda campaign occasioned by the fall of Sālim Rubiyyaᶜ ᶜAlī, and there were no naval deployments in the Indian Ocean of the kind that occurred in 1979. The US had no leverage in the crisis, and, since the latter did not threaten any neighbouring states, there was no occasion for demonstrations of US military presence in the region. There were reports on 18 January, a few days after the crisis began, that the USA had offered to deploy fighter planes in Oman, to defend that country 'against any aggression from Iran and South Yemen', and the timing of the offer, although justified by the redeployment of a US aircraft carrier previously used to protect Oman, may well have been connected to the crisis in Aden and the fear of renewed South Yemeni–Oman hostilities.[137] But, although such a move could have led to precisely the kind of minatory deployment seen in earlier crises, nothing seems to have eventuated, and the immediate moves by the new South Yemeni leadership to reassure Oman of their good intentions would appear to have removed the overt reasons for such a US move.

This indifference to events in the PDRY was, however, a temporary one and concealed the extent to which the crisis in Aden, precisely because it showed how weak the regime was and the difficulties that the Russians faced there, reopened official US curiosity about the PDRY. This was not such as to suggest the reopening of diplomatic relations, but rather an interest that looked for a way in which the USA could take advantage of the leadership crisis. What this led to were a series of statements by US officials in which the USSR was attacked for its role in the crisis itself, and even accused of backing those opposed to ʿAlī Nāṣir. Thus, in late February CIA Director William Casey gave his view of events in the PDRY:

We recently witnessed a sudden and dramatic display of Gorbachev's application of the Brezhnev Doctrine in its South Yemen satrapy. As you may be aware, the Soviets succeeded in establishing a Marxist-Leninist regime in South Yemen in the early 1970s. They soon established a naval base and communications centre there to support their operations in the Indian Ocean. Recently, ʿAlī Nāṣir, president of South Yemen, began to draw away a little from the Soviets and seek more help elsewhere. Less than a month ago, hardline pro-Soviet elements in his government initiated a *coup* against ʿAlī Nāṣir. The *coup* soon escalated into a bloody civil war between military and hardline elements loyal to President ʿAlī Nāṣir and those of the hardline pro-Soviet camp. Now the hardline Yemen Vice-President happened to be in Moscow 'for consultations'. The Soviets sat and watched the blood flow for a few days, while evacuating Soviet dependents from the country. Neighbouring countries, North Yemen and Ethiopia, sought to help the South Yemen government. A few days later, it appeared that the pro-Soviet rebels were gaining the upper hand. Moscow thereupon warned both North Yemen and Ethiopia not to help the government forces. Moreover, Moscow ordered Soviet fliers, using Mig-21s given to the South Yemen government, to pound beleaguered government forces. And Soviet transport planes started bringing in additional weapons for the hardliners. To tie things up, the South Yemen Politburo then met – perhaps at Moscow's suggestion – and declared the Vice-President, then sitting in Moscow, to be the country's new President. Now this is not new. The Soviets removed two puppets in Afghanistan in 1979, and probably were behind the murder of Maurice Bishop of Grenada in 1983. The message in all these cases is clear: leaders of governments installed by Moscow who seek improved relations with the west do so at their peril.[138]

In similar vein, on 8 April 1986 Under Secretary for Political Affairs Michael Armacost included the PDRY with Afghanistan, Angola, Nicaragua and other Third World states in a list of crisis states where the USSR had been implicated:

Under Gorbachev's leadership, Moscow's involvement in Third World regional conflicts has not diminished. Indeed, there is some evidence that it has intensified ... In South Yemen, the Soviets intervened in January in an attempt to preserve a dominant role in that country and to protect access to port and air facilities needed to project military power in the region. First, they forced their clients to repatriate an opposition leader, then they abandoned him in the midst of political conflict. The result was a bloody civil war, the full human toll of which is still unknown. Thus, the Soviet determination to consolidate and, where possible, extend their influence in the Third World persists.[139]

The 1987 edition of the Pentagon's annual publication, *Soviet Military Power*, added a further voice to this Administration denunciation of the Soviet role in the PDRY:

In the brief civil war between rival Marxist factions in South Yemen in 1986, Moscow provided direct support to the hardliners, who eventually emerged on top. This support included Soviet pilots flying combat mission on behalf of the hardliners. Also, a battalion of Cuban troops, airlifted by the Soviets from Ethiopia, spearheaded the drive in Abyan Province that led to the expulsion of President Al-Ḥasani's main force across the border.[140]

It was statements such as these, made with exiguous regard for accuracy, that constituted the major US response to the PDRY crisis. This diplomatic and political position appears, in retrospect, to have been mainly for propaganda purposes, i.e. it was not related to the PDRY as such, or to what really happened there and why, but was a function of the desire to denounce the USSR with whatever charges could be made to sound plausible. It rested in part upon the ambiguity of the term 'intervention': that the Soviet Union had played some role in the ending of the crisis was evident, but the broader implication of the term, that Soviet troops had played an active or combat role, was specious.

At the same time that US officials were criticising the USSR for 'intervention', however, evidence began to emerge that the Reagan Administration itself, its interest reawakened by the January crisis, was now debating whether to play a more active role in the PDRY. The cornerstone of Reagan's policy in the Third World, the 'Reagan Doctrine', was that the USA should aid anti-communist guerrilla and resistance movements where these operated and, if necessary, create them if they did not yet exist. By early 1986 there were at least four of these that the USA was backing: Cambodia, Afghanistan, Angola and Nicaragua. The CIA had already been involved in assisting the Khartoum-based exile radio station, and had launched the unsuccessful 1981–2 sabotage campaign. In April 1986 Vice-President George Bush, during a visit to North Yemen, made reference to events in the PDRY and to the threat Aden posed in the region: 'We are concerned both about the violence of the uprising itself and about the possibility of a regime in that country that does not respect the rights and territory of its neighbours.'[141] During the same visit to the YAR Bush is also reported to have met with representatives of the opposition in exile, presumably *al-Tadjammuᶜ al-*

Ḳawmī, the coalition of former FLOSY and right-wing NLF leaders headed by Makkāwī and Ḥaytham, and to have promised them military aid.[142] Such aid would have been very much part of the broader assistance being given to guerrilla opponents of Soviet allies in the Third World under the 'Reagan Doctrine'. In the short run, little appears to have come of this, and the YAR authorities would probably have shown themselves as reluctant to be drawn into a war with the PDRY for Makkāwī and his supporters as they were on behalf of the much more substantial forces of ᶜAlī Nāṣir. Less conspiratorial US observers believed that the main reason Bush had gone to the YAR was to show support for the oil exploration work of the Hunt Company, who hailed from Bush's home state of Texas. Certainly, in the months that followed there were no indications that an active anti-YSP guerrilla movement had emerged in the South. At the same time, the statements by Casey and Armacost, and the Bush involvement of April 1986, reflecting as it did the Administration's search for areas of vulnerability in the Soviet alliance system in the Third World, indicated how the January 1986 crisis had reawakened a dormant US interest in the PDRY.

For their part, the new leaders in Aden had little reason to alter their long-standing policy on relations with the USA. There was, at first, some suggestion on the part of the new YSP leadership that, out of a desire to improve relations with Peninsula states and to counter reports of a more radical foreign policy, Aden would now be willing to re-establish relations with the USA. But, even if made after collective deliberation, such statements would appear to have been designed to head off any possible US actions against Aden rather than open a substantially new chapter in relations with Washington. Certainly, the 23 January State Department 'warning' to the USSR was met with strong criticism in Aden, which used it to argue that it demonstrated American support for ᶜAlī Nāṣir: 'What does such a US statement mean? It clearly means that the United States has declared its clear stand on the events in the PDRY and has unambiguously supported the conspirators led by ᶜAlī Nāṣir and encouraged them to persist in their conspiracy against the political legitimacy represented by the YSP Political Bureau . . . '.[143] The statement went on to warn against any US intervention, of which there was no sign, and to claim that were the USA to move against the PDRY as it had acted against Grenada in 1983 then the USSR would come to Aden's assistance, under the terms of the 1979 treaty. If by this the new YSP leadership meant to imply that the USSR would sent its own forces to defend the PDRY, then this was almost certainly misleading. The USSR has always refrained from making such a commitment, and no such guarantee is contained in the published text of the 1979 treaty: but the USSR would be expected to provide military supplies to the PDRY in the face of any attack from outside.

This last statement was, therefore, an exaggeration but it may have been designed, as was the highlighting of a possible American attack, to rally domestic support to the new leadership. Similarly, political considerations of an indirect kind may have lain behind another significant initiative which Aden took vis-à-vis the USA in April 1986, when the PDRY made strong statements denouncing the US raid on Libya. These may well have been designed not so much to influence US policy, as to promote an improvement in Libya–PDRY relations, strained since 1984. During the escalation of the crisis in the Gulf, in 1987, the PDRY on more than one occasion condemned the US naval deployments in the Gulf, and US attacks on Iranian vessels, while, out of deference to Kuwait, it supported the latter's right to invite foreign ships into the Gulf to protect its shipping. During 1986 and 1987 the increased US role in the Middle East, as evident both in regard to Libya and the Gulf, certainly aroused opposition in Aden. So too did the rise to prominence within the Reagan Administration, first as National Security Adviser and then as Secretary of Defense, of Frank Carlucci. Carlucci was a former deputy director of the CIA, who had been expelled from Tanzania in 1965 after being accused of interference in that country's internal affairs and he was the man revealed as having been the instigator of the 1981–2 CIA destablisation attempts.

On the eve of the twentieth anniversary of the PDRY's independence there was no sign of improved US–South Yemen relations: Washington saw no reason to open an embassy in a capital where it would not be able to exert any influence, and where a US presence might upset Saudi Arabia. On its side Aden identified three major areas of difficulty affecting any improvement in relations: continued US hostility to the PDRY regime itself, as embodied in the policies associated with Carlucci; concern that any US embassy in Aden would only engage in 'mischief'; and the US position on Palestine.[144] The course of the US–PDRY relations after January 1986 therefore continued, as before, to be strongly shaped by regional and local considerations, as well by the overall state of US–Soviet relations. In bilateral terms, there was little to discuss and little incentive to seek improvement. Both Aden and Washington felt more secure in not having diplomatic relations.

4 The enigmas of Yemeni 'unity'

The question of Yemeni 'unity' is one of the most complex and important in modern Yemeni history. For most Yemenis, it has, since the 1950s, been an article of nationalist faith that the two Yemeni states should unite and that this could be attained in the foreseeable future. No political leadership has been able overtly to contradict this, and all political currents have sought to mobilise the popular sentiment on unity, for their own purposes. At the same time, the issue of Yemeni unity, like that of Arab unity more generally, has been a cause of considerable friction between the Yemeni states, both because of disagreements on how this unity is to be achieved and because each has used the commitment to unity as a legitimation for interference in the internal affairs of the other. The two revolutions produced states of diverging, contrasted character and each upheaval located within the other, refugee communities hostile to the orientation of the other state. The ideal of Yemeni unity is that the movement in favour of this goal can and should promote a reconciliation and fusion of the two states. The reality has been that each state, jealous of its own power, has used unity the better to strengthen its own position and contain the influence of the other.

The issue of unity has also been a source of disagreement within each of the two Yemens. In the YAR the Zeidi North has, in general, been less enthusiastic about unity than the Shafei South, whose ideological and religious orientation has been similar to that in the western part of the PDRY. Those outside the Yemens hostile to unity, such as Saudi Arabia, have been able to play on this. In the south, there has been significant disagreement within the leadership over how far, and in what way, to promote unity. One division has been, roughly, between those willing to place a high value on supporting resistance in the YAR, and those who were willing to find some compromise with YAR leaderships: not surprisingly, those within the PDRY leadership who were originally from the YAR (including ʿAbd al-Fattāḥ Ismāʿīl, Muḥammad Saʿīd ʿAbd Allāh) or who were from areas bordering the North (such as ʿAlī ʿAntar) tended to favour a more militant policy. Sālim Rubiyyaʿ ʿAlī and ʿAlī

Nāṣir Muḥammad, by contrast, favoured a more conciliatory stance. This issue contributed greatly to the PDRY leadership divisions from 1977 onwards.

There was, however, another spectrum of debate within the PDRY deriving from different evaluations of the two states. The dominant position within the PDRY was that the South was in some sense 'socialist' and the North 'feudal' or at best 'capitalist': unity would, therefore, depend upon the extension of the 'socialist' system to the North. In one of the early discussions of unity, Sālim Rubiyyaᶜ ᶜAlī is reported to have placed two conditions on unity to YAR President al-Iryānī: that he liquidate the 'bureaucracy' and that he liquidate the 'bourgeoisie'. Al-Iryānī, a man who knew his country well even if he was not versed in Marxist theory, is said to have replied that he would be only too happy if someone would give him either a bureaucracy or a bourgeoisie to liquidate: the fact was, he said, that the YAR did not yet have either. Discussion of this kind suggested that the problem of unity between the two Yemens, like that between the two Germanies, would rest upon the resolution of which social system was to prevail over the other. The prospect of unity was, therefore, remote. There was, on the other hand a second, minority trend, within the PDRY which took a different approach: it argued, equally in the name of Marxism and with perhaps greater realism, that it was exaggerated to pretend that the South, with only a fifth of the total Yemeni population, was socialist already. Since, on closer examination, there was no fundamental difference in social system between North and South, there was less problem about unity than was initially thought. Unity should be pursued as a primary goal, at the inter-governmental level, and there should not be a policy of promoting revolutionary change in the North. A consolidated, progressive, capitalist Yemen, incorporating the strong points of the two countries, would create a more prosperous and independent entity, and was best suited to defending the position of the Yemeni people. As, in the aftermath of the 1986 crisis, the army became more central in the South, this too fostered a growing similarity of regime. This, more sober but also more enthusiastic, position on Yemeni unity was not to prevail, however, not least, of course, because it could not resolve the central aspect of the Yemeni situation, one inherited from the Sultanic and colonial divisions of early centuries: this was that two Yemeni states existed, each with its distinct and indissoluble interests. It was this fact of two states that, irrespective of socio-economic comparisons and unity negotiations, was to dominate relations between the two Yemens throughout the post-1967 period.

The origins of the call for unification of the two Yemens lie in the interconnection from the late 1940s onwards of the nationalist movement in Aden and the reformist Free Yemeni movement in the North. Despite claims of later Yemeni historians to this effect, the Free Yemeni Movement, had not, when it began to develop in the 1930s, considered greater Yemen as one unit; the Free Yemenis had concentrated on calls for change in the North. Following the defeat of the 1948 uprising in the North, the Free Yemenis had been allowed to operate in Aden, in part because the British authorities saw them as a useful counterweight to the Imam in the North: at this point it was the Imam who in furtherance of dynastic goals promoted the idea of Yemeni unity and claims to the South. Right up to 1962 the problem of Yemeni unity was to be bedevilled by the fact that it was the conservative leader of the North, the Imam, who was the most active proponent of Yemeni unity. Nonetheless from the early 1950s onwards the Free Yemenis espoused union with the 'Occupied South' and encouraged by more radical elements in Aden and by Egyptian denunciation of the British presence in the south, the United National Front, founded in Aden in 1955, made explicit this call for union of the two Yemens.[1] Such an appeal was presented at the time as part of the broader unificatory drive of Arab nationalism, and Yemeni unity was seen as a step on the path to broader Arab unity. But the effect of this proclamation was to make the goal of Yemeni unity an intrinsic part of the nationalist movement in the South from the mid-1950s onwards.

The aspiration to 'unity'

Proposed as an article of central importance during the political conflicts of the 1950s and 1960s, the call for unity became an enduring component of the PDRY's foreign policy. It was affirmed in every congress of the Front and of the Party, in the speeches of political leaders, and in both South Yemeni constitutions. It was, at the same time, an ideal which appeared to find widespread support within the population of South Yemen, as well as from both government and population in the North. The 1965 Charter, the basic document of the NLF prior to independence, begins by evoking the greatness of the ancient pre-Islamic Yemeni civilisations, and the 'natural and integral unity' (*waḥda tabīʿiyya mutakāmila*) of North and South Yemen, which binds the people of these two areas together. As a result, there is 'unity of the land, unity of language, unity of the daily efforts of life, unity of interests, and unity of destiny' (*waḥda al-arḍ wa waḥda al-lugha wa waḥda al-muʿānāh al-yawmiyya lil-ḥayyā wa waḥda al-maṣlaḥa wa waḥda al-maṣīr*). The Charter argues that this unity was expressed in political form both in the states of the pre-Islamic epoch and, during the Islamic period, by the establishment of a succession of states on Yemeni territory.[2] In analysing the contemporary situation, the Charter stressed the contribution which the 1962 revolution in North Yemen had made to the revolution in the South, although it saw political unity in overall Arab, more than specifically Yemeni terms. The Resolutions of the 1968 Fourth Congress of the NF spelt out the link that ties the revolutions of North and South:

> Although we have carried out the expulsion of the colonialist and have eliminated the semi-feudal rule of the Sultans in our republic, we should remember that our national freedom will not be entirely complete without the victory of our revolution in the North and without the realisation of unity of the Yemeni region.[3]

The 1970 Constitution stressed that the 'Yemeni people has struggled heroically against imperialism and colonialism, and against the reaction of local feudalism represented by the Imamic and Sultanic regimes' and continued:

> Despite the exceptional and unnatural conditions which appeared to divide the Yemeni region into two parts, this division was not able to stop the unity of joint national struggle in both North and South of our Yemeni region.
>
> Thus the Yemeni masses in the South struggled with the Yemeni masses in the North shoulder to shoulder in order to bring down the Imam's regime and establish the Republican regime.
>
> And similarly the Yemeni masses in the North struggled with the Yemeni masses in the South shoulder to shoulder in engaging in armed struggle against the British colonialist presence.
>
> This struggle resulted in the revolution of 26 September 1962 which brought down the reactionary Imamic regime in the Yemeni North and united all national and democratic forces which established the Republican regime.
>
> The success of the long struggle which our Yemeni people undertook against the colonialist presence was crowned with the detonation of the armed struggle against the British occupation and the Sultanic regime which began on 14 October 1963 and united all sections of the working people – workers, peasants, intellectuals, petty bourgeois and all sections of the noble people – under the leadership of the National Front.[4]

The 1970 Constitution went on to assert that conditions were now improving for the complete 'liquidation' of the division into two Yemens, and the return to the natural unity of the region.

The Fifth Congress of the NF, in 1972, took policy towards the North a step further. The 1968 Congress had taken place at a time of continued hope of finding a common front with the YAR authorities, and of assisting them to defend themselves against the royalists. In 1970 the YAR government had reached a compromise with the royalist and Saudi Arabia and, since 1971, there had been guerrilla war in the North by radical republicans supported by the South. Thus, whereas the 1968 Congress resolutions had called for the establishment of links with the republican forces in the North as a co-operative step towards achieving the unity of the Yemens, the resolutions of the 1972 Congress proposed the goal of a 'United Democratic Yemen'.[5] This shift in PONF policy reflected the change of South Yemen's name instituted by the 1970 Constitution: this had signalled an end to the limited restriction of aim of the Aden government which now claimed to present not just South Yemen – the state's title from 1967 to 1970 was People's Republic of South Yemen – but rather the first part of a government that would in time encompass the whole of Yemen in one united democratic Yemen – the People's Democratic Republic of Yemen.[6]

The 1972 Congress left open how this united Yemen was to be achieved: it did not specify if this was to be through state-to-state or through revolutionary activity. As always, the specific organisations to which the PONF was to extend support in the YAR were not named, whereas they were for some other areas towards which the Front expressed a commitment, such as Oman. Nonetheless, the 1970 Constitution and the 1972 Congress resolutions were clear in so far as they indicated a shift away from unity through dealing with the YAR government and towards unity through the alliance with opposition forces in the North.

The resolutions of the 1975 Unification Congress were even less explicit. No mention was made of the aim of a United Democratic Yemen, or of the instruments for achieving this goal. The Unification Congress's statement simply read:

> As regards issues pertaining to the unity of the Yemeni people and ensuring achievement thereof on a democratic basis, and with a content ensuring the progress and prosperity of the Yemeni people, the UPONF will continue to exert diligent and relentless effort for achieving the noblest aims of our Yemeni people. It also expresses with satisfaction its conviction in the correctness of the policy pursued as regards the cause of Yemeni unity. It considers continuation on the same path as being harmonious with the aspirations of the Yemeni people who are the ones primarily affected by such unity.[7]

The 1978 YSP Congress reaffirmed these basic guidelines: the linkage between the two revolutions, the aim of a United Democratic Yemen, and the leading role which the YSP itself would play in the movement towards this goal.[8] This orientation was also restated in the preamble to the new, second, Constitution of 1978. This reasserted that there was a link between the 26 September and 14 October revolutions and then went on:

> All this affirms that despite the unnatural situations of the false division of the Yemeni land and people, its struggle in the two parts is dialectically related in its unity, not only against imperialist and reactionary conspiracies against the Yemeni homeland, but also for the purpose of finally liquidating the division and restoring the natural situation for the democratic unity of Yemen . . .

> The struggle of the Yemeni people will continue until the realisation of all the tasks of the national democratic revolutionary stage, the strategy of the Yemeni revolution, including the construction of the United Democratic Yemen under the leadership of its allies and the rest of the groups of the democratic and national movement – in our Yemeni homeland.[9]

The 1980 YSP Congress approached the matter rather differently. The long-term goal was now said to be a 'free, democratic, united and prosperous homeland'. This was an apparent dilution of the earlier call for a United Democratic Yemen, and the Congress declarations stressed that the means through which this could be reached was through official, inter-governmental contacts, rather than the increased strength of the YSP or revolution. Less stress was laid on the achievement of revolutionary goals inside the PDRY, and more on the defence of national sovereignty, the raising of living standards, and the guaranteeing of political liberties.[10]

Apart from such proclamations, the reality of relations between North and South Yemen was, despite the adherence to the goal of unity, far from harmonious; 'unity', in the sense of a fusion of the two states, remained a distant aim throughout the post-independence period. While on two occasions, in 1972 and 1979, agreements on implementing unity were signed by the Presidents of the two states, progress on putting such agreements into practice was both slow and limited: on both occasions, at least one of the signatory states wanted to use the agreement to buy time and fend off pressure from the other – the PDRY in 1972 and the YAR in 1979. Moreover, the periods of negotiation and collaboration between the YAR and the PDRY were offset by phases of overt conflict between the two governments, who waged war against each other in 1972 and 1979. Beyond the course of diplomacy as such there have lain deeper domains of divergence: in foreign policy, in structure of government and society, and in internal socio-economic organisation. The history of relations between the two Yemens after 1967 was, therefore, one of the both antagonism and co-operation, as the forces making for unity and co-operation were offset by those stimulating division and antagonism.

These divisions had their origins in the history of the Yemens and, more recently, of Yemeni nationalism itself. The idea of Yemen as a distinct entity is not recent or simply factitious. Settled civilisations had existed in the South Arabian region for some millennia, and the term 'Yaman' had been used to denote this region since, at the latest, the time of early Islam.[11] But this generic 'Yaman' had long contained many subdivisions – religious, economic and political. No Yemeni 'nation-state' existed, only dynastic realms of greater or lesser extent. In the twentieth century, with two states in existence, an independent Imamate in the north and a British-ruled entity in the south, the fluidity of real divisions was evident in the political terms used for the area, which had been remarkably permanent. It was only in the 1940s that a nationalist movement active in both states had come into existence, and only in the 1960s that the term 'Yemeni South' (*Djunūb al-Yaman*) came into common political parlance.[12] Even when such a Yemeni nationalism did emerge, however, it was associated with very different processes in the two Yemeni states: a republican anti-autocratic revolution in the North, followed by a civil war, and an anti-colonial upheaval in the South. If the South had to some extent an experience analogous to that of other Third World countries ruled by colonialism, the North underwent something more comparable to the anti-absolutist upheavals of Europe, in which nationalism postulated an egalitarian unity of all members of the nation, advocated against the hierarchies and divisions of the old order.[13]

While the tensions within Yemeni nationalism in part derived from the histories of the two Yemeni states, Yemeni nationalism itself was characterised by three major distinctive features. The first of these was the dual affiliation of this nationalism – to both Arab and Yemeni entities; the second was its social radicalism; the third the emphasis on 'unity'. The dual affiliation can be found in other Arab countries – Egypt, for example – and it has also been evident in the modern history of the Yemens, where writers and politicians have at times emphasised their inclusion in the Arab world, and at other times stressed their distinction as Yemenis from other Arab countries.

The ambiguities raised by this dual affiliation, and a gradual shift in the way the duality was handled, were evident not just in NF policies, but also in the terminology used to identify South Yemen's place in the wider world. The 1965 Charter lays stress upon the Arab more than upon the Yemeni context of the NLF's activity. It does talk of the geographical unity of North and South, of the revolutions in North and South, and of the role of 26 September in stimulating resistance in the South; but it lays greater emphasis upon the role of the Egyptian revolution of 23 July 1952 in initiating a new phase of the Arab national movement.[14] It refers to 'our Arab people in North and South Yemen' and when it talks of unity it uses the term 'Arab unity', and places unification of the Yemeni region within that context, presenting 'the unity of our Arab people in North and South of the Yemen region as a step towards liberated Arab Unity'.[15] It not only talks of the Arab homeland (*waṭan*) but also of an Arab people (*sha*ᶜ*ab*), and it argues that the 14 October revolution in the South 'is part of the Arab revolution in the west and east of the homeland'.[16] Where the Charter does qualify the term 'unity' this is not by introducing a regional or geographic restriction, but a political one, unity being qualified as 'socialist' and 'revolutionary'.[17]

Discussion of unity in texts of the post-1967 period involves a geographical contraction of the terms used, away from the Arab and towards the more restricted Yemeni dimension. In these post-1967 texts the term 'people' now refers not to the Arabs as a whole, but to the Yemenis, and it is *their* unity which is called for. The overall semantic development of relevant political terms in party and state documents after 1967 tends towards such a contraction. Yet the modification of the Arab dimension is not absolute, in that the commitment to an Arab identity and politics remains; and if some limitation of scope is implied in the shift from the Arab to the Yemeni, a compensating expansion of reference is evident in the transference of loyalty from the Egyptian revolution of 1952 to another extra-Yemeni event, the Russian revolution of 1917. The 1965 Charter did make some mention of the Bolshevik revolution, in acknowledging the importance of 'the victories of socialist revolution in the world':[18] but these were not given the pride of place later allocated to them in NF statements; in these the dual affiliation of 1965 to the Arab world/Yemen is gradually displaced by a new couplet, socialist camp/Yemen.

This semantic change can be followed, in some detail, in the official documents of state and party over the post-independence period. In the 1970 PDRY Constitution, Article Two states: 'The Yemeni people is one people and is part of the Arab nation with one Yemeni citizenship.'[19] The terms used here and in the Preface refer to the whole Yemen as a district (*iḳlīm*), a term also used in the Charter, one subdivided into two halves (*s̲h̲aṭrayn*). The Yemenis themselves are now stated to be a people (*s̲h̲aᶜab*), while the Arabs, the 'people' to whom the Yemenis belonged in earlier documents, are now described by the broader term *umma*:[20] *umma* means 'community' and has a connotation of the Islamic community as well as of the wider Arab one. Despite this membership of a wider community, the Yemenis have a specific *d̲j̲insiyya*, a word that means both citizenship and nationality. The Constitution of the YAR adopted in the same year also asserts the commitment to Yemeni unity. Article Six states: 'Yemeni unity is a legitimate right of all sons of natural Yemen, and it is their shared duty to attain it by legitimate means.'[21] But the affiliation is stated differently. Thus Article One states: 'Yemen is an Arab and Islamic state' and 'the Yemeni people is an Arab and Moslem people and part of the Arab and Moslem communities', where the term used is *s̲h̲aᶜab*.[22] The Constitution does not assert membership of an Arab nation, but does claim an Arab *and* Islamic identity, of Arabic language and Islamic religion.[23]

The revised 1978 Constitution of the PDRY introduces further new terminology. The two Yemeni states are now stated to be each a *shaʿṭr* of a single Yemeni *waṭan*.[24] *Waṭan* is the conventional term for 'homeland' in modern Arabic and is used of the Arab world in the 1965 Charter: its application to Yemen in 1978 is thus a stronger assertion of Yemeni affiliation than that contained in the 1970 Constitution. While the 1978 Consitution reaffirms that the Yemeni *shaʿab* is part of the Arab *umma*, it does not provide a term for what the territorial entity in which the Arabs live is to be called. The conventional term *waṭan*, used in the Charter and in much Arab nationalist discourse, is no longer available. Thus, while in the 1970 PDRY Constitution the word *waṭan* is avoided altogether, the contrast merely being between two categories for the population – Yemeni *shaʿab*, Arab *umma* – the 1978 Constitution now attributes the term *waṭan* to the two Yemens, and the less powerful word *iḳlīm* is dispensed with. The semantic shift in the two Constitutions was such that in the 1970 Constitution the term *shaʿab* was transferred from the Arabs to the Yemenis, and in that of 1978 the term *waṭan* was similarly re-allocated, just as the two documents laid greater overall stress on Yemeni unity as opposed to its Arab counterpart, by contrast with the 1965 Charter.

Similar semantic changes can be seen in the documents of the South Yemen party, but here the process is less clear-cut. Thus, if the 1970 state Constitution talks of an Arab *umma*, the 1972 PONF Congress still talks of an Arab *shaʿab*. In party documents the term 'national' when applied to 'liberation' is used both about Yemeni *and* about more general Arab activities: the implication is that the *waṭan* in which this liberation is being aspired to is both the Yemen itself and the whole Arab world.[25] In the same way, the different states of the Arab world are referred to each as a *ḳuṭr* – a zone, section, or region – of a wider entity.[26] This is the term commonly used in Arab nationalist discourse, by, for example, Baʿthists, when the intention is to stress that each specific state is but part of the wider Arab world. But two quite specific terms often used in Arab nationalist writing are applied to South Yemen, or at most the two Yemens, and not to the Arab world as a whole: these are *bilād* or homeland, the normal patriotic term for a particular state, and *ḳawm*/*ḳawmī*, nation/national. Whereas *waṭan* refers to a territory, *ḳawm* refers to people. So in the South Yemeni party usage the words *waṭan* and *ḳawm* have distinct connotations: the former is applied to both Yemeni and Arab areas, the latter only to the population of the Yemens.

The second specific feature of Yemeni nationalism has been that it has contained a strong element of social radicalism.[27] In the North, this resulted from the origins of the movement in the resistance to the Imam, and the accession of this opposition to power in the September 1962 revolution.[28] The civil war was fought by the republicans to defend a state that proclaimed a new national and popular identity, and rejected the forces that sought to restore the monarchy. The fact that the latter were supported by Saudi Arabia, a kingdom, while the former were backed by Egypt, a republic, not only internationalised the war but also led each side to see its own social and political cause as a nationalist one as well, i.e. as directed against the external supporter of its internal enemy.[29] It was for this reason that in 1963 YAR President Sallāl opened an Office of the Arabian Peninsula to promote revolution in Saudi Arabia itself, although, as he was later to say, this was itself more of a reaction to Saudi support for the royalists than an indication that any Arabian-wide upheaval was possible. After the end of the civil war in 1970, the lines of division in the North ran not so much between republicans and royalists but between more and less radical factions of the republican camp, and this was the context in which the combination of nationalist with internal political conflict continued. Once the Egyptians had departed from the YAR in late 1967, the more moderate republican faction sought a compromise with both the royalists and Saudi Arabia, whereas the radicals remained partisans of greater militancy on both counts.[30]

In the South, the development of a nationalism of a more conventional Third World mode, one of hostility to colonial rule, did not preclude it from also having a socially radical side. For the very pattern of British colonial control, one that maintained the existing rulers in place in the hinterland under indirect rule and sought the co-operation of the merchants of Aden, encouraged the nationalist movement to regard these local Arab allies of the colonial power as *both* social *and* national enemies. The character of British colonial rule in the South, coupled with the identification of Yemeni nationalism with the cause of the republican revolutionaries in the North, thereby produced an interrelationship of social radicalism and national assertion in South Yemen that was to endure beyond the weakening of the radical forces in the North.

Time and again, official statements of the NF and by its leaders qualified the unity they were seeking as 'progressive', 'popular' or 'revolutionary'. Thus during the first major conflict between North and South after independence, in February 1969, an official statement gave Aden's view of Yemeni unity: 'Yemeni unity . . . is a unity of the toiling people, and must be made by them . . . This unity must be progressive and must not be racial or regional in character, and must be hostile to colonialism and reaction.'[31] Speaking a few days later, Ḳaḥṭān al-Shaʿabī listed what he saw as the basic points underlying unity. The first principle was that 'The unity between North and South must have social progress as its aim.' The other goals were: to 'eradicate colonialism and foreign occupation from our countries'; to 'work in co-ordination for the removal of the colonialist wherever he may be'; 'to strike openly at imperialism in the Arab nation'; to 'eradicate feudalism, and achieve a socialist society ... The agrarian reforms carried out in the South must also be carried out in the North.'[32]

The third distinctive feature of Yemeni nationalism was the fact that it posed the question of 'unity', of calling for and seeking to establish a unification of two separate states. Many modern states have acquired independence on territory less than they claim as rightly theirs or have in other ways (e.g. as a result of war) found themselves in possession of less territory than they feel is legitimately theirs. This involves the problem of irredentism. An irredentist element does exist in Yemeni nationalism as advocated by the South, with regard to the three provinces taken by Saudi Arabia in 1934.[33] The land boundaries of South Yemen with Saudi Arabia and Oman also remain contentious, even apart from the issue of the Kuria Muria Islands.[34] But the focus of Yemeni nationalism has been not on these *irredenta*, so much as on the need to unify two separate and independent Yemeni states. Here there are far fewer examples of similar cases: the post-war divisions of the two Koreas and the two Germanys and, between 1954 and 1975, the two Vietnams, may provide the nearest recent analogues. The issues of Italian and German 'unity' in the nineteenth century may also be relevant. In all these cases reunification formed a widely upheld if for a long time at least unattainable national goal, sustained by forces that were otherwise in disagreement. But in the recent cases the original division and its subsequent maintenance were twentieth-century creations, the result above all of the impact on these countries of the east–west conflict that evolved after 1945. In the Yemeni case, the division pre-dated the colonial occupations of the nineteenth century: the Imams had not ruled a united North and South since the early eighteenth century. The consolidation of the division between the two states in the late nineteenth century was a later development, the result of strategic rivalry between Britain and the Ottoman empire that developed in western Arabia.[35] The post-1967 division then compounded this by introducing different social and political systems, and foreign policy orientations and influences on either side of the intra-Yemeni frontier.

As already noted, the history of attempts to produce Yemeni 'unity' and the survival of disunity can be attributed to the multiple determinations of the division. The result has been that the two Yemens have experienced different social evolutions in the past two decades, a difference further compounded by the influences of Arab politics upon them. These factors – international, regional and internal – have reinforced the division of the two states and have made it all the more difficult to achieve substantial and lasting progress towards 'unity'. Yet, for all the historical implantation of the division and the divergent characters of the two states, 'unity' remained a professed goal of both states, with many practical implications.

Relations with the YAR: six phases

The pursuit of the South Yemeni state of the policy of unity with North Yemen can be analysed as falling into six distinct periods or phases in the years 1967–87. The first phase, beginning in 1967, was one of initial enthusiasm for closer co-operation on both sides; it ended in 1970 with a confirmation of difference, in the compromise peace in the YAR and the proclamation of a 'Democratic Republic' in the new constitution of the South. The second phase, 1970–2, was one of increasing tension between the two states, leading to the first inter-Yemeni war, of September-October 1972, and the subsequent Cairo and Tripoli agreements on unity. In the third phase, 1972–7, negotiations between the two states on the subject of unity continued. Yet little substantial progress was made, and this phase ended abruptly – with the assassination of YAR President al-Ḥamdī in October 1977 and the rapid deterioration of the overall situation in the Southern Arabian Peninsula and Red Sea areas at that time. In phase four, lasting from 1977 to 1979, there was increased tension between the two states, together with worsening relations between Aden and Saudi Arabia: this period culminated in the second inter-Yemeni war, that of February 1979, and the subsequent signature of the Kuwait agreement on unity in March 1979. In phase five, 1979–86, there was, initially, PDRY support for guerrilla forces operating inside the YAR. But these were defeated in 1982, and state-to-state negotiations became more important. In December 1981 the two Presidents went a step beyond the 1979 Kuwait agreement and signed a new 'Agreement on Developing Co-operation and Co-ordination between the two parts of Yemen'. The ending of guerrilla activities inside the YAR in 1982 was accompanied by the establishment of a Supreme Yemeni Council, comprised of representatives of the two states (which was to meet for the first time in August 1983) and by the proclamation of a draft constitution of a united state. The crisis of January 1986, however, opened a sixth phase with new areas of conflict between the two states.

PHASE I: 1967–1970

When the PRSY became independent, both it and the YAR took a number of measures to reflect their commitment to unity. Each set up Ministries of Yemeni Unity Affairs (that of the YAR replacing the

Ministry of Occupied South Yemeni Affairs) and on 7 December 1967 Aden lifted pre-existing restrictions on entry of YAR citizens to the PRSY: entry was now permitted to all holding a YAR identity card.[36] Because they claimed to be one country, they did not establish diplomatic relations of exchange embassies: neither, therefore, had official representatives in the capital of the other. Initially both sides declared themselves in favour of Yemeni unity, and in the weeks immediately after independence volunteers from the PRSY went north to support the republicans resisting a royalist attempt to capture Sanaᶜa. In February 1968 YAR and PSRY forces co-operated in operations against royalist troops. President Ḳaḥṭān al-Shaᶜabī justified this saying, 'North and South are to us one region. Whoever interferes in the North is interfering here in the People's Republic of South Yemen. Whoever attacks Sanaᶜa is attacking Aden.'[37] But new divergences were appearing. The moment of independence of South Yemen had coincided with changes in the YAR: for the British withdrawal from the South on 30 November came a month after the Egyptian withdrawal from the North, and after a *coup* on 5 November. The former brought the NLF to power in Aden, the latter brought a new government under representatives of 'the third force', a grouping that lay between republicans and royalists and wanted to encourage a compromise peace.[38] The ending of the Sanaᶜa siege, in February 1968, opened the door for conflicts later in the year within the republican camp. As a result, those forces opposed to a compromise peace with the royalists and more sympathetic to the PRSY went into opposition: these included the militia who had defended Sanaᶜa, known as the Popular Revolutionary Forces, and the North Yemeni followers of the MAN who in June 1968 formed *al-Hiẓb al-Thawrī al-Dīmuḳrātī* – the Revolutionary Democratic Party.[39]

Tensions in the YAR resulted in two intra-republican clashes, one in August and the second in December 1968. The result of these was that the PRF, the Revolutionary Democratic Party and peasant leagues affiliated to them were defeated, and the government in the YAR, under General Al-ᶜAmrī as Prime Minister, began to seek a rapprochement with Saudi Arabia and with the royalists. This came in March 1970 when Premier Muḥsin al-ᶜAynī led a YAR delegation to the Islamic Conference at Jeddah, and there signed, on 28 March 1970, an agreement with Saudi Arabia to end the war. A coalition government was created and in July 1970 diplomatic relations between the YAR and Saudi Arabia were re-established.[40]

This settlement of the war in the YAR caused differences between the two Yemeni states, particularly as it coincided with the radicalisation of the regime in the South itself after June 1969. In 1968 relations between the two states had initially been cordial: in addition to co-operation on security, the Aden Nationality Law allowed citizens of the YAR to acquire PRSY citizenship more speedily than other Arabs.[41] In May 1968 Ḳaḥṭān al-S͟haᶜabī re-affirmed the PRSY's commitment to 'mass unity between the revolutionaries' of the two Yemens.[42] In June 1968 the YAR premier announced that the two states would set up a Joint Council of Ministers and the PRSY President made a strong statement in support of unity.[43] In July the PRSY Foreign Minister went to Sanaᶜa for the first official visit of a PRSY representative and both sides at that time proclaimed their support for the goal of unity. Speaking at the end of July YAR President al-Īryānī declared:

> There can be no doubt that unity of the two parts of our cherished Yemen – North and South – is a popular demand in both areas. All citizens, here and there, are equally and enthusiastically pressing for unity. We consider that unity between the citizens of North and South actually exists: there are neither barriers nor limits to exercising it. The feeling exists that our soil is one. We have the same history, language, religion, traditions, customs and blood. We share common principles and a common destiny. The revolutions of North and South are being exposed to aggression perpetrated by the same enemy, and they are facing the same imperialist and reactionary forces. All this is our road to unity. All these ties – rarely present among peoples ruled by the same State under the same flag – make it incumbent on all of us to advance at a rapid, yet prudent and measured pace towards formal unity.[44]

But the clashes in the North during the following month marked a set-back for Aden's YAR allies, and the flow of refugees from the PSRY to the YAR created a strong opposition constituency there. In November, the YAR and the PRSY signed an agreement on economic co-operation in the fields of finance, banking, commerce, customs, and anti-smuggling operations, and a Joint Economic Department of the two states was set up. But it seems that no practical results followed from this and the death of the pro-Aden opposition leader ᶜAbd al-Raḳīb ᶜAbd al-Waḥḥāb in January 1969 led to two months of polemics between both states.

It was the YAR which broke the skein of formal fraternity. In a statement in early February 1969, the YAR Foreign Minister blamed the PRSY for the failure to bring about the unity, and listed YAR proposals for implementing this: a joint delegation at the UN, and the convening of a national conference with representatives from North and South. He alleged that the PRSY government had been set up by the British, and that it was now pursuing a path of 'rigidity, escapism and absolute rejection'. He also accused the Southern authorities of carrying out border attacks on the YAR, in which a number of people were killed.[45] Later statements accused the Aden government of sending arms, 'plotters' and 'assassins' to the towns of the YAR, an apparent reference to the Southern support for the radical republicans in the North.[46] Southern replies argued that it was Aden which had taken the initiative in working for unity, particularly on economic co-operation, but that the North had rejected this.[47] The underlying divergence of the two states was alluded to in one PRSY statement which stated: 'The regimes in Aden and Sanaᶜa differ, for in Sanaᶜa the regime is feudalist and clannish and in Aden there is a national progressive regime.'[48] But it was interference in each other's affairs that constituted the main issue: Southern statements drew attention to what they saw as YAR support for opponents of the PRSY government, while the YAR confirmed its backing for FLOSY, repeating the charge that the NLF had been put in power by Britain.[49] Three months later, in May 1969, Ḳaḥṭān al-S̲h̲aᶜabī recognised the depth of the difference between the two states, but expressed the hope that it would find a resolution: 'The revolution in our Northern Yemen has been affected by a reversal that many of us did not expect. But this reversal . . . will not remain for long, for the revolutionaries are still in good health.' Opposition forces in the North were, he said, 'planning to restore the revolution and set up a national democratic government in Sanaᶜa'.[50]

Although relations later improved somewhat, the advent of the left to power in June 1969 entailed that the political differences between North and South were now, in reality, greater than ever before. Yet this underlying polarisation of the two regimes did not at first lead to a complete break in joint efforts towards unity. The dispute of early 1969 subsided and in March 1970 Ministers from both states visited the other to discuss bilateral co-operation. The Presidents of the two countries met at Nasser's funeral in September 1970 and in November Muḥammad ᶜAlī Ḥayt̲h̲am, the PDRY Premier, visited Taᵓiz for two days of discussions with the YAR Premier Muḥsin al-ᶜAynī. On this occasion Ḥayt̲h̲am declared:

> We are one people in one region and must work and struggle as a Yemeni people towards achieving the natural Yemeni unity. We have come here to lay a foundation, in fact to try and lay a foundation of co-operation between the two countries, as the first step towards the unity of the people of Yemen and the unity of their territories.[51]

And on his return the PRSY Premier declared: 'The realisation of Yemeni unity is an historical responsibility borne by the political leaderships of both sides of the Yemen.' As a result of this meeting new committees were set up to discuss a number of matters of joint economic interest: currency and customs standardisation, and industrial co-ordination and banking co-operation. In his 1971 new year's message to

Ḥaytham Muḥsin al-ᶜAynī declared that 'unity between the two parts of Yemen would certainly be achieved shortly by means of development and progress'.[52]

This apparent progress in inter-governmental co-operation was more than offset by a growing underlying divergence between the two Yemeni states, one evident in at least three respects. First, the political and social character of the two regimes, already distinct in November 1967, had now been rendered even more so by the political changes that had subsequently taken place in each. The elimination from government of the radical republicans in the North, and the formation of the coalition of third force and royalists in 1970 contrasted with the eviction of the Sultans and Sheikhs in the South, the alienation of much of the urban commercial class, and the advent of the NF 'Left' to power in June 1969. Secondly, the two states had increasingly divergent foreign policies: this did not apply to Yemeni unity itself – both maintained formal adherence to this as a goal; nor did it apply to Arab affairs as a whole. Rather it concerned attitudes to the most important neighbour of each, namely Saudi Arabia. For the process of reconciliation of the Saudis with the YAR, which reached fruition in July 1970, contrasted with growing conflict between Aden and the Wahhabi kingdom: Saudi Arabia was from 1968 onwards backing opposition to Aden on the frontier, and in November 1969 there came the al-Wadiah border clash between the two states. The Yemens were also at loggerheads owing to the conflict between political forces in the YAR. While the YAR sent a delegation to the March 1970 Islamic Conference, South Yemen was absent. PRSY Foreign Minister al-Bīḍ gave his country's reasons for this course of action as the fact that the Conference represented 'a new form of colonialism condemned and rejected by the Arab people during the fifties and as a falsification of the real differences of opinion'.[53] In July 1970, when the YAR and Saudi Arabia exchanged diplomatic recognition, ᶜAlī Nāṣir Muḥammad was reported to have stated that 'the role of Saudi Arabia did not differ from the role of Israel in fighting the liberation movements'.[54] In November 1970, on the third anniversary of independence, President Sālim Rubiyyaᶜ ᶜAlī denounced 'the reactionary Saudi regime and its mercenaries' for creating problems between the two Yemens.[55]

These divergences found expression in a third dimension of disagreement between the two states, namely in the constitutions which each drew up in 1970. The constitution of the PDRY was drawn up during 1970 and announced in November on the occasion of the celebration of the third anniversary of independence. In its implications for the North–South relations, this constitution marked an important change. The Aden government ceased to call its territory by the name 'South Yemen'. It changed this to 'People's Democratic Republic of Yemen'.[56] The implication of this alteration, at least as it was read in Sanaᶜa, was that Aden no longer presented itself as the capital of *part* of Yemen (i.e. South Yemen), but rather as the capital of the *whole* of Yemen, one part of which was already under 'popular democratic' control: unity would not now come about by a fusion of the two states, but by an extension of Aden's system of government to the whole of Yemeni territory. The YAR government criticised this change as 'a grave step' and recalled its representatives at the Aden independence celebrations.[57]

Parallel problems arose when the YAR's constitution was finalised on 28 December 1970. While the PDRY made Islam the state religion, the YAR derived the Constitution from Islam (Article 2) and envisaged the establishment of a Consultative Council of 159 members, to be chosen by indirect elections, with a further 20 members nominated by the President.[58] Seats for 'southern delegates' had been kept open in the National Assembly set up by Al-ᶜAmrī in the period 1969–70 and this practice continued in the new Consultative Council: thus not only the manner of selection of the members, but also the implicit claim that this Council represented the whole of the Yemens was seen in the South as a claim by the YAR that it, as much as the PDRY, claimed to speak for the whole country. This latent challenge of the YAR to the PDRY's legitimacy was to be taken a step further in August 1971 when Premier Al-ᶜAmrī constituted a government that included within it representatives of the FLOSY leadership in exile from South Yemen.[59]

The emphasis in this first phase of inter-Yemeni relations was, consequently, upon relations between governments: each government sought for some time to find common ground with the other. But this focus was not exclusive. The combination of domestic and international events, and the reaction of each to, indeed the involvement of each in the internal politics of the other led to deadlock on unity and to rising antagonism. Virtually no steps towards unity were taken and the constitutions of the two states shifted conflict to a terrain on which each state sought to achieve unity by claiming to supplant the other. By 1971 this political and constitutional claim was being put into effect by the enhanced encouragement that each began to give to rebel forces in the other's domain.

PHASE 2: 1970–1972

Although this second period of inter-Yemeni relations was one of growing conflict, it began with continued negotiations between the governments, and mutual expressions of goodwill. Thus at the first meeting of the new PDRY legislature, the Supreme People's Council, in

August 1971, President Sālim Rubiyyaᶜ ᶜAlī sent a message to the YAR's Consultative Council 'stressing the unity of the Yemeni region and the need to create a suitable atmosphere to achieve that unity and to ensure the continued operations of the economic committees formed earlier' (i.e. in November 1970).[60] The emphasis of the unity policy in both parts of Yemen had, however, shifted: first, towards greater attempts by each side to undermine the other; secondly, towards direct confrontation between the armies of the two states.

The events of 1968–9 had weakened the organised groupings of the radical republicans in North Yemen, but there remained a considerable body of opinion hostile to the 1970 settlement. The RDP, established in 1968, remained in existence, and it received support from the NF in Aden.[61] In January 1971 a second grouping, the Yemeni Revolutionary Resistance Organisation, began guerrilla operations around the area of Damt, in the south of the YAR, and, in the subsequent months, it continued military activities on a low level with Southern support.[62] Throughout 1971 and 1972 armed groups backed by Aden maintained operations along the frontier between the two countries. For its part, the YAR began to provide facilities to a number of groupings of South Yemeni exiles who were forming with Saudi and other Arab encouragement. Thus the border conflict that had been taking place between the South Yemenis and the Saudi Arabians from 1968 onwards had now spread, by 1971, to encompass the YAR–PDRY frontier.[63]

Events took a more serious turn in 1972. New governments formed in both states omitted what had until then been the significant Ministry of Yemeni Unity Affairs and on 21 February 1972 an important YAR tribal leader, Sheikh ᶜAlī bin Nādjī al-Ḳadr, was killed on the PDRY side of the frontier together with two other tribal leaders and 65 other people.[64] The YAR authorities, in a statement issued on 11 March, claimed he had been lured over to a banquet and then murdered;[65] the PDRY insisted that he had been leading an attack upon its territory, with 2,000 men, as a part of a 'Saudi–US plan to attack the PDRY and occupy Bayhan'.[66] This incident was followed by tensions along the frontier involving the armies of the two states. During the summer two further developments helped to maintain tensions: one was the supply to the YAR of substantial quantities of arms by two states concerned to counter the PDRY, namely Saudi Arabia and Libya;[67] the other was the formation of a comprehensive exile grouping in the YAR involving all the main factions of the South Yemeni opposition, the United National Front of South Yemen.[68] Throughout 1972 Radio Free Yemeni South, based in Saudi Arabia, broadcast reports of UNF actions inside South Yemen.[69] In September, Libya announced that it was donating to the Front five million dinars promised earlier in the year as aid to the PDRY.[70]

The stage was set for the full-scale war between the two countries that began on 25–6 September, when irregular forces in the YAR attacked the PRSY, and the guerrillas backed by Aden increased their activities inside the YAR.[71] The inter-state war was limited in duration and geographical extent. Heavy fighting ended on 2 October, and after further mediation a lasting cease-fire was agreed on 19 October.[72] The fighting was itself confined to the border region, with the YAR forces advancing on the PDRY town of Dhala, and the PDRY forces seizing the YAR town of Qataba and shelling a number of others.[73] On 6 October the YAR also occupied the island of Kamaran in the Red Sea, a former quarantine station occupied by Britain in 1918 and handed to the PDRY in 1967.[74] (The PDRY later waived its claim to this island.) Fighting on both sides, however, exemplified the wider aspects of the conflict: irregulars supported the armies of the two states, and the YAR forces had received substantial logistical support from both Saudi Arabia and Libya, the two states opposed to the government in Aden, while the PDRY was armed by the USSR. At the same time, the response of several states in the Arab world to the outbreak of war in South Arabia was to attempt mediation, not only because the war posed a direct threat to their security or strategic interests, but also because of the opportunities which such mediation posed for these states to present themselves as upholders of Arab unity. The Arab League mediation team that arrived in Aden on 4 October and reached Sanaᶜa on 8 October included representatives of Egypt, Libya, Algeria, Syria, and Kuwait.[75]

Negotiations were held in Cairo from 21–28 October, and through these two agreements were reached. The first, which the Premiers of the two states, al-ᶜAynī and ᶜAlī Nāṣir Muḥammad, signed, covered a cease-fire. It stipulated that all troop concentrations withdraw from the frontier, that the borders reopen, that both sides withdraw from the areas occupied since 26 September, that all refugees wishing to return be repatriated, that all sabotage operations be stopped and that all military training camps for refugees be closed.[76] The second was an agreement on unity, an Agreement between the Governments of the Two Parts of Yemen. This envisaged a single Yemeni state, with one flag, one presidential body, and unified legislative, executive and judicial authorities. Joint technical committees were to be set up to unify institutions for the two states: they were to complete their work within a year.[77] Later, Presidents al-Iryānī and Sālim Rubiyyaᶜ ᶜAlī met in Tripoli, the Libyan capital, and in discussion with Colonel Ḳadhāfī they signed a more detailed agreement on unity. This indicated that the future Yemeni Republic would have Sanaᶜa as its capital, Islam as its religion of state and Arabic as its official language. It would 'aim at achieving socialism', create a 'national democratic' system of government and a unified political organisation, modelled on the party then ruling Libya, the Arab Socialist Union. The Tripoli Agreement also envisaged the establishment of eight joint technical committees, dealing with: the constitution, foreign affairs and diplomatic and consular representation, economics and finance, legislative and judicial affairs, educational, cultural and information affairs, health affairs, military affairs, and administration and public utilities.[78]

While the Agreement was greeted enthusiastically by Libya and some other Arab countries, and led to considerable diplomatic activity between the two states, it remained little more than an aspiration. No clear timetable for the implementation was established; despite the Tripoli Agreement's emphasis on the need to hasten implementation of the Cairo Unity Agreement, Cairo's stipulation that a constitution be drawn up within a year was not repeated, the constitutional committee merely being urged to report 'as soon as possible'.[79] Secondly, while both governments appeared to endorse the Agreements, there were also reservations on both sides, vis-à-vis each other and vis-à-vis the very 'unity process' itself. The text of the Tripoli Agreement reflected the influence of Ḳadhāfī and embodied a number of political positions that seemed to be closer to the stance of the South than of the North: the call for socialism, the support for the 'people of the Arabian Gulf', and the aim to establish a political organisation modelled on Libya reflected this.[80]

In general the content of the Agreement, and the outcome of the war, represented a certain victory for the radical nationalist camp in the Arab world over the conservative positions of Saudi Arabia. But for this reason it could not command assent within the YAR as a whole, nor be accepted by Saudi Arabia with equanimity. The PDRY government was also not able to ensure the support it might have liked: some NF members in Aden doubted the wisdom of attempting to find a compromise with the YAR, and the USSR's press, in contrast to the enthusiasm expressed in Peking, met the news of the Tripoli Agreement with reserve, mentioning the measures to stop the fighting, and efforts to 'normalise relations', but not the agreement on unity.[81] The three post-war agreements of 1972, the two of Cairo and the Tripoli one, therefore followed a cease-fire between the states, and a declaration of some willingness to explore co-operation between the countries. But these declarations marked the limits to which the 'unity process' was able to go at that time, rather than the start of closer relations between the two Yemeni states.

PHASE 3: 1972–1977

In the immediate aftermath of the 1972 war the 'unity process' appeared to be achieving some specific results. The cease-fire itself did hold, and by the end of November 1972 air and road traffic between the two countries had been resumed.[82] On 2 December the YAR government banned the anti-NLF United National Front of South Yemen.[83] The committees, envisaged under the Agreement, began meeting in December 1972 and continued to meet with frequency into the early part of 1973.[84] But other trends were now beginning to assert themselves. Opposition to the Tripoli Agreement emerged into the open first in the YAR: on 28 December 1972 Prime Minister Muḥsin al-ᶜAynī was forced to resign. The reason he gave for resigning was the obstruction of the unity process by the Consultative Assembly.[85] The Prime Minister who replaced him, ᶜAbd Allāh al-Hadjrī, was known to be a more conservative leader, who was himself critical of the negotiations with the South.[86]

The response of the PDRY was at two levels: it continued the official negotiations with the YAR government, but at the same time Aden continued aid to the guerrilla forces that had been operating since 1971 against the YAR government. By March 1973 the guerrilla opposition was claiming that it was active in six out of nine provinces or *liwāt* of the YAR, and was presenting itself as embodying a combined national and social resistance to the policies of the al-Hadjrī government.[87] Around the same time, forces hostile to the PDRY government were reported to be gathering across the YAR border, and there was increased Saudi–South Yemeni tension: leaders of both Yemeni states emphasised that the unity discussions were being threatened.[88]

An additional issue of dispute arising between the two states at this time concerned the northern frontiers of the YAR. Under the 1934 Treaty of Taʾif between the Imam of Yemen and Saudi Arabia, the latter had acquired possession of the three provinces of ᶜAsir, Jizan and Najran.[89] The South Yemeni position was that these were provinces of North Yemen, and hence any future united Yemen, and that the Treaty of Taʾif was valid for only forty years. It was therefore the PDRY's view that in 1974 these three provinces should be returned to the YAR and that it was the YAR government's responsibility to make its claim public.[90] When YAR Premier al-Hadjrī visited Saudi Arabia in March 1973 he did the opposite, i.e. acknowledged Saudi Arabia's right to permanent control of these three provinces.[91] This constituted a further issue of dispute between the two countries, leading to denunciations by the PDRY of the YAR position. The curious logic of Yemeni unity found its expression in the PDRY's policy on irredentism: while it chided another state, the YAR, for conceding these provinces to Saudi Arabia, Aden was content to allow the YAR to occupy part of its own territory, the Kamaran Islands.

Later in 1973 unity discussions appeared to be reviving. The level of guerrilla activity on both sides of the frontier seemed to have declined, and on 4 September 1973 the two Presidents met in the context of the Non-Aligned Movement Summit in Algiers, in the presence of Algerian President Houari Boumedienne. In their joint statement they agreed to prolong the one-year deadline originally fixed at Cairo the year before, emphasised their continuing commitment to the unity process and stressed the need to stop the encouragement of 'sabotage'.[92] This recognised the fact that a major practical obstacle to the continuation of talks in the context of the joint committees was guerrilla activity in both states. The Algiers statement led to renewed meetings of the joint committees, and on 10 November 1973 President Sālim Rubiyyaᶜ ᶜAlī visited Sanaᶜa; it had taken six years for one Yemeni head of state to visit the capital of the other.[93] A year after the Tripoli Agreement it therefore seemed that, despite the delays and the political divisions within both states, the minimal points of the 1972 peace agreements had been reached: the two states were not at war or near it, they had withdrawn support for the guerrillas in each other's states, they had weathered the initial criticism of their reluctant patrons in Moscow and Riyadh, and the process of inter-governmental discussion was continuing.

In the early part of 1974 there were new discussions between the committees: there was neither substantial progress nor setback in the unity negotiations. But in June the process suffered an apparent reverse. On 13 June 1974 there was a *coup d'état* in the YAR in which al-Īryānī, a known champion of unity, was replaced by a new military Command Council under Colonel Ibrāhīm al-Ḥamdī. The Command Council re-affirmed the YAR's commitment to unity in its first pronouncements, but this assertion was offset by strong affirmations of support for Saudi Arabia. While the response of the PDRY authorities was initially neutral, and they re-affirmed their commitment to the unity process, their private view was at first that al-Ḥamdī was supported by Saudi Arabia and that his acquisition of power meant an end to progress on unity.[94] However, for the next two years the committees continued their deliberations and agreements were reached by the Economic and Financial Committee in February 1975 and by the Military Committee in the summer on the border.[95] Guerrilla harassment of each state had apparently ceased, and during 1976 YAR ministers began to talk with more emphasis on unity; this was in relation to greater economic and tourism collaboration, rather than the wider political unity envisaged in 1972.

The course of the unity issue was at this stage increasingly determined not by the state of relations *between* the two Yemeni states, but by the divisions *within* them, and in particular those within the YAR. While the underlying conflict inside the PDRY leadership, between President Sālim Rubiyyaᶜ ᶜAlī and Secretary-General ᶜAbd al-Fattāḥ Ismāᶜīl was continuing, this was contained at this time: the President was apparently more in favour of the unity policy than the Secretary-General, and he saw in the possibility of an alliance with the North a means of balancing the influence of his rivals in the PDRY. But this conflict was not as influential a factor as the situation in the YAR. Here al-Ḥamdī was preoccupied with establishing his authority: after coming to power in 1974, apparently with some Saudi support, the new President then proceeded to work towards establishing greater central government control over the pro-Saudi tribes and in so doing lessening the political influence of Saudi Arabia.[96] In such circumstances it would have probably have added to his troubles had he, at this juncture, initiated new negotiations with the South.

Unity policy therefore became itself one part of the internal conflicts of the YAR. Elements within the YAR government began to oppose unity with the South, and in January 1976 the YAR Chief of Staff Aḥmad Ḥuṣayn al-Ghashmī went so far as to say that he envisaged unity between the YAR and *Saudi Arabia*.[97] Throughout much of this period two former FLOSY opponents of the NLF in South Yemen, ʿAbd Allāh al-Aṣnadj and Muḥammad Sālim Baṣindawa, occupied influential positions in the YAR government. Al-Ḥamdī for his part sought to placate the Saudis and he was helped in this by the establishment of diplomatic relations between Aden and Riyadh in March 1976. But he also sought to encourage the emergence inside the YAR of political forces that would assist him in his campaign to strengthen central government.[98] In this way the internal politics of the YAR sustained a commitment to unity, not so much by persisting in the inter-governmental negotiations, as by allowing political forces allied to the PDRY to emerge once again within the YAR. These forces combined in early 1976 to form the National Democratic Front (*al-Djabḥa al-Dīmuḳrāṭiyya al-Waṭaniyya*).

The NDF was established on 11 February 1976 through the fusion of five groups that had emerged from the latter period of the civil war and its aftermath: the Revolutionary Democratic Party, the Organisation of Yemeni Resisters, the Popular Democratic Union, the Popular Vanguard Party, and the Labour Party.[99] The first two of these were former branches of the MAN, and therefore close to the NF in Aden. The third and fourth were, respectively, the YAR branches of the pro-Soviet communist and formerly pro-Syrian Baʿth parties, the equivalents of the two groups that had merged in the South. The Labour Party, founded in 1969, was itself a coalition of independent Marxists, former Baʿthists and members of the republican militias that had fought in the conflicts of the 1967–8 period.[100] According to its programme, the NDF aimed to establish 'a national democratic state' in the YAR, and to promote national and state control of the economy. It had a cautious policy on unity, calling for greater co-operation between the YAR and the PDRY, but it was explicit in condemning Saudi influence in the YAR, and in supporting the PFLO in Oman as well as the opposition in the Gulf region.[101] The NDF programme made no mention of 'socialism', or of the international influence of the USSR, although this was implied in the final paragraph, which called for a strengthening of relations between the YAR and the 'socialist countries'.[102] The merging of five radical groups within the YAR into a single National Democratic Front would seem to have been itself facilitated by the unification in the PDRY of the three political constituents of the UPONF at the Sixth Congress of the NF, in the previous October. In essence, the NDF's programme was a transposition to the YAR, in milder form, of the political programme adopted some months earlier by the UPONF in the South.

The emergence of the NDF provided al-Ḥamdī with a lever with which to strengthen his own position within the YAR and it was presented as an index of greater willingness on Sanaᶜa's part to find common ground with the PDRY. In 1977, this enabled a relaunching of the discussions at the highest governmental level that had more or less ended with the June 1974 *coup*. On 15–16 February 1977 the two Presidents met in the border YAR town of Qataba and agreed to establish a Ministerial Council that would meet every six months, and implement the 1972 unity agreement.[103] It would include the two Presidents and officials responsible for defence, the economy, trade, planning and foreign affairs. A month later, on 22–23 March, the Presidents of the YAR, PDRY, Sudan and Somalia met in Taᶜiz to discuss the growing crisis in the Red Sea area.[104] The common declaration issued, which called for peace and non-interference by outside powers, was important for the two Yemeni states in that it established their joint desire to maintain a foreign policy independent of these external powers. Neither Saudi Arabia nor the USSR endorsed the Taᶜiz statement. This pattern of meetings was repeated later in the year when on 13–14 August the two Presidents met again, in Sanaᶜa, and the officials repeated the positions of March on the need for peace in the Red Sea.[105]

However, the pressures on the YAR President proved to be too great. While no concrete steps towards unification of the two states had taken place, he had created hostility amongst conservative forces in the YAR by two policies that pertained to the unity issue: first, the tolerance of the NDF from 1976 onwards, and the more general strengthening of the central government against the tribes; secondly, the establishment of what appeared to be a more co-ordinated Yemeni foreign policy in response to the crisis in the Horn of Africa. In his speech on the anniversary of the September 1962 revolution, he alluded to the unexpected degree of agreement he had reached in the February meeting with Sālim Rubiyyaᶜ ᶜAlī.[106] On the night of 11–12 October 1977, two days before he was due to leave for his first official visit to Aden, indeed the first by any YAR head of state to the South, al-Ḥamdī was assassinated.[107] He was apparently a victim of the tensions which his unity policy had occasioned, and with him died the hopes of a cautious but sustained unity policy that had been maintained by al-Īryānī and al-Ḥamdī himself since the 1972 Tripoli Agreement.

PHASE 4: 1977–1979

The death of al-Ḥamdī initiated a new period of tension between the two Yemeni states. Aden denounced the YAR President's murder and implied that Saudi Arabia was responsible for it.[108] The new President, al-Ghashmī, declared that he remained committed to unity, and the PDRY appeared to believe that negotiations on unity could continue.[109] But whereas Aden had trusted al-Ḥamdī in part because of his internal policies, so now the YAR President appeared in a hostile light as he proceeded to reverse the domestic policies of al-Ḥamdī: the northern tribes were conciliated, while in May 1978 a revolt by officers formerly loyal to al-Ḥamdī, under Colonel ᶜAbd Allāh ᶜAbd al-ᶜĀlim, was crushed by al-Ghashmī's forces.[110] The rebels retreated to Aden. Thus by the middle of 1978 not only had the inter-governmental unity process been frozen, but the conflictual interaction of unity and political conflict within the two Yemeni states had been revived, in a manner not seen since the first part of 1973.

Events once again took a more dramatic turn. As tensions rose between the two states, the political situation in the PDRY came to a crisis. In the early part of 1978 the powers of President Sālim Rubiyyaᶜ ᶜAlī were further reduced, and one of the factors that appears to have contributed to his demise was the failure of his policy of accommodation with the YAR. Then a dual crisis occurred: in circumstances that have not been adequately explained, President al-Ghashmī of the YAR was killed by a bomb on 24 June, while two days later Sālim Rubiyyaᶜ ᶜAlī lost his life, along with a number of his followers, in the attempted *coup d'état* in Aden. The YAR authorities blamed the PDRY for sending a bomb to al-Ghashmī disguised as a present from the Southern to the Northern President.[111] The majority faction in the PDRY accused Sālim Rubiyyaᶜ ᶜAlī of having engineered the explosion, both to avenge the death of al-Ḥamdi, and to provoke a crisis in the YAR from which he could possibly have benefited.[112] Whatever the precise truth, and the degree of linkage between the two events, the death of the two Presidents within two days of each other, was a striking indication of the sensitivity of the politics of those states to the pressures of the other, and the degree to which internal, inter-Yemeni and wider foreign policy issues intertwined particularly through the Yemeni unity question itself.

In response to the death of al-Ghashmī Saudi Arabia took measures within the Arab League to isolate the PDRY: thus the inter-Yemeni conflict rapidly acquired a wider, Arab, dimension. The PDRY's participation in the Ethiopian war effort against Somalia earlier in the year and later against the Eritrean guerrillas also served to antagonise Arab sentiment. Aden's response was to support the opposition within the YAR that had been in conflict with the government from October 1977 onwards: the NDF expanded guerrilla activity in the southern and central regions, and acquired radio facilities in Aden.[113] In October 1978 there was a nearly successful *coup* against the new YAR President ᶜAlī ᶜAbd Allāh Ṣāliḥ, after which the defeated conspirators, Nasirists, Baᶜthists and followers of al-Ḥamdī, led by Lieutenant-Colonel Mudjāhid al-Kuḥḥālī, fled to Aden.[114] There, together with the rebels who had gone to Aden in the previous May, they formed the 13th June Front: in January 1979 this Front joined the NDF.[115]

Relations between the two Yemeni states were now at a consistently worse level than at any time since 1972. The YSP Congress of October 1978 was outspoken in its support for the opposition in the YAR, and was addressed by NDF leader Sulṭān Aḥmad ᶜUmar.[116] At this time a force of Northern tribesmen was welcomed in the streets of Aden.[117] Guerrilla resistance in the YAR reached its peak in October–December 1978.[118] But, on this occasion, although the PDRY was diplomatically on the defensive, it appeared to have the advantage in the South Arabian arena itself. Although they had acquired their own radio station after the June crises, South Yemen Freedom Radio, the exile forces opposed to Aden, still grouped to some degree in the YAR, were far weaker than in 1972; Libya was supporting Aden rather than Sanaᶜa; and the PDRY's armed forces were now better trained and armed than those of the YAR. In this situation, with the YAR government apparently weak, the NDF gained ground in the rural districts. In February 1979 fighting broke out between the regular armies of both sides.[119] The dynamic of diplomatic conflict between the states and social conflict within each now led to a direct interstate war on the 1972 pattern, but now it was the South which took the initiative, claiming that the situation in the YAR was close to being 'a comprehensive social revolution'.[120] Fighting lasted from 24 February to 3 March, and NDF forces, backed by the regular forces of the PDRY, occupied Qataba and a number of other towns in the southern region. At one point it appeared that the PDRY forces would be in a position to march on Taʾiz, the YAR's second city, and thereby directly challenge the YAR government. But after the 16 March cease-fire agreement both sides withdrew forces from each other's territories. This paved the way for a meeting of the two Presidents in Kuwait on 28–30 March. At Kuwait, a new agreement on unity was signed.[121]

The second inter-Yemeni war was in some respects similar to the first: a relatively short, border conflict, involving both irregular and regular forces, and brought to an end through Arab League diplomacy. The differences were, however, also considerable. As mentioned, the preceding period had been one of considerable NDF activity in the southern part of the YAR and it would appear that this time it was the PDRY which pushed the conflict towards direct war: the Aden leadership apparently hoped that it could in this way strike at the government of ʿAlī ʿAbd Allāh Ṣāliḥ. The precarious state of the new YAR regime, and the incidence of military *coups* in 1978 itself, may have strengthened this view within the NDF.[122] The second war therefore represented, as did the first, an attempt by one state to achieve unity by the deployment of its own forces in a direct assault upon the other. But this time it was the PDRY which was seeking to do so. The other important difference between the two wars was in the nature of the international response: on this occasion both Arab and world powers responded vigorously and openly to what was, in military terms, a subaltern affair. The second inter-Yemeni war was far more internationalised than the first, and while Aden had enjoyed some diplomatic advantage prior to the war this no longer applied. Saudi Arabia was joined by Egypt, Syria and Iraq, formerly allies of Aden's, in putting pressure on the PDRY not to advance on Taʾiz and to agree to a cease-fire. Syria and Iraq both told Aden it could not 'export revolution' to the YAR.[123] The USA also took a part in the conflict: Carter ordered a US naval task-force to the Red Sea and on 9 March announced an emergency airlift of $390 million worth of arms to support the YAR army.[124] The US government indicated that it was not prepared to allow the PDRY to win.[125] Conflict between the Yemens was, therefore, now invested with a strategic and symbolic importance at the Arab and world levels that had not previously been the case; it was, in part, this enhanced significance that prevented what might otherwise have been a decisive PDRY advance to capture Taʾiz.[126] This would have enabled the South to establish a form of 'unity' in alliance with the NDF over the part of the YAR they both held.

The meeting of the two Yemeni Presidents, ʿAlī ʿAbd Allāh Ṣāliḥ and ʿAbd al-Fattāḥ Ismāʿīl, in Kuwait on 28–30 March was the first between the heads of state of the Yemens since Rubiyyaʿ ʿAlī and al-Ḥamdī had met in Sanaʿa in August 1977: both their predecessors were now dead, and the new incumbents seemed improbable candidates for reconciliation. The President of the YAR was a semi-literate army officer, reputed to be implicated in the murder of al-Ḥamdī, who had shown himself a determined opponent of the pro-Aden forces inside the YAR.[127] ᶜAbd al-Fattāḥ Ismāᶜīl, himself an emigrant from the YAR, was a strong believer in Aden's alliance with the USSR and did not express, in his public statements, the support for unity through government-to-government negotiations which Sālim Rubiyyaᶜ ᶜAlī had voiced. Nevertheless the two Presidents issued a Joint Statement on Unity which re-affirmed the Cairo and Tripoli Agreements of 1972 and which provided a new means of implementing the goal of unity: this was to set up a Constitutional Committee that would draft a constitution for the united state within four months. Whereas in the Tripoli Agreement of 1972 responsibility for implementation had been placed with the eight specialist committees, Clause 5 of the new agreement stipulated that it was now to be the task of the two Presidents themselves to ensure that this agreement was to be accomplished within the stipulated time.[128]

Whatever its long-term practicability, the Kuwait Agreement did have, like its antecedents, certain immediate consequences. Fighting between the armies of the two states had ceased, and the borders reopened. In a significant conciliatory move, the YAR President reorganised his cabinet and dismissed the former FLOSY leaders who had been members of several Northern governments since 1972.[129] Later, during September, in an even more surprising move, ᶜAlī ᶜAbd Allāh Ṣāliḥ's government began receiving new military supplies from the USSR, thereby in effect reducing the importance of the military co-operation agreement which Carter had so publicly accelerated in March.[130] Yet, while relations between the two governments therefore improved, the underlying conflicts endured: during 1979 the NDF remained a significant and active force in the YAR, and the inter-governmental negotiations did not proceed at the rapid pace envisaged in the Kuwait Agreement. A repeat of the ambiguous aftermath of 1972 seemed to be likely.

PHASE 5: 1979–1986

If the immediate postwar situation of 1979 resembled that of 1972 in certain key respects – rapid proclamation of unity agreement and ceasefire, followed by continued guerrilla resistance in the YAR and slow implementation – it was nonetheless distinct from its predecessor in a number of respects. The YAR had launched the 1972 war, and been blocked, and it was now the turn of the PDRY to face the consequences of having its strategy frustrated. The relative diplomatic strengths of the two states reflected this: although the PDRY now had diplomatic relations with Saudi Arabia, these had been frozen after the June 1978 crisis, and influential external states, particularly Iraq and Syria, that might in other circumstances have backed the PDRY, were now keen to consolidate the unity process in order to check the PDRY's influence, as well as counter-balance Egyptian and Saudi influence. The internal situations of the two Republics were also different. The anti-PDRY forces based in the North were weaker than in 1972–3, and the pro-Aden forces of the NDF constituted a major problem for the Sanaᶜa government. But the NDF had also to face the consequences of the war's outcome, and, while it maintained its organisational and military presence in the countryside of the southern central YAR, it now had to engage in the political arena and bargain for power with the centre. The experience of many guerrilla movements, from Greece in 1944–45 to El Salvador and the Philippines in the 1980s, is that such a transition may be extremely difficult: once the decision to compete in the political arena is taken, the strength and dynamic of the guerrilla campaign may be lost, while the state's forces conserve their coercive potential and initiative. Aden's pursuit of 'unity' in negotiations with President ᶜAlī ᶜAbd Allāh Ṣāliḥ was, therefore, matched by sustained and evident support by the PDRY for the YAR President's radical opponents in the NDF.

Relations between the YSP and the opposition in the North were, moreover, affected by another development which had taken place during the war itself, on 5 March. This was the formation within the NDF of a new vanguard party, the Yemeni People's Unity Party – *Ḥizb al-Waḥda al-Shaᶜabiyya al-Yamaniyya*, known colloquially as *hoshi*, its Arabic acronym.[131] The YPUP was made up of the five parties that had, in February 1976, come together to form the NDF; but, whereas hitherto they had retained their separate identities within the Front, and had been joined by other groups opposed to the YAR regime, now they were to form a single, centralised, party. This fusion of the five YAR groups had obviously been made possible by the formation of the YSP in the previous October, just as the original formation of the Front in early 1976 had followed the establishment of UPONF in the South a few months previously. The YPUP was therefore the political ally of the YSP, the long-run intention being for it to attain power in the North and then fuse with the YSP. Its own programme made clear that it was committed to 'scientific socialism', that it was enthusiastically supportive of the USSR and the PDRY, and that it presented itself as the 'vanguard of the working class' and its allies in the North. Like the YSP, it called for unity on a 'national and democratic basis', but it stressed that this could only come about through 'class struggle', and the conflict 'between revolution and counter-revolution'. The commitment which the YSP now had to a fellow party in the North marked a definite shift in its overall approach, and was to establish a claim and an involvement more formal than any that had previously existed. Even after the 1982 accords, the support by at least some within the YSP for the YPUP was to complicate relations between North and South, as well as relations within the YSP itself.

Despite support from Aden and the NDF's strength on the ground, the balance of advantage had begun to shift away from Aden and its allies from the March 1979 war onwards. The ability of both governments to pursue the Kuwait Agreement was initially inhibited by domestic difficulties which each encountered. The YAR President, while able to conciliate the NDF by negotiations with the South, ran the risk of antagonising the pro-Saudi tribal forces of the YAR north by so doing, and Saudi threats to suspend aid to the YAR in 1979 indicated where Riyadh's priorities lay.[132] The unexpected return in late 1979 of the YAR to its traditional policy of purchasing weapons from the USSR, and the drastic reduction in implementation of the arms agreement negotiated with the USA and Saudi Arabia during the February war, also constituted issues of dispute between the YAR and Saudi Arabia. Anxious as he was to consolidate power at the centre, and to outmanoeuvre the NDF, ʿAlī ʿAbd Allāh Ṣāliḥ was nonetheless initially seriously constrained by the weakness of his own government internally and Saudi suspicion of the unity process. He also faced the continued challenge of the NDF: not until he had contained it, and built a stronger army, did he feel confident to pursue unity discussions with the South. All in all, ʿAlī ʿAbd Allāh Ṣāliḥ used the Kuwait Agreement to buy time.

Inside the PDRY there was no overt, organised, anti-YSP opposition, and while the USSR was not enthusiastic about the unity discussions, it did not exert the leverage over PDRY finances and society on this matter which Saudi Arabia did in the YAR. There was, however, another factor within the PDRY which complicated the unity discussions, namely the suppressed but still vital conflict within the PDRY's state and party between officials of Northern and Southern origins. How far this really did constitute a line of cleavage, and how far it was only rumoured to do so, cannot, on available evidence, be ascertained. But by the late 1970s the question of origin had become a significant issue in PDRY politics, with the North–South issue forming part of the wider factional dispute that reached its peaks in the attempted *coup* of Sālim Rubiyyaʿ ʿAlī in 1978 and the removal of ʿAbd al-Fattāḥ Ismāʿīl in 1980.[133] This constellation of issues came about in two ways. First, the economic hardships and diplomatic isolation of the PDRY were blamed by some Southerners on the fact that their country was ruled by a government that included many emigrants from the North. The replacement of Sālim Rubiyyaᶜ ᶜAlī, a Southerner, by ᶜAbd al-Fāttāḥ Ismāᶜīl, a Northerner, contributed to this, and the decision to advance in the 1979 war occasioned criticism from within the army.[134] At the same time, those in the PDRY from the North were much less willing to reach conciliation with the existing government there: their representatives, both in the PDRY state and party, and through the NDF, wanted to replace or at least significantly alter the policies of the YAR government. The Southerners apparently inclined towards a more moderate approach, and to reining in the NDF as far as this was practicable.

An important further precondition for implementing the Kuwait Agreement was the establishment of a minimal degree of trust: ᶜAlī ᶜAbd Allāh Ṣālīh was, after all, a man opposed to al-Ḥamdī, and whom supporters of the South tried to kill in October 1978. He and the PDRY had been at war in February 1979. The PDRY government had, since 1977–8, been supporting a wide-spread guerrilla movement in the YAR itself. It was therefore necessary that each President should feel confident about pursuing the talks. ᶜAlī ᶜAbd Allāh Ṣāliḥ had to some extent mended his fences with the Saudis by 1980, and the replacement of ᶜAbd al-Fattāḥ Ismāᶜīl by ᶜAlī Nāṣir Muḥammad in April 1980 acted as a solvent on the PDRY side. Soon afterwards, YAR Premier ᶜAbd al-ᶜAzīz ᶜAbd al-Ghanī had visited Aden and a joint communiqué published on 6 May announced a decision to found joint economic projects, in the fields of industry, minerals, land and maritime transport, and to co-ordinate national development plans.[135] When President ᶜAlī Nāṣir Muḥammad visited the YAR in June 1980 these commitments were embodied in a series of economic and cultural agreements between the two sides. In particular, it was decided to set up joint companies in the fields of maritime transport, overland transport and tourism.[136] The communiqué talked of greater economic integration – of co-ordinating development plans, discussions on monetary and banking union, increased inter-Yemeni trade, and freedom of travel between the two countries.

Progress in inter-governmental relations was, however, limited by the continued conflict between the YAR government and the NDF/YPUP. After substantial fighting in late 1979, the two parties to the dispute reached an agreement on 31 January 1980. This allowed the NDF some political freedom in the YAR, in return for an ending of armed conflict and the closing of its radio facilities in Aden.[137] The January 1980 agreement was welcomed by the PDRY and contributed to the improved relations between the two states.[138] There were, however, those within the YAR government who opposed any such compromise with the NDF, and the Front was, for its part, seeking to consolidate its position on the ground to ensure that it could not be compelled to make concessions by pressure from the PDRY. The result was that, despite the January 1980 agreement and improved PDRY–YAR relations, in the latter part of 1980 fighting flared again and continued till the spring of 1982. The YAR government gained the upper hand and in April 1982 the NDF was forced to suspend guerrilla opposition. It had to withdraw roughly 2,000 fighters to the PDRY in return for promises of limited political freedom of action in the YAR.[139] It was at this point that the PDRY signally refused to provide military assistance to the NDF, despite appeals from the latter and the desire of some within the YSP leadership, such as ᶜAlī ᶜAntar, to do so.

The renewed fighting in 1980–2 between the YAR government and the NDF, and the refusal of the Sanaᶜa government to accept compromise with the Front, meant that progress in relations between the two states was slow. New agreements were reached only in October 1981, after the two Presidents met in Kuwait and when, in the next month, ᶜAlī ᶜAbd Allāh Ṣāliḥ agreed for the first time to visit Aden. The YAR President had just been received in Moscow and it can be assumed that the USSR was discouraging the NDF. It was reported at the time that the YAR President then demanded and received assurances about reduced PDRY backing for the NDF.[140] Many Yemenis believed that it was indicative of ᶜAlī ᶜAbd Allāh Ṣāliḥ's view of his hosts that while he travelled to Aden by plane he preferred to return home by car. This visit by President ᶜAlī ᶜAbd Allāh Ṣāliḥ to Aden culminated in the signing of a new YAR–PDRY agreement, which took the discussions on unity further than they had ever previously gone. This envisaged the establishment of a Supreme Council (*al-Madjlis al-Yamanī al-ᶜAlā*) chaired by the two Presidents. It was to meet every six months on a regular basis, surpervise the work of the unity committees and have a Joint Ministerial Committee comprising the premiers, foreign ministers, interior ministers, supply and planning, education ministers and the chiefs of staff of the two sides. A Secretariat, based in Sanaᶜa, with an office in Aden, was to handle the administrative work of the Council. The agreement also envisaged the continuation of economic, cultural and foreign policy co-ordination between the two states. The text of a new constitution, in 136 clauses, was also, it was reported, drawn up.[141] The issue of the NDF was not mentioned, but when ᶜAlī Nāṣir Muḥammad visited the YAR in May 1982, at a time when the NDF was ending its guerrilla actions, the press statement alluded to this: it stated that the two sides

> succeeded in coming to an agreement to overcome the instability and the difficulties that obstruct the realisation of the aspirations of our people in the two parts of the homeland for a stable and peaceful life leading to the reunification of our country.[142]

In effect, the PDRY had to accept that the North Yemeni government was, for the time being at least, the sole viable interlocutor within the YAR, and that, for this reason, the NDF could not be supported further. Thus ended the policy which the Southern government had been pursuing since independence, of simultaneous negotiation with Sanaᶜa and support for the radical opposition.

The ending of the conflict within the YAR and between Aden and Sanaᶜa in early 1982 was a product of numerous factors, the exact importance of which it is still too early to assess. The situation on the ground itself turned against the NDF in the early months of 1982 and this was the decisive reason for the ending of the period of conflict. It became evident to the PDRY that the protracted period of instability in the North initiated by the death of al-Ḥamdī in 1977 had not, despite several apparently near successes, been able to install a regime more favourable to the South: neither military revolts at the centre, nor guerrilla pressure, had dislodged the post-al-Ḥamdī rulers. But several other considerations may have weighed in bringing about this result. The situation within the South itself had deteriorated, both as a result of leadership conflicts over the North and in the aftermath of severe floods in March 1982. The position of the Soviet leadership was clearly negative, as signalled by the warm reception of ᶜAlī ᶜAbd Allāh Ṣāliḥ in Moscow in October 1981, and the ensuing substantial supplies of Soviet arms to him, which he used against the NDF. But PDRY leaders were later to allude to a further dimension, namely the emergence of a long-run plan by the YAR, Saudi Arabia, Egypt and the USA to topple the regime in Aden.[143] This had reportedly been devised in Sadat's time, and had involved substantial sabotage inside the PDRY by infiltrated groups, to be followed by a YAR/Saudi invasion. At one point, it is claimed, the YAR leader telephoned to Aden to announce that he was going to launch such a war: but the death of Sadat in October 1981, followed by the arrest within Aden of 17 members of a CIA-trained sabotage group, prevented the full import of this plan being realised. Whatever the truth of this, the fear of such a concerted challenge certainly played a part in the thinking of the PDRY leaders, and led them to calculate that the costs of continued intervention in the YAR were too high to sustain.

In the period between 1982 and 1986, relations between Sanaᶜa and Aden remained peaceful, and there were three meetings of the Yemen Supreme Council, the joint body with a secretariat based in Sanᶜa through which ongoing negotiations on areas of co-operation were to take place. A contributing factor to this process may have been the further development of Soviet–YAR relations, leading in 1984 to Sanaᶜa signing a Twenty Year Treaty of Friendship and Co-operation with Moscow, similar, though not identical, to that between Aden and Moscow, signed in 1979. The most important agreement between the PDRY and the YAR was reached in January 1985, when a joint economic zone along part of the borders of the two countries was created, to share the production and exploitation of oil resources found there and which had begun to be exploited on the northern side.[144] The two Yemeni states also sought to co-ordinate in areas of foreign policy, and this was especially noticeable in the exertions they both made to overcome the divisions that emerged, after 1983, in the Palestinian resistance movement. But despite these advances, very little of substance was achieved: the constitution remained in draft form, 'under study by the Presidents', as official phrasing put it; there was, in practice, very little real economic collaboration between the two states and the development of port facilities at Hodeida in 1982 lessened YAR dependence on Aden – IMF statistics give a total of $50 million worth of trade between the two states in 1985; freedom of movement of citizens of one country to the other remained remote. Each also continued to allow opponents of the other to remain discreetly, in their respective capitals. Those in Aden were from the NDF and the YPUP; those in Sanaᶜa from *al-Tadjammuᶜ al-Ḳawmī*, comprising FLOSY leaders such as Makkāwī and al-Asnadj and ex-NLF elements such as Muḥammad ᶜAlī Ḥaytham. The growing divisions within the South also appear to have contributed to the slow pace of discussions, and it is perhaps indicative that the last, third, meeting of the Yemen Supreme Council took place in December 1984, more than a year before the explosion in the PDRY. As in earlier periods, the policy of promoting Yemeni unity consisted of peaceful coexistence, and a small amount of foreign policy and economic co-ordination, but also stimulated dissension within each state.

From the South's perspective, the early 1980s saw an overall shift of advantage away from Aden and towards the YAR. Contrary to the expectations of many, ᶜAlī ᶜAbd Allāh Ṣāliḥ had after 1978 been able to establish his authority in the YAR and, slowly, to broaden the base of his regime. He had used the Kuwait Agreement of 1979 to buy time, and had, by 1982, been able to force Aden to abandon support for the NDF and the YPUP: this in itself had strengthened his hand in the North and provoked dissension in the South.

In addition, the comparative economic and social performance of the two states was causing unease in the South. While the provision of social services in the PDRY was far superior to that in the North, the availability of consumer goods was higher in the cities of the North, as a result of emigrants' remittances and imports, and the opening of a YAR colour TV service in 1982, able to broadcast directly to the South, served to project a distinctively attractive image of the YAR into the PDRY. So too did the provision by ʿAlī ʿAbd Allāh Ṣāliḥ of an emergency electricity generating station, at a time when Aden's power supply problems were widely attributed to Soviet failure to complete the al-Ḥizwa station, initially planned in 1972. The Northern discovery of oil in 1984, however limited in real quantity, also served to provide the North with an advantage in terms of popular appeal. Well before the 1986 explosion in the South, therefore, it was evident that the PDRY was no longer in the stronger position vis-à-vis the North that it had enjoyed in the latter part of the 1970s.

PHASE 6: 1986–1987

The 1986 crisis in the PDRY took the leadership in Sanaʿa as much by surprise as other outsiders: the signs of factional disagreement in the South had been noted in the North, but the YAR authorities appeared as confused as others after the fighting broke out. ʿAlī Nāṣir does appear to have warned ʿAlī ʿAbd Allāh Ṣāliḥ that something might occur, and it was to the YAR that he and his supporters retreated as the fighting wore on: but there is no evidence of any YAR role in either the onset or course of the conflict.

While there may have been some immediate thoughts of intervening, the response of the YAR was by 17 January to try to mediate in the conflict; but it would also seem certain that Sanaʿa was anxious that its interlocutor the President might be replaced by forces more hostile to accommodation with the North. Some consideration was, apparently, given to intervention on the side of ʿAlī Nāṣir, but there were substantial influences against this. The USSR and Kuwait, both influential in Sanaʿa, warned against any YAR intervention, and, once it became evident that the bulk of the PDRY's armed forces had turned against ʿAlī Nāṣir, the army in the YAR itself made known to the President its reluctance to move into the South. Towards the end of January, lorries carrying relief supplies donated by the YAR and the PLO tried to reach Aden, but they too were turned back: the result was that, despite its close involvement in the affairs of the PDRY, the YAR did nothing to affect the outcome of the January fighting.

Nonetheless, the January 1986 crisis produced a major hiatus in relations between Aden and Sanaʿa.[145] Tens of thousands of supporters of ʿAlī Nāṣir fled to the YAR and continued to arrive during the following months. ʿAlī Nāṣir was able to conduct political business in the North, where he constituted his supporters as the 'Legitimate Leadership' (*Ḳiyyāda Sharīʿiyya*) of the Central Committee of the Yemeni Socialist Party'. He put forward his own proposals for resolving the inner-party conflict, based on the convening of a new YSP Congress. Over the following months, he published a weekly paper, *Kifāḥ al-Shaᶜab* (Struggle of the People), gave interviews, convened meetings of his supporters, and travelled to other capitals, notably Damascus, Algiers and Addis Ababa, from his headquarters in Sanaᶜa. This welcome accorded to ᶜAlī Nāṣir clearly alarmed the South, but there were also factors in the new PDRY regime which concerned the North. Several of those now prominent in the leadership were exiles from the North associated with support for the NDF and YPUP in the years up to 1982, and subsequently: this was particularly true of Muḥammad Saᶜīd ᶜAbd Allāh, or ᶜMuḥsinᶟ, who now held an important organisational position in the YSP Central Committee Secretariat. The NDF and YPUP had divided during the January crisis, and one faction, associated with Sulṭān ᶜAḥmad ᶜUmar, had sided with ᶜAlī Nāṣir. But others, including Djayr Allāh ᶜUmar, who had been secretary-general of the YPUP in the preceding years, played a prominent role in the new regime. As had happened so often in the past, both Sanaᶜa and Aden kept the opponents of the other in reserve, as part of the delicate balance between the two states.

From the beginning, however, there were limits on the degree of conflict which the January 1986 crisis occasioned. Clandestine radios were started up, but only for a few weeks. In September 1986, there were reports that ᶜAlī Nāṣir's supporters were engaged in military preparations against the South: they are reported to have tried to shoot down a PDRY helicopter, before the YAR authorities prevented them. When, in the aftermath of death sentences on his supporters in Aden in December 1987, ᶜAlī Nāṣir threatened to launch armed resistance to the PDRY government, the YAR Foreign Minister ᶜAbd al-Karīm al-Īryānī, was quick to state that this would not occur from YAR territory. The new regime in Aden, for its part, averred that it was continuing the policies established prior to January 1986 and that a union of the two states, 'on a peaceful and democratic basis', remained its goal. The crisis in the PDRY therefore had its impact on relations with the YAR and presented Sanaᶜa with the difficult question of what to do with the tens of thousands of political refugees on its soil: but this did not lead to armed conflict between the two, either during or after the fighting in Aden.

Throughout 1986 relations between the two Yemens remained tense, as negotiations continued on what to do about the exiles in the YAR. In 1987, however, there were some improvements, culminating in a visit to Sanaᶜa in July 1987 by ᶜAlī al-Bīḍ, the YSP Secretary General. This meeting served, he stated, to overcome 'the obstacles that were set up in the period after the events of the 13th January conspiracy'.[146] Al-Bīḍ's, and other, visits temporarily reduced the threat of military conflict and both sides benefited from a lessening of tensions: the YAR now had some difficulties with Saudi Arabia, concerning border clashes in disputed areas of the north, while the PDRY leadership was facing substantial problems at home. But the al-Bīḍ visit also demonstrated that no compromise on the exiled PDRY leadership was possible: the YSP had just held its Congress, at which ᶜAlī Nāṣir's remaining associates had been purged, and the trial of the former President's supporters was reaching its conclusion in Aden, with the pronouncement of death sentences. There was talk of a 'resumption of the unionist dialogue', but in any effective sense this did not occur: a cold and precarious peace prevailed.

Three issues, in particular, served to underline the differences between Aden and Sanaᶜa. The first was that of ᶜAlī Nāṣir and his supporters, who continued to be joined during 1987 by high-level defectors from the South. It proved impossible, despite the efforts of Kuwait, the YAR and the Soviet Union and others to get a compromise acceptable to both sides, and the execution in December 1987 of five close associates of ᶜAlī Nāṣir, despite appeals from ᶜAlī ᶜAbd Allāh Ṣāliḥ and many allies, including the leaders of Kuwait, Cuba, the GDR and the PLO, was indicative of Aden's unyielding resolve in this regard. There were plans for ᶜAlī Nāṣir to move his base to another Arab capital, such as Algiers, or to Addis Ababa, much as former YAR Presidents, al-Sallāl and al-Iryānī, had spent years in Damascus and Baghdad: but even this, which could have contributed to some improvement between Aden and Sanaᶜa, did not occur. A second issue concerned the international situation in the Middle East as a whole: while the YAR's relations with Saudi Arabia remained temperamental, Sanaᶜa did in broad terms associate itself with the bloc of states opposed to Iran. It sent some Soviet military equipment to Iraq, at least in the early stages of the war, and in November 1987, following the Amman summit of the Arab heads of state, the YAR, in common with Saudi Arabia, Kuwait and other states, re-established diplomatic relations with Egypt.[147] The PDRY, while critical of Iran's attacks on Kuwait, was not so associated with the pro-Iraqi bloc, and was evidently far more reluctant to restore relations with its erstwhile foe in Cairo.

The third, and most important, question concerned with the unity negotiations themselves, and the stronger bargaining position of the North. In broad terms, the situation of 1979 was now reversed: the YAR found itself in an enhanced position vis-à-vis the South and was therefore pressing for a rapid conclusion of an agreement to merge the two states. The PDRY, in a more precarious political and economic situation, was reluctant to risk entering such an agreement rapidly; as a delaying tactic, it wanted any draft constitution to be discussed and amended by public discussion in both countries, whereas the YAR wanted any agreement between the two Presidents to be ratified by the respective legislatures.

The YAR authorities spoke of uniting the two states within two or three years, those in the PDRY of a five-year period. In practice, both sides reconciled themselves to the fact that unity was a long way off. As one YAR official put it: 'Except by some historic accident, unity will only come about over a long period of time . . . Reunification will not be realised through grandiose discussions, but is more attainable through slowly creating concrete links, beginning modestly with areas such as trade and tourism.'[148] The experience which so many other proponents of unity integration had lived through, in Europe as much as in the Arab world, that collaboration on specific, 'functional', issues is more realisable than the merging of states, has been reproduced, with much disillusion, and not a little bloodshed, in the Yemens. Even here, however, mutual suspicion and competition had their impact: the discovery of oil in a region bordering both states but where the frontier was disputed contained the potential for disputes, as evident in November 1987, just as the near simultaneous start of oil production in both states created a new dimension for competition between them.

Sources of the 'unity' policy

This chronological account of YAR–PDRY relations may provide some basis for identifying underlying features of the unity policy, both why it apparently failed, but why it was at the same time sustained. The problem to be overcome, the division of the Yemens, has been analysed above as reflecting not one but several historical factors which combined to produce the situation that prevailed after 1967. One was the absence of a single state or administrative region inherited from pre-colonial times, and the prevalence of tribal, religious and regional differences. The second was the impact of the two colonialisms, Turkish and British, and the delimitations of the two administrative areas. The third was the difference in the social and national upheavals of the 1960s, and the different states that emerged from them towards the end of the decade. The fourth was the imposition on to the South Arabian region of wider rivalries, between Saudi Arabia and more radical Arab states, and between east and west. Each on its own would have constituted a substantial obstacle to unification of the two states: together these four factors reinforced a division that proved more effective than the declarations of the two states' leaders.

The same factors that sustained the division at the same time go some way to suggesting reasons why, despite its impracticability, the official call for Yemeni unity remained strong in the YAR as well as in the PDRY. In the first place, the assertion of a common Yemeni identity by political leaders served to strengthen the legitimacy of each state with their own populations against outside powers *and* against each other. It reinforced legitimacy against outside states, particularly Saudi Arabia, because Sanaʿa and Aden could pose as the champions of a local independence against richer, intrusive, states.[149] At the same time, this quest for legitimacy was, on occasion, competitive: each state presented the other as being under the domination of an external power (Saudi Arabia or the USA in the case of the YAR, the USSR in the case of the PDRY) and so each could suggest to its own population that it was the true defender of national interests.[150] The second function of asserting a Yemeni identity was integrative, since the problem of unity was not just between these two states; both Yemeni states faced considerable difficulties in binding their own societies together, in overcoming the tribal, regional and religious divisions within them inherited from earlier epochs, as well as the political divisions of the contemporary Arab world that were translated to them. In each state, national economies and modern state structures had to be developed at the time when the old order was ending, in 1962 in the North, in 1967 in the South. Assertion of a Yemeni identity therefore served to assist this integrationist process.

A third function was practical: Yemeni unity could be seen as bringing certain important benefits, and the proclaimed quest for Yemeni unity had its own limited advantages. A unified Yemen would have created a state of up to nine million people, the most populous in the Arabian Peninsula, with both a significant cultivated area and a considerable reserve of manpower. The limited resources, human and natural, of the two Yemens would to some extent have complemented each other. Short of full unity, moreover, the quest for unity had its benefits: it had the advantage of allowing limited co-operation in some fields – education, economics, movement of individuals between states. In this sense 'unity' was but an exaggerated way of denoting a measure of co-operation between states. At the same time it allowed for a consultation in foreign policy that lessened the danger of war. In private discussions, officials on both sides stated that the most important point in the Yemeni unity policy of the two states was that it enabled them to avoid war, and this argument was given additional force by the implication that the two wars between the Yemeni states had been the result of external influence.[151]

For all the element of co-operation, however, the call for unity had another, antagonistic, dimension, in that it served as a means for each state to pursue its rivalry with the other. In this sense the national and social components of Yemeni nationalism remained interlocked not just by compounding each other within each state, i.e. by the casting of social enemies as national ones, but in the sense that both issues led to conflict: each state became implicated in the internal conflicts of the other state by asserting the claims of national unity. The concept of 'non-interference' in the internal affairs of the other had weak salience. Throughout the period after 1967, each state committed itself to the pursuit of 'unity': but this pursuit of a common goal reflected particular interests – the political and social priorities of the governments in Aden and Sanaʿa and their search for allies within the other state. At one level, the involvement led to diplomatic negotiations with the counterpart governments on areas of co-operation and compromise; but it also involved each in supporting the rivals of the other, in order to bring pressure upon them, or even overthrow them. Each Yemeni state therefore pursued unity at these two levels: at that of diplomatic negotiation and government-to-government discussion, and that of encouraging upheaval in the neighbouring state that might bring a more friendly government to power. Consequently, if in one sense the encouragement of change in the other state was a product of the commitment to national unity, on the grounds that the governments of similar outlook could the more easily unite, it was also the case that the commitment to unity provided a means of prosecuting an interrelated social and political conflict within both Yemens that had been in train since 1962.

This complex combination of the social and political on one side and the national on the other may in some degree explain the history of relations between the two Yemens after 1967. The position held until independence by nationalists in the South was that since the division of the two Yemens was a product of colonialist division, unity would become possible once the British had departed. This did not take place, and by 1970 both states were in open political conflict with each other. The ensuing years yielded apparently inconsistent behaviour by both sides: two wars, in 1972 and 1979, each of which was followed by a unity agreement; support for guerrillas operating in the other state while conducting negotiations with the other government.

Marked as it was by uncertainties, South Yemen's policy towards North Yemen involved, therefore, more than just conceptual slippage about the nature of the national entities involved, the historical antecedents of the two distinct states or the goals of the unity policy. It also involved uncertainty about the *means* by which this unity could be brought about, and the channels through which a unity policy could be pursued. The South's commitment to unity resulted in the use of at least three different political instruments, with three correspondingly different strategies: negotiation with the YAR government, support for rebels within the YAR, and direct deployment of the South Yemeni state and army itself against the YAR. This variation of instruments was to continue throughout the period after 1967. It was a response to changes within the political situation in the YAR, but it also reflected the differences of opinion within the South Yemeni regime, and the various pressures to which both regimes were subjected by outside forces, Arab and Soviet. The paradoxical combination of tenacity and oscillation in Yemeni policy was therefore a reflection not only of the definitional and historical uncertainties of this policy, but also of the manner in which policy on unity was the resultant of conflict *between* the two states, and *within* them, as well as that of interplay of unity with broader strategic issues that had affected the two Yemens since the mid nineteenth century. The intersection of the unification issue with east–west conflict in the post-1945 period, one also evident in the cases of Germany, Korea and Vietnam, became part of the Yemeni unity question as well.

Analysis of the history of the 'unity' issue can look at it in two dimensions: either as a goal-directed activity, where the aim is unity, in which sense the process was frustrated; or as one pursued for other more limited reasons, without it being necessary to achieve unification. In the latter sense, the pursuit of Yemeni unity, on both sides of the frontier, was an important, practical and in some measure successful component of the PDRY's foreign policy, as it was of the YAR's, throughout the post-1967 period. If it had not continued to serve some functions, the goal of unity would not have been maintained.

5 Regional orientations: 'solidarity' and accommodation

The major revolutions of modern history, with the partial exception of the Mexican, involved the revolutionary states in alliance with opposition forces in, and armed conflicts with, their neighbours and other proximate states: France, Russia, Cuba, Vietnam, Iran all underwent this experience. South Yemen too followed this path. Indeed one of the most remarkable aspects of the South Yemeni case was the extent of its revolutionary 'solidarity' and embattlement in the post-revolutionary phase, the range and persistence of its conflicts with other states in the Arabian Peninsula and surrounding regions over more than a decade. Given its exposed strategic position, its economic vulnerability and limited resources, the extent of its persistence in such conflict with its neighbours and in a revolutionary foreign policy was striking.

This commitment to revolution in the Arabian Peninsula was not something given great prominence in the official documents of the pre-independence period. The 1965 Charter had reiterated radical Arab nationalist themes of that period, calling for freedom from colonial rule and 'progressive Arab unity', but its only specific commitment was to support the Palestinians.[1] The shift towards a more socially revolutionary position and to change in the Peninsula was, however, evident from independence itself, and especially when, after some initial optimism on the South Yemen side about establishing relations with Saudi Arabia, it became evident that the two states were in conflict. Speaking at the Fourth Congress, in March 1968, ᶜAbd al-Fattāḥ Ismāᶜīl stressed the role of the PRSY as a support of revolution throughout the Arabian Peninsula.[2] In a major statement in May 1969 President Ḳaḥṭān al-Shaᶜabī, whose government had been challenged by Saudi-backed rebels, emphasised that he too subscribed to this view:

> As for Saudi Arabia, its attitude towards us was clear from the start and the attitude of our revolution to Saudi Arabia was clear. Winds of change will certainly blow from this revolution . . . The principle of this revolution will spread over the entire Arabian Peninsula.[3]

In the same speech he affirmed the support of the PRSY for the oppositions in North Yemen and Oman, and for the Palestinian resistance. At the Fifth Congress, in March 1972, ʿAbd al-Fattāḥ Ismāʿīl declared that the 'success of the Congress would affect the whole Peninsula and would light the way for all strugglers and progressive people'.[4] For the revolutionaries of the NF, their own revolution was a model for others in the Arabian Peninsula, and the security of their revolution depended upon the success of kindred revolutions elsewhere. As Aden radio declared in November 1971:

> The battles being fought by the revolution of the Front for the Liberation of the Occupied Arab Gulf aim at independence for the people of the Gulf. The people of the PDRY believe their own independence to be at peril so long as pockets of colonialism remain in the Arabian Gulf.[5]

This support for revolutions elsewhere involved the PDRY in the first instance in conflicts with the three states with whom it shared a land frontier: North Yemen, Saudi Arabia and Oman. In the cases of North Yemen and Oman this led Aden to more than a decade of intermittent military engagements, both with the forces of the neighbouring state and in support of guerrillas operating in these states. As discussed in chapter 4, the North Yemeni case involved a simultaneous pursuit of negotiations with the incumbent governments, an advocacy of a policy of unity with the other state and support for that state's opponents. The case of Oman was a more conventional case of support for a guerrilla movement in a neighbouring state, not one overlain by the issue of 'unity': but the geographical location of that state on the Persian Gulf itself meant that the PDRY's role in aiding the Omani opposition came to affect its relations with many other states. This in part explains the degree of conflict with Saudi Arabia: while the PDRY did, until 1976, aid Saudi opponents of the monarchy, as the Saudis did exile opponents of the PDRY, the level of South Yemeni–Saudi mutual threat was at a much lower level of military activity than on the YAR and Oman frontiers. The confrontation between the PDRY and the KSA was much more directly a political one between two states, neither of which accepted the legitimacy of the other, or the other's overall orientation in foreign policy, than a dispute that took the form of protracted military conflict.

Throughout the first two decades after 1967 the PDRY pursued what, in the context of the Russian revolution, has been termed a 'dual policy':[6] that is, a combination of developing diplomatic relations with states while simultaneously providing support to radical opponents of those states. In some cases, such as Oman up to 1982, the support for the opposition was such that no diplomatic relations were envisaged, but in the majority of cases the PDRY both exchanged embassies with countries and backed revolutionary allies within these states. If this revolutionary policy was true for remoter states such as Iraq, Somalia, and Ethiopia, it was most palpably true in dealings with the PDRY's three Peninsula neighbours – the YAR, Oman and Saudi Arabia.

Oman: conflict and normalisation

For the first fifteen years after independence South Yemen maintained no diplomatic relations with the neighbouring Sultanate of Oman and was in a state of substantial conflict with it. In certain respects the dispute with Oman was less serious than that with Aden's two other land neighbours: Saudi Arabia posed a far more serious *military* threat to South Yemen, given the air power at its disposal, and it provided shelter for significant numbers of South Yemeni refugees who were used by Riyadh to raid the South Yemeni frontier areas at moments of tension; North Yemen posed a *political* problem, since it was a state with which Aden proclaimed its desire to unite, and whose internal developments were followed with great care by government and population alike in the South. It was with Saudi Arabia and North Yemen that border wars actually broke out, and these countries, by virtue of their greater proximity to the main populated regions of the PDRY thereby presented a potentially larger menace.

Yet the disputes with North Yemen and Saudi Arabia were, in other ways, of a lesser dimension than that with Oman: they were intermittent, where that with Oman was continuous, and the Omani dispute involved Aden in a far clearer and more persistent attempt to alter the system of government in a neighbouring state than was the case in either the YAR or Saudi Arabia. In terms of its place within the PDRY's foreign policy as a whole, policy towards Oman occupied a special position, as the greatest single commitment to encouraging revolution in another state undertaken by the Aden government; and this commitment occupied a similar place in evaluations of South Yemeni foreign policy by other states, regional and from further afield, who endorsed the stability of existing governments in the Arabian Peninsula. Hostility to the PDRY in the Arab world and the west was to a considerable extent a result of what was regarded as Aden's 'destabilising' role in Oman.

The guerrilla movement which Aden supported in Oman conducted substantial and sustained military activities in the southern, Dhofar, province of the Sultanate from 1965 to 1975.[7] Intermittent guerrilla actions were claimed until at least June 1981.[8] The Dhofar area, of around 30,000 square miles, and with a population of around 50,000, was in many ways more part of Saudi Arabia than Oman: its geography and climate were linked to those of South Arabia, and the population spoke a variety of pre-Arabic dialects similar to those spoken in the Mahra region of

South Yemen and on the island of Socotra.[9] But from the latter part of the nineteenth century, Dhofar had been part of the Sultanate of Oman and, while in some earlier periods the term 'Yemen' encompassed Dhofar, with few exceptions no modern Yemeni politicians claimed it as part of historic Yemen.[10] Dhofar's distinct character did, however, provide the context in which tribal resentment of rule from Muscat could develop, and the proximity of South Yemen meant that the rebel forces in Dhofar could obtain support from across the frontier.[11]

The war that began in 1965 was organised by a coalition of Dhofari exile groups who in 1964–5 formed a Dhofar Liberation Front.[12] This included both Nasserist and radical members of the MAN, and from the time of the First DLF Congress and the first guerrilla actions in June 1965 the Front appealed for support from the NLF in South Yemen.[13] The extent of involvement of the South Yemeni MAN with the Dhofari guerrillas prior to November 1967 is not known, but there must have been contact, and in October 1966 British forces did raid the Yemeni border town of Hauf and arrest a number of people there in an attempt to stem the flow of arms to Dhofar.[14] Once the PRSY became independent in 1967, supplies and base facilities became available to the DLF on a more regular basis.[15] The Dhofar revolt was not, however, a direct consequence of the situation in South Yemen, in the way that the outbreak of guerrilla warfare in South Yemen in October 1963 had been a result of the war in the North. The groups which formed the DLF in 1964–5 had come together from Dhofari exiles working in the Persian Gulf and other parts of the Arab world, and built their support inside Dhofar on the basis of the resentments and tensions that had existed there for decades.[16] Prior to 1967, the fact that Dhofar had a common frontier with South Yemen provided a line of logistical support more than a source of political or military impulsion.

In the ten years of its guerrilla campaign, the Dhofari rebel movement went through a number of organisational changes. In September 1968, at a congress reportedly held at Hamrin in the central Dhofar, the DLF changed its name to the People's Front for the Liberation of the Occupied Arab Gulf (PFLOAG).[17] This term included not only all of Oman, but also the states of Trucial Oman (later the United Arab Amirates), Bahrain and Qatar, and, it was sometimes suggested, Kuwait.

The new organisation adopted political and social programmes of a more explicitly revolutionary character, reflecting both the influence of the radicalised sections of the MAN in the Mashriḳ and that of China, which in 1967 became a significant supplier of arms, training and political literature to the Front.[18] It announced that 'organised revolutionary violence' was 'the sole means' of waging its struggle, and declared its desire 'to work towards the unification of the revolutionary tool of the popular masses in the Occupied Arabian Gulf as the healthy and revolutionary prelude to the unity of the area'.[19] This congress, presented as the second congress of the PFLOAG, was followed by a third, in June 1971, in the western Dhofari town of Rakhyut, and then in December 1971 by the fusion of the PFLOAG with another group of former MAN members, the National Democratic Front for the Liberation of Oman and the Arabian Gulf.[20] This merger produced a new name for the organisation – the People's Front for the Liberation of Oman and the Arabian Gulf (still PFLOAG) – and a programme that gave more attention to political work and, alongside the military campaigns, to the diffusion of a 'national democratic character' drawn up at the third congress.[21] The difficulties which the Front then encountered in spreading its campaign to other parts of the Gulf led it, in 1974, to modify its goals again, and in July 1974 the PFLOAG divided into two parts – a People's Front for the Liberation of Oman, and a People's Front in Bahrain.[22] The former was to continue the guerrilla struggle in Oman, the latter to persist in that underground political work in Bahrain which MAN and later PFLOAG members had undertaken since the latter part of the 1950s. With the virtual defeat of the guerrillas in 1975 PFLO continued as an organisation based primarily in exile.[23] But it failed to develop new strength inside the country, and the majority of its members and leaders returned to Oman: its greatest weakness had been its inability to extend itself into northern Oman, and the death of Aḥmad ᶜAlī in a clash in the north in 1972 marked the turning point in the PFLOAG's campaign. At its congress in 1982 the PFLO sought to develop modified political positions that corresponded to the new, and weaker, situation in which it found itself. This involved greater stress on political as opposed to military activities, and on the need to build a broad alliance of all nationalist forces within Oman, a United Omani National Front.[24]

This political evolution of the guerrilla movement was a reflection, in part, of the changes in the military situation in Dhofar itself. The first two years of the guerrilla movement (1965–7) had involved mainly scattered actions in central Dhofar. But with the imminence of independence in South Yemen the Sultan's Armed Forces tried to establish positions in the western part of Dhofar, near the frontier, in order to counter what was expected to be greater assistance from the NLF.[25] This pre-emptive policy did not succeed, however, and in August 1969 the last of the SAF positions in western Dhofar had fallen to the guerrillas.[26] The focus of fighting then shifted to central and eastern Dhofar and by the middle of 1970 the government forces had lost control of all of Dhofar except for the capital, Salala, and the Jurbaib plain surrounding it. At this point, in July 1970, the reigning Sultan Said bin Taimur was deposed in a military *coup*, with British support, and his son Qabus became Sultan.[27] Sultan Qabus, using oil revenues that had first become available in 1967, and promising social reform to the population, reorganised the army and began, in 1971, to take the offensive against the guerrillas. In 1972 SAF re-established positions in western Dhofar, and in 1973 PFLOAG shelling of the Salala air base ceased. In November and December 1973 several thousand Iranian troops were deployed by the Shah in support of Sultan Qabus.[28] A set of three defensive lines was then constructed on an axis running from the desert to the sea – Hornbeam, in early 1974, Hammer, in December 1974, and Damavand, in January 1975 – each one further west than the other. Their function was to inhibit guerrilla supplies from reaching the Dhofari interior from South Yemen. In October and November 1975 the last remaining PFLO forces in western Dhofar were defeated, and, with a few insignificant exceptions, the remaining guerrillas withdrew to South Yemeni territory.[29] While sporadic operations continued, PFLO had ceased from late 1975 to be a significant military force inside Dhofar.

The PDRY played an important role in this guerrilla war, and the consequences of this policy were to endure long after significant fighting ended in Dhofar. In the first place, South Yemen provided the guerrillas with military aid and base facilities. While the first weapons used by the DLF had come overland from the Gulf, or from supplies available as a result of the civil war in North Yemen, or were captured from the SAF, from 1967 onwards the PRSY aided the guerrillas directly, as well as serving as a transit area for supplies coming from other sources – first China and later Russia and Libya.[30] After independence, the PFLOAG was granted many facilities in the PDRY. The guerrilla base and training camps were on South Yemeni territory, and the guerrillas also organised refugee camps, schools and hospitals in the border region.[31] The Front office in Aden served as a centre for political and propaganda work directed at the outside world: and the guerrillas were given time on Aden radio for broadcasts to Oman.[32] Successive South Yemeni government statements and Front congresses repeated support for the guerrillas in Dhofar, and Aden also provided significant diplomatic support to the guerrillas, in the Arab League and elsewhere. Thus South Yemeni delegations visiting other countries made a point of urging their hosts to support the Front, and they on occasion took delegates from Oman with them as part of their own delegation. South Yemen also sought to give diplomatic backing to the PFLOAG campaigns in 1971 that aimed to keep Oman, Bahrain, Qatar and the Amirates from receiving recognition from international bodies, such as the UN and the Arab League.[33] Until 1982, therefore, the PDRY's support for the Omani guerrillas was overt, sustained, and comprehensive.

This commitment to the Oman guerrillas involved South Yemen in a number of costs additional to that of the actual aid given to the Front. First among these was the tense military situation along the frontier between Dhofar and the eastern frontier region of the PDRY, which on several occasions led to incidents between the armed forces of the two states. As a precaution, the PDRY tended to station only police and militia, not army units, along the frontier. The first clash came soon after independence in early February 1968 when South Yemen claimed that Oman was 'massing' troops on the frontier.[34] There were no reports of actual fighting on this occasion, however, and the gradual retreat of SAF forces from western Dhofar, with the exception of positions in the desert north of the populated mountains, meant that border tensions on land declined. But according to PDRY sources, 'British', i.e. SOAF, planes were from 1970 carrying out flights over PDRY airspace: in the period between June 1970 and May 1972 these flights amounted to a total of 119.[35] In 1972, moreover, conflict on land and sea recurred as a consequence of the SAF campaign to re-establish its presence in western Dhofar in what was termed 'Operation Simba'. The PDRY account is that in April 1972 British ships violated South Yemeni territorial waters in the region of the frontier, and that on 4 May Omani land and air forces attacked the Wadi Habrut district, a PDRY position north of the mountains.[36] While SOAF planes hit positions inside the PDRY, the Omani fort on the eastern side of the frontier was destroyed by PDRY forces in response. According to Omani sources, South Yemenis participated in a cross-border attack at Habrut on 5 and 6 May.[37] Later in May 1972, at a point nearer the coast, fighting between SAF and PFLOAG forces was followed by SOAF bombing attacks on the village of Hauf itself, inside the PDRY. A number of offices and facilities belonging to the PFLOAG were hit in these air attacks.[38]

This outbreak remained isolated, but it initiated a new period of Oman–PDRY conflict. Beginning in 1972 South Yemeni-based artillery using 85 mm Soviet guns with a range of several miles continued to hit SAF positions inside Dhofar,[39] while the ground fighting was concentrated in the central and eastern parts of Dhofar. PFLOAG sources alleged that this was connected to events nearer the PDRY in that an offensive against their positions in eastern Dhofar in early September 1972 coincided with the launching of the first inter-Yemeni war.[40] There were also repeated statements by both PFLOAG and PDRY officials to the effect that Saudi Arabia was stationing forces on its frontier with the PDRY with a view to pushing through to the sea, thus cutting Dhofar off from the western part of the PDRY.[41] In November 1973 Oman alleged that South Yemeni troops and an aircraft had been in action in Dhofar, a charge Aden denied.[42]

The final occasion when serious conflict occurred on the Oman–PDRY frontier was in the latter part of 1975 when fighting spilled over the frontier as a result of the SAF offensive in western Dhofar that in effect ended the war. Between 17 and 21 November 1975 SAF artillery attacked PDRY guns at Hauf and Jaadib, and SAF planes hit PFLO and PDRY government positions at Hauf on 17 October.[43] PDRY shelling of Omani positions continued until 8 March 1976.[44] Soon afterwards a *de facto* cease-fire came into operation on the Omani–PDRY frontier. This coincided with the establishment of diplomatic relations between Saudi Arabia and the PDRY, on 9 March, and it was widely reported, in unofficial coverage, that such a cease-fire was a condition of Saudi recognition of the PDRY.[45] In discussions with PFLO, the South Yemenis justified this on the grounds that they needed to ensure the safe return of militia elements still inside Oman. Significant military assistance across the frontier did end and, while some isolated individuals from PFLO remained within Oman, the remaining forces inside the PDRY had no further regular contact with them. The cease-fire held. PDRY sources indicated that the Saudis had at first made it a condition of their recognition that *all* PDRY support to the PFLO ceased.[46] This did not occur. PDRY political support for the PFLO was maintained: until 1982 the Front continued to maintain offices, camps and schools in the PDRY, as well as to enjoy the diplomatic and radio facilities which it had previously been allocated.[47] The PDRY authorities did continue to allow some guerrillas to cross the frontier, but not to involve PDRY forces in clashes with the Omanis. The commitment to the Omani guerrillas was therefore substantial, costly and prolonged: but it also had clear limits.

The PDRY backed the PFLOAG but was only rarely involved in waging the war on Omani territory. The one occasion when PDRY forces did cross the frontier in any significant numbers as PDRY units, i.e. on their own, was in the May 1972 clash at Habrut. This was, however, a case of a direct conflict between the forces of the two states, an isolated incident, removed from the main theatre of operations. In late 1975 PDRY forces did, for the only time, fight unannounced alongside the guerrillas.[48] The PDRY did, however, play an important back-up role for the guerrillas in at least four other respects: as supplier of arms, as guardian of the PFLOAG's rear positions, as provider of long-range artillery support for operation inside western Dhofar, and as periodic supplier of militia forces for short-term operations inside Oman itself. The cost to the PDRY was, however, far greater than the diversion of forces and funds to this border conflict in the far east of the country, since the PDRY paid a major diplomatic cost in overtly and consistently aiding the Omani guerrillas throughout the period of their war. This support alarmed the oil-producing states of the Gulf: the Dhofar war was a threat to them and they further exaggerated its significance for their own reasons (as the PDRY did for its) for good measure. It certainly postponed the speed with which relations could be established with these states. It also increased the diplomatic isolation of the PDRY within the Arab world as a whole: Aden's attempts in 1971 to prevent the entry of Oman into the Arab League and the UN were failures, and showed that it had no support within the international community on this matter, even from the Soviet bloc. Such isolation was, moreover, something which the Sultanate, after 1970, actively sought to encourage. The degree of isolation which the PDRY, in supporting the Omani guerrillas, underwent can be gauged from the tone of the appeal which PFLO itself directed to the Arab states during the final Omani government offensive in late 1975:

> We have addressed ourselves to our Arab brothers by every available means of communication with facts and logic, providing them with proof and evidence of our awareness of the dangerous situation in this region. We appealed to them in the name of Arabism and humanity, but the brothers were deaf, dumb and blind, unable to comprehend anything. Yet here we have the invaders again escalating their crimes against our people.[49]

Not only were the PDRY's relations with conservative Arab states of the Peninsula affected, but so too were Aden's relations with the then emergent power of the Persian Gulf, Iran. While Iran had formally recognised the NLF regime, it sent an embassy to Aden and the Shah despatched his forces to Oman with the express purpose of countering South Yemen's influence;[50] the result was that from 1973 onwards, until the Iranian troops were withdrawn at the time of the Iranian revolution, Iranian planes and forces were deployed near the South Yemeni border, and on one occasion, in November 1976, an Iranian plane was shot down over South Yemeni territory.[51] The issue of Dhofar also played an important part in keeping relations with the west at a low level: Britain was not willing to improve relations, and the USA was not interested in re-establishing them, as long as the PDRY's hostility to the Sultanate continued.

The cost which the PDRY was prepared to pay for its commitment to the Omani guerrillas was striking enough during the years when the guerrilla movement was functioning within Dhofar. Aden changed its policy as a result of changes on the ground in Oman, not vice-versa. It is unlikely that the agreement on establishing diplomatic relations with Saudi Arabia would have been possible had the guerrillas not already been defeated: there is no indication that the PDRY altered its policy towards the PFLO, by reducing support, and so hastened the defeat of November 1975, but it was this result on the ground that enabled the establishment of Aden–Riyadh diplomatic relations in March 1976.[52] However, even after the effective end of the guerrilla war the PDRY continued overtly to support the PFLO for a further six years. This was evident from the fact that until 1982 the Front maintained its office publicly in Aden, its facilities in the area near the Omani frontier, and its use of Aden radio. Well after March 1976, PDRY officials time and again reiterated their support for the PFLO.[53] A modification was noted in the formulations of the 1978 YSP Congress, which did not mention the Omani guerrilla organisation by name in its resolutions as previous Congresses had done; but ʿAbd al-Fattāḥ Ismāʿīl did mention the PFLO in his political report and a PFLO message of support was reported at the 1980 Congress.[54] Any shifts of nuance were not matched by an ending of the support and public coverage which the PFLO received in PDRY government and press materials in the late 1970s.

After the Dhofar war ended, however, a gradual shift in PDRY positions on Oman itself, as distinct from the Front, was noticeable. The balance within the 'dual policy' swung gradually towards diplomatic contact with Oman. Mediation between the PDRY and Omani governments had been attempted by a number of Arab governments from the early 1970s onwards. From 1971, both governments sat in the Arab League, and in May 1974, after a meeting of Arab Foreign Ministers in Tunis, an Arab League delegation was despatched to mediate between the two countries. This delegation comprised the Arab League Secretary-General, Mahmud Riad, and representatives of Tunisia, Algeria, Kuwait, Egypt and Syria.[55] The factor which occasioned this diplomatic initiative was the introduction of large numbers of Iranian troops into Dhofar in the previous December. This Arab League mission was not, however, successful. Its terms of reference were that it should mediate between the governments of Oman and the PDRY. But while the Omani government received the mission, the PDRY refused, on the grounds that it was not involved in the dispute.[56] The position of the PDRY was developed in the statements of the PFLOAG, which argued too that there was no dispute between the governments of the two states, South Yemen and Oman. Rather the conflict was one between two forces *within* Oman itself, the legitimate representatives of the Omani people on one side, the PFLOAG, and two foreign occupying forces, Britain and Oman, together with their client regime, that of Sultan Qabus, on the other.[57] As a PFLOAG statement put it:

> We reject the allegation that Democratic Yemen is a party to the dispute now going on in Oman between our people and the foreign invaders. Our people liberated much of the territory inside the southern region of Oman in the first years of the revolution, and the military operations which are launched against the British bases in Salalah are only launched from these liberated areas . . .
>
> The People's Front has on several occasions and in its national democratic programme stated the just demand of our people that the colonialist occupation,

> all foreign interference and all military bases which threatened the security of our people and the Arab nation should be ended . . .
>
> Instead of forming a fact-finding commission, the Arab League was in duty bound to ask Qabus to expel the Iranians and the British, and to abolish all military bases.[58]

The Front not only insisted that the Arab League adopt these positions, but also invited the League to send a fact-finding mission to the guerrilla areas. It rejected any mediation between itself and the Qabus government, and it called for the expulsion of Oman from the Arab League.[59] As a result, the 1974 mediation effort ended in failure, and an attempt to revive the mission in March 1975 was also inconclusive.[60]

A number of individual Arabian Peninsula countries had also been trying from 1973 onwards to mediate between Aden and Muscat. Kuwait sought to use its diplomatic links with Aden and its provision of aid to modify Aden's stance, but at first this Kuwaiti initiative only led in 1974 to a strain in Omani–Kuwait relations, and it had no apparent impact on PDRY policy. In November 1974 the PDRY restated its refusal to have diplomatic relations with Oman.[61] Saudi Arabian attempts to get a change in PDRY policy were more successful in that they brought about a border truce; but they too failed to produce any movement towards diplomatic relations and Saudi influence on South Yemen declined again in 1977 as a result of the overall deterioration of relations between the two states. In the latter part of the 1970s, PDRY–Oman relations remained peaceful but frozen, and both sides continued to criticise the other for its alliances with third parties – the Omanis denouncing the PDRY for its alliance with the USSR and drawing international attention to Soviet military facilities there (the extent of which they often exaggerated), the PDRY criticising Oman for granting military facilities to the US. When Oman supported Egypt's policy of signing a peace treaty with Israel in 1978–9, this brought a further element to the dispute between the countries.

The very persistence of conflict between the two states nevertheless involved South Yemen in an unstated adjustment of its policy towards Oman. One of the first PDRY statements to be made on relations with Oman after the effective defeat of the guerrillas was made in 1977. Hitherto, the official Adeni position was one of supporting the *victory* of the Front, a position affirmed at the October 1975 Unification Conference.[62] Under the influence of the attempts by Saudi Arabia and others to mediate, from 1976 onwards, Aden apparently altered its stance to one of laying down conditions for recognising the Omani state. Thus it enunciated a new set of principles which seemed to mark an initial departure from one of simple support for a PFLO victory. At a meeting to commemorate the twelfth anniversary of the start of the guerrilla movement in Oman, ᶜAbd al-Fattāḥ Ismāᶜīl denied that there was negotiation with Oman, stating that

the PDRY adheres to its position in support of the Omani revolution . . . The starting-point of any political settlement in Oman is the complete withdrawal of the Iranian forces, the liquidation of the military bases, and freedom for the Omanis to determine their own destiny.[63]

This represented a modification of Aden's position in two respects: first, it was insisting not on the replacement of the Sultan by the PFLO, but on some less clearly defined democratisation or self-determination; secondly, it introduced specific foreign policy conditions into the negotiation procedure, rather than the more absolute one of supporting a complete change of regime. The position of the PDRY in 1977 was still, however, that no negotiation with the Sultanate was then possible. Nonetheless, by the late 1970s Aden had begun to talk of negotiation with Muscat, albeit on conditions that were then not capable of being met. In 1979, the PDRY posed three conditions for improving relations with Oman: that it end all facilities for foreign forces, that it cease hostile actions along the common frontier of the two states, and that it 'return to the Arab fold', i.e. renounce its support for Egypt and the Camp David agreement.[64] In June 1980 ᶜAlī Nāṣir Muḥammad said that mediation depended 'on the return of the Sultanate to the Arab ranks opposed to the parties to Camp David'.[65]

These conditions appeared to be ones that Oman would not meet and to signify a continuation of the cold war between the two countries. But the 1979/80 PDRY conditions were significant by omission: they did not, by that time, make any mention of the PFLO as a party to the dispute. The ending of the guerrilla war had not produced an agreement between Oman and the PDRY, nor had it ended PDRY backing for the PFLO. But it did produce a shift in the underlying PDRY position, from presenting the PFLO as the legitimate government to posing demands directly to the Muscat government. This was a change that made it easier, at a later stage, for Aden and Muscat to come to an agreement. The defeat of the guerrillas in 1975, therefore, had its consequences on the PDRY position, albeit in these partial shifts – first the frontier cease-fire, then the modification of diplomatic position.

A series of new elements were now introduced into the conflict in the period 1979–81, and by July 1980 the PDRY was prepared to say that it had agreed to mediation with Oman.[66] On the one hand, PDRY criticism of Oman increased, as the Muscat government went further than previously in granting use of military facilities to the USA and developing an alliance with Egypt. A bases access agreement was signed with the USA in April 1980 and, from 1981 onwards, Oman held joint manoeuvres with the USA on Omani territory.[67] In practice, this brought US forces in significant numbers to within a few miles of the South Yemeni frontier for the first time and US equipment was reported to have been stationed at Thamrit, a base about fifty miles from South Yemen,[68] as well as at other Omani bases. Consequently, in 1981, relations between the two states seemed, if anything, to have deteriorated: in March, June and December 1981 there was tension and minor conflict along the frontier.[69] In this period South Yemeni statements repeatedly denounced the US presence in Oman. But as early as June 1981 a PDRY statement enunciated two points that could provide the basis for an agreement: (a) the PDRY accepted mediation efforts by Kuwait and the UAA; (b) 'Democratic Yemen had', it was stated, 'always been eager for Arab solidarity against the Arab nation's principal enemies, imperialism and Zionism. Yemen had been calling for priority to be given to pan-Arab issues over secondary issues.'[70] The PDRY now put the blame for the failure of mediation on to the Sultanate.[71]

In June 1982 Kuwait arranged for a meeting between Deputy Foreign Ministers of the two states. While many previous unannounced meetings had been rumoured, this would have been the first public bilateral meeting of representatives of the two neighbouring countries. This meeting did not take place, in part because the PDRY side did not accept the status of the Omani representative.[72] But on 3–7 July talks did take place in Kuwait between the directors of the Arab world departments of the two Foreign Ministers and preliminary agreement was reached on four topics for discussion: (1) non-interference in the internal affairs of the other, and respect for sovereignty in discussing the border issue; (2) the question of a foreign presence and military bases in each other's countries; (3) a halt to media campaigns against each other; (4) an exchange of diplomatic representation.[73] After further negotiations, an agreement was signed on 27 October 1982 between the Foreign Ministers of the two countries, allowing for the settling of remaining issues between them, and a future exchange of diplomatic representatives.[74] This agreement was known as the *Kuwait Agreement of Principles*: it led to a closure of the radio facility in the PDRY used by the PFLO, on 6 November 1982, the day the PDRY ratified the agreement, and it brought to an end overt PDRY government criticism of Oman.[75]

Official PDRY statements justified the agreement with Oman by reference to the need for Arab unity in the face of the Israeli threat. Thus a statement on 26 October declared that

> normalising relations between the PDRY and the Sultanate of Oman is one of the PDRY's goals in securing the stability of the region and avoiding the hostile

dangers that threaten our peoples as a result of the growing imperialist military presence and the US and Israeli plots against our Arab peoples.[76]

Subsequently the PDRY Foreign Minister was reported to have declared 'that his country had the right to do what was commensurate with its welfare and the welfare of the region's states and that there was nothing contradictory in that'.[77] PDRY statements stressed the importance of 'security and stability' in the region, and the need for Arab unity in the face of dangers posed to the Arab world by Israel and the USA.[78]

The *Kuwait Agreement of Principles* assented to by the Foreign Ministers of the two states, and later ratified by both governments, certainly brought some benefits to the PDRY government: it ended a state of military alert on the eastern frontier, opened the frontier to trade and migration that had been in existence for centuries but which had been virtually blocked since 1968, and relieved Aden of a political commitment that no longer made the sense it had, both practically and morally, when the guerrillas were a significant force within Oman itself. Most importantly of all, perhaps, the PDRY gained diplomatically, by ending a conflict that had antagonised other Arab states, including, in particular, the Arab oil-producers whose economic assistance Aden required.

On the other hand, the Kuwait Agreement represented a setback for Aden's long-standing policy towards Oman and continued to underline the limits of South Yemeni influence. PDRY policy towards Oman had undergone a number of setbacks since independence. An initial one, in 1967, was the failure of the newly independent PRSY government to secure continued control over the Kuria Muria Islands, retroceded by the UK to Oman. The second, in 1971, was the failure of the PDRY to win backing for its stance on recognition of Oman, to prevent the entry of Oman into the Arab League and the UN, and to win support from any other states for this. This failure was compounded by the Arab League mission's refusal to accept PDRY and PFLOAG conditions for mediation in 1974–5. The third was the defeat of the guerrillas on the ground in late 1975 and the acceptance of a cease-fire in March 1976, albeit one which Aden never officially acknowledged.[79] Even in the negotiations of the final years of overt conflict, the PDRY was forced to abandon some of the conditions it had laid down. Thus, after the Kuwait Agreement, Oman did not terminate its support for Egyptian diplomacy towards Israel, and American forces continued to use Omani facilities. Immediately after the Oman–PDRY accord, South Yemen criticised Oman for allowing US military manoeuvres to continue but it did not renounce the agreement itself. Even the reason given to justify the Kuwait Agreement, the need to co-ordinate Arab strategy towards Israel, was without meaning, given the great differences of policy that existed between Aden and Muscat and the overall inability of the Arab world to evolve a coherent, let alone effective, policy towards Israel at this time. The PDRY continued to back the PLO, and a 'rejectionist' stance hostile to Egypt, while Oman declared itself in favour of Arab diplomatic recognition of Israel.[80]

As in the post-1982 relations with the YAR, there appeared to be little follow up after the signing of initial agreements between Aden and its Omani foes. Some official visits were exchanged, and the border commission met repeatedly: but up to the end of 1987 no embassies were established in each other's capitals and a lukewarm tolerance prevailed. The 1986 crisis in the PDRY posed an immediate challenge to the Aden–Muscat relationship in that it was initially feared that the new leadership in Aden might revitalise the PFLO. But this was, in objective terms, an illusion, since the PFLO no longer had a significant political or military following inside the Dhofar, and, for its part, the new YSP leadership was quick to reassure Oman that relations would remain as correct as they had hitherto been. Such was the continuity of PDRY–Oman relations that, in contrast to the YAR, there was no tension after January 1986, and the diplomatic encounter of the two states appeared equally unaffected by a sudden border clash in early October 1987 in which at least ten soldiers were killed: neither side made any public statement about the incident, and it appears that some British contract personnel involved on the Omani side were disciplined as a result.[81] The one issue of enduring dispute concerned the land frontier, where the PDRY claimed that a total of 7,000 square kilometres, in two triangular sections, had been transferred from South Yemeni to Omani jurisdiction by the British Political Agent in al-Gheidha in 1965. The PDRY was not, publicly, pressing the issue of the Kuria Muria Islands, but the disputes over territory, and over the authority of a British Political Agent to redefine the frontier in this way, were a major cause of the inability of the two countries to reach a solution to their frontier problem.

The 1982 outcome drew attention to the fact that South Yemeni support for the guerrillas, although overt, had been granted within certain constraints. Two are most evident. First, Aden had always been careful about the degree of direct military assistance it gave to the Front, and it had not committed the forces it could have to supporting the guerrillas and it kept its regular armed forces at one remove from the frontier: it can be argued that at the height of the PFLOAG's power, between 1969 and 1971, a quick, substantial, intervention by PDRY regular forces in support of the guerrillas would have given victory to the latter in Dhofar by enabling the PFLOAG to capture Salala. But the diplomatic and strategic consequences of such a forward strategy, and the possibility that other outside forces would then have intervened on the side of the Sultanate, may have prevented the PDRY from ever maximising its support for the rebels. South Yemen never committed its own forces in a major cross-frontier intervention in Oman as it did in 1979 in North Yemen, and the lesson of North Yemen, in 1979, only confirmed the need for such prudence. The second limit was political. The Aden government had long sought to provide political support to the guerrillas: but its own experiences with Egypt during the 1963–7 guerrilla war against the British in South Arabia had made the NF leaders cautious about seeking to inflect other guerrilla leaderships.[82]

Yet, despite the policy of non-interference in the guerrillas' activities, it seems that from the early 1970s onwards the PDRY government was disturbed by some aspects of PFLOAG policy: the lack of activity in the cities of northern Oman and Dhofar, the factionalism within the leadership, which some PDRY officials blamed on the influence of the PFLP of Habbash, the incidence of harsh treatment of the population under guerrilla control, and, later, the exaggeration of the Front's military strength.[83] PDRY stress in 1971 and 1972 on the need for broad alliances in the Gulf was probably a reflection of Aden's sense that the PFLOAG was too sectarian. Between 1968 and 1971, the PFLOAG also went much further than the NF in adopting pro-Chinese political positions.[84] Only in 1971 did the first official PFLOAG delegation visit the USSR.[85] Neither of these factors – the restraint in military support for the Front, the political disagreements between them – led to any overt breach between the two. The defeat of the guerrillas in 1975 does not seem to have reflected any shift in PDRY policy, i.e. any reduction in Aden's support, and Aden continued to pay a considerable price for years to come for its backing to the PFLO. But at no point was the PDRY government willing to risk the survival of its own state by becoming involved in an outright war with Oman that would have run the risk of bringing in other states to support the Sultanate.

Despite these limits, however, the commitment to an overthrow of the government in Oman was a sustained and open one, and was terminated only some years after the Omani guerrillas themselves had been defeated on the ground. It involved the South Yemeni state in considerable foreign policy costs during the decade and a half after independence, and did much to produce that wider confrontation between South Yemen and the other states of the Peninsula and the Persian Gulf, as well as between Aden and the west, that was to confirm the isolation of the South Yemeni government. It is, therefore, worth identifying in summary fashion those factors that may have led Aden to make such a long, expensive and improbable gamble upon the overthrow of the Sultanate of Oman, the underlying sources of this 'solidarity'. First, South Yemen had a state interest in prosecuting the conflict with the government of Oman. There was the issue of the disputed frontier, and of the Kuria Muria Islands in particular, which would have been more likely to find successful resolution in the event of a guerrilla victory. (It is worth noting, however, that when questioned on the matter of the islands in 1970, PFLOAG leaders would not be specific.) South Yemen also had an interest in winning an ally in a neighbouring state with which it could have beneficial economic relations, and towards whom, if the guerrillas did succeed, it would no longer have to adopt an adversary posture. Secondly, as a regime itself committed to revolution, South Yemen derived benefits from being perceived as encouraging this process elsewhere. These included benefits within South Yemen itself, where the process of internal radicalism was presented as cognate with the radicalism of foreign policy. Indeed, while this linkage involved South Yemen in additional deprivations that made the process of internal transformation more difficult and while not a few South Yemenis complained privately about this policy, the authorities overseeing this process tried to derive additional legitimacy from it.[86] Thirdly, the NF's support for the PFLOAG in Oman was part of a wider continuity in MAN organisational commitment that pre-dated the independence of South Yemen, and which also involved ties to the Palestinian and other groups that had once comprised the MAN. It was part of the self-image of the NF leadership that it should remain loyal to the PFLOAG for these historical reasons, and it was also a part of the support which South Yemen won from radical sections of the Palestinian movement that it should continue backing for the PFLOAG. Despite the fact that these other ex-MAN forces were not in power, and hence in a weaker political situation than the NF, such was the need of South Yemen for allies within the Arab world that the backing of these guerrilla groups within the Palestinian émigré communities was important to it. Unfortunately for South Yemen, the MAN connection introduced an extra element of factionalism into the Omani movement, one that may have confirmed the Front's isolation in the Gulf as a whole. Fourthly, the commitment to the Omani guerrillas had certain benefits beyond the Arab world itself. In the initial post-1967 years, China supported the Omani guerrillas: this may have constituted a further encouragement to Peking to provide aid and political support to the PDRY. The USSR did not give political support to the PFLOAG on the scale that China did, but from 1971 the Russians sent some arms, and the threat to the PDRY from Oman, and even more so from Iran, did encourage the USSR to give Aden military aid.

These four reasons in themselves appear insufficient to explain a commitment that was maintained by South Yemen for so long and at such cost. The South Yemeni support for Oman can only be fully accounted for if it is seen as a product of an additional factor, the revolutionary ideology of the NF with its international implications as it developed during and after the independence struggle: this ideology involved both a radical nationalist element, of hostility to British, American and Iranian forces and bases in the Arabian Peninsula, and a radical social element, of opposition to Sultans, merchants, tribal chiefs and other groups in Arabian society considered to be exploitative. In the eyes of the NF, the political and social character of the Omani regime, before and after the fall of Said bin Taimur in July 1970, resembled in several important respects that of the South Arabian Federation which the NF had ousted in 1967. Beyond, therefore, the identifiable concrete benefits which suggested support for the Omani guerrillas, there lay a broader political commitment born of the dual, social and national, character of the South Yemeni revolution itself.

Saudi Arabia: an uncomfortable hegemony

The establishment of diplomatic relations with Oman in 1982 marked the greatest alteration in the PDRY's post-independence foreign policy in that it represented Aden's acceptance of the need for state-to-state relations with this most long-standing foe. But the process of establishing relations with a variety of states in the region had been in train since the early 1970s, and involved, in essence, two kinds of relationship. One was the negotiation of ties with conservative states to which the PDRY had initially been opposed. The other was the search for alliances – military, political and economic – with radical states that were either in place at the moment of South Yemen's independence or which emerged during the years after 1967. The uneven and belated progress of the first process contrasted with a number of advances in the second. After the first years of isolation, South Yemen's search for reliable revolutionary allies amongst the radical states of the region was to provide in many respects an alternative or substitute for the unsuccessful encouragement of revolution among the more conservative and vulnerable components of the area's state system.

The impact of the South Yemeni revolution within the Arabian Peninsula as a whole, and the sustained support by Aden for the Omani guerrillas, led to antagonistic relations between South Yemen and most of the conservative monarchies of the Peninsula. A joint statement of November 1972 was signed by the NF and organisations from Saudi Arabia, Kuwait, Bahrain and the PFLOAG.[87] By far the most important of the Peninsular states in economic and military terms was Saudi Arabia, one of the three states, along with Oman and North Yemen, to share a common border with the PDRY. The difficulty which Aden posed to Saudi Arabia was of a quite distinct character to that posed to the two other neighbours, since the frontier was in desert terrain and at no time did the PDRY provide material support to any significant opposition forces within the KSA. In the early 1970s some small Saudi exile groups, themselves descendants of MAN cells, did have representation in Aden,[88] but none acquired even a radio facility and the major underground guerrilla groupings inside Saudi Arabia that had operated in the aftermath of the North Yemeni revolution had been defeated by the time that the South became independent. During the 1970s there was much speculation about possible PDRY influence via the hundreds of thousands of North Yemeni and South Yemeni migrant workers in Saudi Arabia and, since a number of South Yemenis were involved, there were attempts to link the PDRY to the insurgents who seized the Grand Mosque in Mecca in November 1979.[89] But no evidence of any such linkage of South Yemen to internal dissent within Saudi Arabia has ever been shown, and the comparative tranquillity of the KSA, combined with the very different geographical conditions along the frontier dividing the two states, precluded the kind of South Yemeni involvement with opposition in Saudi Arabia that occurred in the cases of Oman and North Yemen.

South Yemen did, however, pose a certain challenge to Saudi Arabia in other respects. First, by its role in Oman and North Yemen, particularly in the latter, Aden found itself involved in an indirect conflict with Saudi Arabia: a triumph of the forces backed by South Yemen in either of these two countries would have constituted a setback for Saudi Arabia.[90] Secondly, the political orientation of the new South Yemeni regime was in itself a source of difficulty for the Saudis, in that it opposed the principles of monarchical rule and public adherence to a traditional interpretation of Islam that were so central to the Saudi policy. Thirdly, the establishment of military ties between the PDRY and the USSR exposed Saudi Arabia to a potential threat on its southern flank. The KSA had since the 1940s had a military alliance with the USA, and this developed much further in the 1960s and 1970s as Saudi oil wealth and the rise of Arab nationalist forces in the Peninsula combined to increase Riyadh's demand for weapons. Throughout the post-independence period Saudi Arabia had superiority over the PDRY in military terms, because of its superior air power. But the growth of Soviet influence and deployment in Aden, coming as it did with Soviet deployments in Egypt, Iraq, Somalia, and later Ethiopia, then served to promote anxiety in Saudi Arabia itself.[91]

The pre-independence period had already established certain of the parameters of what was later to be KSA policy towards South Yemen. Saudi Arabia had not recognised the legitimacy of British rule in South Arabia and the border between the two entities remained ill-defined: but in May prior to the British withdrawal, King Feisal visited London and attempted to persuade the Labour Government not to continue with the withdrawal policy.[92] For their part, the NF pursued policies that conflicted with Saudi Arabia, because of the latter's support for Britain in 1967 itself, because of Riyadh's involvement in encouraging the pro-Saudi tribal forces in North Yemen, and because of Saudi backing for the rulers of the South Arabia Federation.

In the post-independence period the NF seems initially to have believed that there was some chance of gaining Saudi recognition. Saudi Arabia's delegate welcomed the PRSY's admission to the UN, and a week after independence, when most other Arab governments had recognised the PRSY, the Foreign Minister declared: 'We hope the Saudi Arabian kingdom will soon recognise our young state and establish good relations between us inspired by a spirit of neighbourliness in the interests of our two peoples and states.'[93] However, Riyadh refused to do this and provided refuge and facilities for many of the more influential refugees from the revolution in South Yemen that accompanied the British withdrawal. Saudi Arabia had, by mid-1968, organised the South Yemeni exiles into an active opposition and provided them with radio facilities to broadcast to South Yemen. Open denunciations of Saudi Arabia by Aden began to be made in July 1968,[94] and Saudi statements then repeated the FLOSY charge that the NF had been put into power by Britain.[95]

Saudi ability to influence events in South Yemen was, however, limited by a number of factors. First, the Saudi government was divided about what to do. Policy towards North Yemen had long been controlled by the Governor of Najran and that toward South Yemen was under the command of Prince Sultan, the Minister of Defence since 1960, who directed exile raids from the base at al-Sharura.[96] But King Feisal was not, it seems, fully persuaded of the chances of success of their plan, and as a result the campaign was conducted in a spasmodic mannar.[97] Secondly, the exiles themselves were not a coherent fighting force. They were recruited mainly from tribal refugees and migrants from the YAR who were not trained or organised into a coherent fighting force.[98] Thirdly, the threats from Saudi Arabia served a supportive role for South Yemen itself: the rulers were able to evoke hostility to the Saudi rulers, and the threat from Saudi Arabia, and behind it the US presence in the Kingdom, served as an argument for requesting greater military assistance from the USSR.

In 1968 and 1969 there were a number of clashes along the frontier between the two states, both in the Fourth Governorate, formerly Beihan, and in the more deserted northern regions of the Fifth Governorate, or Hadramaut. These involved only South Yemeni exiles and PRSY government forces.[99] In November 1969, however, clashes escalated into a direct conflict between the forces of the two states when on 26 November PDRY forces occupied a Saudi border post in the al-Wadiah area, about 400 miles north-east of Aden.[100] Between eight and ten days of fighting took place, but superior Saudi air power was used to push the Yemenis back.[101] This conflict reflected a deeper dispute between the two states. The al-Wadiah area had in the past been part of the Qaʾiti Sultanate: as such it was considered by the South Yemenis to be part of one of the Eastern Protectorates and so of their national territory inherited from the pre-1967 period.[102] A dispute between Saudi Arabia and Britain had occurred there in 1954–5. The Saudis, on the other hand, saw al-Wadiah as part of their legitimate territory and as a frontier in the confrontation with the PDRY: following the Wadiah clash, large-scale military construction and deployment of forces took place at al-Sharura, a position lying a few miles behind al-Wadiah.

For the next five years, border clashes and acts of sabotage organised with Saudi support took place within South Yemen. 'Radio Free Yemeni South' continued its broadcasts against the NF. The main arena of the conflict was, however, North Yemen and the barometer of Saudi–South Yemeni relations and radio comment fluctuated in accordance with the degree of threat which South Yemeni policies, both vis-à-vis Saudi Arabia and vis-à-vis other Peninsula states, were believed to pose in Riyadh. The 1969 al-Wadiah clash, a border incident on 20 March 1973 and South Yemeni policies generally in the Peninsula were, however, used within the USA as arguments in favour of supplying arms to Riyadh despite the opposition of the pro-Israeli lobby. In testimony to Congress in 1973, at the height of US concern about the PDRY, Assistant Secretary of State Sisco said that arms sales to Saudi Arabia were not a threat to Israel: the Saudis were, he said, 'looking south, not north'.[103] However, by 1974 a gradual shift in policy could be detected on both sides. The failure of both the direct cross-border raids from the KSA and of the larger offensive, to which Saudi Arabia contributed, in the first inter-Yemeni war of 1972 appear to have led to a change of perspective in Riyadh. Preliminary negotiations seem to have involved the presentation of quite clear conditions on both sides: the Saudis demanded an end to support for the guerrillas in Oman, an end to PDRY attacks upon the Saudi monarch, and the return to South Yemen of those exiled in 1967, together with the restitution of their property. On their side, the South Yemenis asked for the closing down of the Saudi-backed radio station, the establishment of economic links between the two states, and the integration into the KSA of those exiles that would not accept the new regime in the PDRY.[104] Later accounts of the negotiations gave details of additional issues that the Saudis are believed to have brought up: an end to Soviet military, political and economic influence in the PDRY, and the ending of state control of the South Yemeni economy.[105]

On the South Yemeni side, there was also a change of perspective as a result of increased anxiety following the arrival of Iranian combat forces in Dhofar in December 1973. In December 1972, after the inter-Yemeni war and the conclusion of the unity agreement with the YAR, President Sālim Rubiyyaᶜ ᶜAlī had made a strong denunciation of 'the Saudi reactionaries and their masters, the American imperialists'.[106] He alleged that Saudi Arabia was planning to divide the PDRY by invading Hadramaut and pushing through to the Indian Ocean, to seize the port at Mukalla.[107] This would have led to the establishment of a Greater Hadramaut State. This charge was repeated by PDRY leaders during 1973, when a number of substantial border clashes took place on the Saudi–PDRY frontier, between South Yemeni exiles and PDRY government forces and in March the KSA accused South Yemen of again attacking al-Wadiah.[108] In 1974, however, the Aden leadership began to alter its position. During a visit to Cairo in September 1974 President Sālim Rubiyyaᶜ ᶜAlī stated: 'We are trying on our part to establish relations with whoever respects our independence and our national sovereignty and believes in non-interference by states, irrespective of their dissimilar regimes, in our internal affairs.'[109] In the Presidential speech on the anniversary of independence he was more specific:

> All I want from Saudi Arabia is an end to sabotage operations against our country, an end to the supply of weapons to the mercenaries, the liquidation of the mercenary camps on the borders, and a halt to the hostile campaigns. We categorically refuse to be an aggressive state. There is not a shred of evidence that we committed an aggression against Saudi Arabia, but we have much evidence that some Saudi officials have supplied and supported our enemies.[110]

The President's use of the phrase 'some Saudi officials' may have indicated an awareness that policy towards the two Yemens was traditionally in the hands of Prince Sultan and the Governor of Najran, but it was also an indication that a change of leadership in the Kingdom itself might ease relations between the two states. The assassination of King Feisal in March 1975, an event in which Aden played no part, may therefore have been an additional solvent in relations between the KSA and South Yemen, as it was in those between the Kingdom and the United Arab Amirates. Sālim Rubiyyaᶜ ᶜAlī, for his part, was annoyed with the USSR, after the coastal artillery forces, supposedly trained by the Soviet Union, had been found deficient in the 1973 Arab–Israeli war.

The announcement of diplomatic relations, made in March 1976, spoke of the two states having the 'intention to establish normal relations between them on the basis of Arab fraternity, good-neighbourliness, the unity of destiny and non-interference in internal affairs'. It made no mention of respect for each other's territorial integrity or of any other specific political conditions.[111] Both sides did, however, agree to some of the practical demands which the other had put. The PDRY ceased propaganda activities against the Saudi monarchy, together with support for opposition groups. As a result of the end of the war in Dhofar, it was possible for the PDRY to accept a *de facto* cease-fire on the Oman–South Yemeni frontier, without this involving an end to the public support and provision of facilities accorded the PFLO.[112] The Saudis, for their part, recognised the South Yemeni government, silenced the opposition radio and ended armed attacks across the frontier, and allowed for the establishment of economic ties between the two states.[113] The latter involved the offer of economic aid totalling 70 million Saudi rials to the PDRY.[114] It also led to the development of broader economic ties between the two states.[115] This thaw, together with the establishment of diplomatic ties, was of considerable importance for the PDRY. It enabled emigrants to remit money and send goods with less difficulty back to the PDRY, and provided the South Yemeni government with the ability to provide consular and transport facilities to the emigrants for the first time. The opening of direct air links between the two states also enabled South Yemenis to visit Mecca in greater numbers than had previously been the case.[116]

On the other hand, neither side had achieved its full complement of aims. The Saudis had made no apparent headway in repeating in the PDRY what they had earlier achieved in Egypt, Somalia and North Yemen, namely using the inducements of recognition and aid to alter the diplomatic and economic orientations of the country. In addition to the aid offered, which amounted to $50 million, hints of up to $400 million in Saudi aid were reportedly made.[117] Nor had Aden's support for the opposition in Oman ceased. Aden, for its part, won *offers* of limited economic support from Saudi Arabia but none was actually *delivered*; and, while overt Saudi hostility to the PDRY was terminated, it was too early to be sure that the Riyadh government accepted as permanent the results of South Yemeni independence. One particular topic on which agreement was not reached was that of frontiers. As noted, the announcement on the establishment of diplomatic relations did not contain the statement, common in such declarations, on respect for each other's territorial integrity, and it does not appear that either state sought to have its view prevail in the preliminary discussions, so great was the divergence between their two positions. The question of the frontier fell into two parts. There was, first, the problem of the Saudi–PDRY frontier, a boundary never properly defined and the site of the al-Wadiah clash of November 1969. Saudi Arabia had shown itself reluctant in relations with other states to define its frontiers and this had not impeded a general improvement of relations between them – Oman and the Amirates being cases in point. In late 1982 discussions on the joint border were reported to have begun.[118] The failure of the two sides to find agreement, or even to agree to appoint a boundary commission, may therefore have reflected a common desire to avoid a contentious point at this stage. But the Saudi–PDRY dispute involved another border question, namely that of the Saudi–YAR frontiers. For, given its claim to represent the whole of Yemen, the PDRY had made this issue, of the frontiers between what were in practice two other states, a matter of concern in its own foreign policy. This dispute concerned something far more substantial than the desert areas along the Saudi–PDRY boundary: it involved the PDRY claim that three provinces of Saudi Arabia – Jizan, Najran and ʾAsir – were Yemeni territory. This issue, although dormant, remained a source of PDRY resentment against the KSA, and a further obstacle to the resolution of all outstanding differences between the two states.[119]

The remaining incompatabilities did not take long to emerge. Sālim Rubiyyaᶜ ᶜAlī visited Saudi Arabia in July 1977 and some improvement in relations was noted. The joint communiqué spoke of the need to unite Arab ranks.[120] But by the end of 1977 relations between the two states deteriorated once again. As a result of the crisis in the Horn of Africa, Saudi aid to the PDRY was blocked, and tension along the common frontier grew. The PDRY held Saudi Arabia responsible for the death of YAR President al-Ḥamdī.[121] In June 1978 there occurred the death of YAR President al-G͟has͟hmī and the leadership conflict inside the UPONF: the victorious faction led by ᶜAbd al-Fattāḥ Ismāᶜīl implied that former President Sālim Rubiyyaᶜ ᶜAlī had been involved in secret contacts with the Saudis and had been contemplating acceptance of the Saudi terms rejected in the 1976 agreement.[122] Saudi Arabia, for its part, accused Aden of having killed al-G͟has͟hmī and the USSR and Cuba of having organised the fall of Sālim Rubiyyaᶜ ᶜAlī.[123] Saudi Arabia encouraged a move inside the Arab League on 2 July to have the PDRY suspended from membership and to have all political and economic ties to it broken.[124] This suspension, accompanied by a restarting of the propaganda war between the two states, lasted until the PDRY was readmitted to full membership of the League at the Arab League meeting that followed the signing of the Israeli–Egyptian peace treaty in March 1979.[125] But, accompanied as this readmission was by continued conflict in North Yemen and between North and South Yemen, the ending of this intense period of Saudi–PDRY diplomatic hostility did not produce a resolution of all conflict between the two states. For both the PDRY and

Saudi Arabia perceived the other as part of a menacing strategic alliance, with the USSR and USA respectively, and the increased military deployments of these two outside powers in the Peninsula at the end of the 1970s occasioned hostile comment from Riyadh and Aden.[126] Both states, too, continued to suspect the other not only of supporting its respective clients in the YAR, where conflict lasted until 1982, but of backing underground activity within their own states. Thus, Saudi officials suspected, and publicly alleged, a supposed PDRY role in the seizure of the Mecca Grand Mosque in November 1979. The PDRY in 1982 arrested and later sentenced a group of seventeen returned exiles who had been trained for sabotage missions by Saudi, British and US experts inside Saudi Arabia.[127]

An element of normalisation was possible, however, after the restoration of political and economic ties in 1979. Saudi Arabia received a visit by President ʿAlī Nāṣir Muḥammad in June 1980 and discussions on a resumption of economic aid took place.[128] The PDRY President visited the KSA again in August 1982 for discussions on the Israeli invasion of Lebanon in June.[129] The underlying compromise of 1976 therefore continued to provide the structure within which the two states regulated their affairs. The PDRY ceased to anticipate major upheavals within Saudi Arabia, the KSA was compelled to accept the socio-economic and strategic orientations of the PDRY. Beyond these guidelines, however, the character of relations between Aden and Riyadh depended to a considerable degree not on their bilateral relations as such, but on the state of affairs in other states in which the two countries had a joint interest – North Yemen, Oman, the Horn of Africa.

It was the relatively more stable situation in these areas, combined with the growth of areas of common concern, that enabled Aden and Riyadh to return by 1980 to the kind of basic if limited understanding that had been worked out in 1976. The balance of advantage and disadvantage in this accommodation was the converse of that in the resolution of relations between South Yemen and Oman. In relation to the latter, it was the PDRY which was compelled to accept the permanence and legitimacy of the regime in the neighbouring state. None of the major demands made by the PDRY in regard to Oman, either before or after 1976, were met. In the settlement with Saudi Arabia it was the latter which was forced to accept the legitimacy of the PDRY. The only major 'concession' obtained from Aden, the termination of support for the Omani guerrillas, had already in practice been achieved by the very fact of the PFLO's defeat on the ground at the end of 1975. None of the other two major Saudi objectives – the severing of ties with the USSR, the restoration of private enterprise in the PDRY – were met. In the face of an apparently equal or even weaker neighbour, the PDRY had to give ground. In the face of the much stronger KSA, South Yemen to some degree prevailed.

Relations with the KSA continued to be relatively correct, if distant, throughout the early and middle 1980s. The isolation of Egypt and the growing threat of Iran meant that the old Saudi–PDRY divide had been superceded by new divisions, and the KSA continued to provide economic assistance to the PDRY. The hidden but continuous conflict of the two over influence in North Yemen continued, and part of the success of Aden and Sanaʿa in improving their relations can be explained by reference to a desire by the YAR to counterbalance Saudi pressure by improved ties to Aden. During the 1986 crisis in Aden the Saudis appeared to be as surprised and cautious as the other Peninsula states, and they, like Kuwait, were apparently reassured by the appointment of Ḥaydar al-ʿAṭṭās as President. Their deeper reservations about the regime in Aden were not, of course, overcome and it was perhaps typical of the Saudi response that their policy after January 1986 was to maintain links with both sides. Financial and some military help was given to ʿAlī Nāṣir and his supporters in the YAR, and it is believed that Saudi influence played some role in ensuring that Sanaʿa did not reach a more rapid rapprochement with Aden:[130] on the other hand, Riyadh provided economic assistance to Aden, to help with revitalising the economy, and to ensure that its position there was not eroded. Aden posed no visible threat to the KSA, and judicious donations to both factions in the PDRY conflict ensured that Saudi influence was maintained across the, greatly weakened, spectrum of South Yemeni politics.

The smaller Gulf states

Relations both with the Sultanate of Oman and the KSA also bore on the question of Aden's relations with the other states of the Peninsula, the four smaller entities along the Persian Gulf, namely Kuwait, Bahrain, Qatar and the Amirates. All four of these had working relations with Saudi Arabia, and after the change of Sultan of Oman in 1970 relations between that country and Saudi Arabia developed too.[131] In May 1981 the five smaller states were to join Saudi Arabia in establishing the Gulf Co-operation Council. But they also had some margin of variation in their foreign policies, a factor that became evident in their somewhat diverse dealings with the PDRY.

When South Yemen became independent in 1967 only Kuwait was already a fully independent state: it immediately recognised the PRSY. In his annual address a year later the Amir of Kuwait declared of PRSY: 'We wish this fraternal state success. We also hope that the fraternal PRSY will succeed in putting an end to the civil war which hampers its progress to the better life we wish it.'[132] Despite Saudi hostility to the PRSY, owing to the latter's support for a PFLOAG that implicitly included Kuwait within its concept of the 'occupied Arab Gulf', Kuwait appears to have believed that its interests would be best served by keeping diplomatic contacts with Aden open, and providing economic aid, of which by the end of 1980 a total of $37 million had been spent.[133] During the 1970s Kuwait was the only Peninsula state apart from the YAR to maintain regular air links with Aden.[134] Such indeed was the import of this contact with Aden that in 1974, in protest at Kuwait policy, the Omani government expelled the Kuwaiti *chargé d'affaires* from Muscat. Kuwait continued to maintain ties of diplomacy, aid and communication with Aden throughout the troubled years of the late 1970s and, after several failed attempts, it was to play an important mediating role between the PDRY and Oman. In February 1981 the Amir of Kuwait paid an official visit to Aden during which the Amir endorsed the movement towards Yemeni unity.[135] Aden's atypically warm relations with Kuwait continued to prosper during the 1980s: Kuwait was energetic in dissuading other states from intervention during the January 1986 crisis, and in 1987 Aden went out of its way to criticise Iran for attacking Kuwaiti ships.

In 1967 the other three Gulf states were still British Protectorates and the policy of South Yemen towards these was initially one of undifferentiated hostility. All were part of the 'occupied Arab Gulf' which the PFLOAG was seeking, from 1968, to liberate from British control. When, in 1971, Britain began to prepare to leave the remaining entities by the end of the year, South Yemen reacted critically. It asserted, as it did in the case of Oman, that the independence granted to rulers long supported by Britain, and to be backed by treaties after independence legitimating a continued British military role in the region, was not a genuine one.[136] The PRSY became engaged in a futile diplomatic campaign, designed to prevent both the three new Gulf entities and Oman from obtaining international recognition. Thus in July 1971 the PDRY Minister of Information and Culture, ʿAbd Allāh al-K͟hāmrī, stated that the establishment of the 'spurious Federation' of the Amirates 'confirms that British colonial policy has been oppressively and forcibly trying to bring this colonialist toy into being in any form'.[137] He stated that Britain wanted, in reality, to perpetuate the division of the area into small states. In early September 1971 the PDRY Foreign Minister Muḥammad Ṣāliḥ ʿAwlaḳī went on a tour of several Arab states – Egypt, Libya, Algeria, Syria, Iraq – in an attempt to win their support for opposition to the entry of Oman, Qatar, Bahrain and the Amirates to the Arab League.[138] He was reported to have stated that 'these countries were not independent because foreign interests dominated them'.[139] At the same time the Aden authorities publicly re-emphasised their support for the PFLOAG. This support they justified on two grounds: that the Front wanted a *genuine* independence for the Gulf, in contrast to the 'fake' independence being granted by Britain, and that the Front wanted to *unify* the Gulf, as opposed to the fragmentation being brought about by British policy.[140] The new cabinet of ʿAlī Nāṣir Muḥammad appealed to other Arab states to support the PDRY's stand on the revolutionary movement in the Gulf.[141]

However, the PDRY's policy evoked little support either within the states concerned or in the wider Middle East. The four states were admitted to the Arab League, and while Iraq shared some misgivings about Oman no other Arab state backed the PDRY's position on the Sultanate.[142] When on 30 November Iran seized three islands belonging to the Amirates, the PDRY, in common with some other Arab states, condemned this action, and held Britain and the USA responsible.[143] But again, there was little in practice that the PDRY could do, and the PFLOAG had no active presence in the Amirates, its only significant following outside of Oman being a political one in Bahrain. When the four Persian Gulf states applied for admission to the United Nations, the PDRY alone voted against them.[144] Thus, not even amongst the socialist states was there any support for Aden's stance and in the UN votes the Soviet Union and its allies accepted the independence of the Amirates, Qatar, Bahrain and Oman.[145]

During 1972 and 1973 the PDRY maintained its criticism of the four states of the Gulf that it had failed to keep out of the Arab League and the UN. In a speech on the financial difficulties facing the PDRY in July 1972 Premier ʿAlī Nāṣir Muḥammad was reported as saying that:

> the crisis could not be solved either by the flirtations of the Amirates in the Gulf or by reaction, at the expense of our people in the Gulf and the Peninsula and that we would continue to support the Gulf's revolution and the revolution of the Arabian Peninsula.[146]

However, within a few months of the 1971 entry of these states into the international bodies concerned, some modification of the official NF position on them was noticeable. It was in relations with three non-Omani Gulf states that the first developments were noticeable. The Fifth Congress Resolutions of 1972, while endorsing the 'armed popular revolution in the Arabian Gulf', did not restate the position of the previous year on the illegitimacy of the smaller Gulf states or mention them by name,[147] and the spate of denunciations of the 'imperialist agents' in November and December 1972 criticised only Saudi Arabia and Oman.[148]

A change became explicit two years later in November 1974, in a speech on the seventh anniversary of South Yemen's independence in which President Sālim Rubiyyaᶜ ᶜAlī made an appeal for improved relations with the other Gulf states, apart from Oman:

We have excellent relations with certain Gulf states, such as Kuwait, which has given us much support and aid. Following Iran's military intervention in Oman, we had to determine who was our arch enemy and to destroy him . . . It is inevitable that we should negotiate and establish relations with the United Arab Amirates and some Gulf states. Such a relationship must be based on a clear-cut basis – non-interference in each other's internal affairs, non-aggression and mutual respect. There is no reason for the existence of enmity between us and the other Gulf states if those states preserve their independence and reject any foreign presence in their territory. Our duty is to struggle against the foreign presence in the Sultanate of Oman.[149]

This led to some divergences with the PFLOAG: but, after a meeting with ᶜAbd al-Fattāḥ Ismāᶜīl in 1974 at which the new PDRY policy was spelt out, PFLOAG/PFLO criticisms of Bahrain had to cease. This change in PDRY policy, distinguishing Oman from the other Gulf states, was made possible by two developments. The one, which the President stated, was the Iranian intervention in Oman in December 1973 which brought a direct threat to the borders of South Yemen. The second, also a result of the Iranian intervention and preceding the announcement of the change in South Yemeni policy, was the dissolution of the PFLOAG, and the emergence of a guerrilla movement confined to Oman, the PFLO, in July 1974.[150] The entity continuing PFLOAG policies which did come into existence in Bahrain, the Popular Front in Bahrain, did not call for armed resistance, and while PFB–NF links were continued, the PFB did not receive any public backing from Aden, or radio facilities.[151] No organisations were reported as existing in Qatar and the Amirates. This itself reflected the fact that despite its name the PFLOAG existed as a guerrilla force only in Oman.

The PDRY had, therefore, by the end of 1974 made some concessions in the hope of establishing relations with three of the Gulf states whose legitimacy it had earlier disputed. In accordance with this policy, Foreign Minister Muṭiyyaᶜ visited the three states in early 1975.[152] This change of policy did not, however, lead to as rapid an evolution of relations as might have been expected. The Amirates did begin, from 1975, to provide economic aid to the PDRY, and in March 1977 Sheikh Zayyid of Abu Dhabi, the President of the Amirates, visited Aden.[153] Like Kuwait, Abu Dhabi maintained some links with Aden throughout the 1977–9 period when Aden's links to Saudi Arabia were broken again. But the other two Gulf states, Bahrain and Qatar, were more reluctant to provide aid, and for a number of years diplomatic relations were not established with any of the three. The formal PDRY position was that it was *South Yemen* which, as the state which had been independent earlier, had to make the first move in exchanging recognition and which, as of 1977, refused to do so. As the South Yemeni Foreign Minister stated in 1977 of the Gulf states: 'The British are still there. It is only oil that enables them to look independent. In fact, they are just as artificial as they were in 1971, and there is no need for us to accord them formal recognition.'[154] Relations with the Amirates were finally established in 1981,[155] and an embassy was opened in 1983.

Elements of reservation would, however, appear to have operated on the side of the Persian Gulf states as well. They were throughout this period influenced by both Saudi Arabia and Iran, and they may on their own account have remained apprehensive about PDRY involvement in Oman. The Amirates had in general more leeway in determining their own foreign policies than Bahrain and Qatar and this was why they were able to go some of the way along the road taken by Kuwait in opening and maintaining links with Aden. It can be surmised that Aden was avoiding the issue of recognition, in the hope that by offering to extend recognition in the future it could obtain greater economic assistance and diplomatic concessions from these states, and possibly win their support for the campaign to isolate Oman. In fact, Aden did not win any such concessions. The Gulf states, with the exception of Kuwait, participated with Saudi Arabia in providing some assistance to the Sultanate while attempting to avoid implication in the deployment of Iranian troops there.[156]

After the fall of the Shah, however, a different situation emerged, when the Iranian revolution was seen as a threat by the oil-producing Arab states of the Peninsula.[157] After the war between Iraq and Iran began in September 1980, Saudi Arabia, Kuwait, Bahrain, Qatar, the Amirates and Oman came together in May 1981 to form the Gulf Co-operation Council. The GCC envisaged creation of a combined military force, and it was seen by Aden, as well as Tehran, as being a threat to its security. The PDRY therefore disagreed with the GCC, on the grounds that it included Oman with which, at that time, Aden was in a continuing state of hostility.[158] The GCC, however, developed a diplomatic strategy to reduce disagreement with Aden. One of the main topics of discussion at its first summit was the security situation in the south of the Arabian Peninsula, a topic raised by Oman.[159] As a result, the GCC encouraged negotiation with Aden and in September 1981, coincident with preparations for direct negotiations between Oman and the PDRY, discussions also took place between the GCC and the PDRY.[160] These talks do not appear to have led to any specific agreements, but they did signify a decision on both sides to lower the level of tensions between the GCC and one of the two Peninsular states not to participate in it. These discussions, a decade after the issue of negotiation between South Yemen and the Gulf states arose, therefore marked a further step in the reconciliation of the PDRY with the smaller Gulf states. By the mid-1980s, Aden had diplomatic relations with all the GCC states.

Regional involvements: the Horn of Africa, Iran, Palestine

If in this way Aden's conflict with Saudi Arabia and Oman led to tensions with the other states of the Persian Gulf and, in the period up to 1974, to support for the spread of guerrilla war to some of the smaller Arab states of the Gulf, the PDRY's foreign policy also involved a search for allies elsewhere in the region, beyond the states immediately bordering the PDRY. It entailed support for guerrillas operating against the Shah of Iran, and to a tempestuous relationship with the rival nationalist tendency of Baᶜthism, in power from July 1968 onwards in Iraq. The image diffused in some western discussion of South Yemen and Iraq as two prongs of a radical threat to the Peninsula contrasted with a history of recurrent antagonism between these two competitors for radical hegemony. In 1976 the PDRY denounced 'the fascist Baᶜth Party of Iraq' for interference in the PDRY's internal affairs and Iraq's agreement a year earlier on an end to hostilities with Iran,[161] and in 1979 and 1980 ambassadors were recalled after Iraqi embassy personnel killed an Iraqi exile in Aden.[162] In 1985 there was a major trial in Aden of pro-Iraqi Baᶜthists: but despite this, and PDRY links to Iran, relations with Baghdad improved a degree or two. On the Red Sea side, the PDRY maintained a continual if discreet interest in the affairs of the Horn of Africa: until 1974 it backed the guerrillas in the Ethiopian province of Eritrea[163] and developed a close political relationship with the military regime in Somalia.[164] After the fall of Ethiopian Emperor Haile Selassie in September 1974, Aden sought to establish an allegiance with the PMAC, the military regime that replaced the emperor. South Yemen's influence in the heartlands of the Arab world was certainly limited, by reason of its geographical distance and exiguous resources alike: but even here, South Yemen sought to develop a distinct policy of influence. It aided the more radical currents within the Palestinian resistance movement, and became increasingly critical of the policies pursued by the Egyptian government under Anwar al-Sadat. It also sought to develop close relations with those Arab states that seemed most opposed to Sadat, namely Libya and Syria.

In addition to these three core areas of its radical foreign policy – the Persian Gulf/Arabian Peninsula, the Horn of Africa, the Arab–Israeli complex – the PDRY also gave support, political and in some cases material, to revolutionary groups elsewhere in the Third World: to the Polisario guerrillas of the Western Sahara, whose 'state', the Saharan

African Democratic Republic, Aden recognised in 1978,[165] to exiled guerrillas from Chile and other Latin American countries,[166] to some urban guerrillas from western Europe introduced by part of the Palestinian movement into the PDRY during the Presidency of Sālim Rubiyyaᶜ ᶜAlī,[167] and, prior to their assumption of power in 1975, to the guerrillas operating in the three countries of Indo-China.[168] Tempered over time as this wide-ranging commitment was by pressure and external realities alike, it constituted for some time a sustained defiance of the international status quo.

The commitment to a radical policy beyond the immediate region underwent a distinct evolution in the decade and a half after independence. In the Arabian Peninsula, and particularly in those states bordering the PDRY, the initial attempt to promote change or to defy established governments led later to some accommodation with the neighbouring regimes. The building of ties with Kuwait and the Amirates, the establishment of relations with Saudi Arabia in 1976, the signing of the Kuwait agreement with Oman in 1982, and the ongoing if fitful negotiations on Yemeni unity marked this process of adjustment. It was one that came about without major changes of the kind Aden envisaged in the political and social composition of the states involved.

By contrast, the change in the PDRY's relations with the wider range of regional states beyond the Peninsula tended to reflect the fact that substantial changes did take place within these countries. In other words, whereas South Yemeni foreign policy began in 1967 by seeking allies amongst revolutionary and other movements that had not yet come to power, and were in various degrees of opposition and clandestinity, this orientation changed over time. This occurred, on the one hand, because its initiatives in the neighbouring states were blocked, but also because the PDRY was able to establish alliances with movements that had, like it, emerged from internal conflicts to assume state power, albeit further afield.

This process was evident in several instances. Soon after the independence of South Yemen, there occurred the military *coup* in Libya on 1 September 1969, in which the regime led by Colonel Ḳadhāfī came to power. Although Ḳadhāfī was initially hostile to South Yemen – he encouraged the North Yemeni attack on the PDRY of September 1972 and even offered aid to the Sultan of Oman[169] – he had by the mid-1970s become an active diplomatic supporter of the PDRY.[170] In December 1977 Libya, together with Syria, Iraq, the PLO and Algeria, formed a 'Rejection and Confrontation Front', a group of states that opposed Sadat's peace initiatives. Egypt broke diplomatic relations with Aden on 5 December 1977 in protest.[171] Although Iraq soon withdrew, and pursued a separate path, this 'Rejection Front' continued to act as a forum for the proposing of an alternative Arab foreign policy line to that of Egypt, and to the advocacy of a policy of closer alliance with the USSR.

The revolution in Ethiopia in 1974 brought a similar opportunity to the South Yemenis, albeit one that took three years to mature. While Aden had earlier supported the Eritrean guerrillas, by 1976 all PDRY aid to them and to the EPRP, left civilian opponents of the PMAC, had ceased.[172] In 1977–8 PDRY military forces played a role in defending Ethiopia against the Somali attack: some South Yemenis were killed in that war.[173] Close military, state, economic and party relations between the two countries developed after that time. In December 1979 the two states signed a Treaty of Friendship and Co-operation;[174] in August 1981 a Tripartite Pact between the PDRY, Ethiopia and Libya was signed.[175] This Pact envisaged economic support by Libya for the two poorer members, and military assistance between the member states in the event of an attack upon either by an outside power: this was particularly relevant for the two Red Sea states, Ethiopia and the PDRY. The Tripartite Pact also constituted a defiance of the conservative states of Egypt and Saudi Arabia predominant in the Red Sea area for some years previously, and provoked criticism from them.[176]

The third revolution which brought the PDRY a new ally was the Iranian. Prior to 1979 Iran and South Yemen had had no direct relations. As already discussed, the PDRY had strongly opposed the Iranian presence in Oman and in November 1976 the PDRY had shot down an Iranian Phantom plane overflying its territory.[177] Aden had provided aid to some Iranian exiles up to 1978 and Iran had in 1976 played host to a visit by the exiled former South Yemeni Premier Ḥaytham. Aden early on welcomed the revolution as it developed and the fall of the Shah in January 1979.[178] After initial requests for diplomatic contact from Aden had not been met, relations were established on 23 April 1980 and in June 1982 the first Iranian ambassador to Aden arrived.[179] The PDRY remained neutral in the Iran–Iraq war, blaming its outbreak on 'imperialist' influence,[180] and its relations with Tehran did not seem to be immediately affected by the deterioration in Soviet–Iranian relations that began in 1982. For its part, Iran was glad to find an interlocutor in an Arab world otherwise largely opposed to it, and the PDRY was able to win economic support from Iran, in the form of contracts to refine Iranian oil in Aden.[181] These three breakthroughs in regional relations – with Libya, Ethiopia and Iran – therefore consituted a contrast with the development in Arabian Peninsula relations, a contrast made possible by the upheavals within those countries that followed the emergence of the independent state in South Yemen in 1967.

These three positive developments were, however, subject to increasing strain by the mid-1980s. Relations with Libya, apparently consolidated by the 1981 Tripartite Pact between it, the PDRY and Ethiopia, began to deteriorate in 1982–8. Libya had also been substantially involved in sending arms to the NDF in North Yemen, and must have opposed Aden's settlement with the North in 1982. Following the split within the Palestinian resistance movement, Libya supported the rebel group backed by Syria against ʿArafāt, while the PDRY, adopting a less factional stand, tried, with Algeria, to promote unity. The result of the differences was that Libya cut off all financial aid to Aden by early 1984, and a visitor to Aden in February 1984 could see that work on the Libyan-financed medical school in Khormaksar had ceased. Libya subsequently withdrew its embassy from Aden allegedly for financial reasons, but stopped short of breaking diplomatic relations. Contacts between Tripoli and Aden resumed in 1985 and 1986 and in the aftermath of the January crisis in the PDRY Tripoli tried to mediate between Aden and Sanaʿa: a meeting of the two Yemeni Presidents in Libya, in July 1986, was not a success, and served only to confirm the Yemenis' sense of Libyan policy as rash and unproductive.

The 1986 crisis in the PDRY was, however, to occasion a protracted period of tension in relations between Aden and Addis Ababa, and in so doing to prompt the most public divergence between Ethiopia and the USSR since the consolidation of relations in 1977. ʿAlī Nāṣir Muḥammad had developed close ties with Mengistu during the years prior to the crisis, and in December 1985 he made an unannounced visit to Addis: it can reliably be assumed that he at least to some extent made the Ethiopian leader privy to his plans and secured a degree of commitment from him. The fact that Mengistu himself had come to power in early 1977 through measures against his colleagues in the PMAC not dissimilar to those ʿAlī Nāṣir was now contemplating against his rivals in the YSP Politburo did not escape subsequent observers. When the crisis erupted in Aden, Ethiopia sided with ʿAlī Nāṣir: on 17 January, by which time the USSR had swung to a neutral position, *The Ethiopian Herald* reported that the PMAC had declared 'its readiness to extend every assistance to those who stand for the development of socialism under the vanguard leadership of the Yemeni Socialist Party headed by Comrade ʿAlī Nāṣir Moḥammed'. As late as 31 January, the Ethiopian press was supporting ʿAlī Nāṣir, by now clearly defeated. During the fighting he flew to Ethiopia, and warships of the PDRY navy, which had backed the President in the fighting, took refuge in Ethiopian ports once the conflict turned against ʿAlī Nāṣir. There were indications that at one point the Ethiopian navy was itself preparing to sail to back ʿAlī Nāṣir, but that technical difficulties delayed the ships' departure: one can only surmise that, had they indeed set sail, serious Soviet pressure would have been brought to bear to stop them, as it was on the YAR and on PLO forces stationed in that country. Only in 1987, once it was evident that the situation in Aden had restabilised, was it possible for the two states to normalise relations.

In the aftermath of the January 1986 crisis, relations between the PDRY and Ethiopia were therefore tense, more so than between any other country and Aden with the exception of the YAR. ᶜAlī Nāṣir and his supporters continued to have access to Addis Ababa, and the South Yemeni fleet remained on the western side of the Red Sea. But, with the passing of the months, contacts were resumed, the ships were returned, and by the time of November 1987 celebrations in Aden full state and party contacts had been re-established. In effect, Ethiopia had little choice but to accept that a successor regime was in place in Aden: while it continued to offer hospitality to ᶜAlī Nāṣir, it could not prejudice its overall security by persisting in hostility to his successors. The Ethiopian authorities may, indeed, have been encouraged in this by parallel evolutions in PDRY foreign policy subsequent to January 1986: restored relations with Somalia, with the foreign ministers of the two countries exchanging visits for the first time since the 1977–8 Horn of Africa crisis; improved relations between the PDRY and Sudan, following the fall of Nimeiri in April 1985; and low-level contacts between Aden and some of the Eritrean guerrillas, with whom Aden had broken in 1976 out of solidarity with the Ethiopians. Whatever the reluctance, both Ethiopia and the PDRY needed to restore the working relationships which the January 1986 crisis had placed under such strain.

The normalisation of relations between Addis Ababa and Aden only took place over a period of several months. In February 1986 Mengistu met YSP Secretary-General al-Bīḍ in Moscow, where both were attending the CPSU Congress: but the Ethiopian leader was not willing to yield to al-Bīḍ's requests for a return of the five ships, let alone for the handing over of ᶜAlī Nāṣir. In June 1986 an Ethiopian military delegation visited Aden, to begin the normalisation process, and later in the year the naval vessels were returned. ᶜAlī Nāṣir continued, through 1986 and 1987, to be permitted to visit Addis, but as the months elapsed relations between Ethiopia and the PDRY also improved. By the time of the September 1987 Ethiopian revolution celebrations, when al-Bīḍ led a YSP delegation to Addis, the process of normalisation had, for the time being at least, been completed.

The difficulties the PDRY faced in relations with Iran were less overt, and throughout the middle 1980s cordial exchanges continued between Tehran and Aden. The economic links with Iran were helpful for Aden, not least in providing some oil for the refinery to process. But the sharpening of tension in the Gulf war in 1986 and 1987 made it increasingly difficult for the PDRY to avoid some friction with Tehran. While Aden opposed boycotts and other forms of pressure on Iran, and agreed with the Islamic Republic in condemning the entry of US ships into the Gulf, the PDRY had also to meet its obligations on the Arab side. Insofar as it held the view that the war should cease immediately, it implicitly agreed with Iraq; but it also had special obligations to Kuwait, a country that had accepted South Yemen from 1967, had provided substantial financial support, and had assisted Aden to restore its diplomatic position after the January 1986 events. PDRY officials therefore found themselves in 1987 condemning US ships for responding to the Kuwaiti invitation to 're-flag' the latter's ships, while at the same time condemning Iranian attacks on Kuwait and Kuwaiti-bound vessels. When the Arab states met in Jordan in November 1987 to censure Iran, and to lift the embargo on diplomatic relations with Egypt imposed a decade before over Sadat's visit to Jerusalem, the PDRY was not able, as Syria was, to absent itself. The pressures in the region arising from the Gulf war, and the PDRY's own precarious position, made alignment with Tehran more difficult.

One further significant area of accommodation and policy change was in the PDRY's relations with the Palestinian resistance. As part of the MAN, and as a component of the Arab nationalist milieu more generally, the NF came to power with a clear and radical stance on this issue. The 1965 Charter supported the Palestinian movement, and denied the legitimacy of an Israeli state.[182] After independence the PDRY developed policy in two additional respects. First, whereas most Arab states had recognised the PLO, led by al-Fatḥ, as the main representative of the Palestinians, the South Yemenis gave their main support to two former MAN branches, the PFLP and the PDFLP.[183] The 1964 Arab League decision to set up the PLO had been taken prior to the independence of the PDRY and so did not commit Aden to accepting its leadership. Secondly, although it did little about it, the PDRY also challenged the free passage of Israeli-bound shipping going through the Bab al-Mandeb Straits. In 1971 the PDRY permitted a group of PFLP guerrillas to attack an Israeli-bound tanker in the Bab al-Mandeb,[184] and in the October 1973 war South Yemeni artillery on Perim island, together with Egyptian naval units, imposed an undeclared blockade at the mouth of the Red Sea for about four weeks.[185] In 1974–5 there were discussions with Egypt about stationing Egyptian forces on Perim island but no agreement was ever reached.[186]

All three of these particular components of the PDRY's radical stance on the Arab–Israeli conflict – its denial of Israel's legitimacy, its particular stance on the Palestinian resistance, and its stance on Israeli-bound shipping – were in time altered. In 1973 the PLO was allowed to open an office in Aden, and Aden then backed the Yāsir ʿArafāt leadership within the PLO. ʿArafāt paid his first visit to South Yemen only in February 1977.[187] Given his reliance on Saudi funds, it is unlikely he could have risked a visit before 1976. In 1982–3 when Libya and Syria criticised ʿArafāt and backed a dissident faction within the PLO, Aden at first continued to support ʿArafāt.[188] The PDRY also came in time to adjust its policy on the form of a final solution for the Arab–Israeli dispute. While in common with almost all other Arab states, with the exception of Egypt and Oman, it refused to accept the right of an Israeli state to exist, Aden concentrated on calling only for Palestinian self-determination.[189] This shift, noticeable but unannounced, brought the PDRY position a little closer to that of the USSR, and it may be inferred that Soviet advice played some part in causing this adjustment in Aden's stance. A similar unannounced adjustment took place in the PDRY position on freedom of navigation in the Red Sea. After the 1973 blockade there were no further cases of PDRY interruption of the flow of ships to and from the Israeli port of Eilat, and by the time of the Kosygin visit to Aden in September 1979, Aden was prepared to accept the freedom of navigation for ships from 'all adjoining states'.[190] The very explicit defense of international freedom of navigation with regard to the Persian Gulf expressed at the June 1987 YSP Conference had definite, if unstated, implications for the Red Sea as well.[191]

In one sense, these changes were of secondary importance, in that South Yemen played in practice a small part in the fate of the Palestinian movement and in the process of Arab–Israeli negotiations. The PDRY was too remote and too impoverished to exert significant influence: if Algeria found it so difficult to play more than a diplomatic role, it can be seen that South Yemen, equally distant and with much fewer assets, found its influence even more restricted. Aden's only direct impingement was via the Bab al-Mandeb, and this only took effect on two occasions, in 1971 and 1973. But the PDRY did provide some inputs into the Palestinian movement – of diplomatic backing, both individually and as part of the Rejectionist Front, of military training facilities, and of refuge, for up to several hundred Palestinian fighters evacuated to the PDRY from Beirut in September 1982. Support for the Palestinian cause was a central plank in the PDRY's foreign policy, albeit one that was, until the 1978 Congress, placed after that of Oman in the listing of foreign policy guidelines.

The PDRY's role in the Palestinian movement was, however, greater when this is seen in an intra-Arab context, than if it is evaluated in terms of Aden's contribution to the Arab campaign against Israel. In 1976 the

PDRY detached military forces to another Arab country, when it contributed units to the Arab Deterrent Force stationed in Lebanon. While these did not play a combat role, they did constitute a significant South Yemeni contribution to the inter-Arab attempt to restabilise the situation in Lebanon, and protect the PLO and other independent Arab nationalist forces there from Syrian and Israeli pressure. In 1982, following the withdrawal of Palestinian forces from Beirut, the PDRY, like the YAR, played host to some of the PLO forces and thereby acquired a more direct involvement in the Palestinian issue. In the period after the overt split in al-Fatḥ, in 1983, Aden played a major diplomatic role in seeking to restore the unity of the Palestinian movement, and, with Algeria, was responsible for getting the majority of the rival factions to Algiers in April 1986 to agree on a measure of co-ordination. On this, more than perhaps any other issue of Arab politics since 1967, South Yemen was a central and effective actor.

The PDRY's policy towards the Palestine issue was significant in the way in which its evolution symbolised that overall adjustment in Aden's external relations which took place after the period of initial militancy. The adoption of a verbally militant and diplomatically isolated policy in the first years after 1967 gave way to one that was both more cautious and more in harmony with that of other states and organisations involved in the issue. The most evident, and most immediately relevant, of these policy adjustments was, however, not to be found in relation to the major international issues of the Middle East, in which the remote PDRY played a small part, but in relation to those conflicts within the Arab Peninsula itself that had brought the PDRY into direct conflict with neighbouring states.

6 In search of allies: the USSR and China

When the PDRY celebrated the twentieth anniversary of its independence in November 1987, pride of place amongst the invited delegations was given to the representatives of the USSR, and the PDRY authorities were keen to emphasise their commitment and gratitude to the Soviet Union for all that it had contributed to the consolidation of the post-1967 regime. The alliance with the USSR was in many ways the most important component of the PDRY's foreign policy and, despite some tensions and disagreements in the relationship, there was no sign from 1969 onwards that any leadership in Aden had seriously contemplated major alterations in it. The USSR was essential for the security of the regime, and as a source of political and socio-economic guidance. On their side, the Soviet leaders were committed to the PDRY as the closest of their Arab allies and as one of the 'states of socialist orientation' that, together with Nicaragua, Mozambique, Angola and Ethiopia, were potentially socialist states. Soviet leaders and writers had their reservations about the policies pursued by the PDRY internally and were not above giving hints as to how they thought Aden should approach certain problems: this was evident enough in the speech of welcome made by Gorbachev to YSP Secretary-General ʿAlī al-Bīḍ when the latter visited Moscow in February 1987.[1] Nonetheless, the USSR had made a long-term commitment to the regime in South Yemen that neither pressure from the west nor the internal conflicts of the PDRY itself were sufficient to interrupt.

The NF's decision to establish and develop relations with the socialist countries in the post-independence period was, at one level, a straightforward one. Both the USSR and its allies, and China, had given support to the nationalists in South Arabia during the independence struggle, by criticising British policy and, in the case of the USSR at least, supplying arms through Egypt and North Yemen. As already noted, it is not clear how far direct links between these states and the Front existed before independence, but the one NF delegation is known to have visited China early in 1967 and some NF–USSR contacts already existed via Egypt and the PDU.[2] Within the Front the ideologies and policies associated with the two states had acquired some followers, and both Soviet and Chinese versions of Marxism were available in translations from these countries and in publications acquired through the MAN networks in North Yemen and Lebanon.[3]

Beyond their long-standing support for Arab nationalism both the USSR and China enjoyed a particular prestige because of the backing they had given to the YAR in the period after 1962.[4] They were therefore regarded by many not only as allies of Arab and Yemeni nationalists in the struggle against other external powers, such as Britain and the USA, but also as potential allies in conflict with conservative forces within the Arabian Peninsula itself, the royalists and tribal leaders in the North, and, beyond them, the Saudis. In addition to such revolutionary affinity, the PRSY turned in November 1967 to the socialist countries for a more immediate reason, namely the pressing needs of the post-independence situation. Faced with a large budget deficit, and with military tension along all three of its land borders, the new government in Aden had to move with some speed and decisiveness to consolidate its power. As relations with Saudi Arabia and with the west deteriorated, the Front was therefore encouraged to establish close ties with those distant supporters with whom, till then, it had established only tenuous contact.

Yet if the reasons for adopting this general orientation towards the eastern countries were clear, there were a number of uncertainties about how far and in what precise direction this policy should go. There were, first of all, divisions within the ranks of the NF itself on the degree of alignment to be established with the east, and how far the PRSY should abandon balance in relations between the two power blocs. Ḳaḥṭān al-S̱haʿabī favoured pursuit of some balance, and sought until his fall in June 1969 to maintain ties to Britain, the USA and West Germany; but his more radical opponents did not. Their advent to power therefore opened the way to establishing stronger ties with Russia and China. But the radicals too were divided and the issue of relations with the east remained part of the overall conflict on policy with the Front throughout the post-1967 period. President Sālim Rubiyyaʿ ʿAlī sought to maintain good relations with China, and he visited Peking in 1970 and 1974. He also sought to apply what he thought as Chinese models of political mobilisation to South Yemen. ʿAbd al-Fattāḥ Ismāʿīl, on the other hand, was already a strong supporter of the USSR and the period of his Presidency, from 1978 to 1980, was the one in which Soviet–Yemeni ties became closer. His successor, ʿAlī Nāṣir Muḥammad, did not return either to the policies of Ḳaḥṭān al-S̱haʿabī or Sālim Rubiyyaʿ ʿAlī; but he did slightly lessen the degree of identification of the PDRY with the USSR.

For their part, the Soviet authorities had to evaluate their commitment to South Yemen in the light of several distinct considerations. First, they had to assess the reliability of the NF – how far it could be depended upon to retain power, and how far it would follow what the Russians regarded as a judicious foreign policy line, one neither too accommodating to the west, nor so adventurous that it would provoke a western counter-attack. It evidently took some years before the Russians, who had had more than a few disappointments in the Arab world over the years, could feel sufficiently confident of the Aden authorities. Secondly, the Russians had to calculate what they could afford to offer: they could provide weapons for the PDRY's armed forces, but they could not and would not offer a firm guarantee to come to the PDRY's defence if it was attacked. Such a guarantee was given only to Warsaw Pact members, and was not even accorded to such allies as Cuba or Vietnam. At the same time, while the Russians were prepared to give some economic aid, this was neither of the quantity nor the quality that the PDRY expected and needed. Whatever either side wanted, there were consequently objective limits on what the USSR could provide. Thirdly, there was the overall situation in the Arabian Peninsula, Red Sea and Persian Gulf regions. The independence of the PDRY coincided with the beginnings of a more active US deployment in that region. The pace of Soviet military activity in the Indian Ocean, and more particularly in South Yemen, was to some degree dictated by what Moscow saw as the growth in the US presence. Exactly how far Soviet deployments in the PDRY were a counterpoint to US activities is impossible to say, since the evidence on Soviet policy and decision-making is not available. But the record of the Soviet build-up in Aden does on several occasions seem to be one of response to, and rivalry with, that of the USA in the adjacent countries and waters. As in the Indian Ocean itself, so in the Arabian Peninsula: while the Russians could not match the US deployments with equal deployments of their own, they nonetheless acted to strengthen their position and extend their military reach when and where the USA was also doing so. Each of these three considerations – the Soviet assessment of the PDRY regime, the capabilities of Soviet power, and the strategic rivalry with the USA – all contributed to shaping the direction and pace of Soviet–South Yemen relations.

Moscow and Aden: initiating an alliance

The evolution of Soviet dealings with South Yemen can be analysed in terms of the four Presidencies that marked post-independence politics in the Republic since each involved a distinct phase of Soviet–PDRY relations. At the moment of independence, *Pravda* in an article entitled

'Victory of the People', welcomed the departure of the British and gave a guardedly positive analysis of the new regime:

Imperialist propaganda, first of all British propaganda, is now trying to assert that Britain is voluntarily granting independence to South Arabia even before the set date.

Actually, the situation is otherwise. The history of Aden is a history of more than four centuries of struggle by the people of Aden against conquerors, from the Portuguese to the British. The independence of Aden has been won in stubborn struggle through the united efforts of the whole South Arabian people – the workers of Aden, the rebels of Dathina, Kathiri and Quaiti and the partisans of Radfan.

All the patriotic organisations and parties of Aden made a contribution to the common struggle for independence: the Aden TUC, the NLF of the South Arabian Peninsula and the FLOSY.

Under the pressure of the national-liberation forces of South Arabia, which were supported by the progressive Arab countries and all progressive mankind, the British government adopted a forced decision to withdraw from South Arabia.[5]

Pravda went on to ascribe the NLF–FLOSY conflict to 'fanning' by British colonialism and quoted Ḳaḥṭān al-Sha'abī and unnamed FLOSY leaders as calling for an end to the dispute. (Other Soviet coverage repeated this emphasis on the need for unity among the nationalist groups.[6]) *Pravda* concluded with a cautious prognosis:

As for the future governmental structure of the newly independent country, Sha'abi noted that South Arabia will be a republic with all the institutions of a people's democracy, i.e. a union of popular forces will be created, not a 'formal capitalist democracy'.

The people of Aden, after traversing a long road of struggle, have won independence. But they will have to exert considerable efforts to defend and strengthen the independence they have won. Success to you, heroic people of Aden![7]

The USSR recognised the PRSY two days after independence, on 2 December 1967, and later in that month a Soviet mission arrived to set up a Soviet embassy. The first permanent diplomatic staff arrived in February 1968[8] and the first Soviet ambassador, Vladimir Startsev, in November.[9] Unlike almost all other countries, the USSR did not have to take permanent possession of an existing building, but was allowed to build a large new compound overlooking the sea on the eastern side of the Khormaksar isthmus, with no adjacent buildings, near to the international airport, and with extensive residential facilities.[10] Discussions must have proceeded rapidly on the most important matter of concern to the PRSY, namely security, for within three months of independence, in early February 1968, a military delegation led by Minister of Defence 'Alī al-Bīḍ visited Moscow.[11] No actual agreement was announced at the time, but on his return al-Bīḍ dismissed the British technicians serving with the armed forces and in March the first Soviet military delegation under General Alexander Negrasky came to Aden for a four-day visit 'during which it studied the Republic's military requirements'.[12] In August the two countries signed a Technical and Military Assistance Agreement, the first accord of any kind between the USSR and the PRSY.[13] Further military missions visited the USSR in November and December.[14]

The USSR continued the pace of contacts with the new Republic despite the divisions within the South Yemeni leadership, and the apparent shift of power to the more moderate sections of the Front after March 1968. During the height of the May 1968 crisis the Soviet ambassador made a point of calling on the Minister of Defence to offer support.[15] In June 1968 a group of Soviet ships, the first such flotilla to visit the Indian Ocean, paid a visit to Aden and this was repeated again in January 1969 when a second Soviet naval visit to the area was paid.[16] Throughout the latter part of 1968 delegations visited the capitals of the two states to discuss military, economic and cultural matters: the visit of Defence Minister ᶜAwlaḳī resulted in the Technical and Military Agreement. The first arms came in July 1968 and in January 1969 a major consignment of Soviet military equipment arrived, comprising 'ten Mig-17 fighters, air-to-surface missiles, anti-aircraft guns, portable radar equipment, ammunition and spare parts'.[17] A Soviet military mission, reported to include fifty members, reportedly accompanied these supplies.[18]

The first top-level South Yemeni visit to the USSR was by President al-S͟haᶜabī who spent eleven days in the Soviet Union in January and early February 1969. During his visit an initial Economic and Technical Assistance Agreement was signed: under it, the USSR agreed to help the PRSY create a modern fishing industry by building a new fleet, constructing a fish cannery and setting up a training and research centre in the PRSY.[19] The USSR agreed to train South Yemen personnel in the USSR, while South Yemen agreed to Soviet technical missions studying the waters around the PRSY. Al-S͟haᶜabī's visit also led to the signing of a Scientific and Educational Agreement, and in subsequent years the number of Yemenis studying in the eastern bloc as a whole rose considerably.[20]

The increasing reliance of the PRSY on the USSR for support in the military field, and the growth of economic and cultural ties, did not lead so rapidly to the consolidation of a closer overall alliance between the two countries. As noted, Soviet coverage of the initial NF governmental programme was favourable but restrained, and the conflicts of the first post-independence Presidency were treated carefully in Moscow. Soviet commentators were sceptical about the NF's radicalism.[21] The Soviet press reported on the problems facing President Ḳaḥṭān al-Shaᶜabī, but stressed again the need for unity among the 'patriots' in the PRSY.[22] While the Programme of the Fourth Congress of March 1968 was, in general, treated favourably, reports also pointed to problems within the NF and to the enormous social and political problems South Yemen faced.

With the inception of the second Presidency, that of Sālim Rubiyyaᶜ ᶜAlī, in June 1969, relations began to improve further. Soviet publications made favourable comment on what they called the 'June 1969 Reshuffle', and on the declarations of the new leadership about relations with the USSR and support for national liberation movements,[23] while others criticised impatient 'leftists'.[24] The decisions taken immediately after the 'Corrective Move' were not, however, given the kind of coverage in the Soviet press that would suggest Moscow was convinced the new leadership had really purged itself of such extremist tendencies. Nonetheless, an NF delegation, led by Secretary-General ᶜAbd al-Fattāḥ Ismāᶜīl, attended a meeting in April 1970 on the one hundredth anniversary of Lenin's birth, and in the Soviet report the Front was classified as one of the 'national democratic parties and organisations' attending the ceremonies.[25] Two months later, in June, ᶜAbd al-Fattāḥ Ismāᶜīl stated that the USSR had agreed to provide assistance in training party cadres and providing educational courses.[26] Another NF delegation visited the USSR in July 1970 to study training methods in the CPSU and, from December 1972 onwards, with the opening of a College of Socialist Sciences and of a school for the *Ashid* or Youth Union,[27] Soviet instructors were teaching NF members in South Yemen on a regular basis. In December 1972 a second agreement, on CPSU–PONF cooperation, was signed.[28]

A certain improvement in Soviet-South Yemeni relations came in the latter part of 1970 and in the following two years. In December 1970 *Pravda* reported warmly on the new constitution and the proclamation of the PDRY:

> A progressive state that has taken firm anti-imperialist stands has sprung up on the very frontier of the mighty Anglo-American Persian Gulf oil 'empire'. This state has become an example for the peoples of Arab territories where the oil monopolies and their feudal vassals are still active. The Yemenis already are rendering the courageous partisans of the neighbouring Sultanate of Oman support in their struggle.[29]

The report went on to say that Yemenis 'speak gratefully' of Soviet assistance, and that the USSR was involved in building irrigation dams in Lahej and in seven other districts. Twenty artesian wells had been drilled to provide water to co-operatives and state farms, and Soviet tractors and motor vehicles could now be seen in the streets of Aden.[30]

As this report indicated, the USSR had by now come to accept what it may earlier have thought of as South Yemen's more adventurist foreign policy initiatives in backing the Dhofar guerrillas, where Chinese influence had been strong between 1968 and early 1971. Yet while Soviet correspondents visited Dhofar in 1969 and 1971 and reported favourably on the movement there,[31] even in this convergence differences remained. Soviet writers did not endorse the overall PDRY position on the Gulf in 1970–1: they criticised, but did not condemn, the British policy of transferring power to the rulers of the three smaller states of the Gulf[32] and they did not join the PDRY in refusing to recognise these states.[33] Whereas the South Yemenis talked of the 'Arab Gulf', the Russians maintained their use of the term 'Persian Gulf', in press reports and in USSR–PDRY communiqués.[34] Thus, a *Pravda* correspondent who visited Dhofar in 1971 had to render the name of the guerrilla organisation not as it was in Arabic, the People's Front for the Liberation of the Occupied Arab Gulf, but as the 'People's Front for the Liberation of the Occupied Zones of the Persian Gulf'.[35] Nevertheless, while the PDRY's opposition to British policy in the Gulf itself remained ineffective, and hence posed no problems for Soviet–Yemeni relations, the USSR did from 1971 onwards begin giving public support to the Dhofar guerrillas following a PFLOAG's delegation's visit to Moscow in September 1971, permitting substantial transfers of Soviet arms to them via South Yemen.[36] By 1971 a working basis of Soviet–Yemeni agreement therefore existed on what was, at that point, the most militarily active of South Yemen's three borders.

Further development of Moscow's relations with Aden took place during high-level South Yemeni visits in 1971–2. ᶜAbd al-Fattāḥ Ismāᶜīl attended the Twenty-Fourth Congress of the CPSU in February, and this was followed by ᶜAlī Nāṣir Muḥammad, then Defence Minister, in April 1971, ᶜAlī Nāṣir Muḥammad again, now Prime Minister as well as Minister of Defence, in September 1971, and then by Sālim Rubiyyaᶜ ᶜAlī, the President, in November 1972. The first two visits by ᶜAlī Nāṣir Muḥammad appeared to concentrate on defence matters. In the April 1971 visit, he was reported to have met with Marshal Grechko, the Soviet Minister of Defence, Marshal Zakharov, the Chief of General Staff of the Armed Forces, Admiral Gorshkov, the Commander-in-Chief of the Navy, and Marshal Yepishev, Head of the Main Political Administration of the Soviet Army and Navy.[37] During the September 1971 visit he met Alexei Kosygin, the Soviet Prime Minister, as well as other Soviet ministers concerned with areas of bilateral relations, Marshal Grechko, and the Minister of the Fishing Industry, A.A. Ishkov.[38] No agreements were reported after the first visit, but following the second visit, an agreement was signed on 'further development of economic and technical ties in the fields of irrigation, the fishing industry and the training of cadres'. This included construction of a fish cannery, whether the one already agreed to is not clear, and creating and equipping a training centre for vocational-technical education.[39] By February 1972 *Tass* reported that around thirty small-scale projects promised in the February 1969 Agreement had been completed.[40] President Sālim Rubiyyaᶜ ᶜAlī's visit in November 1972 was the occasion for the signing of a further Economic and Technical Co-operation Agreement under which the USSR agreed to construct a thermal power station for Aden, and a hospital, and to assist in geological surveys of an unspecified kind.[41] In addition, the communiqué issued on the completion of Sālim Rubiyyaᶜ ᶜAlī's visit stated: 'An agreement was also reached on the Soviet Union's continuing provision of assistance to Democratic Yemen in strengthening the republic's defence potential.'[42]

This rapprochement between Aden and Moscow was the result not only of increased Soviet confidence in the PDRY, but also of a shift in Aden itself. It appears that for some time after June 1969 Sālim Rubiyyaᶜ ᶜAlī had been reluctant to pay an official visit to the USSR and had, instead, preferred to visit China in August 1970.[43] But the change in China's foreign policy in the region – its ending of aid to the Eritrean and Omani guerrillas, its improved relations with Iran, its support for Sudanese President Nimeiry in his conflict with the Communist Party in July 1971 – all contributed to altering the new President's opinion.[44] Most important, perhaps, for both the PDRY and the USSR, was the deterioration in conditions in the Peninsula itself. The USSR had, as noted, sought to balance its relations with the YAR and the PDRY. In a pointedly even-handed statement in 1969 Soviet Foreign Minister Andrei Gromyko had stated: 'We have good relations with Iraq, the YAR, the PRSY and other Arab states'.[45] When fighting broke out between Saudi Arabia and the PRSY in November 1969 the USSR did not take sides. By 1972, when the USSR had come more clearly to endorse the Adeni position, it blamed the tensions in South Arabia not on the YAR but on 'aggressive forces' and 'imperialist plans'.[46] An *Izvestia* commentary in late August discussed what it regarded as the US policy of 'relying on reactionaries in the Arab world' to divide the Arab peoples and weaken their struggle against imperialism:

> Such an unenviable role is being played by Saudi Arabia, for instance, which initially helped the Yemeni reactionaries in their struggle against the republican authorities after 1962 and then started fanning all kinds of discord between the Yemeni Arab Republic and the People's Democratic Republic of Yemen.[47]

The Soviet press reported the inter-Yemeni war of September 1972, but without openly blaming North Yemen.[48] Soviet policy was to help the

PDRY to survive without prejudicing other ties it had. The visit of President Sālim Rubiyyaᶜ ᶜAlī in November, an occasion probably prompted by Aden's anxieties after the war, provided an occasion for the USSR to endorse what it termed 'the measures that Democratic Yemen has taken to end military operations on the border between the PDRY and the YAR and the conflict between the two states'.[49] The communiqué went on: 'The Soviet Union supports the PDRY's efforts for the normalisation of relations between the two Yemeni states and for ensuring favourable conditions for the Yemeni peoples' development along the path of national progress.'[50]

Such convergence did not mean, however, that complete agreement between the two sides existed. As far as Yemeni matters were concerned, the USSR still hoped to maintain some influence in the YAR. It continued to provide some military aid to the Sanaᶜa government at a time when the Adeni authorities were assisting guerrilla opposition in the North and, in his speech welcoming Sālim Rubiyyaᶜ ᶜAlī, Premier Kosygin stressed that the YAR was a country 'friendly to the Soviet Union'.[51] The USSR was also cautious about what it supported – 'normalisation of relations between the two Yemeni states', rather than Yemeni unity, the policy espoused in Aden and which was at that time also explicitly endorsed by China.[52] On broader Arabian Peninsula matters some divergence was also evident. Thus the communiqué issued on the occasion of ᶜAlī Nāṣir Muḥammad's second visit in 1971 stated: 'the two sides exchanged opinions concerning the present situation in the Persian Gulf region and confirmed their solidarity with the peoples of the Persian Gulf'. It did not mention any conservative Arab state by name,[53] nor did it specifically endorse the Omani guerrillas of the PFLOAG as the PRC–PDRY statement of 1970 had done. A similar generic declaration of support was contained in the November 1972 communiqué which backed 'the anti-imperialist struggles of the peoples of the Arabian Peninsula and the Persian Gulf against the intrigues of the international oil monopolies', without mentioning Oman or the PFLOAG.[54] These visits drew attention to a somewhat warmer Soviet appreciation of internal developments in the PDRY. But Soviet observers were aware of the conflict between Sālim Rubiyyaᶜ ᶜAlī and his opponents. While they may have drawn comfort from the Fifth Congress of 1972, with its adoption of a set of positions more consonant with Soviet policy, they must have been disappointed by the 'Maoist' mobilisations of July, the 'Seven Glorious Days' and the Maoist echo in Sālim Rubiyyaᶜ ᶜAlī's appeals for 'self-reliance'.[55] In contrast to the attention given to the Fifth Congress, the 'Seven Days' received no coverage in the Soviet press.

Nevertheless, a greater degree of endorsement was evident. The

October 1971 visit by ᶜAlī Nāṣir Muḥammad was the occasion for Kosygin to state:

The Soviet Union gives support to the People's Democratic Republic of Yemen in its struggle to consolidate its independence. We shall do everything necessary so that the agreements concluded between our countries on co-operation will be successfully fulfilled in the interests of the peoples of our countries and the cause of peace.[56]

The communiqué stated that the Soviet Union 'expressed its high appraisal of the anti-imperialist and anti-reactionary foreign policy course of the government of the People's Democratic Republic of Yemen'.[57] As yet words such as 'progressive' or 'socialist' were not used. The statement of November 1972 went further and specified support for the PDRY's internal policies as well:

The Soviet side stated that the Soviet Union highly appreciates the activity of the National Front and the People's Democratic Republic of Yemen government in eliminating the onerous colonial legacy, constructing the national economy and carrying out progressive social, economic and political transformations. At the same time, the great importance of the fact that the National Front and the People's Democratic Republic of Yemen base this activity of theirs on the support of the broad masses of people was emphasised.[58]

Official visits were also used by the PDRY delegations to express their thanks to the Soviet Union for the assistance given. While the Yemenis did not oblige their Soviet hosts by at any time making criticisms, implicit or explicit, of Chinese foreign policy, and while NF Congresses continued to call for relations with *all* socialist countries, they did indicate that the alliance with the USSR had pride of place in their orientation as a whole. In October 1971 ᶜAlī Nāṣir declared:

people in our country are well aware of the fact that if it were not for the firm friendship that links our country with the socialist camp, headed by the Soviet Union, we would not have succeeded in overcoming and solving the problems that were created for us by colonialism and those which at present neo-colonialism, in collaboration with reaction, is trying to create.[59]

In December 1972, on a visit to attend celebrations on the occasion of the fiftieth anniversary of the formation of the USSR, ᶜAlī Nāṣir Muḥammad hailed the USSR as 'a true friend of the Arab peoples', but combined this, in accordance with what was still NF policy, with a call for the unity of the 'world revolutionary forces', a policy for which he invoked the authority of Lenin.[60]

The guidelines for close USSR–PDRY relations had therefore been established by the end of the fifth year of South Yemeni independence: agreements in the military, economic, cultural and party spheres had been signed and were being implemented. The PDRY and the USSR now shared common positions on a range of international issues which were regularly evoked in their joint statements – on Indo-China, southern Africa, Palestine. Some areas of differing emphasis remained – on Yemeni unity, and Oman in particular. And the Soviet characterisation of the stage of development of the PDRY remained cautious.[61] The PDRY had not ceased to develop relations with China, but these were evidently not as close as those with the USSR and by 1972 divergences between Aden and Peking became more evident. In addition to unstated Sino-Yemeni disagreements on emphasis, there was a clear public divergence over the secession of Bangladesh in December 1971. While China and the great majority of Muslim states opposed the secession and backed Pakistan, the PDRY was the first Arab state to recognise the new Dacca government, a policy in common with that of India and the USSR.[62] Yet, despite these disagreements with Peking, a greater resolution of the disagreements between the USSR and the PDRY, as within the South Yemeni government itself, was to take another six years to come about.

The relationship consolidated

The spate of official contacts continued throughout 1973 and 1974, with both ᶜAlī Nāṣir Muḥammad and ᶜAbd al-Fattāḥ Ismāᶜīl making visits in each year. Defence evidently remained of great importance. At the end of ᶜAlī Nāṣir Muḥammad's visit of March 1973 the communiqué stated that the two sides had 'examined questions of strengthening the defensive capability of the PDRY'.[63] Similarly, the communiqué on the occasion of ᶜAbd al-Fattāḥ Ismāᶜīl's visit in July 1974 made mention of 'measures for the future strengthening of the defence capabilities of the PDRY'.[64] The same communiqué reported a new Agreement on Technical and Economic Co-operation, the third such agreement, as well as a programme of cultural and scientific co-operation for 1974–5.[65]

The Russians took advantage of these encounters to restate their positive, if cautious, evaluation of developments within the PDRY. They slightly increased the degree of commitment they were able to declare for South Yemen, while at the same time appearing to urge the South Yemenis to settle their differences with their neighbours. During the September 1974 visit of ᶜAlī Nāṣir Muḥammad, Kosygin stated that the PDRY 'can count firmly on the unfailing support of the Soviet Union in its efforts to carry out progressive social and economic reforms', but he coupled this with a plea 'to normalise the situation in the southern part of the Arabian Peninsula'.[66] What exactly was meant by the latter phase is not clear, but it is evident from the communiqué that the Soviet and Yemeni positions on the region diverged. The statement merely reports: 'Opinions were also expressed on the situation in the Near East, particularly in the southern part of the Arabian Peninsula.'[67]

It would seem from the communiqué that the USSR was concerned at the degree to which the PDRY was exposed in that region. In June 1974 there had been a *coup* in the YAR, in which Chairman al-Iryānī, intermittently engaged in negotiations with Aden since 1972, had been ousted. The new President, al-Ḥamdī, was still an unknown quantity. He was at first believed to have been put in power by Saudi Arabia which had been disconcerted by the slight rapprochement of Aden and Sanaʿa. Both South Yemenis and Russians were therefore worried about their tenuous relations with the YAR. Kosygin's advice may also have concerned Saudi Arabia, and the Soviet belief that Aden should establish diplomatic relations with it, something which finally occurred in 1976.

What appears inconsistent, however, is that the emphatic Soviet caution on the YAR and Saudi Arabia should have coincided in the 1974–5 period with a definite increase in Soviet support, political and military, for the Dhofar guerrillas.[68] The Soviet press reported favourably on the August 1974 Congress of the Front, which limited the organisation's scope to Oman, as opposed to 'Oman and the Arab Gulf'.[69] This change was in harmony with Soviet policy: the USSR distinguished between Oman, a state very closely allied to Britain and the USA, and the other, somewhat more autonomous, Peninsular and Gulf states.[70] The sharpening in Soviet attitudes to Oman appears to have been dominated by diplomatic and strategic considerations, rather than by the situation on the ground where guerrilla activity was ebbing. The Iranian intervention in 1973, and the Omani decision to grant base facilities to the USA, were apparently the sources of this greater Soviet irritation.[71] As a result of this divergence, Soviet press coverage reached a crescendo in October and November 1975 at the very moment when the PFLO was finally being crushed. A *Pravda* report on 23 October 1975 talked of 'an armed struggle against the puppet monarchist regime and the colonialists' which had been going on for ten years. 'The Arab patriots are not alone', it stated,[72] a point repeated a few days later in an article in the military paper *Krasnaya Zvezda*, which also reported that the PFLO was 'using the latest equipment for the first time, including highly efficient anti-aircraft missiles'.[73] Yet this change in Soviet policy, although apparently contrary to the drift of its policy on 'normalisation' elsewhere in the Peninsula, served to reduce still further the gap between itself and the PDRY. The establishment of diplomatic relations between South Yemen and Saudi Arabia in March 1976, a development that involved a tacit agreement on a cease-fire along the South Yemeni–Omani border, nonetheless resolved this question in practice. Soviet commentators welcomed this development.[74] 'Normalisation' along all three of the PDRY's frontiers was now under way.

In 1976 and 1977 the pace of official visits continued. ᶜAbd al-Fattāḥ Ismāᶜīl attended the 25th CPSU Congress in March 1976, and returned on a party mission in July 1976.[75] Foreign Minister Muḥammad Ṣāliḥ Mutiyyaᶜ visited Moscow in May 1977,[76] and ᶜAlī Nāṣir Muḥammad in July. No major new agreements were announced in 1976–7. The outlines of the main areas of co-operation had been established, and the halt in new agreements may also have been a result of the increasingly polarised situation within the Aden government itself, which made it more difficult for it to negotiate with the Russians and for the latter to rely on it.[77] The Soviet Press did not, however, cease to declare its concern about developments in South Yemen: in April 1977, it once again started to criticise Saudi Arabia by name, because of the latter's opposition to the new revolutionary government in Ethiopia and its attempt to use its relations with pro-Soviet governments in Somalia and South Yemen to wean them away from the USSR. An important *Izvestia* commentary quoted the French paper *L'Aurore* on Saudi attempts to win Somalia and South Yemen to the conservative camp, adding: 'The heightened interest Riyadh is showing in unification trends in the two Yemens, as well as its attempts to play a role as intermediary between certain Middle Eastern states, should be viewed in this light.'[78] When Mutiyyaᶜ visited the USSR in May 1977 some divergence between the two states was evident in that the *Pravda* report spoke only of an 'exchange of opinions' on the Red Sea.[79] The two did, however, agree on the call to make the Red Sea a zone of peace, as well as on the independence of Jibuti. In November ᶜAbd al-Fattāḥ Ismāᶜīl went to Moscow to attend celebrations of the sixtieth anniversary of the Bolshevik revolution and at the end of 1977, when the PDRY joined with other radical states at the Tripoli conference of rejectionists to oppose Sadat's visit to Jerusalem, *Pravda* reported favourably on this and on the way in which the meeting of rejectionist states had 'rebuffed' attempts to divide the Arab states from the USSR.[80] By then any anxieties about Saudi influence in the PDRY must have been allayed.

In 1978 a period of even closer Soviet–South Yemeni collaboration began. ᶜAlī Nāṣir Muḥammad visited Moscow in February 1978 and the final communiqué reported on a 'complete coincidence of both states' positions on questions of the struggle for peace and people's security, for universal and total disarmament and for a further relaxation of international tension'. The communiqué recorded the joint position of the two sides on the Arab–Israeli question, where they condemned the separate negotiations being conducted between Egypt and Israel, and on the Horn of Africa, where they called for a settling of the Ethiopian–Somali conflict, then at its height, 'on the basis of good-neighbourliness and anti-imperialist solidarity'.[81] The tense international situation in the Middle East must therefore have figured prominently in these talks, but defence matters were also discussed, since ᶜAlī Nāṣir Muḥammad visited the Soviet Ministry of Defence on 3 February for discussions with Marshals Ustinov, the Minister of Defence, and Ogarkov, the Chief of the USSR Armed Forces General Staff.[82] The Soviet press, in articles accompanying the visit, gave prominence to the economic assistance which the Soviet Union had given to the PDRY.[83] Yet it appears that no new agreements were signed during this visit.

The internal crisis of June 1978 was given considerable coverage in the Soviet press. No mention was made of western accusations that the Soviet Union had played a part in instigating or determining the outcome of the crisis. But Saudi Arabia was accused of 'attempting to take advantage of the assassination of the President of the YAR to make unsubstantiated and false accusations against the PDRY', and on 27 June *Pravda* repeated Radio Aden statements by UPONF concerning 'the failure of an attempted *coup* by former chairman of the South Yemeni Presidency Council, Sālim Rubiyyaᶜ ᶜAlī'.[84] Later, ᶜAbd al-Fattāḥ Ismāᶜīl was quoted as saying that the late President had tried to 'sow doubt about the correctness of our relations with the socialist community and above all with the Soviet Union'.[85] With growing criticism in the Arab world of South Yemen, *Pravda*, in an official commentary entitled 'Dangerous Interventionist Intentions', made the strongest statement to date of support for the PDRY:

> Now that the attempted *coup* in the PDRY by Sālim Rubiyyaᶜ ᶜAlī, the former chairman of the Presidency council, has been smashed, those who pushed him into that venture are trying to achieve their ends by other means. According to reports, Saudi Arabia is actively preparing for armed intervention against the PDRY, in hopes of overthrowing the progressive regime, which Riyadh finds objectionable . . .
>
> Saudi Arabia is trying to provoke an attack on South Yemen by the Yemeni Arab Republic in order to create a pretext for armed intervention against the PDRY . . .
>
> What the forces of reaction and imperialism succeeded in doing in Zaire's Shaba province must not recur in the south of the Arabian Peninsula.
>
> The sovereign People's Democratic Republic of Yemen is not alone. Progressive forces will not abandon her in her troubles.[86]

Internal and external factors therefore combined to produce a situation in which the USSR voiced greater support for the PDRY: the change in

South Yemeni leadership on the one hand, the greater external pressure on the other, led to a new degree of Soviet commitment. While no binding defence agreement was known to have been reached, the phrase about 'not abandoning' the PDRY implied some, albeit unspecified, Soviet commitment to help Aden in the event of attack. In October 1978 the Founding Congress of the YSP was given favourable coverage in the Soviet press: after listing the achievements of the PDRY in the fields of socio-economic reform and strengthening the state sector, *Pravda* went on:

> The creation of a vanguard party in the PDRY reflects the will of the country's popular masses. They welcome the policy approved by the YSP Congress, of further development along socialist lines, and they favour a stronger alliance with the USSR and other socialist states.[87]

For the first time, therefore, Soviet writers were reflecting the thesis, already articulated in South Yemen, that the PDRY was in some measure moving towards 'socialism', that it was, in Soviet terminology, a 'state of socialist orientation'.[88]

Soviet coverage of the second inter-Yemeni war, of February-March 1979, was, as in 1972, relatively restrained. In private, the Russians opposed military action against the YAR, and the Soviet leaders sent letters to a number of Arab leaders to this effect. In public, stress was laid not on the role of the YAR government itself, but on the aggravation of the conflict by Saudi Arabia and the USA.[89] Carter's decision to send nearly $400 million worth of US arms to the YAR was described as an attempt to divert the attention of the Arab countries from the Egyptian–Israeli negotiations.[90] Less mention was made of the deployment of US ships in the region of the war, and of unpublicised US threats to intervene if the PDRY's forces continued to advance. Only the rarest mention was made of the role in the fighting, and in YAR politics more generally, of the left-wing guerrillas backed by South Yemen, the NDF.[91]

With the war over, the leadership crisis in the PDRY apparently settled, and the USSR skilfully offering itself as supplier of arms to the YAR instead of the USA, a number of further major agreements were signed between the USSR and PDRY. In June 1979 ʿAlī Nāṣir Muḥammad attended the Comecon annual meeting in Moscow and it was announced that the PDRY had joined the CMEA as an observer.[92] Three Third World communist countries were already full members of the CMEA – Mongolia, Cuba and Vietnam – and the PDRY now shared observer status with five other pro-Soviet socialist or 'socialist oriented' states in the Third World – Angola, Afghanistan, Laos, Mozambique and Ethiopia. Its delegations henceforward attended the annual regular session of the Council, held each June in different member countries' capitals.

In September 1979 Soviet Premier Alexei Kosygin visited Aden, the first visit by a top-level civilian Soviet official.[93] A new economic agreement was signed during his visit and it provided the occasion for a general restatement of Soviet and South Yemeni views on the Red Sea area. In October 1979, ᶜAbd al-Fattāḥ Ismāᶜīl, now President of the PDRY, led a delegation to the USSR, and this marked a new high point of Soviet–South Yemeni collaboration. In a speech at the ceremonial banquet, Soviet leader Brezhnev paid tribute to his guests:

> The people of Democratic Yemen have inscribed more than one glorious page in the history of the national liberation movement. From the first guerrilla detachments in the mountains to the victory of the anti-imperialist uprising, the winning of independence and the proclamation of a course aimed at building socialism – this has been the path traversed by the South Yemeni people. And they traversed it under the leadership of their revolutionary vanguard, now united in the Yemeni Socialist Party . . .
>
> True to Leninist principles of foreign policy, the Soviet Union attaches special significance to the development and consolidation of relations with those countries that, like us, adhere to the ideals of freedom, independence and peace and take an intransigent attitude toward all manifestations of hegemonism.
>
> Especially close to us are countries that are not only our allies in the struggle against imperialism, in the struggle for peace, but also think as we do and have set as their goal the building of a society free from the exploitation of man by man. These countries have no truer or more reliable friends than the Soviet Union and other states of the socialist commonwealth.[94]

On his side, ᶜAbd al-Fattāḥ Ismāᶜīl expressed thanks for the assistance given by the USSR, mentioning in particular the fields of economic aid, training cadres and prospecting for petroleum.[95] On this occasion the two sides concluded three new agreements. One was a plan for CPSU–YSP collaboration in the period 1980–3, an upgrading of the inner-party contacts that had been in train since at least 1970. The second was a new protocol on economic and technical co-operation, the contents of which were not announced. The third, and most important, was a Treaty of Friendship and Co-operation, to run for twenty years.[96]

The twenty-year treaty was a significant step in Soviet–South Yemeni relations. Beginning with Egypt and India in 1971, such treaties had been later signed with Iraq, Somalia, Angola, Mozambique and Afghanistan.[97] In January 1979 a treaty of friendship and co-operation was signed with Ethiopia and in October 1980 one was signed with Syria. These treaties differed from those signed with members of the Warsaw Treaty Organisation which involved a commitment to mutual aid in the event of an attack upon them in Europe, and agreements with core members of the communist bloc in the Third World, such as Mongolia, Cuba and Vietnam. They did not include explicit guarantees of mutual support in the event of an attack upon one of the parties, as the Warsaw Pact did, or commitments to massive economic aid. But they did involve a commitment to close co-operation in the fields of foreign policy, economics, and culture, and to maintaining common positions on specific important areas of foreign policy.

Within the overall common characteristics of these treaties of friendship and co-operation, some variations were, however, noticeable. Thus, the USSR–PDRY treaty included, as Article 5, the statement that 'The high contracting parties will continue to develop co-operation in the military field on the basis of the relevant agreements concluded between them for the purpose of strengthening their defence capability.'[98] This was a somewhat stronger statement than that on military co-operation contained in Article 10 of the USSR–Ethiopia treaty.[99] Similarly, the first Article of the USSR–South Yemeni treaty talked of 'the unbreakable friendship between the two countries', a phrase absent from the comparable section of the USSR–Syria treaty.[100] What was most surprising about the signing of the USSR–PDRY treaty, however, was its timing: for some years previously the PDRY had let it be known that it did not intend to sign such a treaty, pointing out that such treaties had not in fact guaranteed the continuation of close relations with the USSR on the part of the country concerned.[101] Of the three Arab League states which had signed such treaties Egypt had repudiated its treaty in 1974, Somalia had done so in 1977, and Iraq's relations with the USSR had deteriorated considerably in the latter part of the 1970s, although Baghdad did not actually repudiate the treaty. Some South Yemeni sources were later to state that the signing of the treaty had come as a surprise in the PDRY, and that President ʿAbd al-Fattāḥ Ismāʿīl had exceeded his brief in unilaterally signing this agreement without prior consultation with the YSP leadership as a whole.[102]

The diplomatic contacts of the period after June 1978 had certainly involved greater collaboration than hitherto between the PDRY and the USSR, and this was evident in the agreement to join the CMEA and the signing of the Treaty of Friendship and Co-operation. In 1979 and 1980 substantial new economic agreements were signed and these led to increased Soviet aid and exports to South Yemen.[103] There was also a more active military liaison, as the USSR increased its level of naval and air deployment in the PDRY. Admiral Gorshkov, the Chief of the Soviet Navy, who had visited Aden for the first known time in May 1974, paid a subsequent visit in May 1978.[104] In May 1979 a major Soviet naval force, including helicopter-carriers and a cruiser, visited Aden as part of a show of force in the western Indian Ocean.[105] In June 1979 General Yepishev, head of the Central Political Department of the Soviet Army and Navy, visited Aden. For some time Soviet long-range reconnaissance aircraft, of the Ilyushin-38 and Tupolev-16 varieties, had been operating out of Aden over the Indian Ocean and Persian Gulf. In October 1979 western reports spoke of a large airlift of troops, bringing two brigades or 10,000 men together with some armoured vehicles and artillery from bases in southern Russia on temporary deployment in the PDRY and Ethiopia.[106] While the Soviet ability to supply the PDRY and Ethiopia by air had been evident for some time, and had been demonstrated during the air transport of supplies to Ethiopia in November and December 1977, this deployment of Soviet combat troops on manoeuvres in the PDRY was a new development. It gave some force to the Soviet assertion that the PDRY was 'not alone' and, coming but two months before the Soviet intervention in Afghanistan, may have in some measure offset in the minds of Moscow's allies the impact of the more forward American deployment in that region which the Carter administration was by then elaborating.

The fall of ʿAbd al-Fattāḥ Ismāʿīl, in April 1980, certainly marked a crisis in USSR–PDRY relations, albeit one that was subsequently overcome by both parties. The evidence available does suggest that complaints about the quantity and quality of Soviet economic assistance had played a part in weakening support within the PDRY for President Ismāʿīl's approach. In particular, the Soviet failure to complete the al-Hizwa electricity generating plant outside Aden occasioned Yemeni criticism.[107] It also seems that the Soviet ambassador Fedotov intervened with the Central Committee of the YSP to ensure that ʿAbd al-Fattāḥ Ismāʿīl was allowed to leave the country, and not imprisoned or, as some members of the leadership desired, executed. A Presidential visit to the USSR had been scheduled for the following month, and, after some negotiation by the PDRY to ensure that the delegation was properly received, President ʿAlī Nāṣir Muḥammad did visit Moscow on 27-29 May 1980.[108] During this visit two new agreements were signed: one set up a Standing Commission on Economic and Technical Co-operation, the other was a new agreement on constructing the al-Hizwa thermal power station.[109] If the former marked a further institutionalisation of the economic links between the two states, the latter involved one of the sensitive issues in the USSR–PDRY relations. Although the USSR had agreed to construct the station during the Presidential visit of 1972, and official Soviet reports indicated that it had been completed, little work was in fact done, and there had been substantial power shortages in Aden towards the end of the 1970s.[110] These, as noted, had been blamed on the USSR, and had contributed to the conflict in which President ʿAbd al-Fattāḥ Ismāʿīl had fallen. Reports from Aden suggested that there had been some tension in PDRY–Soviet discussions of the project since the Soviet minister responsible claimed that, according to reports *he* had received, the project was already completed.

The May 1980 communiqué gave special emphasis to the growing tension in east–west relations, and condemned current US policy in the Middle East, one, it was said, of 'setting up a network of military bases and knocking together aggressive blocs'.[111] The communiqué also declared support both for the Democratic Republic of Afghanistan, calling for a political solution there, and for Iran, where the attempt by the USA to rescue its diplomatic hostages had recently failed. Nothing, however, was said about the situation in South Arabia, beyond a general attack upon US military bases in the Persian Gulf, apparently an implicit reference to Oman. The silence on South Arabia may in part have reflected improved Soviet–YAR relations. The Soviet press had recently paid more attention to the question of inter-Yemeni relations, and Soviet arms supplies, to the tune of $600 million, were now being provided to the YAR, the first significant deliveries since 1970. An *Izvestia* commentary of 6 April 1980 stated that the USA was

> doing everything it can to exaggerate the contradictions, many of them pure invention, between the Yemeni Arab Republic (North Yemen) and the PDRY (South Yemen) and is going all-out to impede the incipient trend toward those countries' reunification.[112]

The same article argued that the US arms despatched to YAR in 1979 were intended to create 'a situation the US may at any time use to undermine Arab anti-imperialist unity or use against Riyadh'.

This belated interest in the cause of Yemeni unity, and the new concern for the susceptibilities of Saudi Arabia, may be explained by the diplomatic context of the time in which the USSR had, after a decade of relative exclusion, regained some influence in the YAR, and was even hoping that Saudi Arabia would now agree to the restoration of diplomatic relations with Moscow.[113] Expectations of such an agreement with Saudi Arabia were not borne out, but relations with the YAR continued to improve and in October 1981 President ʿAlī ʿAbd Allāh Ṣāliḥ of the YAR paid an official visit to Moscow, the first by a YAR President since that of ʿAbd Allāh al-Sallāl in 1964.[114] In the final communiqué, the YAR supported the Soviet call for turning the Red Sea and Indian Ocean into a zone of peace, and, in line with Soviet declarations, opposed outside bases and intervention in the Persian Gulf. But, in keeping with the practice observed hitherto in USSR–PDRY communiqués, no mention was made of inter-Yemeni relations.[115]

The situation had, however, changed by the time of the next visit of ʿAlī Nāṣir Muḥammad to the USSR in September 1982. Postponed from May

1982 because of floods in the PDRY, this visit involved one of the last public engagements of Soviet President Brezhnev, who met the PDRY President at the airport. Though no new agreements were reported to have been signed, the communiqué issued on 16 September did mark a shift in certain respects from that of two years before. It made explicit mention of the PDRY as advancing 'along the road of socialist orientation' and reported that 'the Soviet side highly assessed the deep socio-economic transformations carried out in Democratic Yemen'.[116] Beyond stating common positions on the Middle East as a whole, and Lebanon in particular, the communiqué also recorded that discussions had taken place on YAR–PDRY relations and reflected Soviet interest in ending the NDF uprising:

> The South Yemen side informed the Soviet delegation of the steps that were being taken by the leadership of the PDRY and the Yemen Arab Republic to promote good-neighbourly relations between the two countries, and to achieve a united Yemen by peaceful means. The Soviet side was pleased at this development of relations between the PDRY and the YAR.[117]

While the 1982 communiqué, therefore, made note of the unity talks between the YAR and the PDRY, it did not state that the USSR itself favoured the idea of unity between the two states, only that it approved of 'the development of relations' between Aden and Sanaʿa. 'Normalisation' remained the key term and when later in the year South Yemen and Oman established diplomatic relations, Soviet writers commented favourably on this.[118]

A 'state of socialist orientation'

Prior to the crisis of 1986, the evolution of Soviet–PDRY relations appeared, after almost two decades, to have reached a point of relative stability and continuity, one that had survived both the rapid change of political conditions in the region surrounding the PDRY, and the attempt by conservative Arab states to weaken the Aden–Moscow bond. It had also, so far, survived the endemic factionalism within the PDRY itself, a factionalism that owed little to the influence and role of the USSR as such, but which nonetheless posed challenges and difficulties for the USSR in dealings with its South Yemeni ally.

In the political sphere, Soviet evaluation of South Yemen had improved gradually over the years, from the first cautiously positive reporting after independence to the endorsement of the PDRY's 'socialist orientation' in 1982. Soviet evaluation of this change rested upon certain criteria developed in the general Soviet literature on Third World states: the destruction of the previous ruling class, the degree of state control of the economy, the growth of the co-operatives, and, above all, the spread of the vanguard party.[119] It is unlikely, however, that these internal criteria, although analytically primary, would in themselves have constituted sufficient basis for Soviet confidence had they not also coincided with the convergence of Soviet and South Yemeni military and foreign policies.

Yet in both these domains substantial difficulties remained and continued to lead to Soviet caution about the stage reached by the PDRY on the 'socialist oriented' path. In the initial post-independence period, Soviet concern had focussed on the factionalism in South Yemen and on the 'left extremisms' of some of the NF factions.[120] Soviet writers also stressed the PRSY's economic problems.[121] Then, during the Presidency of Sālim Rubiyyaᶜ ᶜAlī, Soviet concern was expressed indirectly – in appeals for 'normalisation' in South Arabia, and in the failure of the Soviet press to report and thereby lend support to certain South Yemeni developments. With the fall of Sālim Rubiyyaᶜ ᶜAlī in 1978 it became possible for the Soviet press to voice criticisms of the former President's policies. Thus Soviet analysis of the June 1978 crisis argued that Sālim Rubiyyaᶜ ᶜAlī had tried to conspire with 'imperialism' and weaken the ties between the PDRY and the USSR.[122] And after the YSP Congress in October 1978 Soviet commentators used the resolutions of the Congress to validate their claims that 'left-extremist measures' in agriculture had slowed the growth of production and had antagonised small traders.[123]

Despite the correction of these 'left-extremist' mistakes, attributed to Sālim Rubiyyaᶜ ᶜAlī, Soviet writers still continued to paint a rather sombre picture of the situation in the PDRY. In an indication of the ideological problems still confronting the PDRY fifteen years after independence, the Soviet author Alexander Guskov wrote in 1982:

> It is no secret that the prospects of the revolution depend to a large extent on the shaping of national self-consciousness, cultivation of a new attitude to labour, and elimination of tribalism and other remnants of the past and of the influence of bourgeois ideology.[124]

Or, as another Soviet commentator wrote:

> Of course, there is no ground to deny the fact that, in the progress of socialist construction, the revolutionary authorities of the PDRY did not confine themselves to the solution of the problems linked with the overcoming of the incredible backwardness of the country, but also ventured to take radical measures without sufficient socio-economic foundations, seeking to do away with the socio-economic backwardness at one stroke.[125]

The same author discussed two objections that critics of the PDRY might raise: the continuation of a private sector, and the acceptance of aid from conservative Arab states.[126] Both policies were justified, the author argued, at the phase of socialist orientation, provided the revolutionary party maintained its control of power and its overall orientation. Reports published by Soviet writers after January 1986 were to identify negative aspects of the liberalisation process, but these were only hinted at earlier on.

Another Soviet author, appraising the results of the first fifteen years, pointed to certain objective constraints on the PDRY's ability to develop the economy: the small population, the low level of 'national-ethnic consolidation', the fall in living standards as a result of the closure of the canal and the British withdrawal in 1967, and the destruction and dislocation associated with the guerrilla period itself.[127] This appraisal singled out certain problems which still persisted in hindering the PDRY's development: inadequate food production, the shortage of skilled labour and the disproportionate amount of labour in non-productive as opposed to productive activity, and the 'demonstration effect' of oil-producing economies on the PDRY. But the author also expressed hope that some areas of the South Yemeni economy – fishing, oil, and foreign aid – were showing positive signs and he added: 'The leftist excesses of the early 1970s have been finally overcome.' By this he seemed to mean, in addition to other issues, that the strong opposition to developing the port and the re-export trade had receded.[128]

The Soviet Union did, from 1968 onwards, play a role in both shaping the development of the PDRY economy and in providing aid for it.[129] As of 1980 Soviet aid included 24 main projects of which ten had already been completed. These included water-storage dams and machine-repair stations, and the boring of dozens of irrigation slits. A report of 1980 made particular mention of three Soviet projects: the joint Soviet–Yemeni permanent fishing expedition, the thermal power station in Aden, and the fish cannery in Mukalla.[130] It stated that Soviet economic aid was 'pursuing a policy of helping to develop the branches most important to the formation of the national economy and to raising the people's well-being in Democratic Yemen'. By the end of 1982 the number of Soviet-aided projects in the PDRY had reportedly risen to fifty, and involved co-operation in industry, power development, agriculture, transport, exploration for minerals, training of Yemeni specialists, and public health.[131] More generally, Soviet advisers assisted with the drawing up and implementation of the planning mechanisms, and with the establishment of administrative machinery through which the YSP directed the economy.

Yet the economic relationship between the two countries was far more limited than that in the military and political spheres. Soviet aid accounted for about one third of the total disbursed aid provided to the PDRY in the period 1967–80, and was *in toto* around $152 million, as compared to $84 million from China, and another substantial amount from eastern European countries.[132] Compared to the amounts supplied to more favoured core bloc allies in the Third World, such as Cuba, Mongolia or Vietnam in the same period, aid to the PDRY was very small, both absolutely and as a proportion of the total aid given to them.[133] As Table 2 indicates, total Soviet aid to the PDRY at a little under $300 million, in the 1967–87 period, represented a small contribution compared to that to Third World communist states, and even to other non-revolutionary Middle Eastern ones. Similarly, while the volume of Soviet exports to the PDRY rose after independence, the 1977 total of $17.5 million still accounted for only 3.2 per cent of the PDRY's total imports in that year.[134] South Yemeni exports to the USSR stood in 1976 at $527,000, a negligible proportion of the total.[135] These figures, however, understate the degree of trade between the two countries in two respects. The import figures appear to omit imports of military goods, an important component in the overall balance of trade. And while earnings from exports to the USSR were extremely low, and paid in non-convertible currency, Soviet aid did enable the PDRY to earn quantities of hard currency by exporting fish to Japan and the west. Soviet statistics gave the annual average of PDRY earnings from Soviet-Yemeni co-operation in the fishing field as $5.6 million in the late 1970s, or about 60 per cent of total PDRY export earnings.[136]

The limitation of non-military, economic, relations between the PDRY and the USSR would seem to have been a result of several factors. In the first place, both states agreed that South Yemen should maximise its earnings of foreign exchange and its receipt of aid in dealings with western or Arab states. The USSR encouraged the PDRY to seek trade and aid there, and, as noted, Soviet writers criticised those who saw this as a dangerous policy to pursue. Soviet policy in general was that the states of socialist orientation had to rely on sources other than the USSR.[137] Secondly, despite the growth of a strategic alliance between the PDRY and the USSR, South Yemen remained a 'socialist-orientated' not a socialist state, and was not therefore deemed to be eligible for the kinds of large aid programmes given to the core Third World members of the bloc, such as Cuba and Vietnam. Soviet observers, like their British predecessors, emphasised the meagre material base of the PDRY and the continued poverty of the country.[138]

But in addition to these considerations there were other factors restraining the growth of economic relations, ones that additionally inhibited both sides from further developing the interaction. On the Soviet side, there was a general reluctance, after the first enthusiastic aid

Table 2: *Soviet gross aid disbursements by recipients ($m.) 1976–1983*

	1976	*1977*	*1978*	*1979*	*1980*	*1981*	*1982*	*1983*
Total Soviet aid to all LDCs	*1727*	*1778*	*1865*	*2225*	*2684*	*2756*	*2804*	*2917*
Core socialist states	*1310*	*1342*	*1416*	*1779*	*2290*	*2365*	*2335*	*2605*
Cuba	400	400	400	400	450	500	500	500
Vietnam	500	500	500	750	850	900	950	1025
Afghanistan	40	42	37	34	276	235	142	312
Cambodia	—	—	19	85	134	100	115	110
Laos	40	20	30	30	50	70	38	38
Mongolia	330	380	430	480	530	560	590	620
Others	*416*	*436*	*448*	*434*	*378*	*374*	*427*	*312*
of which								
Middle East	*186*	*184*	*187*	*152*	*132*	*123*	*95*	*83*
Iran	65.0	50.0	50.0	6.3	9.6	5.6	16.5	12.1
Iraq	55.0	55.0	57.5	60.5	37.2	17.5	29.5	17.5
PDR Yemen	6.6	9.0	8.8	10.6	10.3	18.0	16.5	21.0
Syria	28.0	31.0	28.8	24.8	30.5	30.0	21.7	23.7
Turkey	30.5	36.8	38.5	39.6	38.2	42.0	10.7	8.0
AR Yemen	1.3	0.8	1.2	1.5	1.9	4.5	0.5	1.1

Source: Extracted from *Soviet, East European and Western Development Aid 1976–83*, Foreign and Commonwealth Office, Foreign Policy Document, No. 108, n.d.

programmes to India and Egypt in the early 1960s, to provide aid to the Third World, and particularly to Arab states. This inhibition was to be found in Soviet officials as well as amongst the Soviet population.[139] Soviet aid programmes for the PDRY were certainly an index of Soviet interest in South Yemen, but they may also have aroused anxieties in the USSR about further expenditures in countries that were not, in the longer run, considered to be sufficiently appreciative of what they had received. Such an inhibition may also explain the emphasis, repeated time and again in Soviet press coverage of South Yemen and in the communiqués and reports of PDRY delegations' visits to the USSR, of the 'gratitude' and 'appreciation' shown by the South Yemenis for their aid. Yet the South Yemenis also had their own inhibitions as a result of the realisation that developed of the low quality and unreliable delivery pattern of the Soviet aid programme. The supplies provided in irrigation were found to be deficient. The fishing agreement was seen by many Yemenis as exploitative of them, as a result of Soviet over-fishing. And the Soviet failure for several years to build the Aden thermal power station at al-Hizwa originally promisedin a 1972 agreement but unfinished a decade later brought considerable criticism of the Soviet programme as a whole.[140] When a Japanese firm built another power plant in eighteen months, even senior YSP personnel were heard to express doubts as to the self-evident superiority of socialism to capitalism.

In contrast to these restricted relations in the economic sphere, the PDRY and the USSR developed substantial military relations and the post-independence state became almost wholly reliant on arms from the USSR. Military delegations had been exchanged in the first three months of 1968, the first Soviet arms arrived in June 1968, and the first agreement was signed in August. Later in 1968 a South Yemeni military delegation spent one month visiting the USSR, a visit which had, in the words of the Defence Minister, 'laid the foundations for stronger relations' between the two states.[141] As early as 1969, at the anniversary celebrations in October, all arms in the military parade were reported to be of Soviet origin,[142] and throughout the 1970s a process of modernisation and expansion took place. Soviet advisers served in the PDRY, along with Cubans and East Germans, and thousands of Yemeni officers, and the leading personnel in the armed forces, spent time in the USSR on training courses. Precise evaluation of the Soviet military supplies to the PDRY is impossible, given the restricted nature of the information available, but attempts have been made to establish an outline of the known flows of Soviet and Soviet-bloc arms to Aden in the post-independence period.[143] Similarly, an exact total for the value of the arms supplied or what they cost to the PDRY cannot be estimated, but for the years 1977–80, i.e. when the USSR upgraded its relations with the PDRY, the value of arms provided is estimated to have come to $964 million, in constant 1975 prices. One US source gave a total of over $2.2 billion for 1967–85.[144] The 1977–80 figure, if accurate, was equal to around ten times the total of the PDRY's hard currency exports in this period, and equal in value to between 75 per cent and 100 per cent of all non-military imports in the same period. Whatever the details, the overall result of this flow was that the PDRY acquired, soon after independence, a new armoury, a new internal organisation for the armed forces, and a new political orientation for the army.[145]

Soviet statements usually referred to Moscow's policy of 'strengthening the defensive capabilities' of the PDRY, and it seems that this was considered to be the main function of Soviet arms deliveries. The main threat to the PDRY was believed to come from Saudi Arabia and the latter's receipts from the USA were far superior in quantity and quality to those delivered by the USSR to the PDRY. Although the Omani armed forces were inferior to those of the PDRY, Oman could call on

Table 3: *Imports of major weapons to Middle Eastern countries, 1971–85*

Country	Percentage of total exports of major weapons to the Third World, 1971–85	Index points, 5-year averages 1973	1978	1983
Iraq	*8.0*	100	272	743
Iran	*7.7*	100	107	19
Syria	*7.2*	100	62	154
Egypt	*7.2*	100	40	138
Israel	*5.3*	100	78	60
Saudi Arabia	*4.3*	100	394	668
Jordan	*1.7*	100	339	421
Kuwait	*1.2*	100	482	385
United Arab Emirates	*0.9*	100	169	299
Yemen, South	*0.6*	100	363	119
Oman	*0.6*	100	178	293
Yemen, North	*0.5*	100	12,363	3,295
Qatar	*0.4*	100	561	3,158
Lebanon	*0.3*	100	152	500
Bahrain	*0.1*	100	996	6,073
Total	*45.9*	100	112	160
Total value: 131,238				

Note: Shares are based on SIPRI trend indicator values in US $m. at constant (1985) prices.
Source: SIPRI data base. In Michael Brzoska and Thomas Ohlson (eds.), *Arms Transfers to the Third World 1971–85*, p. 16.

other states in the Peninsula to support it. The armed forces of the YAR were also, for much of the post-1967 period, inferior to those of the PDRY, but in the last part of the 1970s Soviet arms supplies to Sanaʿa increased, in some degree compensating for those provided to Aden.

The USSR's military interest in the PDRY had, however, a second dimension, namely that of using South Yemen in the context of the Soviet Union's global deployment. From 1968 onwards Soviet ships were permanently stationed in the Indian Ocean, and visiting fleets also paid periodic visits to the region. These used Aden on a regular basis and the Soviets purchased food and water and refuelled.[146] They changed crews, brought in by plane. The USSR maintained mooring buoys off the island of Socotra, south of Aden. The Soviet air force also used Aden for overflight to destinations in Africa; this was particularly important during the thirteen-day emergency airlift to Ethiopia in November and

Table 4: *Soviet deliveries of major weapons to countries with which a treaty of friendship and co-operation has been signed*

Country	Date of Treaty	Percentage of Soviet deliveries of major weapons to the Third World 1981	1985	1981–5
Afghanistan	1978	0.2	5.2	2.5
Angola	1976	2.7	4.2	4.2
Ethiopia	1978	1.0	1.4	1.1
India	1971	18.2	12.4	15.2
Iraq	1972	12.3	29.3	21.5
Mozambique	1977	0.2	0.2	1.3
North Korea	1961	0.2	6.9	2.4
Syria	1980	22.2	21.5	25.1
Vietnam	1978	10.6	4.2	4.7
Yemen, South	1980	1.8	0.2	1.0
Total		69.4	85.5	79.0

Source: SIPRI data base. In Michael Brzoska and Thomas Ohlson (eds.), *Arms Transfers to the Third World 1971–85*, p. 44.

December 1977 when Soviet planes stopped at Aden to refuel on their way to Addis Ababa. From 1975 onwards, the Soviet air force also used Aden for deploying reconnaissance planes, and other forms of reconnaissance, electronic and visual, may also have been carried out from Aden.[148] While Soviet forces staged exercises, however, the Soviet Union did not maintain its own forces in the PDRY on a regular basis, as it had previously done in Egypt and Somalia. The loss of Egyptian bases in 1974 and of Somali bases in 1977 may have enhanced the utility of Aden to the USSR, especially as the US naval and air deployment in the western Indian Ocean was also increased after 1973. Despite repeated allegations in the western press of Soviet 'bases' in the PDRY, no base facilities comparable to those in Egypt and Somalia were provided by South Yemen: talk of submarine pens was specious; and the Soviet dry dock, moved from Berbera in Somalia in November 1977, was later taken to Ethiopia after remaining in Aden for some months. In the middle 1980s Soviet naval deployment in the western Indian Ocean decreased somewhat, and the shadowy competition begun in 1973–4 eased.

In the field of foreign relations, the USSR and the PDRY adopted similar positions on many questions throughout the post-independence period, and the two countries, together with their ruling parties and attached specialist bodies and committees, often declared agreement on the major issues of the day. On some issues in particular, the PDRY stood out with the USSR against the majority of other Arab states – support for

Bangladesh in 1971, for Ethiopia in 1977, for the Babrak Karmal government in Afghanistan in 1980 and for a boycott of the 1984 Los Angeles Olympics being outstanding instances.[149] On others, the USSR and the PDRY endorsed the consensus of the radical states in the Arab world: this was particularly so on the Palestine question, a matter that recurred prominently many times in communiqués between the two states. Yet, despite this convergence, there were several issues of importance on which some disagreement could be noted with certainty, and others on which latent indications of some divergence were also present.

Two issues of divergence on international questions concerned Cambodia and the western Sahara: Aden recognised the opposition coalition established by Prince Sihanouk after 1970, whereas the USSR refused to do so till 1975;[150] Aden recognised the SADR in 1978, a step Moscow persistently refused to take.[151] On the Arabian Peninsula, the USSR's policy was in some respects more cautious than that of the PDRY throughout the post-1967 period. Thus, although the Soviet Union did on some occasions mention the issue of Yemeni unity, it laid much less stress on this than did the South Yemenis or, for that matter, the Chinese. In private, Soviet officials stated that they did not believe in the policy of Yemeni unity.[152] Even more so, the USSR did not back the guerrillas in the YAR fighting the central government. At one point, during the aftermath of the 1979 war, the Soviet press did quote NDF guerrillas, but no official support for them was ever voiced, and while NDF representatives did visit the USSR on unannounced visits no NDF delegation, or delegation of anterior guerrilla groups, was ever publicly invited to the USSR. Overall Soviet policy remained one of support for the YAR government, and of trying to wean it from Saudi Arabia.[153] Indeed, from late 1979 onwards, the Soviet Union was, as it had been in the 1960s, supplying the YAR government with the weapons to crush internal dissent, this time from the Aden-backed guerrillas of the NDF.

Soviet policy toward the guerrillas in Dhofar was a little more forthcoming. The first Soviet journalists visited Dhofar in May 1969 and a PFLOAG delegation visited Moscow in September 1971: but strong support was noted only at the very end of the guerrilla war. Even here, however, the USSR was reticent about endorsing the Front in Dhofar, and in dealings with the guerrillas, as with Aden, the Soviet press and state insisted on using the term *persidski zaliv*, 'Persian Gulf', in contrast to the usage by the radical Arabs of the neologism 'Arab Gulf'. Its rendering of the PFLOAG's name involved it in various circumlocutions. Soviet commentators were also initially concerned about Chinese influence among the guerrillas.[154] Soviet policy was one of opposition to US and British influence in Arabia, and to Iran's external military role, but it remained based on the hope of establishing relations with all states of the region, including the Arabian monarchies. For these reasons the USSR did not join with the PDRY in opposition to the independence of Bahrain, Qatar, and the United Arab Amirates in December 1971, and it sought, from the early 1970s onwards, to encourage 'normalisation' between the PDRY and Saudi Arabia. Section 7 of the 1979 Treaty, which committed both parties to 'the settlement of international dispute by peaceful means' may have had particular implications in Arabia as part of a Soviet attempt to influence South Yemen's policy towards its neighbours.

On other regional developments a measure of divergence was also noticeable. Some disagreement on the Horn of Africa was evident in the communiqués issued in May 1977. Policy also diverged on the Iran–Iraq war, since by 1982, during the second year of the war, the USSR was openly arming and favouring Iraq, while the PDRY, whose relations with Iraq had long been bad, had improved its relations with Iran. There was, in addition, an underlying disagreement on the Arab–Israeli question. The USSR had, from 1948, accepted the need for partition in Palestine, for two states to be created, one for Israelis and one for Palestinians. Soviet statements on the Middle East explicitly repeated their view that an Israeli state should remain in existence after any peace settlement, and that Israel was a legitimate member of all negotiations. Soviet policy also supported the right of Israel to free passage through the Red Sea. On one specific aspect of this question Soviet and South Yemeni policy did converge even in the early post-independence period: neither recognised the PLO as the sole legitimate representative of the Palestinians, albeit for different reasons. While the PLO did not open an office in Aden until 1973, it did not do so in Moscow until 1981, when it was recognised by the USSR as the representative of the Palestinians.[155] It was only in the joint communiqué of September 1982 that the USSR and the PDRY explicitly endorsed it together.[156] Prior to this, however, Soviet influence on the PDRY was apparent in a shift of position on the two major areas of disagreement. From the YSP Congress of 1978 onwards, the PDRY called merely for the withdrawal of Israel from the occupied territories, and the establishment of a Palestinian state, and in the joint communiqué after Kosygin's visit in September 1979 the two sides talked of 'strict respect for the rights and interests of all the littoral states and non-interference in their internal affairs, as well as due consideration for the interests of international shipping'.[157] This change in Yemeni policy was not, however, taken to the point of the PDRY explicitly accepting the legitimacy of an Israeli state. In common with the other rejectionist states, the PDRY refused to make such a public statement, and Soviet commitments to this effect were not explicitly reproduced in joint statements of the two sides.[158]

Soviet relations with the PDRY therefore encompassed a wide range of activities and, despite the overall agreement between the two states, some areas of disagreement did remain. At the same time, however, the USSR ensured that other countries of the Soviet bloc also contributed to development in the PDRY, on the basis of a division of labour elaborated by the Warsaw Pact states for the Third World as a whole. Czechoslovakia provided aid in modernising the TV service, Hungary in the medical field. The GDR helped draft the 1970 constitution and to establish the Ministry of State Security in 1974. It also helped in a number of economic projects.[159] Cuba provided help with training the militia, from 1973 onwards, and provided air force pilots during much of the same period.[160] After ʿAbd al-Fattāḥ's visit to Cuba in 1972, Cuba provided medical aid, and the first two Cuban doctors arrived in December of that year.[161] Cuba also advised on the establishment of local Popular Defence Committees and on the electoral system brought into being in 1977.[162] Later hundreds of South Yemeni teenagers went to study on Cuba's Isle of Youth. While Cuba was singled out for special praise, along with the USSR, at the 1987 YSP Conference, Cuba was also one of the countries that publicly appealed for clemency at the end of the trial of ʿAlī Nāṣir's supporters, in December 1987. Bulgaria provided agricultural assistance, and built a large new hotel in Aden.[163] While the PDRY was most closely influenced by Cuba, and a number of important official visits were exchanged, published agreements bound the PDRY most closely to other eastern European states. Thus, after signing of the twenty-year Treaty of Friendship and Co-operation with the USSR in November 1979, the PDRY signed similar treaties with the GDR (November 1979) and Czechoslovakia (September 1981).[164] This process of consolidating relations with the eastern bloc states allied to the USSR went together with the strengthening of treaty links between the PDRY and other pro-Soviet states nearer Aden, namely Ethiopia and Libya. The fall of ʿAbd al-Fattāḥ Ismāʿīl in April 1980 did not, therefore, interrupt a process of further integration into the Soviet bloc that had been initiated in 1978 and had involved strengthening relations at the economic, military and political levels. The 1986 crisis led the USSR to play a *more* direct role, as a way of protecting its already considerable investment in South Arabia.

Moscow and crisis management: January 1986 and its aftermath

The Soviet role in the January 1986 crisis was an important and controversial one.[165] Such an outbreak of conflict in a major Third World ally posed serious problems for the USSR – in how it reacted, in limiting the damage to its interests and international position, and in preventing east–west tensions from exacerbating, and in turn being exacerbated by, the conflict in the country concerned. Soviet policy during the crisis was, therefore, not only a test for the USSR–PDRY relationship, and for Soviet policy in the Peninsula more generally, but also an illustration of broader Soviet policy on the handling of problems in Third World allies. In addition it served, to a limited extent, to demonstrate something of the new, more open, approach to foreign policy that was to become characteristic of the early Gorbachev period, in that as part of the evacuation of thousands of Soviet and other foreign nationals from Aden, Soviet Foreign Ministry officials in Moscow allowed western diplomats unprecedented access to their decision-making procedures.[166]

At the same time, many other actors had an interest in what the USSR did and in presenting Soviet policy in a particular light. Thus, both factions within the PDRY itself sought to win Moscow over to their side, while in the Arab world and in the west there were many who sought to use the Aden crisis as a way of causing the USSR maximum damage in propaganda terms – either by arguing that Moscow had in some way organised the conflict and was consequently responsible for the killings, or by presenting Soviet policy after 13 January as some form of military intervention. Such accusations were, with a delay of some days, to become particularly common in Washington: there a number of senior administrative officials were to be heard charging that Soviet conduct in the PDRY crisis of 1986 was comparable to the invasion of Afghanistan in 1979 and to other Soviet actions, real or imagined.[167]

The reality of Soviet policy in the 1986 PDRY crisis would appear to have been rather different in three significant respects. First, the USSR was taken by surprise and did not incite or have foreknowledge of the leadership explosion. While much public discussion of Soviet and US policy in the Third World has been based on the presumption that each must be completely responsible for everything that happens in a Third World ally, or for what such allies may do in the international arena, it should by now be evident that some untoward events can occur without the foreknowledge of the strategic ally: both the USSR and the USA have had ample experience of such things happening. The USA had experience enough of this in Indo-China. As far as the USSR is concerned, this is what occurred in Afghanistan in the period 1978–9, and in Grenada in 1983. These junior allies presented the USSR with major internal crises that then had international repercussions.[168] Secondly, once it became evident that ᶜAlī Nāṣir had lost control, the short-term Soviet response was to seek to restabilise the situation and ensure a return to normality under as broad a successor leadership as possible: only this could make it possible to preserve the regime itself and limit the chances of the crisis acquiring an international dimension. Thirdly, there was a more long-term response, evident through the rest of 1986 and through 1987, of strengthening Soviet control over the policies of a junior ally, in order to ensure that the factionalism and confusion that led to earlier crises would not recur. One can speak, in this sense, of a broader model of Soviet responses to crisis in junior allies: Moscow responds to the errors of a relatively autonomous leadership in these allies by imposing greater control, combined with stronger guarantees. This was evident in Cuba after the disastrous economic policies of the 1960s. It was seen in its most acute form in Afghanistan in December 1979, where it led to direct military intervention. It was also seen *within* the USSR in the imposition of stricter control on Central Asian republics, especially Uzbekistan and Kazakhstan, between 1984 and 1986. The South Yemeni case is another example of how Moscow reacts to such developments: the parallel with Afghanistan rests not upon whether there was, or was not, a direct Soviet military role in the January 1986 crisis, but rather in the broader pattern of increased Soviet authority in response to such a crisis in a Third World ally, overriding some of the susceptibilities of local and national party personnel.

An indication of this change in Soviet relations towards the PDRY came with the appointment after the January crisis of a new Soviet ambassador. All six of the previous Soviet envoys to Aden had been professional diplomats, with experience in the Middle East: three had earlier served as ambassador in the Sudan.[169] The most prominent of these, Vladimir Poliakov, had gone on to be a leading Middle East expert in the Soviet Foreign Ministry. In 1986, however, the incumbent Vladislav Zhukov was replaced, at the end of his term, by Albert Rachkov, a career party official: Rachkov had served two periods in the Central Committee apparatus in Moscow (1965–9, 1974–80), and had since 1980 been Second Secretary of the Turkmenistan Communist Party. Since 1981 he had been a candidate member of the CPSU Central Committee. (Following his failure in Aden, Zhukov was prematurely retired.) This shift from diplomat to party official with experience in a Soviet Muslim republic had been seen earlier in Afghanistan, during the factionalist outbreak in 1979 that preceded the Soviet intervention: the career diplomat Puzanov was replaced in October by Fikryat Tabeyev, a member of the CPSU Central Committee and, since 1960, Secretary of the Tatar Autonomous Republic. In Ethiopia, too, Soviet ambassadors in the 1980s were party officials. The appointment after January 1986 of a CPSU functionary as chief Soviet representative in Aden indicated greater unease, and a greater willingness to exert direct influence.

In the months preceding the January crisis the USSR was actively trying to contain the problems within the YSP. As already indicated, Moscow in the first half of the 1980s made clear its support for the general line of ʿAlī Nāṣir's policies: both internally and internationally there was, in Moscow's eyes, no realistic alternative to some liberalisation of the economy and to peace with the PDRY's neighbours. But the USSR was concerned at the enduring division within the YSP between ʿAlī Nāṣir and ʿAbd al-Fattāḥ, and from 1984 onwards encouraged a process of reconciliation to take place. ʿAbd al-Fattāḥ returned to Aden in early 1985 from Moscow, with the support of the Soviet authorities, and they encouraged ʿAlī Nāṣir to use the October 1985 Congress to broaden membership of the YSP's governing institutions in order to complete the process of reconciliation. The result was that the new Central Committee contained not only supporters of deposed President Sālim Rubiyyaʿ ʿAlī, who tended to support ʿAlī Nāṣir, but also cadres loyal to ʿAbd al-Fattāḥ. Earlier outbreaks of factionalism, in May and October of 1985, occasioned considerable mediation efforts by the Soviet ambassador, Vladislav Zhukov: but while the Soviet representatives in Aden were certainly aware of the disagreements within the YSP leadership, they do not seem to have envisaged that matters could take the sanguinary form that they were to do in January. Up to 13 January 1986 Soviet policy remained one of urging compromise and unity on a YSP leadership that had rather different intentions. The parallels here with Afghanistan and indeed with Ethiopia are striking: despite the dependence for ultimate survival of these regimes on the military and political support of the USSR, the leaderships in all three of these countries paid scant attention to repeated Soviet calls for an end to factionalism.

Soviet policy during the crisis itself can be divided into three phases. Between 13 January and 16 January Moscow continued to acknowledge ʿAlī Nāṣir as President of the PDRY and to lend credence to his account of events – thus on January 14 *Pravda* repeated ʿAlī Nāṣir's claim that four YSP leaders, including ʿAbd al-Fattāḥ, had been executed, as 'counter-revolutionaries'.[170] On 15 and 16 January the Soviet media continued to refer to ʿAlī Nāṣir's opponents as 'putschists'.[171] While subsequently some Soviet officials suggested that Moscow broke with ʿAlī Nāṣir on 14 January, it was only on 17 January that it became publicly clear that a second phase had opened: during this period the USSR sought to mediate between the two factions in Aden, inviting representatives of the two sides to negotiations at the embassy, while in Moscow Prime Minister al-ʿAṭṭās and Foreign Minister al-Dālī, who had flown to the Soviet capital from Delhi, were involved in high-level talks with CPSU leaders. After a meeting with Yegor Ligachev and Boris Ponomarev, leading CPSU officials concerned with international relations, TASS reported the 'serious concern' expressed about the situation in the PDRY, the need to find a political solution to the problems there, and the 'impermissibility' of outside interference. The solution still seemed, at this stage, to be some form of compromise: 'Emphasis was placed on the earliest possible normalization of the situation in the PDRY and the restoration of unity in the ranks of the YSP, which would be in the highest interest of the party and the people'.[172] An article in *Pravda* on 24 January by a senior commentator Pavel Demchenko reported for the first time on the evacuation of Soviet citizens from Aden and spoke, in neutral terms, of 'disagreements in the country's party and state leadership'. Demchenko also provided a cautious assessment of the overall background to the crisis: 'In recent years, the republic has achieved considerable successes in both the social and economic area and the political sphere. But, needless to say, there are also difficulties: they include a social factor – the traditional heterogeneity and tribal fragmentation of society, inherited from past eras. They also include the subversive actions of foreign reactionary and imperialist forces.'[173] Such stress on the socio-economic underpinnings of YSP factionalism was to provide the basis of much subsequent Soviet commentary on the January 1986 crisis.

A third phase of clear support for the new YSP leadership began on 24–5 January, and was followed by intensive Soviet diplomatic and material support for the successor regime. Soviet officials in Aden appear to have decided that neither side was abiding by ceasefire agreements reached through the mediation efforts of the Soviet embassy, but with the establishment of a new party and state leadership between 24 and 27 January, the USSR now had an alternative set of interlocutors with which to engage. Quite apart from relevations about his role in precipitating the fighting, it was now clear that ᶜAlī Nāṣir was no longer a credible leader because he had, in effect, lost. By the end of the month the first planes and ships bringing in relief supplies to Aden had arrived, and in the following weeks the Soviet Union made great efforts to compose and consolidate the new regime in Aden. It would appear that military equipment destroyed or used in the fighting was quickly replaced, and emergency food and medical supplies were sent in from late January onwards. Within a few weeks of their leaving, Soviet diplomatic staff and advisers, civilian and military, had returned to Aden. Some Arab and, later, US reports claimed that Soviet military experts had sided with ᶜAlī Nāṣir's opponents in the later stages of the fighting, but such claims are unsubstantiated and improbable.

By the end of January Moscow had, therefore, decided to back the new leadership, despite its former commitment to ᶜAlī Nāṣir and the fact that those YSP cadres closest to the USSR, namely the former leaders of the

PDU, had also sided with ʿAlī Nāṣir. The practicalities of the situation dictated this choice. There then followed a series of high-level visits by Soviet officials to Aden that, over the next year and more, suggested that Moscow had decided to play a much more active role in directing the South Yemeni state than had previously been the case. These included: Ivan Kapitanov, chairman of the CPSU Central Auditing Commission a body responsible for inner-party discipline, in July 1986; CPSU Politburo member Geidar Aliev, on two stopover visits flying to and from the funeral of Samora Machel in Mozambique, in October 1986; Nikolai Talyzin, chairman of the State Planning Committee in March 1987; the Deputy Defence Minister and Commander-in-Chief of Soviet Ground Forces, General Yevgeni Ivanovski, in April 1987; and General Alexei Lizichev, head of the Main Political Directorate of the Soviet army and navy, in October 1987. It can be asumed that these led to a strengthening of Soviet influence throughout the apparatuses of state, party and the armed forces within the PDRY. On their side, the new PDRY leaders paid several visits to the USSR in the months after the January crisis: ʿAlī al-Bīḍ, the new party secretary, visited Moscow in early February 1986 and met then with Gorbachev, Ligachev and other senior Soviet officials; Prime Minister Nuʿmān was in Moscow in June; al-Bīḍ visited Moscow again in early February 1987, when he was an official guest of Gorbachev and treated to a Kremlin banquet; Defence Minister Colonel Ṣāliḥ ʿUbayd Ahmad visited the USSR at the invitation of the Soviet Minister of Defence in May 1987. The pace and level of these visits suggests that Soviet–PDRY relations were, if anything, more active after than before the January 1986 crisis.

Soviet policy in the post-January period would seem to have comprised at least four major issues. The first goal was the encouragement of unity within the ranks of the PDRY. In the aftermath of January 1986 the Russians faced two kinds of problem – that of reconciling the new YSP leaders with at least some of those who had supported ʿAlī Nāṣir and gone into exile with him, and that of maintaining the fragile collaboration of the individuals and factions thrown together by the crisis itself. In the period up to November 1987, at least, Soviet pressure seems to have been reasonably successful in ensuring the success of the second goal, but the first was much less attainable. From late January 1986 onwards Soviet coverage of South Yemen stressed the need for unity within the ranks of the PDRY, and when al-Bīḍ met Gorbachev in February 1987 this was indicated as having been a central issue in the talks. Gorbachev declared that the Soviet people had been 'saddened' by the events of January 1986 and had tried to help the PDRY 'to overcome the crisis and speedily put an end to the bloodshed'. He urged al-Bīḍ to 'rally the party and the people together in building a progressive democratic state' and stressed the need for 'normality in the country'.[174] Soviet emissaries were directly in touch with ʿAlī Nāṣir in exile, as part of the attempt to assist this process. But little came of it: the two factions within the YSP were far too divided, and the new YSP leadership itself was unwilling to follow Soviet promptings in this regard. The problem of factionalism, which the Russians rightly identified as lying at the core of the crisis in the PDRY, therefore continued. If Soviet advice had failed to prevent the January 1986 explosion, it was even less likely to be able to heal the fissures which that crisis itself had created. In late 1987, when the YSP leadership followed the twentieth anniversary of independence celebrations by announcing death sentences on fifteen of those on trial in connection with the January 1986 events, it was apparent that the USSR did not approve of this move. It was left to GDR leader Honecker and Fidel Castro to make public appeals for clemency, along with ʿAlī ʿAbd Allāh Sāliḥ, Yasir Arafat and the Amir of Kuwait, amongst others: but the Soviet press did not report on the death sentences and subsequent five executions, and the CPSU secretariat envoy Karen Brutents brought a letter from Gorbachev asking for clemency and raised Soviet concern when he met the YSP leadership on 21 December. The YSP reply, that some executions were needed to assuage protests by the families of those killed by ʿAlī Nāṣir, and in particular by the family of ʿAlī ʿAntar, is unlikely to have convinced the Soviet envoy, who could see to what extent the conclusion of the trial and executions had contributed to extending the isolation of the PDRY within the Arab world and communist bloc.

The second goal was the strengthening of the PDRY's economy: not only was this the precondition for any broader consolidation of the regime and the winning back of a degree of popular support, but it was all the more necessary because of the deteriorating economic position, as a result both of declining oil revenues elsewhere in the Peninsula and of a reluctance by migrants to remit money after the fighting. As noted, prior to the 1986 crisis the USSR had provided some economic aid to the PDRY, but this was not such as to make Moscow either the major trading partner of the PDRY or the provider of the majority of the PDRY's aid. Apart from emergency aid, the USSR therefore strengthened the links binding the PDRY to it and to the CMEA and a number of major new economic agreements were signed. The most important, concluded in July 1987, covered long-run Soviet support for the development of the PDRY's oil industry:[175] it was announced in April 1987 that the Soviet team working in Shabwa province had begun producing some oil, but this had to be transported by trucks to Aden, and the 1987 protocol envisaged not only additional drilling for oil but also the construction of pipelines, first to thesea at Biʾir Ali and later to the Aden refinery.[176] An agreement had already been concluded in 1986 for the modernisation of the Aden refinery, first built in the early 1950s. If Soviet policy in the PDRY had one priority after January 1986, it was to promote oil output as a means of strengthening the regime and lessening its economic reliance on the USSR.

Parallel to this internal reconsolidation of the situation within the PDRY, the USSR also sought to prevent any internationalisation of the conflict in its Yemeni ally. Mindful of the US intervention in Grenada less than three years before, in which a factional clash between elements of the New Jewel Movement had opened the door to a successful US invasion and overthrow of the regime, the Russians were particularly anxious to prevent any outside state, Arab or western, from intervening in the PDRY. Following the 23 January meeting in Moscow between al-ʿAṭṭās, al-Dālī and members of the Soviet leadership, the TASS report emphasised: 'A special point was made of stressing the purely internal nature of developments in the PDRY and the need to prevent any outside interferences in its affairs in future, too'.[177] The speed with which Soviet military supplies were despatched to Aden once fighting had subsided illustrated how deep this fear probably was.

At the same time, the Soviet Union took diplomatic measures to ward off those who might be considering intervention. Thus Soviet communications with North Yemen, including, it was reported, a personal message from Gorbachev to ʿAlī ʿAbd Allāh Sāliḥ, cautioned the YAR leadership against any action towards the South:[178] the Soviet ambassador to the YAR saw President Sāliḥ on 16 January, the Soviet First Deputy Foreign Minister Viktor Maltsev arrived in Sanaʿa on 31 January. The unusual openness towards British and other western diplomats in Moscow over the evacuation of their nationals from Aden during the fighting may have been designed to reassure them about Soviet intentions. Soviet charges about 'foreign' involvement in the conflict, echoing similar charges from the PDRY itself, were unsubstantiated, but did serve to draw attention to what Moscow saw as the danger of external intervention. This concern, however, was not confined to the period immediately after January 1986 since throughout the subsequent period the precarious condition of the YSP leadership, and the evident desire of ʿAlī Nāṣir and his people to regain power, must have kept the issue of external intervention alive. Reports some time after the crisis that the USA was now considering support for exiled guerrillas operating against the YSP can only have fuelled this anxiety. Thus, in an attempt to counter any possible drive to topple the Aden government, Moscow encouraged the continuation of good relations by the PDRY with other Peninsula states, especially

Kuwait and Saudi Arabia, the border talks with Oman, and a slow reduction in tension with the YAR. The USSR's own relations with Oman took a step forward, in August 1987, with the announcement of plans to open a Soviet embassy in Muscat, and Soviet backing for Kuwait over the tanker war in the Gulf must have helped to reassure the Peninsula's rulers that Moscow was not planning another revolutionary offensive through Aden.

In limited terms, the Soviet policy of 'normalisation' and restabilisation was a success: the YSP leadership remained apparently united, it was able to re-establish control over the country, its external relations were continued on pre-existing lines, and, while much of the population remained alienated from the regime, no significant internal threat materialised. The difficulties which the January 1986 crisis had occasioned with some states, notably the YAR and Ethiopia, had been largely overcome by the end of 1987. However, many problems remained, as the Russians themselves were well aware. In regard to ᶜAlī Nāṣir, the Russians refused to do what they had done following the fall of Sālim Rubiyyaᶜ ᶜAlī, namely endorse in full the criticism by the new PDRY leadership of its predecessor. When al-Bīḍ attended the 27th Congress of the CPSU in February 1986 and included in his speech a criticism of ᶜAlī Nāṣir, this section of his statement was, by prior agreement between Russians and Yemenis, not translated. In subsequent accounts of how the crisis had developed, Soviet writers did mention both ᶜAlī Nāṣir's role in the events of 13 January, and the extent to which under his leadership negative trends had developed within the PDRY's economy. But these observations fell far short of what was being articulated in Aden. The trial of ᶜAlī Nāṣir's supporters which was held amidst much publicity in Aden over several months in 1987 was not covered in the Soviet media, and Moscow was privately critical of the decision to execute some of those involved. Similarly, while South Yemeni officials roundly denounced any suggestion that tribal factors had played a role in the outbreak of factional fighting in January 1986, Soviet writers repeatedly stated that this, while by no means the sole factor in sparking the crisis, had played a definite role, with the added implication that recognition of the dangers of tribalism was all the more necessary because the January crisis had exacerbated inter-tribal tensions.[179]

The Soviet leadership used events in the PDRY to underline the importance of socio-economic and internal political factors in dealing with Third World revolutions, an ever-present problem since the crisis in Afghanistan had been brought on by neglect of precisely these questions, by a lethal mixture of factionalism within the ruling party and arbitrary imposition of reforms on society without. In speaking to al-Bīḍ in

February 1987, Gorbachev struck a characteristically admonitory note: he stressed the need for a flexible policy in the PDRY and praised a policy that 'carefully takes into account the realities, economic possibilities of a country, the level of historical development of a society, political consciousness and culture of the people, its traditions, peculiarities and, of course, the internal situation of the state'.[180] YSP leaders were not, moreover, slow to notice the significance of the fact that, at a meeting of communist and socialist party delegations attending the 1987 seventieth anniversary of the revolution celebrations in Moscow, the YSP was not invited to speak, where representatives of the Syrian Baᶜth, and a host of European social-democratic parties, were so honoured. Overall, subsequent Soviet analyses of the situation in the PDRY restated those reservations about the general level of development of the country and its society which had underlain much of the analysis of the early 1980s. As in Ethiopia, Afghanistan and other Third World states, Soviet policy was to strengthen the state apparatus, and to provide military support, but to urge caution in the reforms which the regime carried out. Intoxication with the revolutionary phrase was not something Soviet policy-makers were willing to indulge. At times Soviet analysis was quite blunt as in the reflective analysis published in *Pravda* in September 1986 which spoke of the PDRY as 'taking a difficult examination in steadfastness and maturity'.[181] In addition to the usual references to the backwardness of the PDRY, this article also highlighted what could now be openly designated as controversial developments under ᶜAlī Nāṣir: the growth of social stratification in the countryside, including the re-emergence of an agricultural proletariat; the siphoning off of food from border areas to neighbouring states, where it could command a much higher price; and the growth of corruption in state enterprises. *Pravda*'s interim judgement on the examination was cautious indeed: 'Many of the republic's achievements, even if they are modest, are basically steps on an *as yet untrodden* path' (italics added). In October 1987 the chief Soviet economic adviser in Aden, Kadirov, startled his listeners by making a public critique of the politicised nature of South Yemeni economic policy, the first time such Soviet reservations had been so publicly aired or printed in the YSP party press.

If, therefore, the two parties diverged on the causes and solutions of the January crisis, the Russians continued to be anxious about the stability of the YSP regime, as a result of continuing internal conflicts, including those within the leadership, the many costs of the 1986 crisis, and the temptations which the PDRY's weakness presented to external forces. This anxiety was all the greater because, although this could not be admitted openly, one of the many results of the 1986 crisis was an increase in anti-Soviet sentiment in the PDRY. This had been growing prior to the crisis, as public attitudes blamed the USSR for the economic difficulties and shortages within the country, often without reason, but it was dramatically demonstrated during the fighting itself, when tanks apparently under the command of Muḥammad ʿAlī Aḥmad, the governor of Abyan, and therefore loyal to ʿAlī Nāṣir, shelled the Soviet embassy in Aden, one of them scoring a direct hit on the ambassador's office. Reports of Soviet casualties vary – some reliable accounts speak of up to 12 Russian dead, including one woman, whilst others deny any fatal casualties. Whatever the truth about this, the abrupt and public evacuation of so many Russians from their closest Arab ally, the discrediting of Third World radicalism and the fragmentation of the Arab left which the January events occasioned, must have dismayed the Russians greatly, on top of the very real problems which the events brought about. The fact that Moscow's closest allies within the YSP, former members of the PDU, had been forced out of power because of their alliance with ʿAlī Nāṣir was an additional setback. It is not surprising, therefore, that the PDRY leadership missed no opportunity in the months that followed to pronounce their deepest loyalty and gratitude to the USSR, and the appropriate Soviet presence, of state and military officials, was given a special welcome at the twentieth anniversary of independence celebrations in November 1987.[182] For their part, the Russians enjoined more proper behaviour on the YSP leadership, and sought to maintain what position they could in the PDRY, but in private warned their South Yemeni allies that they would not maintain their support if another outbreak of factional fighting occurred. The greater willingness to voice problems and criticisms in general, associated with *glasnost*, compounded this Soviet directness.

The January 1986 crisis notwithstanding, the Soviet commitment to the PDRY remained, in overall terms, positive by the standards of many other Third World involvements. Moscow had not made the economic investments seen in Cuba or even Egypt, and it had been able to insulate the leadership disputes in a way not seen in Grenada. At the same time, despite the undoubted divergences between Moscow and Aden, and the enduring nationalism of the South Yemenis, there had not been the kind of break that had occurred in China or in such Arab states as Egypt and Iraq. Moreover, while in the 1970s, and especially in the aftermath of the 1978 crisis in the PDRY, Moscow's relations with other Middle Eastern states had suffered because of its support for the PDRY, this had ceased to be so during the 1980s and the 1986 crisis caused hardly a ripple in dealings with Arab states, by now more concerned with the threat from Tehran. Similarly, while Washington had used the 1978 crisis in Aden as one of the list of supposed Soviet 'violations' of detente, along with Angola, Cambodia, Afghanistan and Ethiopia, the charges levelled at Moscow after January 1986 made little impression: the PDRY was not seen, or used, as one of the 'regional issues' that preoccupied Soviet–US relations in 1986 and 1987. If Moscow gained nothing economically from the relationship with Aden, apart from some fishing opportunities, it did obtain modest military and diplomatic benefits: the former comprised the refuelling and reconnaissance facilities that Aden offered, useful for the Persian Gulf, Red Sea and northern Indian Ocean; the diplomatic benefits included Aden's role as the staunchest Soviet ally in the Arab world, and as an unfailing supporter of Soviet policies in the UN and Non-Aligned Movement, one of the few Third World states to back it on Afghanistan. If the PDRY was one of the poorest and least significant of the Arab states, it was nonetheless by far the most internationally reliable of the radical Arab regimes, without the unpredictability that characterised Algeria, Syria and Iraq.

The one way that the PDRY could have become a major problem for the USSR would have been for it to have engaged in foreign policy initiatives that provoked great Arab hostility or a direct US intervention in the region: this was something that it was in the PDRY's capacity to occasion, and which Moscow, having for fifteen years or more stressed the need for 'normalisation', was determined to prevent. The balance-sheet of two decades of Soviet–South Yemeni relations was therefore, for both sides, positive: Moscow ensured the security of the YSP regime, and provided guidance on the overall range of state and party policies; Aden provided the USSR with diplomatic and military advantages that were of recognisable importance for Soviet strategy, and remained committed to pursuing a set of socio-economic policies based on Soviet theories of socialist orientation and development.

Relations with China: disapproval and tenacity

In the initial period after independence China appeared to have acquired a position of influence in South Yemen as great as that of the USSR. The Chinese press hailed the independence of the country, and carried favourable reports of the new government, as well as of the praise which South Yemenis were quoted as according China and its leader, Mao Tsetung.[183] An agreement on diplomatic relations was signed on 31 January 1968, and a Chinese embassy was finally opened, in July 1969, with one of China's most experienced Arabian experts, Li Chi'ang-Fen, serving as ambassador.[184] The delay may have been caused on the South Yemeni side – Ḳaḥṭān al-Shaʿabī may not have wanted to anger the west further by opening a Chinese mission – or on the Chinese side – the Foreign Ministry was convulsed by the Cultural Revolution and all ambassadors to the Arab world, except the one to Egypt, had been recalled in 1966–7. But even before this embassy opened, a PRSY delegation, headed by Foreign Minister Ṣayf al-Ḍāliʿī, had visited Peking in September 1968 and had signed two agreements, one on trade and one on economic and technical co-operation. At this stage, China offered the PDRY a long-term interest-free loan of $12 million, to cover five years of development projects.[185] Miltiary aid – rifles, machine-guns and anti-tank weapons for 5,000 soldiers – was also offered, but it is not clear that it was ever delivered. In August 1970 a PRSY delegation headed by President Sālim Rubiyyaʿ ʿAlī visited China, and a further loan of $43 million was offered under a new Economic and Technical Agreement.[186]

An interesting insight into Chinese views of South Yemen can be gleaned from the confidential minutes of the 1968 Peking discussions between leading Chinese officials and the PRSY delegation. Repeatedly, the Chinese return to the point that South Yemen is at an early stage of its development and must not adopt excessively radical policies. Thus the Chinese Deputy Premier and Foreign Minister Chen Yi:

> There exist facts and events which you must study objectively and scientifically, for your every claim about constructing socialism and raising slogans which are impractical and provocative offer, by their nature, sharp weapons to your adversaries, with which they can fight you and incite against you the local forces which surround you.[187]

He later tells the South Yemenis to be wary of 'infantile' leftists and to stick to the policies of the 'national democratic' phase of the revolution, rather than trying to initiate a transition to socialism. While the Chinese officials enjoined on South Yemen a policy of self-reliance, they advised them *against* trying to imitate the policies of the Cultural Revolution.[188] Such caution was, of course, very similar to that being enjoined on Aden by the USSR.

In the first decade after independence, Chinese aid was directed to a number of projects: constructing a textile mill at al-Mansura, outside Aden, building a road along the 315 miles to Mukalla, constructing a hospital in the Crater district of Aden, and expanding the salt works in the Khormkasar district of Aden. Three further aid agreements were signed: in July 1972, on the occasion of a visit by Secretary-General ʿAbd al-Fattāḥ Ismāʿīl;[189] in November 1974, when President Sālim Rubiyyaʿ ʿAlī paid a second visit to Peking;[190] and in April 1978 when Prime Minister ʿAlī Nāṣir Muḥammad made an official visit.[191] By the end of 1980 China had provided aid estimated at $84 million;[192] this represented nearly

Table 5: *China's aid commitments to Third World countries 1949–1975 (in US $ millions)*

Middle East		Africa (selected countries)	
Algeria	70	Ethiopia	84
Egypt	110	Ghana	42
Syria	16	Somalia	131
North Yemen	47	Tanzania	411
South Yemen	78	Zambia	212
Sudan	117		
Middle East total	438	Africa total	1,036

Source: John F. Copper, *China's Foreign Aid*, London, 1976, pp. 71, 89.

20% of China's aid programme in the Middle East. Chinese aid personnel in the PDRY were generally liked, for their modest and hard-working image, and the fishermen of Aden bay had a special debt of gratitude because they could sell to the Chinese the shellfish which Islamic practice prevented the local population from eating.

On a number of issues, China and South Yemen saw eye to eye. China, like the USSR, had had relations with the YAR after 1962 and seemed to have derived from it a certain experience of how to conduct relations in the Yemens. China, even more than the USSR, apparently believed in being even-handed between the two Yemens, and this led it, on a number of occasions, to give explicit support to the policy of Yemeni unity.[193] China was also able in 1970 to win PRSY support for one of the most important issues of dispute between it and the USSR, namely the issue of Cambodia: the PRSY, unlike the Soviet Union, recognised the Royal Government of National Union of Kampuchea, headed by Prince Sihanouk, as opposed to the military regime of General Lon Nol, recognised by both the USA and the USSR. In August 1973 the Foreign Minister of Sihanouk's coalition visited Aden.[194]

Despite increasing reliance on the USSR, South Yemeni leaders were for a long time willing to acknowledge their debt to China. Speaking on his 1968 visit, Ṣayf al-Ḍāliʿī stated that China's war of liberation 'offers an example for the people of all countries fighting to break away from imperialism and win freedom'.[195] In 1970 Sālim Rubiyyaʿ ʿAlī stated:

> We, the people of South Yemen, have benefited from the advanced experience of the Chinese people in defeating our enemies, the colonialists and reactionaries, and in frustrating the aggressive schemes against the revolution. . . . We are grateful to the friendly Government and people of the People's Republic of China for their material and more support to us the people of South Yemen.[196]

In 1972, ᶜAbd al-Fattāḥ Ismāᶜīl, someone generally known for his sympathy for the USSR, acknowledged that before independence 'China also gave us unstinted assistance, thus enhanced our fighting capacity and inspired us to continue our struggle until victory'.[197] In the Seven Days demonstrations of July 1972 Sālim Rubiyyaᶜ ᶜAlī echoed Chinese views on economic development.[198]

The two sides also agreed, in the initial period, on a number of specific issues pertaining to the region: both supported the guerrillas in Oman and Eritrea,[199] both backed the Palestinians to the extent that they did not acknowledge the right of an Israeli state to exist,[200] both denounced Iran and had, at first, no relations with it.[201] Only in August 1971 did Peking and Tehran exchange diplomatic recognition.[202] Whereas the Soviet press used the term 'Persian Gulf', Chinese papers made some concession to Arab sensibilities and referred to the 'Persian (Arab) Gulf'. Yet, from the beginning, there was also a major disagreement, on the USSR. The *Renmin Ribao* editorial greeting independence in November 1967 raised this point immediately: 'The British imperialists will not lightly give up their colonial interests . . . The US imperialists and Soviet modern revisionists too will attempt to get a foothold there.'[203] During the 1968 visit, Foreign Minister Chen Yi told his visitors that the USSR was 'colluding' with the USA and would betray the Arab peoples as it had Cuba in the 1962 missile crisis: 'In the present new international conditions the Soviet revisionist renegade clique will surely sell out the interests of the Arab people still further.'[204] In 1970 Tung Pi-wu, Chinese Vice-Chairman, addressed Sālim Rubiyyaᶜ ᶜAlī on the dangers of the 'so-called "Superpowers"' and in 1974 Teng Hsiao-ping was to be found welcoming, during Sālim Rubiyyaᶜ ᶜAlī's second visit, the 'decline' of the super-powers' influence.[205]

There were in South Yemen some who sympathised with the Chinese revolution, who looked favourably on its internal system, and who shared some of its criticisms at least of the USSR. In 1971 President Sālim Rubiyyaᶜ ᶜAlī encouraged his people 'to benefit from the experience and sincerity of the Chinese people'[206] and in 1972 he advanced a policy of 'self-reliance' for the PDRY that appeared to be influenced by China. But despite apparent Chinese encouragement at no point did the South Yemeni leaders lend open support to the criticisms which the Chinese were then making of Russia. Successive Congresses of the South Yemeni Front, from 1968 through to 1975, had stressed the need for *unity* in the socialist bloc, and the dangers of division. This message was repeated time and again by South Yemeni politicians. In 1968 Ṣayf al-Ḍāliᶜī declared in Peking:

All revolutionaries and progressives in the world are rising as one to deal with imperialism and colonialism. Since the enemy's making its dispositions everywhere in Asia, Africa and Latin America, we, progressive revolutionaries of the whole world, should all the more clench our fists in the face of imperialism and colonialism. Otherwise, we would leave openings in our ranks which imperialism might use to preserve its strength and carry out conspiracies.[207]

The final communiqué stated that talks had been conducted 'in a sincere, frank and friendly atmosphere', an indication of disagreement.[208] After the 'Corrective Move' of June 1969 the Chinese appear to have hoped that, despite its more explicit support for the USSR, the new leadership would be sympathetic to them and Chinese leaders later stated that they 'welcomed the revolutionary measure of 22 June'.[209]

In this initial period both sides gave support to the other on particular issues: China agreed to recognise the PRSY's 'sovereignty over all its territories and islands', an apparent reference to the Kuria Muria Islands, and the PRSY supported PRC entry into the UN.[210] The fact that Sālim Rubiyyaᶜ ᶜAlī chose to visit Peking, in 1970, before making a visit to Moscow, in 1972, must also have encouraged the Chinese. Most surprisingly, the 1972 visit by ᶜAbd al-Fattāḥ Ismāᶜīl involved less dissonance in public stance than by the earlier two visits, of Ṣayf al-Ḍāliᶜī and Sālim Rubiyyaᶜ ᶜAlī. The final communiqué stated that it had been 'crowned with complete success'.[211]

Yet by the early 1970s divergences between the two had already begun to appear. PDRY support for the USSR over Bangladesh in December 1971 stood in marked contrast to its siding with Peking over Cambodia a year before. China ceased aid to the Eritrean guerrillas in 1970 and in 1971 Haile Selassie visited Peking, at a time when the PDRY was still arming the Eritrean guerrillas. China supported the guerrillas in Oman between 1968 and 1971 and the 1970 communiqué pledged 'firm support to the people's armed struggle of the PFLOAG'.[212] As late as June 1971 Chou En-lai was reported to have commended the PDRY for its 'support for the people's revolution' in the Gulf.[213] But similar support was not voiced in the 1972 communiqué, despite mention of it in their speeches by the South Yemeni delegation.[214] By then China had already begun to alter its policy on the Gulf: Peking's military aid to the PFLOAG ceased in 1971 and, whereas ᶜAbd al-Fattāḥ Ismāᶜīl had during his 1972 visit to Peking denounced 'conspiracies against the Arabism of the Gulf', a reference to Iran, in 1973 China gave support to Iran in its campaign against 'subversive activity' in the Gulf, i.e. the PFLOAG.[215] When Sālim Rubiyyaᶜ ᶜAlī visited Peking in 1974 he returned to the theme in an apparent attempt to convince his hosts: 'The PDRY supports and aids the people of Oman in their struggle for the realisation of their legitimate objectives', he stated, and he referred to the fact that 'the international situation has become more complicated'.[216] But his host Teng Hsiao-ping did not mention Oman, and, as in 1972, it was not alluded to in the communiqué. Four years later, in 1978, China recognised the Omani Sultanate and later sold it some arms. In 1983 the Chinese Foreign Minister visited Oman as did Vice-Premier Yao Tilin in 1985. No Chinese officials of such rank ever visited the PDRY, the highest-ranking being Li Ximing, Minister of Urban and Rural Construction, who was in Aden in March 1985. Overall, the level of Chinese visitors to the PDRY was inferior not only to that for Oman, but also by comparison with Somalia, the YAR, Kuwait, the Amirates and Iran.

The central issue of disagreement, however, was Soviet influence in the PDRY itself. As early as 1971 Chinese Premier Chou En-lai mentioned the PDRY as one of several countries in which Soviet military influence was increasing.[217] By contrast, Chinese officials and press reports praised the YAR for the measures it had taken after 1970 to reduce its relations with the USSR.[218] China laid stress on measures to reconcile relations between Peninsular states and, more than the USSR, singled out such developments as the YAR–PDRY unity agreement of 1972, the Saudi-PDRY agreement on diplomatic recognition of 1976, the 1982 constitutional agreement between the YAR and the PDRY, and the Omani–PDRY declaration of 1982 as positive developments.[219]

It was with the June 1978 crisis that Chinese coverage of events in the PDRY became markedly more critical. A roundup of international press coverage on the June 1978 crisis commented: 'Articles and commentaries exposing Soviet intervention outright or by implication point out that this crime is aimed at undermining security and stability in the Red Sea and Gulf regions.'[220] The 1979 inter-Yemen war was blamed on Soviet interference:

> Differences between Arab countries, including those that have a historical basis, can be settled through friendly negotiations. But, since the Soviet Union labelled some Arab countries as 'reactionary' and others 'progressive', their differences have been aggravated and have even led to the use of force. It should be noted that in every event which involved bloodshed, the Soviet Union supported one side and opposed the other . . . The Soviet Union has ulterior motives for fanning up the dispute between the two countries.[221]

A later report, on the March 1979 YAR–PDRY unification agreement, went further and provided the fullest analysis hitherto produced of how China viewed the situation in the PDRY. The 1972 unity agreement had, it said, not been realised because of Soviet sowing of dissension between the two Yemens. Signs of inter-Yemeni rapprochement were interrupted in 1978 by the death of the two Presidents: 'It was widely known that the

Soviet KGB and Cuban mercenaries were behind the two deaths', it was claimed.[222] The article argued, against all historical evidence, that the division between North and South Yemen was the result of Britain's having imposed the 1934 Treaty of Taʿif on the Imam, but recalled that resistance to it had continued:

> The smashing of feudal and colonial rule should have provided favourable conditions for national unification. But as soon as the tiger left, the wolf – those who wanted to manipulate the Arabian Peninsula and the Gulf oil resources and control these strategically important areas – came along. Such external forces used a variety of guises to exploit differences and contradictions between tribes, religious factions and political parties. With arms or economic aid as bait or with ideology as a tool, they supported one side against the other. Fishing in troubled waters they tried to establish control through agents in order to stop Yemen's unification.[223]

According to this analysis the Soviet aim was not to promote Yemeni unity but to control the southern entrance to the Red Sea. This was especially the case as, so the article wrongly alleged, the main shipping channel through the Bab al-Mandeb lay between the mainland and the PDRY-controlled island of Perim.

By the end of the 1970s Sino-PDRY divergences affected virtually the whole range of major foreign policy issues: not only did China support Iran and Somalia, but it endorsed Egypt's rapprochement with Israel. China had, by then, warmer diplomatic relations with the YAR and Oman than it had with the PDRY, a preference reflected in the higher ranking of PRC representatives visiting the YAR. From 1974 onwards the pace of diplomatic relations between the two countries slackened. PDRY Foreign Minister Mutiyyaʿ visited Peking in 1977, as did Premier ʿAlī Nāṣir Muḥammad in April 1978, but while the latter did lead to a new economic agreement these were not followed by the signing of joint communiqués as had resulted from the PDRY leaders' visits of the early 1970s. A PDRY envoy despatched to explain the circumstances of the June 1978 events was received by the Chinese; but, from the evidence of Chinese press coverage, his version of events was not accepted.

Yet an element of restraint and continued interest was shown by both sides. Relations between China and South Yemen never reached the point of open animosity evident in the late 1970s in relations between China and such Soviet Third World allies as Cuba, Vietnam, Mongolia, and Afghanistan. The PDRY press abstained from explicit criticisms of China, although the 1978 and 1980 YSP Congresses did not repeat the policy enunciated at earlier Congresses of developing relations with all socialist countries 'without exception'. Inside the PDRY itself, the Chinese experts working on aid programmes continued to be the object of considerable esteem and affection, despite the growing gap in international alignment of the two states.[224] It appears that on only one occasion, a visit to Ethiopia in 1979, did a South Yemeni leader, ʿAbd al-Fattāḥ Ismāʿīl, openly criticise China: this incident was quickly contained. On their side, the Chinese were careful as to the form their criticism took. They did not criticise the PDRY leadership as such, but blamed the USSR and, to a lesser extent, Cuba for developments that China opposed. They pursued a similar policy with regard to Ethiopia. Thus the 1978 leadership crisis in the PDRY and the 1979 inter-Yemeni war were alleged to be the result of Soviet influence, and the Chinese press continued to look for signs of positive development in South Arabia, in the reconciliation of the PDRY with its three neighbours, Saudi Arabia, North Yemen and Oman – in 1976, 1979 and 1982 respectively. Reporting on the improved YAR–PDRY relations of 1982 Chinese reports went out of their way to stress that the PRC did not endorse the activities of the NDF which had, it was said, 'carried out disruptive anti-government activities in some cities of North Yemen'.[225] Chinese emphasis lay, as it had done throughout the post-1967 period, on improvement of relations between the two Yemeni states.

This measure of restraint in Chinese policy became more evident in the 1980s, as China's own hostility to the USSR diminished somewhat and with it hostility to Soviet allies in the Third World. Thus there was some lessening of tension between China and Cuba, and Chinese criticism of Soviet allies in the Third World, Vietnam and Afghanistan excepted, decreased. This was reflected in China's relations with the PDRY. Although from the mid-1970s onwards, the South Yemenis had refrained from statements friendly to China, and made no gestures of appreciation in their party Congress declarations, the Chinese economic commitment endured. In 1983–4 China unilaterally offered to reschedule the PDRY's debt to it, and rebuilt, free of charge, those sections of the Aden–Mukalla highway washed away in the floods of 1982. During the 1986 crisis in the PDRY the Chinese attitude was reserved, in contrast to the coverage of the 1978 crisis, when Moscow had been blamed by China for interfering in South Yemen's affairs. The January 1986 crisis broke out as the Prime Minister and Foreign Minister of the PDRY were on their way to an official visit to China: while they had to abandon this particular visit, PDRY delegation led by the new Prime Minister, Yasin Nuʾman, visited China in March 1987 and signed several economic agreements including one on debt rescheduling.[226] The 1986 crisis appeared, therefore, not to have affected relations between Aden and Peking. It was treated by China as a purely internal matter.

The growing divergence between the PDRY and the PRC arose from the very different situations in which they found themselves, and the resulting difference in the policy requirements of the two states. If China's main preoccupation was its conflict with the USSR, the PDRY was primarily concerned about its conflicts with its neighbours. For a certain period, from 1967 until the early 1970s, Chinese foreign policy also involved opposition to the west, to the USA in particular, and hence support for the radical causes which the PDRY also backed in the region. Even at this time, however, the PDRY refused to follow Chinese urgings all the way and criticise the USSR, because of Aden's need for Soviet military support in its confrontations. But, side by side with this disagreement, the two states, China and South Yemen, did have certain convergent policies from 1967 to 1971. With the changes in Chinese policy attendant upon the end of the Cultural Revolution at home in 1969 and China's 1971 entry into the UN abroad, China ceased to support most guerrilla groups in west Asia and turned instead to the construction of a diplomatic alliance with all those Middle Eastern and Third World states that were opposed to the USSR – South Africa, Israel and South Korea excepted. Thus Iran, Ethiopia and Egypt became states to which China drew closer, and as a result relations with Aden grew cooler. This foreign policy divergence after 1971 therefore compounded China's already existing inability to meet the PDRY's security needs and so to drive the two countries further apart.

This distance was not, however, the product of any specific conflict between the two states, as was the case with, for example, China's relations with Mongolia, Vietnam or Afghanistan, and it did not therefore lead to an overt breach of the kind that occurred between China and these three neighbouring countries. It did, however, confirm an underlying strategic reality of South Yemen's position. The very fact that it was not a country bordering China or in the vicinity meant that China could never have provided military support, in supplies and guarantees, that was available from the USSR. The PDRY was never, for military reasons above all, a candidate for alignment with China against the USSR in the international arena. But, by the same token, the PDRY's alignment with the USSR did not constitute a direct threat to the PRC, in the way that that of the three neighbouring states aligned with Moscow did. Hence China did not feel itself compelled to reach that degree of hostility and breach with Aden that it did reach in dealings with Hanoi, Kabul and Ulan Bator.

Moreover, despite their own differences with each other, and their conflicting policies towards South Yemen, both the USSR and the PRC maintained some common views on the evolution of a radical state in South Arabia. Both the USSR and the PRC established relations with

Aden after some years of experience and influence in the YAR. This anterior commitment both tempered their optimism about the possibilities of change in the South, and gave them an alternative point of contact in the region, one which had, albeit in differing degrees, to be balanced against support for the South. Both warmly welcomed the triumph of the NLF in November 1967, and the further radicalisation of June 1969. Both provided comparatively large sums of economic aid in the most difficult years, up to 1975, when South Yemen was receiving support from almost no other source. Most importantly, Moscow and Peking saw the PDRY as a state that had, in some degree, sought to break away from a predominant western-dominated pattern of international policies, and with which they therefore had some affinity.

Conclusions: revolution and foreign policy

A visitor to South Yemen in the years immediately after independence would soon realise that this was an embattled republic, at once cut off from many of the interactions that states normally experience and at the same time itself committed to radical changes in other states. Few airlines bothered to call at Aden, in contrast to the busy passage of colonial times. The port was almost paralysed, and the great passenger liners no longer landed their droves at Steamer Point. The shops of Tawahi and Crater which had relied on tourism and the British base were depressed. Consumer goods were short. No new buildings were under construction and existing ones were in increasingly poor shape. Few lifts worked. There was no foreign private investment, and foreign aid from governments or multilateral agencies was minimal. Entry into and exit from the PDRY was difficult. A dramatic *caesura* in South Yemen's commercial and political relations with the outside world had taken place. From 1976 onwards, it became an offense for a Yemeni to speak with a non-Yemeni without official approval.

The signs of the republic's own militancy were also not hard to see. On the mile-long avenue of Maala, hitherto housing the families of British servicemen, placards hung outside the offices of guerrilla groups now officially welcomed in Aden – the PFLOAG, the PDFLP and the PFLP. Without such public display, but equally enjoying quasi-diplomatic status were representatives of other guerrilla and opposition groups – Eritreans, North Yemenis, Iranians, Iraqis, Chileans. A visitor to a hotel might find himself accosted by men claiming to have liberated large swathes of southern Ethiopia, or by the representatives of an underground grouping from Saudi Arabia. As time passed, these members of revolutionary movements and parties in the region around South Yemen were joined by the delegations from communist countries and associated solidarity organisations. In particular, the influence of Arab Communist parties – those of Lebanon, Iraq, Egypt and Sudan – came to be greater, that of the radicals of the late 1960s less. Conferences on a wide range of topics related to the Third World development, peace, and 'anti-imperialism' succeeded each other.[1] Aden felt itself to be the promoter of a radical new stand in international relations: it was paying a high price for this commitment, one that not all of its inhabitants felt was worthwhile, but it was itself pursuing this path with the vigour and the resources at its disposal. If the preceding analysis has tried to describe some components of this commitment, these concluding remarks may indicate the broader pattern of which PDRY policies were an example.

The triumph of the NLF in November 1967 led South Yemen into a situation of conflict with its neighbours and with other states of the region, in a pattern of antagonism similar to that which other revolutionary countries have experienced, from France in 1789 onwards. The regional conflicts epitomised the manner in which upheaval in one particular state has implications for the overall pattern of international relations. On the one hand, the very fact of a state having brought about significant social and political change at home can produce conflict in foreign relations: those who have lost power internally either try to regain it from exile and with the support of other states, or seek, from within, to encourage external intervention that will restore that which revolutionary change has taken from them. At the same time, an upheaval in one particular country can be perceived by other states as a threat to their interests, whether through fear that the example of revolution within one state will be reproduced by the population in others, or because the new revolutionary state is, or is believed to be, providing aid to opposition forces beyond its own frontiers.

For its part, the revolutionary state has political reasons for stressing this conflict with its neighbours. As in France in the early 1790s, and China in the 1960s, the militancy of the PDRY's foreign policy was, in part, a reflection of competition between radical factions inside the regime. In addition, such a stance can mobilise support by drawing attention to the continuing threat of 'counter-revolution', of the possible return of those recently expropriated and overthrown. It can portray itself as menaced by foreign invasion and subversion, so that all dissent is portrayed as part of externally backed activity. Moreover, the privations of establishing a new order can be blamed on external hostility. At the same time revolutionary regimes have an interest in the development of comparably radical forces in other states, a concern that goes beyond the mere fact of neutralising or pre-empting those they have themselves removed from power. The very legitimacy of the new regime, as one that issued from a revolution, may be enhanced by declarations of support for radical forces elsewhere. Most importantly, the new regime may feel that its own security can best be guaranteed by the emergence in neighbouring states of regimes like itself, i.e. by the overthrow of foes and the establishment of allied regimes. Thus, faced with the hostility of existing states, the new regime may see that further revolutions provide the means by which it itself can survive: military security, economic co-operation, political support – all can flow from the attempted extension of the revolutionary movement beyond the boundaries of the state where the revolution initially occurred.

Revolutions are almost inevitably international events and such a process involves a partisan statement by each group of protagonists of the causes of the confrontation. The revolutionary state ascribes the conflict to the refusal of neighbouring states and other conservative powers to accept the consequences of the political and social developments within its frontiers. The external opponents of the new regime ascribe their hostility to the latter's insistence on 'exporting' revolution, on extending a process of social change, often involving military activity beyond its own national territory. In fact, both sides can be involved in a two-tiered conflict, protecting their internal political system and at the same time seeking to alter that of the other.

However, certain factors can lessen the apparent deadlock of the initial conflict. Revolutionary regimes have shown themselves surprisingly resilient in resisting invasion and subversion from without, despite the confusion in political and military matters attendant upon revolutions and the often depressed economic conditions and consequent political discontent associated with them. In time, therefore, both those expropriated in the revolution and the states allegedly seeking to restore them to power can be compelled or at least encouraged to accept the permanence of revolutionary change in one specific country. On the other hand, the initial optimism of the revolutionary state about the possibility of revolutions similar to its own occurring in these neighbouring states may prove not to be well-founded. The social and political conditions in the one state may not be reproduced in the second. The very fact of a recent revolution in a region will be likely to lead established states to introduce countervailing measures, whether these be reforms designed to forestall their overthrow, or increased capacities for containing opposition. The fact that one state shows itself, and declares itself, to have an interest in the overthrow of another can make such an overthrow the more difficult to attain. The revolutionary state may be restrained in what it can, in practice, do to assist revolutionary forces elsewhere by the calculation that if it becomes to deeply involved in unrest in another state this may provoke a direct state-to-state conflict in which its own survival may be placed at risk. This calculation was recognised by Robespierre in 1793, Lenin in 1918 and Khomeini in 1988; it guided much of South Yemen's commitment to aiding its Omani and North Yemeni allies.

As a result of such considerations – the survival of the revolutionary state, on the one hand, the containment of revolution elsewhere, on the other – it may be possible for a degree of accommodation between revolutionary and non-revolutionary states to occur. The regime arising out of the upheavals of one country remains in place, but the price of its acceptance by other states is a reduction or termination of its support for other revolutionary movements. Both parts of this process involve profound and very real political forces and policy calculations. The reasons why revolutionary states do seek to extend or 'export' their revolutions, and to offer 'solidarity' to others are substantial, and go beyond the realm of mere enthusiasm and rhetoric. The factors leading them to make later accommodations are equally forceful, and involve some recognition of the limits both of their own power, and of the forces they are supporting. The internationalisation of revolutions and its limits go beyond the surrounding region. A revolutionary regime can seek to realign itself vis-à-vis the predominant forces in international politics, to sunder or weaken the links that it had prior to a revolution and to establish new ones with states more sympathetic to, and supportive of, its goals. Yet such a realignment also has its limits: the bonds that tied it to the formerly dominant powers may not all be broken, in part because beneficial aspects can be retained and renegotiated. Similarly, the new allies may not be able to offer all that the revolutionary state requires, in security and economic support, and may establish boundaries to the kind of alliance that is created. The passage from one 'bloc' to the other may be real enough, but not entail an absolute separation from one and integration with the other, as official presentation might suggest. The degree to which revolutionary regimes can themselves be drawn into rivalries and conflict, evident in Sino-Soviet and Sino-Vietnamese relations, is also evident in the PDRY's uneasy dealings with Ethiopia, Libya and Iraq.

To a considerable extent, this general model has been the path followed by South Yemen in the first decade and a half after independence. The major goal of any foreign policy, the preservation of territorial integrity and of the ruling regime, was successfully carried out. Despite repeated pressures from without, and manifold weaknesses and divisions within, South Yemen was not overrun by its opponents, and the NF and its successor organisations retained power. At the same time, a wide-ranging reorganisation of the country's polity, economy and society took place, in part to reduce the influence upon them of external forces deemed by the Front to be hostile. The ruling party proclaimed and sustained a number of policies for which it had to pay a high price and from which other states sought to deflect it: support for revolutionary groups in neighbouring and other regional states, and alliance with the USSR and its bloc.

This foreign policy orientation was not, however, as complete or sustained as initial hopes in South Yemen would have indicated. The lessening of external influences upon the country itself was only partly successful, in that the country remained critically reliant on imports of goods and inflows of capital for its economic prosperity and growth. The very location of South Yemen, in an Arabian Peninsula the majority of whose states were enjoying a consumer boom derived from oil revenues, made isolation and austerity all the more difficult to sustain. The tensions involved in such a balancing contributed greatly to the 1986 crisis. At the same time, the models according to which the PDRY did transform its society were ones that, to a considerable degree, reproduced those of other countries, in the Soviet bloc. The commitment to revolution elsewhere, enduring as it was, had limited results: the forces supported by the PDRY in both Oman and North Yemen were defeated, and those initially backed in Ethiopia and Iran were themselves to fall victim to other tendencies within those countries' revolutions. But the upheavals in the region did provide the PDRY with new, albeit uncertain, interlocutors, and in the calculus of revolution and counter-revolution, the PDRY was able to offset its failure to back successful revolution against recognition and acceptance by the other states in the region.

The accommodations of the early 1980s were therefore a reflection of an overall limitation of the revolutionary trend in the South Arabian region, but involved, at the same time, a consolidation of the post-revolutionary regime in the one state where the old order had been most completely overthrown. Such a survival was not itself, however, a necessarily enduring achievement, since internal pressures and conflicts, enhanced by external factors, led to a series of bloody intra-regime crises. The validity of the old revolutionary view, that the survival and development of the South Yemeni revolutionary regime could not be assured as long as other states in the Peninsular had not themselves been through such transformations, appeared, in the light of the crisis of 1986, to retain some validity.

APPENDIX 1. TEXT OF AGREEMENT ON YEMENI UNITY, 28 OCTOBER 1972

The two Governments of the Yemen Arab Republic and the People's Democratic Republic of Yemen:

In the name of the one Yemeni people, and in the name of the Arab nation, arising from the reality of historical responsibility and national responsibility; in the belief that the people of Yemen and their land is one single entity which is indivisible and that this reality has confirmed itself across history, in spite of all efforts to strengthen separatism, create barriers and borders;

In fulfilment of the sacrifice and the struggle of the Yemeni people across history in eradicating the backward monarchical imamate system in the North of the country and imperialist domination in the South; being anxious to strengthen and consolidate the progressive national struggle in Yemen; stressing that the unity of Yemen is the foundation for the building of the modern Yemeni society; assuring democratic freedoms for all national forces which are hostile to imperialism and Zionism and are the foundation for the building of an independent national economy; to safeguard the independence and sovereignty of Yemen from any interference or external aggression; stressing that comprehensive Yemeni unity is also the cause of inevitable destiny, the cause of progress, civilization and prosperity for the Yemeni people, being confident that the comprehensive unity of Yemen, in addition to its being the hope of every Yemeni throughout the land of Yemen, is a basic need to strengthen the pillars of political independence and the building of an independent national economy and is a national necessity because it enables Yemen to participate in the struggle waged by the Arab nation against the imperialist-Zionist alliance, and also represents an earnest measure for the realization of the Arab nation as a whole . . .

. . . The two Governments have agreed to set up a unified state, joining the parts of Yemen, North and South, and this in accordance with stipulations and principles set out below:

Principles and stipulations for the setting up of Yemeni Unity between the Yemen Arab Republic and the People's Democratic Republic of Yemen:

Article 1: Unity shall be set up between the two states of the Yemen Arab Republic and the People's Democratic Republic of Yemen in which shall be dissolved the statal personality of each one into one single statal personality, and the formation of a single Yemeni state.

Article 2: The new state shall have: (i) One flag and one motto; (ii) one capital; (iii) One presidency; (iv) One legislative, executive and judicial system.

Article 3:

(i) The governmental system of the new state shall be a democratic, national republican system.
(ii) The Constitution of the union shall guarantee all general personal and political freedoms for all members of the public and for all their organisations and institutions, national, professional and trade unionist. All necessary measures will be undertaken to ensure the enjoyment of these freedoms.
(iii) The union state guarantees that all the achievements of the two revolutions of September and October shall be safeguarded.

Article 4: As a first step towards the realisation of the union, necessary measures are to be taken to hold a summit meeting for the two Presidents of the two States to examine necessary and immediate measures to complete the union, on condition that the meeting is held at a time determined by the two Presidents of the two Governments.

Article 5: Each of the two Presidents shall choose his personal representative to supervise the work of the technical committees mentioned in Article No. 7.

Article 6: The Arab League shall continue to give necessary assistance for the success of this union and in accordance with the desire of the two States.

Article 7: The summit meeting of the two States shall set up joint technical committees, with an equal number of members from representatives of the two States, to unify the present institutions and statutes in each one of the two States. A period of not more than a year shall be defined for the completion of tasks entrusted to these committees. The year shall begin from the signing of this agreement.

Article 8: The technical committees shall be formed from representatives of the two States on a high-level and from specialists. These committees will be allowed to set up sub-committees to facilitate their work. These committees shall be:

(i) Committee for constitutional affairs, and it shall concern itself with drawing up a Constitution.
(ii) Committee for foreign affairs and diplomatic and consular representation, and it shall concern itself with the unification of the foreign policy of the two countries and drawing up the bases for the foreign policy of the new unified state.
(iii) Committee for economic and financial affairs, and it shall concern

itself with economic matters, customs, economic development and a unified currency system and the budget of the state.

(iv) Committee for legislative and judicial affairs, and it shall concern itself with the unification of laws and the drawing up of unified institutions for the judiciary.

(v) Education, culture and information committee, which will be concerned with educational, cultural and information affairs in all their aspects.

(vi) The military affairs committee, which will be concerned with defence and the armed forces and their unification.

(vii) The health affairs committee, which will be concerned with medical affairs, hospitals and so forth.

(viii) Committee for adminstrative and public service, which will be concerned with the arrangement of local government, state services and their operations.

Article 9: After the completion of the draft Constitution by the constitutional affairs committee, the proposals will be forwarded to the appropriate legislative councils of the two States, to be approved in accordance with the constitutional arrangements of the two sides.

Article 10:

(i) The two Presidents of the two States, under the mandate of the two legislative authorities in the two parts, will arrange a referendum for the Constitution and elections to a unified legislative authority for the new state in accordance with the new Constitution.

(ii) To implement this the two Presidents of the two countries will form a joint ministerial committee, whose membership will include the two Interior Ministers of the two parts, so that they can supervise this work, this to be effected within six months from the date the legislative authorities in the two States approve the draft Constitution. This committee will have the necessary mandate to carry out its duties.

(iii) The Presidents of the two States will invite the Arab League to send representatives to participate in the work of the committee.

Article 11: The legislative councils in the two States will be dissolved immediately after the approval of the new draft Constitution in a popular referendum.

Article 12: When the people approve the draft Constitution, a new state will be proclaimed, in accordance with the Constitution.

Article 13: The rules of the new Constitution will operate immediately after the approval of the Constitution.

Article 14: Implementing what was contained in the statement of the

Arab League mediation committee and complying with the rules of the previous articles, the two parts hereby decide on their total commitment to these provisions and their implementation.

Article 15: Three copies were made of this document. Each side received a copy and the third copy will be kept at the Arab League headquarters.

This document was signed by representatives entrusted for the purpose.

Signing for the Yemen Arab Republic were: Muhsin al-Ayni, the Chairman of the Council of Ministers and Foreign Minister; and Ahmad Jabir Afif, the Minister of Education and Instruction.

Signing for the People's Democratic Republic of Yemen, were Ali Nasir Muhammad, the Chairman of the Council of Ministers and Defence Minister; and Abdullah al-Khamri, member of the Central Committee and Minister of Information.

For the Arab mediation committee: Muhammad Salim al-Yafi, the Chairman of the Committee and Assistant Secretary General of the Arab League; Ibrahim al-Mazhudi, the permanent representative of the People's Democratic Republic of Algeria to the Arab League; Saʾad ad-Din Nuwayrat, the Ambassador of the People's Democratic Republic of Algeria to Sanaʿa; the permanent representative of Kuwait to the Arab League, Hasan Fahmi Abd al-Majid.

This agreement was signed at the headquarters of the General Secretariat of the Arab League on Saturday 21st of Ramadan, 1392, or 28th October 1972.

Source: ME/4133/A/10–13, 1 November 1972; Arabic in Ahmad Jabir Afif, pp. 453–60; SWB translation amended in light of latter.

APPENDIX 2. TEXT OF JOINT KSA–PDRY STATEMENT ON DIPLOMATIC RELATIONS, 10 MARCH 1976

In the Name of God, the All Merciful, the All Compassionate. Proceeding from the spirit of Islamic and Arab fraternity between the two fraternal peoples in the Kingdom of Saudi Arabia and the PDRY; out of a desire to create an atmosphere of mutual understanding to serve their causes and those of the Arabian Peninsula and the entire Arab nation; out of their concern to establish normal relations between them; in affirmation of the importance of safeguarding and consolidating relations among all the states of the region in an atmosphere of mutual respect for the sovereignty of every state over its territory; relations between the two countries were reviewed in the present circumstances which are marked by the Zionist aggression, by foreign interferences and the colonialist activities, in all shapes and forms, in the Arab area in general and the Arabian Peninsula in particular.

In response to the aspirations of the peoples of the two countries towards the best of fraternal and cordial relations and mutual co-operation between them, on the one hand, and between them and their brothers in the Arabian Peninsula on the other hand – the aspirations which are consolidated by religious, historic and cultural ties and by the common destiny; in response to the aspirations of the two fraternal peoples towards progress, prosperity and peace for themselves and security and stability for the Arabian Peninsula; so that they may devote their efforts to opposing the Zionist aggression and to preventing foreign interferences which do harm to the safety and security of the region, they declare their intention to establish normal relations between them on the basis of Arab fraternity, good-neighbourliness, the unity of destiny and non-interference in internal affairs, in a manner that realizes the security and stability of the Arabian Peninsula and the interests of the Arab nation, away from foreign interference.

They also assert their two countries' determination: to have fruitful co-operation in the economic, cultural and other fields, in a manner that ensures their stability and the progress and prosperity of their peoples; to take all the steps necessary for this; and to put an end to various differences between them.

Source: ME/5156/A/8–9, 11 March 1976.

APPENDIX 3. AUTHOR'S INTERVIEW WITH MUḤAMMAD SĀLIḤ MUṬIYYAᶜ, PDRY FOREIGN MINISTER, NOVEMBER 1977

Q. Why is the PDRY pursuing a policy of Yemeni unity?

A. Yemen is one country. Before the advent of imperialism there was nothing called 'South Arabia'. It was the British who divided the area and created something called 'South Arabia'. Then nationalists began to call this country 'Yemeni South', and a political struggle developed as to whether we were or were not part of the Yemen. The nationalists stressed the 'Yemeni-ness' [*al-yamaniyya*] of this country.

Q. If your goal is Yemeni unity, what kind of unity will this be?

A. We are not just one people, we also have social differences between us. The Northerners have their own conception of unity and they tried to impose it, using their army, in the war of September 1972. We then came together with them in the committees set up after the Tripoli Conference, and we advanced our conception of unity in these committees. Any unity work must be under the control of the left. In the past, the Northern regime was stronger than us, but now we are stronger than them. So unity has become a progressive slogan. This is evident from seeing who opposes unity – the Saudis do, since they fear that ten million Yemenis would be the strongest country in the Peninsula.

Q. Is unity possible without a revolution in the North?

A. Yes, it is. There is more than one way to achieve unity. Armed struggle is not the only one. We can use all possible means.

Q. There was guerrilla opposition in the North in the early 1970s. Why did it end?

A. This was not a matter for us to decide. It was up to the organisations in the North.

Q. What is happening in the unity committees?

A. A lot of talking, but not much action. For example, the economic committee decided to set up a joint public sector and co-operatives, but these decisions were not implemented. On the other hand, a number of decisions have been taken which have not been made public.

Q. Is the fact that Kamaran Island was seized by the YAR in the 1972 war an issue between you?

A. It is not a problem. It is Yemeni. The North has it.

Q. What about the issue of the three provinces taken by Saudi Arabia in 1934?

A. We did not discuss this with the Saudis. The problem is one for the YAR to take up.

Q. When did you begin discussions with Saudi Arabia on establishing diplomatic relations? Was the death of King Feisal in 1975 a factor?

A. The negotiations began in 1974. King Feisal's death was not important – talks had begun before that.

Q. And what conditions were laid down before the diplomatic relations could be established?

A. We do not want to antagonise the Saudis. It was *they* who would not recognise *us*, and it was they who stopped their attacks on us. They decided they wanted to discuss with us, and by the end of 1975 the hostile radio broadcasts had ceased.

Q. But the PDRY media, which formerly attacked Saudi Arabia, have also stopped doing so.

A. We have made mutual concessions. Neither side is to attack the other.

Q. What about Oman? Was this not also a subject of negotiation between you and the Saudis?

A. We tell the Saudis to get the Iranians out. We are prepared to have relations with Oman if (a) the Iranians get out and (b) there is an agreement between the Popular Front and the regime. Then South Yemen will talk to Qabus. The Front is weak now, so Qabus could find agreement with it, if he was clever enough.

Q. And what about border clashes? It seems you have at least agreed to stop shelling across the frontier, a cease-fire agreement.

A. There has been no cease-fire agreement on the border, since we were never involved. The bombardments along the frontier were the work of the PFLO. The Iranians had occupied strategic areas along the frontier, and the Front then stopped its activities there. That is why there has been talk of a 'cease-fire'.

Q. What is the state of your relations with the Gulf states?

A. Only with Kuwait do we have diplomatic relations. But we often sit with people from the Gulf – the Amirates are the easiest.

Q. But in 1971 you refused to recognise these states, and now you seem to have changed your position.

A. We existed as an independent state before they did, and it should be our choice when diplomatic relations are established. We said in 1971 that their independence was fake, and the fact is that this is still so. The British are still there – you can see that the moment you get off the plane. It is only the oil that gives them the appearance of independence. We also have the problem of not having sufficient numbers of Foreign Ministry personnel, and we do not need to have formal recognition to deal with them.

Q. In the mid-1970s there was a crisis in your relations with Iraq. Why was this?

A. The issue with Iraq was that in 1975 it proposed a Gulf Security Pact to Iran.

Q. Was there also the fact that the Iraqi Baᶜthi tried to interfere in the PDRY?

A. No. Baᶜth is very weak in the PDRY. There was no interference, and this was not a factor.

Q. What about Iran? Have you had any contacts with it?

A. None, except via Saudi Arabia over the pilot shot down last year.

Q. There appears to be some difference between your position on Israel and that of the USSR. The Soviet Union advocates a two-state solution. You refuse to accept the legitimacy of an Israeli state.

A. The USSR can adopt whatever position it wants on this issue. Our view on the Palestinian question is clear: we accept what the Palestinians accept.

Q. One issue that has arisen recently is that of Perim Island. It has been claimed that the PDRY agreed to lease this island to Egypt.

A. There was never such an agreement. Reports about it were lies. There has been no Egyptian presence on Perim, and we have not been paid anything for this.

Q. Are you willing to open diplomatic relations with the USA?

A. There are no problems from our side. But others may stop them. I met Secretary of State Vance in New York recently, and he may send a delegation here.

Q. What about the UK? Can relations with them improve?

A. The UK does not want to help us. Trade relations have grown, but there has been no reaction on their side. They have a large embassy here, but they seem to spend a lot of time diffusing calumnies about us.

Q. Despite your close relations with the USSR you do not have a Treaty of Friendship and Co-operation with them. Why?

A. We have no such treaty with the Soviet Union because we do not think that such treaties strengthen relations. Look at what happened in Egypt.

Q. Have you given the Soviet Union naval bases in the PDRY?

A. There are no Soviet naval bases here. They said the same things about Somalia as they said about us. But in Somalia's case they proved it with photographs. They have not been able to do that in our case.

Q. How are your relations with China? Are there not significant disagreements with it?

A. There are no problems between us and China. Premier ʿAlī Nāṣir Muḥammad is going there in April of next year. We do not discuss differences of opinion with them.

Q. What is your view of the situation in Ethiopia, and in particular on the question of Eritrea?

A. The Eritrean revolution must not be an obstacle to the Ethiopian revolution as a whole. The Eritreans must reach some agreement with the Ethiopians. The Eritreans must now see that they have to negotiate – they cannot capture Asmara. We are not against Eritrean independence, *if* the Ethiopians agree.

Q. What about Somalia? It is now at war with Ethiopia. You have previously had good relations with Mogadishu, and now you have good relations with Ethiopia. What is your policy here?

A. Somalia cannot take a long war. They are three millions to the Ethiopian's thirty millions. In the end, we think the Somalis will negotiate if they are defeated. The Somalis want us to be with them only, and most Arab states take Somalia's side. But the Somalis are misleading the Arabs about what is happening there. We Yemenis say: you have to negotiate, since you are going to have to live with them for a long time to come. The irony is that the Somalis were favourable to Mengistu before he came to power: it was they who advised us and the Soviet Union to deal with him. The Somalis are now talking about the Western Somalia Liberation Front: but the WSLF just consists of external delegations. The Somalis even arrested them all in 1973–4. We are concerned about the situation there, not least because there are Yemenis living in both Ethiopia and Somalia.

Q. Fidel Castro made a visit here to try and arrange a federation of states in the region. Were you included in this?

A. Castro tried to say to the Somalis that the Ethiopian revolution was just starting, and they should try to solve their differences in a peaceful war. He thought we should all try to help the revolution in Ethiopia. The Ethiopians suggested a federation of Ethiopia, Somalia and Eritrea, but the PDRY was not included in such proposals.

Q. Can the Russians put pressure on Somalia?

A. The Russians have not been able to hold Somalia back. We in the PDRY warned the Russians about this, but they gave bad advice to Mengistu about their ability to restrain Somalia.

Q. Your government has been extensively criticised in the west for human rights violations. In 1975 you invited a delegation from Amnesty International to visit the PDRY: but relations between you and Amnesty have now ceased, and you refuse to reply to their letters. Why is this?

A. We gave Amnesty facilities and received them. But they began to interfere in political issues. So, we shall not reply to them or talk to them. We are a developing country and a developing revolution. There are threats to our revolution, and people are in prison according to the law.

APPENDIX 4. TREATY OF FRIENDSHIP AND CO-OPERATION BETWEEN THE USSR AND THE PEOPLE'S DEMOCRATIC REPUBLIC OF YEMEN, NOVEMBER 1979

The Union of Soviet Socialist Republics and the People's Democratic Republic of Yemen,

Believing that the further development and strengthening of the relations of friendship and all-round co-operation which have taken shape between them meet the fundamental national interests of the peoples of both countries and serve the cause of consolidating peace and security throughout the world;

Desiring to lend every assistance to the development of peaceful relations among states and fruitful international co-operation;

Determined to promote the socio-economic achievements of the peoples of the Union of Soviet Socialist Republics and the People's Democratic Republic of Yemen, and to come out in favour of unity and co-operation between all forces struggling for peace, national independence, democracy and social progress;

Inspired by the ideals of struggle against imperialism, colonialism and racism in all their forms and manifestations;

Attaching great importance to co-operation between both countries in working for a just and lasting peace in the Middle East;

Reaffirming their adherence to the objectives and principles of the charter of the United Nations Organisation, including the principles of respect for sovereignty, territorial integrity and non-interference in internal affairs;

Desiring to develop and strengthen the existing relations of friendship and co-operation between the two countries;

Have agreed as follows:

ARTICLE 1

The high contracting parties solemnly declare their resolve to strengthen the unbreakable friendship between the two countries and steadfastly develop political relations and all-round co-operation on the basis of equality, respect for national sovereignty, territorial integrity and non-interference in each other's internal affairs.

ARTICLE 2

The high contracting parties will co-operate closely and comprehensively in ensuring conditions for the safeguarding and the further development of the socio-economic gains of their peoples and respect for the sovereignty of each of them over all their natural resources.

ARTICLE 3

The high contracting parties will exert efforts for strengthening and expanding mutually-advantageous economic, scientific and technical co-operation between them. Towards this end, the parties will develop and deepen co-operation in the spheres of industry, agriculture, fishing, the use of natural resources, the planning of economic development and in other economic spheres, as well as in the training of local personnel. The parties will expand trade and navigation on the basis of the principles of equality, mutual advantage and most-favoured-nation treatment.

ARTICLE 4

The high contracting parties will contribute to the development of co-operation and the exchange of experience in the fields of science, culture, the arts, literature, education, health, the press, radio, television, cinema, tourism, sports and other fields.

The sides will contribute to the developments of contacts and co-operation between the organs of state power, trade unions and other mass organisations and also to the extension of direct ties between industrial enterprises and cultural research institutions for the purpose of gaining a more profound knowledge of the life, work, experience and achievements of the peoples of the two countries. Both sides will stimulate the development of contacts between the working people of the two countries.

ARTICLE 5

The high contracting parties will continue to develop co-operation in the military field on the basis of the relevant agreements concluded between them for the purpose of strengthening their defence capability.

ARTICLE 6

The Union of Soviet Socialist Republics respects the policy of non-alignment pursued by the People's Democratic Republic of Yemen, which constitutes a major factor in the development of international co-operation and peaceful coexistence.

The People's Democratic Republic of Yemen respects the peaceful foreign policy pursued by the Union of Soviet Socialist Republics, which is aimed at strengthening friendship and co-operation with all countries and peoples.

ARTICLE 7

The high contracting parties will continue to make every effort to protect international peace and the security of the peoples, for further relaxation of international tension, for spreading détente to all regions of the world, for its realisation in the concrete forms of mutually-beneficial co-operation between states, for the settlement of international disputes by peaceful means in order to make the principle of renouncing the use of force an effective law of international life, and for the elimination from international relations of all manifestations of the policy of hegemonism and expansionism. The parties will actively promote the cause of general and complete disarmament, including nuclear disarmament, under effective international control.

ARTICLE 8

The high contracting parties will continue a vigorous struggle against imperialist encroachments in order to eradicate colonialism and racism in all their forms and manifestations.

The parties will co-operate with each other and with other peace-loving states in support of the just struggle of peoples for their freedom, independence, sovereignty and social progress.

ARTICLE 9

The high contracting parties will make every effort to ensure a lasting and just peace in the Middle East and the achievement, for this purpose, of a comprehensive Middle East settlement.

ARTICLE 10

The high contracting parties will contribute to the development of co-operation between Asian states, to the establishment of peaceful and good-neighbourly relations and mutual confidence between them, and to the creation of an effective security system in Asia through co-operative efforts of all states on that continent.

ARTICLE 11

The high contracting parties will consult each other on major international questions directly affecting the interests of the two countries.

In case situations arise which threaten peace or violate international peace, the parties will strive to enter into contact with each other without delay for the purpose of co-ordinating their positions in the interests of removing a threat to peace or restoring peace.

ARTICLE 12

Each of the high contracting parties solemnly declares that it will not enter into military or other alliances and will not take part in any groupings of states or actions and undertakings directed against the other high contracting party.

ARTICLE 13

The high contracting parties declare that the provisions of this treaty do not contradict their commitments under the international treaties now in force and undertake not to conclude any international agreements incompatible with this treaty.

ARTICLE 14

Any question which may arise between the high contracting parties as regards the interpretation or application of any provision of this treaty will be settled on a bilateral basis in the spirit of friendship, mutual respect and understanding.

ARTICLE 15

The treaty will be in force for 20 years from the day of its enactment.

If neither of the high contracting parties gives notice, six months before the expiration of this period of its wish to terminate the treaty, it will remain in force for another five years and will be prolonged each time for another five-year period unless either of the high contracting parties gives written notice of its intention to terminate it six months before the expiration of the respective five-year period.

ARTICLE 16

The treaty is subject to ratification and will come into force on the day of the exchange of instruments of ratification, which will be done in Aden.

Done in Moscow this 25th day of October, 1979, in duplicate, in the Russian and Arabic languages, both texts being equally authentic.

Source: Soviet News, 13 November 1979.

APPENDIX 5. THE OMAN–PDRY AGREEMENT ON NORMALISATION OF RELATIONS, THE 'KUWAIT AGREEMENT OF PRINCIPLES', 15 NOVEMBER 1982

Out of fraternal feeling and sincere willingness to develop normal relations between the PDRY and the Sultanate of Oman, an extended meeting of experts and Ministers of Foreign Affairs was held between 23rd October and 27th October 1982. Those who participated in the meeting were a delegation from the PDRY led by the Foreign Affairs Minister, Dr Abd al-Aziz ad-Dali, and the delegation of the Sultanate of Oman led by the Minister of State for Foreign Affairs, Yusuf al-Alawi Abdullah. Also participating were the UAA delegation led by Abd ar-Rahman aj-Jarwan, Under the Secretary of the Foreign Affairs Ministry, and Sabah al-Ahmad al-Jabir as-Sabah, the Deputy Prime Minister and Minister of Foreign Affairs and Information, who led the Kuwait delegation. [The meeting was held] in the light of the meeting between PDRY and Oman delegations in the presence of a delegation representing the State of Kuwait between 3rd July–7th July 1982. Many meetings were held to review the agenda which included the following items:

1. Agreeing to abstain from interference in internal affairs, and mutual respect for national sovereignty and the border issue.
2. The presence of foreign bases.
3. Media campaigns.
4. Exchanging diplomatic representation.

In an absolutely frank and responsible atmosphere the conferees discussed all the items on the agenda, bearing in mind the urgent need to establish good-neighbourly and co-operative relations between the two neighbours. From this, the following was reached.

1. The two countries are committed to establishing normal relations based on mutual respect, non-interference in domestic affairs and respect for the national sovereignty of both countries, good-neighbourly relations and co-operation in the interests of the two peoples. Moreover, the two sides agreed to solve their differences through peaceful means and not allow any hostile act – that could cause stability and security to deteriorate – to emanate from the territory of either side.

As the two countries stress that neither has any ambitions towards any other territory, the two sides agreed to form a technical committee with the participation of Kuwait and the UAA so that all pertinent documents can be reviewed to reach a permanent solution to the border issue between the two neighbouring countries, in accordance with the borders of the two countries as at 30th November 1967.

2. As for the presence of foreign bases, the two sides agreed not to allow any foreign forces to use their territories for aggression or provocation against the other country.

3. As for media campaigns, the two sides agreed to stop all media campaigns by radio, television and press and all official forms of propaganda and publication against the other.

4. Exchange of diplomatic representation. The two sides stressed the need to improve bilateral relations and open new [fruitful spheres] for co-operation. An agreement was therefore reached on the principle of political relations, to develop [bilateral] relations so that the establishment of relations can be announced after bilateral contacts.

In accordance with this, the two sides agreed to sign this agreement and emphasised that they will be fully committed to the princples mentioned when the two countries ratify them on 15th November 1982, with the aim of turning over a new leaf in the relations between the two countries.

[Signed] Abd al-Aziz ad-Dali, head of the PDRY delegation and Minister of State for Foreign Affairs; Yusuf al-Alawi Abdullah, head of the Oman delegation and Minister of State for Foreign Affairs; Shaykh Sabah al-Ahmad al-Jabir as-Sabah, head of the Kuwait delegation, Deputy Prime Minister, Minister of Foreign Affairs and Information; Abd ar-Rahman aj-Jarwan, head of the UAA delegation and Under Secretary of the Foreign Affairs Ministry.

Kuwait, 27th October 1982.

Source: ME/7184/A/9–10, 1 November 1982.

APPENDIX 6. AUTHOR'S INTERVIEW WITH ʿALĪ NĀṢIR MUḤAMMAD, PRESIDENT OF THE PDRY, MARCH 1983

Q. Last October, after many years of conflict, you agreed to the establishment of diplomatic relations with Oman. You had previously laid down a number of conditions for agreeing to such a recognition, yet, in the end, it does not appear that these were met. How do you see the current state of your relations with the Sultanate?

A. We are now starting to normalise our relations with Oman. They have said in the past that it is because of the policies of the PDRY that there is a US presence in Oman, and the manoeuvres held there by the US Rapid Deployment Force. Now that we have recognised Oman, these excuses no longer hold: yet immediately after we announced the agreement between us, they held further joint manoeuvres with the Americans. Oman is now in a weak position, as it cannot convince its own people or the other countries of the Gulf Co-operation Council of the legitimacy of what it is doing. I recently met some representatives of the GCC and they all said that the stand of the PDRY was correct, and that Oman was mistaken in continuing to carry out such manoeuvres.

Overall, we think that the declaration of principles with Oman was a correct one. It expressed the will of our people: the decision was taken collectively, by the Central Committee of the Party and by the Supreme People's Council. It placed the PDRY in a favourable position in the region, and in the eyes of Arab and world opinion. The PDRY wants peace, and we think that our overall position has been strengthened as a result of this agreement.

The change in Oman is also a response to the will of its people and this is what we have said to the PFLO. We have relations both with Somalia, and with the liberation movements of Somalia. The same is true of our relations with Sudan and even with Iraq. We have relations with ʿAlī ʿAbd Allāh Ṣāliḥ in the North, and with the NDF. So normalisation of relations with Oman does not mean that we have taken a step away from supporting popular movements in the Arabian Peninsula. What we cannot do is be a substitute [*badil*] for them.

Q. When did this process of normalisation with Oman begin?

A. It really began with the resolutions of the Fifth Congress of UPONF, in October 1975. We now hope that following from the declaration of principles it will be possible to exchange diplomatic representatives and to solve the problem of defining our frontiers, through an international agreement. We are insisting on all this going ahead: it is the Omanis who are hesitating to move towards normalisation. We think embassies can be exchanged before any agreement on borders is reached. There are, after all, a lot of border problems within the GCC – Oman has not resolved its border conflict with the Amirates and Saudi Arabia, and there are quite a few others, such as those between Saudi Arabia and Kuwait, the Amirates and Saudi Arabia, Qatar and Bahrain, Iraq and Saudi Arabia, and Kuwait and Iraq. If we had made agreement on borders a condition of opening diplomatic relations with Saudi Arabia, we would have made no progress in resolving our problems. We think we can open embassies and continue discussions on remaining problems.

Q. It is now four years since the fall of the monarchy in Iran. How do you evaluate the Iranian revolution?

A. In general terms, the Iranian revolution is a positive development. We supported the revolution from the beginning and we consider its success to have been a success for us. It is also a success for the Arab liberation movement and for the Palestinian revolution. The liberation movement in the Middle East has recently lost Egypt and, while that loss cannot ever be made up, the Iranian revolution provides some degree of compensation. The success of the revolution is against Zionism and imperialism. We do not want to talk about the mistakes of the revolution – these are an internal matter and can be solved by the Iranian people themselves. We in the PDRY are with them. Unfortunately, the majority of the Arabs did not understand why this revolution came about but without the war these problems could have been solved.

We have expressed our view that there should be a peaceful solution and resolution of the remaining problems. At one point, it would have been possible to resolve these problems through discussion: continuation of the war is in the interests only of imperialism and Zionism, and the losses suffered by Iraq have cost the Arab world considerably. Our view is that, as with Ethiopia, the Arab world should take seriously the question of its relations with the Iranian revolution. On the other hand, Iran cannot change the situation inside Iraq: the opposition in Iraq consists of over fifteen parties, and it is not up to another country to dictate what happens there. The Iranians need allies, and I told them frankly, when I met Prime Minister Musavi, of our views on this matter.

Overall, I must repeat: this was a revolution of the oppressed, and we hope it will succeed.

Q. What is the state of your relations with North Yemen, four years after the signing of the Kuwait unity agreement?

A. Discussions are continuing to achieve the unity of the Yemeni people, but there are a lot of problems on the way. Reactionary forces in the region will not allow this to be achieved, nor will US imperialism. Relations between North and South Yemen are seen as concerning the security of the whole region: Saudi Arabia considers Sanaʿa to be on its front line.

After the 1972 war we signed an agreement on unity, saying it would take effect in one year at most. Eleven years have now passed. At that time, when Muhsin al-Aini was Prime Minister in the North, there were forces within the country that stood against us, and his government fell within a month. These forces were against unity, against dialogue and against the work of the specialist committees set up: the result was that nothing happened.

There is a widespread atmosphere in favour of dialogue now in West Asia, and this is in the interests of South Yemen and of our people. Time is on our side: it is important to continue this dialogue, through summits, communications and meetings of the unity committees, and through the convening of the Supreme Yemeni Council. There should be continuing dialogue on economic co-ordination, to overcome the problems caused by imperialism and reaction. These latter forces are against discussions between North and South and used to make use of the conflict between us in the Central Region of the YAR to further their own interests. Many people benefited from these troubles, including reactionary elements in the North Yemeni government. Dialogue is the benefit of our people and our revolution.

Last year we faced a serious threat from a plan involving the YAR, Saudi Arabia, Oman and Egypt to overthrow the government of the PDRY. This began during Sadat's time and involved a joint operation by Oman, Saudi Arabia and North Yemen. It began with the detonation of explosives by agents who came from Saudi Arabia through North Yemen: the aim was to blow up the oil refinery in Aden and sow confusion among the people, at which point a military operation would start. Officials in the North instructed their embassies that the YAR was going to war with the PDRY, and I received a telephone message from ʿAlī ʿAbd Allāḥ Sāliḥ saying that this was the case. In the end, we caught the saboteurs and put them on trial, and, after the death of Sadat, Mubarak gave instructions for the operation to be called off. He used this issue to indicate that he would not simply follow the policies pursued by Sadat.

Q. How do you evaluate your own position as leader of the PDRY?

A. I was active in the MAN from 1961 onwards, and was involved in military work during the period of armed struggle. At the Fourth Congress in March 1968 I was elected to the General Command of the Front, and in 1969 became first Minister of the Interior and then Minister of Defence. I joined the Politburo in 1970 and have been Prime Minister since 1971.

After Sālim Rubiyyaᶜ ᶜAlī fell, I became President for a few months until December when ᶜAbd al-Fattāḥ Ismāᶜīl was elected to this post: for perhaps the first time in the Third World someone left the highest position in his country without a *coup* or without being killed. We respect the party system in our country, and someone comes to a position like mine only through the closest relations with party and people. As Secretary-General of the Party and President I am happy to say that the situation in our country is improving: we are increasing production, and for the first time are fulfilling our plan targets on schedule. The independence celebrations last October were the most successful and impressive we have ever held.

APPENDIX 7. THE YSP AND FOREIGN RELATIONS: EXTRACTS FROM REPORT OF ᶜALĪ AL-BĪḌ, GENERAL SECRETARY OF THE YSP TO GENERAL CONFERENCE, JUNE 1987

5 *The Yemeni national issue and the struggle of our Party for the reunification of the Yemeni homeland*

The issue of the unity of our Yemeni people, and the elimination of the painful division and conditions suffered by our people in both parts, was and remains one of the most important and prominent issues of destiny. It has been given and is still given all the attention of our Party: the Party has always placed it among its priorities and in the forefront of its struggle for the realisation of those strategic aims of the Yemeni revolution represented by total liberation, social progress and firm unity on a peaceful and democratic basis. It is this unity that should bring to reality the aspirations and cherished hopes of Yemeni toilers to build their new life devoid of injustice, oppression and exploitation of man by man. From this starting point our Party has always been concerned to unite its efforts with all the best and good forces in the Yemeni national arena. We have been and still are linked with them in the struggle for accomplishing this great aim of our people and in realising the unity of the Yemeni homeland – land and people – on a peaceful and democratic basis.

During the past years our party has exerted persistent efforts in a sincere manner with the brothers in the Northern part of the homeland. Together we have been able to realise tangible unity steps which were blessed by our people in both parts. In this direction it must be stated that what has been realised is still below our aspirations. Thus, grave tasks await us and they require joint struggle and efforts along with our brothers in Sanaʿa to attain the aspired goals that correspond to the interests of our people in security, stability, unity, progress and prosperity.

The Central Committee of our Party at its plenums convened after the *coup* conspiracy and before the convening of this Party Conference accorded great attention to the Yemeni national issue. It adopted the measures necessary to realise further steps starting from the mutual confidence shared by our brothers in the North and the results obtained to this day. Foremost among these were the results of the Unity Agreement of 1972, the Tripoli Declaration and the Kuwait Agreement of 1979 and other results that were realised subsequently. All of this requires of the leadership of the two parts continuation of work in the spirit of the joint agreement and statements and of joint co-operation. We, along with the leadership of the northern part, are required to be at a high level of vigilance in order to confront the machinations and conspiratorial acts to which the imperialist forces and their allies may resort, to embroil our Yemeni people in an atmosphere of division and tension. National duty dictates that we proceed in the direction of continued unity efforts, and establish the security and stability that our people aspire to.

The issue of those who fled following the conspiracy events should not be an obstacle to continuation of our unity efforts. We have expressed our readiness to receive all of them in accordance with the General Amnesty Resolution, with the exception of those who are being tried *in absentia*. We have expressed our readiness to provide all guarantees for those wishing to return. This is in accordance with what we have reviewed with our brothers during various meetings and mutual visits. We have affirmed the same in the various official statements of the Party and state, stressing that all of their public rights enshrined in the Constitution are guaranteed, that they will be provided with security guarantees and that they will not be held accountable for what occurred. Anyone who was previously employed will be given work in the various state establishments and organs; they will be given material facilities, restored to their houses or provided with appropriate alternative housing.

We call for the reactivation of the political bodies formed by the two parts of Yemen whose activity came to a halt following the January 13 conspiracy. In this respect we must point out the importance of reviving the work of the Supreme Council and the Joint Ministerial Commission, in the perspective of developing content and aims more responsive to the interests of the broad masses of our Yemeni people.

On the other hand, it is important to point to the positive results obtained by the Unity Committees in the political, economic, educational, cultural, social, legislative, constitutional and military planes. We consider it necessary that these resume their activity in the forthcoming period.

During the past few years some joint companies and joint economic ventures have been formed by the two parts of Yemen. The volume of commercial exchange within the national market has increased. We believe there are broader spheres of joint economic co-operation to be reached by consolidating the effectivity of the existing ventures and exploring the possibility of founding new economic ventures that would benefit the Yemeni people and the Yemeni national market. These will also promote the marketing of goods of Yemeni origin and liberate the Yemeni national economy from subservience to the capitalist market.

It is necessary that a peaceful and democratic atmosphere should prevail so that mass, social, cultural and sporting links between the two parts are deepened and can thereby contribute to, and participate in, the struggle along with all the toiling masses for realising unity and the triumph of the aims of the Yemeni revolution. There must also be exchange of experiences and cultural and creative works that personify the principles and aims of the two revolutions of the Yemeni people.

Among the matters that must be accorded attention by the authorities of the two parts is the movement of citizens and the consolidation of social and family ties. This requires joint co-operation to remove the obstacles that restrict the movement of citizens between the two parts.

The consolidation of unity work at the level of the political and mass bodies not only opens up broad vistas for accomplishing the peaceful and democratic reunification of the homeland, but also enables the two parts of the Yemen to play a role in the liberation struggle of our Arab nation, which is waged against world imperialism and Zionist occupation. In this context, our Yemeni Socialist Party will continue its policy of on-going co-ordination with the brothers in Sanaʿa on the various issues that are of importance to the interests of our Yemeni people and to the future of the struggle of the Arab liberation movement, as well as on all issues that affect the security and stability of the region and serve the cause of world peace.

We realise that the path of struggle for the victory of the Yemeni national cause is not easy. It is a long and arduous struggle filled with difficulties and obstacles raised by the enemies of the Yemeni revolution. However, we are confident that the will of the Yemeni people under the leadership of their best revolutionary forces will, in the end, triumph and forever banish the artificial barriers and division imposed upon our people by the enemies of their freedom, social progress and unity.

6 *The Arab and international situation and our Party's tasks on the foreign plane*

The current international situation is characterised by extreme tension and complexity that seriously threaten the future of human civilisation and the security of peoples. It is a result of the increased aggressive tendency and the war hysteria upon which the policies of the US Administration and its NATO allies are based. On the other hand the concern and anxiety of people over this unnatural situation is increased as it continues to be aggravated by the aggressive policy of world imperialism and its military-industrial complex. The peace movement hostile to war has acquired an increasingly mass character and has included and continues to include more sections of the peoples of the world as a whole, including the capitalist countries. In this direction, the Soviet Union and the countries of the socialist community play an enhanced and comprehensive role, which is always accorded the respect and support of all the forces struggling for peace, social progress, freedom and socialism in the world. Our country has also supported the constructive and peaceful policy of the Soviet Union aimed at realising world détente, the establishment of normal relations between states and peoples, disarmament, averting a nuclear catastrophe, halting the production of new types of weapons of mass destruction, halting nuclear tests and preventing the militarisation of outer space. This responds fully to the interests of all people of the world, without exception. The Soviet Union has submitted a wide number of constructive peaceful proposals and initiatives and shown increased flexibility in the hope of finding a response from the US Administration and its NATO allies. It still continues to pursue this course despite the intransigence of the United States and its insistence upon militarisation of outer space through its so-called Star Wars programme and its pressurising of its partners to join it in this. The cause of world peace has become the number one issue for every person, for whom the issue is life.

From this forum we renew our full support for the Soviet policy of peace and all the proposals tabled by Comrade Mikhail Gorbachev, the latest of these being the Soviet working paper at the Reykjavik summit and the Delhi Declaration. We express our confidence in the inevitable triumph of the cause of peace.

Despite the strivings of the forces of world imperialism to escalate tension and increase the complexity of the world situation, our world is nonetheless witnessing a mighty and increasing upsurge of the struggle of peoples aspiring to liberation, democracy, peace and socialism. We can state that an examination of the events, developments and contradictions of the contemporary world will enable us to appreciate the revolutionary transformations that were launched by the Great October Socialist Revolution seventy years ago. Had not they triumphed and backed socialist and liberation revolutions the world situation would not have been what it is today. The socialist system has been consolidated, its influence expanded, and its prestige and might on the world scene increased. Similarly, the influence of the other sections of the world revolutionary movement has increased. It has also been established that the crystallisation of new trends in the balance of power on the world plane do not permit the return of old colonial relations and direct hegemony over the destinies and capabilities of peoples.

Starting from the fact that our country is an integral part of the world revolutionary movement, we have always taken care to strengthen the bonds of militant solidarity with all forces of liberation, progress and socialism in the world, and to increase our country and party's contribution to the support and backing of the just causes of the peoples struggling against colonialism, neo-colonialism, racism, dictatorships and all the other evils of the world capitalist system.

Over the past eighteen months since the foiling of the bloody 13 January conspiracy, all of our foreign political moves have sought the consolidation of the standing of our Party and country in the world revolutionary movement in particular and the international plane in general. Contacts between the Yemeni Socialist Party and the world communist parties headed by the Communist Party of the Soviet Union have been intensified. Within the framework of the relations of co-operation and friendship between our country and the Soviet Union and the socialist countries, there has been exchange of visits and development of the forms of co-operation in all spheres. Within this context the participation of our party in the work of the XXVII Congress of the Communist Party of the Soviet Union with a high-level delegation headed by comrade ʿAlī Sālim al-Bīḍ, General Secretary of the Central Committee in February 1986, and his official visit to the Soviet Union in February 1987, and fruitful and valuable talks with the Soviet leadership headed by Comrade Mikhail Gorbachev, occupied a prominent position. We are confident that the great qualitative results of the totality of visits, contacts and forms of co-operation between our country and the socialist countries at the party and government levels will become a mighty factor for the uplift of the revolutionary process taking place in our country and consolidation of its triumphant march towards the aspired socialist horizons.

In this regard we wish to avail ourselves of the opportunity provided by the convening of the Party General Conference to hail from this forum all forms of support and backing extended by the Soviet Union and the socialist countries the struggle of our Party and people on the path of socialist orientation. It is also of importance to us that we especially greet the international stand of the Soviet Union during the events resulting from the 13 January bloody *coup* conspiracy, and which had an important influence on preventing foreign interference in the affairs of our country.

While we highly value all of these stands in support of our party and country, we affirm our concern for the continued deepening of the bonds of warm militant relations with the Soviet Union and all the socialist countries in all fields, considering them to be the corner-stone of our party's policy and of the socialist orientation of the country.

Our country has also during the past period been concerned with consolidating its standing at the international level, and developing relations of peaceful co-existence with states of differing social systems in a manner that serves the cause of peace and consolidation of stability in international relations. An important element in this context was the participation of our country in the Eighth Summit of the Non-Aligned Movement in Harare, and the Sixth Islamic Summit in Kuwait, together with the visits undertaken by Party and government delegations of a high-level to a number of friendly countries.

The Arab arena is witness to feverish escalation of the aggressive and conspiratorial plans and policies of the forces of imperialism and Zionism aimed at obliterating legitimate Arab causes, headed by the cause of the Arab Palestinian people, the destruction of the Arab national liberation movement and the linking of the Arab region to the nexus of political, military, economic and cultural subservience to neo-colonialism and the international imperialist system.

Undoubtedly, the situation in the Middle East has become a hot-bed of international tension. The expansionist aggressive policy of the Zionist entity backed by US imperialism and with the collusion of some reactionary circles in the region is seeking to impose capitulatory and liquidationist plans and solutions, with the aim of obliterating the cause of the Arab Palestinian people, since this is the essence of the current conflict in the Middle East. It does not recognise the inalienable legitimate rights of the Palestinian people, foremost among them being the right to return to their homeland, to self-determination and to building their independent national state.

During the past years and in an increasing manner the imperialist and reactionary conspiracies have spiralled. They seek to weaken the Arab national liberation movement with its various regimes and national and progressive forces, by increasing aggressive threats against Syria, Libya and the Palestinian revolution and by reviving hostile activity against Algeria and Democratic Yemen. The bloody 13 January conspiracy undertaken by the opportunist right current which was accompanied by dubious plans and moves proves the extent of this extensive and dangerous attack aimed at destroying the revolutionary positions in the Arab arena.

We do not exaggerate when we state that among the more pressing tasks at present is the issue of consolidating the militant unity of the components of the Arab national liberation movement, mobilisation of the immense struggle potential of the Arab masses and directing it towards firm confrontation of the imperialist and Zionist challenges to our Arab people, and deepening militant solidarity with the Soviet Union and all forces of progress and socialism in the world.

During the past period the foreign activity of our party revolved around this crucial task. Party and official contacts with the Arab Communist Parties, Arab countries and the sections of the Arab national liberation movement were intensified. They aimed at the development of militant relations between our Party and country and all the Arab national and progressive regimes and forces, resolution of the secondary differences within the Arab national liberation movement and especially those afflicting the Palestinian revolution. The efforts of our party and country and those of all the Arab progressive forces concerning the unity of the Palestinian revolution were crowned with success, with the convening of the XVII session of the Palestinian National Council on the basis of its programme hostile to imperialism, Zionism and all capitulatory and liquidationist schemes and solutions.

While we are proud of the success of the Palestinian revolution forces in regaining their unity within the Palestine Liberation Organisation as the sole legitimate representative of the Palestinian people, we affirm our full solidarity with the heroic struggle waged by the Palestinian people and their steadfast revolution for the sake of return to the homeland, self-determination and building their independent national state. We also hail the solidarity of all the forces favouring liberation, progress and peace that support the struggle of the Palestinian people and by various means strive to extend support to their just cause. Among these is the insistence upon establishing a just and comprehensive peace in the Middle East on the basis of solving the Palestinian issue by convening an international conference in which all parties to the conflict take part, including the Palestine Liberation Organisation.

High-level party and official delegations have visited Syria, Libya and

Algeria with the aim of consolidating militant relations between our country and these countries, and increasing co-ordination between them to face the imperialist-Zionist attack against the Arab national liberation movement.

There is no doubt that continuation of the struggle on the path strengthening the unity of the Arab national liberation movement and having its principal contradiction with the imperialist and Zionist enemies supercedes all other secondary efforts that must be at the centre of the activity of all Arab national and progressive forces. This will become one of the important factors of the steadfastness of the Arab national liberation movement and its triumph over the vicious attacks to which it is being subjected at present by the imperialist, Zionist and reactionary circles.

The imperialist, Zionist and reactionary plans and conspiracies against the Lebanon seek to undermine its independence, sovereignty and Arab identity, and to divide it into sectarian statelets. This requires consolidation of the unity of the Lebanese national movement and its alliance with the Palestinian revolution and Syria to confront these plans.

Our party values the efforts exerted and being exerted by the Arab League to consolidate Arab solidarity. It considers the reunification of the Palestine Liberation Organisation to be an important and necessary step towards the convening of an Arab summit and towards regaining the Arab solidarity on the basis of hostility to imperialism and Zionism and the massing of all Arab energies and potentials to confront the capitulatory schemes.

Fraternal co-operation between our country and all Arab countries, and in particular neighbouring Arab countries, acquires vital importance within the framework of our foreign policy. Being concerned for the continuation of existing relations of co-operation on the basis of mutual respect, good-neighbourliness and mutual benefit and non-interference in domestic affairs, our country continues to pursue its course of laying down the foundations of these relations in a manner that serves our region's security and stability and the progress and prosperity of our peoples.

In this direction our country has exerted and is still exerting on-going efforts for the consolidation of fraternal co-operation with all states of the region and to provide all that can safeguard security and stability in the region, and remove all factors of tension and the manifestations of foreign imperialist presence in the Gulf region, the Indian Ocean and the Red Sea. In this regard our country has continued to express its concern over the on-going Iraqi–Iranian war, its escalation and its rise to dangerous levels that threaten the life of the Iraqi and Iranian peoples, and confront the whole region with serious threats. While we renew our call for the immediate halting of this destructive war and the solving of differences between the two warring sides by peaceful means, it is of importance to us to affirm our rejection of all attempts to escalate this war and to exploit it with the aim of finding pretexts to expand the military presence of the USA and its NATO allies under the guise of protecting international navigation in the Gulf.

Our country considers that defending the freedom of international navigation in the Gulf waters requires respect for national sovereignty, and non-interference in the vital interests of all peoples and states of the region; these should not be transformed into a military zone under the hegemony of US imperialism and its NATO allies. There must be respect for international conventions and the resolutions of the United Nations on having all waterways, seas and oceans avoid the dangers of tensions and military confrontations.

The past period since the great victory over the unsuccessful bloody 13 January *coup* conspiracy has witnessed great efforts directed at regaining the prestigious position of our party and progressive regime in the Arab and international arenas, and at eliminating the negative effects that harmed the reputation of our party and country abroad as a result of the nefarious crimes and acts committed by the opportunist right current when executing the heinous conspiracy.

Our foreign political activity at the party and official levels was directed towards the deepening of militant relations with the socialist oriented and Non-Aligned Movement countries and towards expansion of the scope of co-operation and co-ordination with them and towards continued support for the national liberation movements in Asia, Africa and Latin America which struggle for national independence and social progress and against fascism and racism.

In this context relations between our country and Ethiopia have witnessed tangible development. The visits paid by high-level Party official delegations from our country, and the visits of some delegations from Socialist Ethiopia to our country were prominent landmarks on the path of the consolidation of militant relations between our two parties and countries. We will in future continue to march towards developing these relations in a manner that serves the great aims and common interests of the Yemeni and Ethiopian revolutions. We will also exert further efforts towards consolidating the militant unity and common struggle of all socialist-oriented and newly-liberated countries, in order to confront the conspiracies of the foes of world imperialism and its lackeys that seek to suppress the aspirations of the people of these countries and to reimpose colonial hegemony over them.

In this regard we affirm our country's support and backing for the struggle of the Socialist Republic of Cuba, the Democratic Republic of Afghanistan, Nicaragua, Angola, Mozambique, Laos, Vietnam, Kampuchea and the Western Sahara Republic against all conspiratorial plans and acts of armed aggression and the various forms of foreign interference in the affairs of these countries on the part of the world imperialism quarters and their reactionary, fascist and racist lackeys. We also renew our affirmation of our country's support for the struggle of the peoples of South Africa and Namibia against racism and for national independence.

We also underline our support for the United Nations and its various bodies based on the noble aims of its Charter for preserving world security and peace and for eliminating the remnants on our planet of obnoxious colonial and racist phenomena.

A number of principal tasks are posed before us in the course of creative implementation of our Party's foreign policy on the path of consolidating our Party and national democratic regime on the Arab and world planes, on the basis of the principles of peaceful co-existence and proletarian internationalist solidarity affirmed by the programme of the Yemeni Socialist Party.

In the forthcoming period we must redouble efforts for the development and deepening of militant relations with the countries of the socialist community headed by the Soviet Union, in various spheres and in a manner that ensures the qualitative rise of these relations to a more comprehensive and deeper level. We must also work for the consolidation of relations with the components of the Arab and world national liberation movements, with all of its regimes and national and progressive forces, with the Arab countries and all countries of the world in a manner that enhances our country's standing in the Arab and international arenas.

Now more than at any previous time we are required to develop the forms and methods of our work in support of the constructive international policies and initiatives aimed at preserving world peace, and exposing and condemning all aggressive and expansionist tendencies through which the imperialist quarters seek to drag the world into a destructive nuclear war. This requires of the organs concerned with foreign political activity that they consider errors and shortcomings that weaken the effectivity of our work in this sphere, and concern themselves with the qualitative improvement of cadres in the diplomatic corps, and in missions and embassies in the fraternal and friendly countries and international democratic bodies and organisations. There must be an improvement in the work of external information by improvement of its competence, and development of its instruments and topics, so that it becomes an effective implement of foreign political activity.

Undoubtedly, the forthcoming period will witness diligent work based on the experience of our successes and failures. We are confident that the experience and traditions acquired in the sphere of foreign political activity will be assessed by the organs concerned with the aim of producing the best methods and means necessary for the development of the form and content of our work, in a manner that ensures enhancement of the standing of our party and country externally. The accomplishments of our workers must be known. The bonds of friendship and co-operation with all countries and people of the world aspiring to building a new world devoid of all war, injustice and sorrow must be strengthened. We must strive after a world over which understanding, friendship, freedom, progress, socialism and peace prevail.

As we conclude our Report we wish to affirm anew the need to raise the militant effectivity of the various leading party bodies, party members and candidate members, mass organisations and all workers and toilers in formulating practical plans and programmes for carrying out the tasks defined in the Political Report and the conclusions and trends defined in the Critical and Analytical Document and which in a dialectical manner reflect the close links between the direct and strategic tasks.

Source: Edited extract from YSP Central Committee English text

APPENDIX 8: *PDRY: external public debt outstanding as of 31 December, 1982 (in US $m.)*

	Public debt outstanding including undisbursed	Disbursed
Multilateral loans	*422.8*	*212.0*
IDA	125.9	55.1
Kuwait Fund	69.3	55.1
Arab Fund	106.1	51.3
Abu Dhabi Fund	52.8	35.4
Islamic Bank	13.1	0.3
OPEC Special Fund	30.5	14.2
European Common Market	2.9	—
IFAD	22.3	0.6
Bilateral loans	*1,117.4*	*573.0*
USSR	713.7	270.3
China	148.8	133.1
German Democratic Republic	49.6	27.6
Bulgaria	65.0	31.9
Czechoslovakia	30.5	18.0
Hungary	18.3	11.0
Iraq	32.2	25.2
Libya	16.8	16.8
Algeria	31.0	28.7
Denmark	3.8	2.9
Other	7.8	7.5
Total external loans	*1,540.2*	*785.0*

Source: Bank of Yemen.

Notes

Introduction: the foreign relations of South Yemen

1 The earlier academic study of South Yemen had yielded a number of excellent works – by Abdulla Bujra, Said al-Attar, Muhammad al-Habashi, Manfred Wenner, and Jean-Pierre Viennot. Among later major contributions to the field can be included the works of John Duke Anthony, Norman Cigar, Leigh Douglas, Jean Gueyras, Tareq and Jacqueline Ismael, Joseph Kostiner, Helen Lackner, Maxine Molyneux, Vitali Naumkin, Mark Katz, Stephen Page, John Peterson, Robert Stookey, and Manfred Wenner. See bibliography for details.

2 Among other relevant studies see Christopher Clapham, *Foreign Policy Making in Developing States*, London, 1977, and, with special relevance to South Yemen, Bahgat Korany and Ali Dessouki (eds.), *The Foreign Policies of Arab States*, London and Boulder, 1984.

3 On the potential and limits of such reorientations of foreign policy by Third World states see G. White, R. Murray and C. White (eds.), *Revolutionary Socialist Development in the Third World*, Brighton, 1983; P. Wiles (ed.), *The New Communist Third World*, London, 1982; and Richard Fagen, Carmen Diana Deere and Jose Luis Corraggio (eds.), *Transition and Development*, New York, 1986.

4 On the relation between nationalism and revolution see B. Anderson, *Imagined Communities*, London, 1983, chapter 9.

5 On the evolution of policy in this regard after the Russian revolution see E.H. Carr, *The Bolshevik Revolution*, London, 1952, vol. 3, and F. Borkenau, *World Communism*, Ann Arbor, 1962.

6 Robert Freedman, *Soviet Policy Towards the Middle East Since 1970*, New York, 1975; Yaacov Roʿi, *The Limits to Power: Soviet Policy in the Middle East*, New York, 1979; A. and K. Dawisha (eds.), *The Soviet Union in the Middle East, Policies and Perspectives*, London, 1982.

7 For earlier bibliographies of the PDRY see S. Mondesir, *A Select Bibliography of Yemen Arab Republic and People's Democratic Republic of Yemen*, Centre for Middle Eastern and Islamic Studies, University of Durham, Occasional Papers Series, no. 5, 1977, and R. Stookey, *South Yemen, A Marxist Republic in Arabia*, London, 1982, pp. 107–11. Ample bibliographies are to be found in, *inter alia*, the works of Ismael, Katz and Page (see bibliography, p. 293ff).

8 Analyses based on these visits can be found in my following publications: *Arabia without Sultans*, Harmondsworth, 1974; 'The People's Democratic Republic of Yemen: the "Cuban Path" in Arabia', in G. White, R. Murray and C. White (eds.), *Threat from the East? Soviet Policy from Afghanistan and Iran to the Horn of Africa*, Harmondsworth, 1982; and 'The Yemens: Conflict and Coexistence', *The World Today*, August–September, 1984.

9 For development of the idea of a 'Twenty Years' War' from 1962 to 1982 in the southern part of Arabia, see Halliday, 'The Yemens: Conflict and Coexistence', pp. 355–8.

1 Development of foreign policy

1 Accounts of the independence movement can be found in, *inter alia*, Brian Lapping, *End of Empire*, London, 1985, chapter 6; Robin Bidwell, *The Two Yemens*, London, 1983; Fred Halliday, *Arabia without Sultans*, Harmondsworth, 1974; Joseph Kostiner, *The Struggle for South Yemen*, London, 1984; Tom Little, *South Arabia*, London, 1968; Vitali Naumkin, *Al-Djabḥa al-Ḳawmiyya fī al-Kifāḥ min ajli Istiḳlāl al-Yaman al-Djanūbiyya wa al-Dīmuḳrāṭiyya al-Waṭaniyya*, Moscow, 1984; Helen Lackner, *P.D.R. Yemen*, London, 1985.

2 For charges of anterior NLF–British collusion see chapter 1, n.41. A British official, Samuel Falle, at that time Head of the United Nations (Political) Department at the Foreign Office, and later Ambassador to Kuwait, and who visited Aden in May 1967 as Political Adviser to Lord Shackleton's mission, has stated that while on that mission he had secret discussions with NLF officials (interview with Granada Television, End of Empire Series, 1985, quoted in Lapping, *Empire*, pp. 302–3). Falle reports that he asked the NLF to stop killing British personnel, in order to facilitate political discussions, but that they declined to do so on the grounds that such an abstention would weaken their political credibility. While Shackleton had had secret talks with FLOSY, no such contacts with the NLF were possible, and he found the British in Aden ill-informed about them.

3 For the history of British policy in creating a South Arabian entity see Bidwell, *Yemens*, chapters 4 and 6; Little, *South Arabia* chapters 2 and 3; R.J. Gavin, *Aden under British Rule 1839–1967*, London, 1975, chapters 11 and 12; and Kennedy Trevaskis, *Shades of Amber*, London, 1968.

4 Little, *South Arabia*, chapter 8; Kostiner, *Struggle*, pp. 128ff; Harvey Sicherman, *Aden and British Strategy 1839–1968*, Philadelphia, 1972, chapter 3.

5 T. Bernier, 'Naissance d'un nationalisme arabe à Aden', *L'Afrique et l'Asie*, no. 44 (1958); Gavin, *Aden*, chapter 12; Halliday, *Arabia*, pp. 180–9; Little, *South Arabia*, chapters 3 and 4; D.C. Watt, 'Labour Relations and Trades Unionism in Aden, 1952–60', *Middle East Journal*, no. 16 (1962).

6 Gavin, *Aden*, chapter 12; Muhammad O. al-Habashi, *Aden*, Algiers, 1964; and, on the Hadramaut, Abdalla Bujra, *The Politics of Stratification: A Study of Political Change in a South Arabian Town*, London, 1971.

7 Al-Habashi, *Aden*, pp. 72–110 and see the references in nn.1 and 5 above.

8 Halliday, *Arabia*, pp. 187ff.

9 Kostiner, *Struggle*, p. 53; Sultan Umar, *Nazra*, p. 235. On the variant Arabic names of the NLF as given in the *Mīthāḳ* see chapter 3, n.12.

10 Details in Gavin, *Aden*, Little, *South Arabia*, and Sicherman, *British Strategy*.

11 Humphrey Trevelyan, *The Middle East in Revolution*, London, 1970, p. 222.
12 Trevelyan, *Middle East*, p. 226.
13 *Keesings Contemporary Archives*, 16–23 December 1967, p. 22411.
14 748 HC Deb., 19 June 1967, cols. 1126–44.
15 *Aden, Perim and Kuria Muria Islands Act 1967*, HMSO, London 1967.
16 *Keesings Contemporary Archives*, 16–23 December 1967, p. 22412.
17 Reuters despatch, 8 August 1967.
18 Reuters despatch, 2 September 1967.
19 Trevelyan, *Middle East*, p. 247; *Keesings Contemporary Archives*, 16–23 December 1967, p. 22412.
20 Interview with ʿAbd Allāh al-Khāmrī, Minister of Culture and Information, Aden, 12 February 1970.
21 753 HC Deb., 2 November 1967, cols. 338–41.
22 754 HC Deb., 14 November 1967, col. 225.
23 *Keesings Contemporary Archives*, 16–23 December 1967, p. 22413.
24 Trevelyan, *Middle East*, p. 258.
25 754 HC Deb., 14 November 1967, cols. 225–6.
26 Interviews with Lord Shackleton, London, 22 July 1985; and John McCarthy CMG, Counsellor High Commission Aden and Political Adviser to C.-in-C. Middle East (1964–7), Head of Aden Department Foreign Office (1967) and Arabian Department FCO (1968–70), Member of British Delegation Geneva Talks on Independence of South Yemen (November 1967), Exeter, 16 July 1983.
27 Little, *South Arabia*, pp. 181–2.
28 McCarthy interview, 1983.
29 Shackleton interview, 1985.
30 McCarthy interview, 1983.
31 Interview with Patrick Bannerman, Principal Research Officer, FCO, 5 February 1981.
32 E.g. 755 HC Deb., 29 November 1967, col. 437.
33 Interview with ʿAbd Allāh al-Khāmrī, February 1970.
34 *Memorandum of Agreed Points Relating to Independence for South Arabia (the People's Republic of Southern Yemen), Geneva 29 November 1980*, HMSO, London 1968, Cmnd 3504.
35 Little, *South Arabia*, p. 180.
36 Trevelyan, *Middle East*, p. 258.
37 Trevelyan, *Middle East*, pp. 265–6.
38 Interview with Denis Healey, Minister of Defence 1964–8, London, 6 December 1972.
39 Harold Wilson, *The Labour Government: 1964–70*, London, 1971, p. 396.
40 746 HC Deb., 11 May 1967, col. 1704; 753 HC Deb., 2 November 1967, cols. 337–8.
41 Bidwell, *Yemens*, pp. 188–9; for a Saudi claim on this see ME/2838/A/2; for analogous FLOSY charges, see *Sunday Times*, 5 November 1967.
42 Trevelyan, *Middle East*, pp. 258.

43 For an Egyptian evaluation of the UAR's role in the Yemens see ME/ 2650/A/3. K̲h̲āmrī interview, February 1970.

44 748 HC Deb., 19 June 1967, col. 1136.

45 *al-Mīthāḳ al-Waṭani*, Aden, n.d. pp. 84–5.

46 *Mīthāḳ*, pp. 83–4, 89–90.

47 Ḳaḥṭān al-S̲h̲aʿabī, in ME/2637/A/2, February 1968; *Mīthāḳ*, p. 79.

48 *Keesings Contemporary Archives*, 16–23 December 1967, p. 22413.

49 John Peterson, *Yemen, The Search for a Modern State*, London, 1982, pp. 102–3.

50 Ḳaḥṭān al-S̲h̲aʿabī in ME/2701/A/3 (February 1968), is quoted as saying: 'Whoever attacks Sanaʿa is attacking Aden.'

51 Walid Kazziha, *Revolutionary Transformation in the Arab World*, London, 1975, pp. 94–8; SWB/ME/30000/A/3.

52 Interview with ʿAbd al-Fattāḥ Ismāʿīl, NF Secretary-General, Aden, 14 February 1970.

53 Interview with Sulṭān ʾAḥmad ʿUmar, Secretary-General of the Revolutionary Democratic Party, Aden, 8 May 1973.

54 Kazziha, *Transformation*, chapter 5, and Nāyyif Ḥawātma, *Azmat al-T̲h̲awra fī al-D̲j̲unūb al-Yamanī*, Beirut, 1968.

55 ME/4747/A/2, 5 November 1974.

56 Kostiner, *Struggle*, Naumkin, D̲j̲abḥa, ʿUmar, Naẓra.

57 K̲h̲āmrī interview, February 1970.

58 Interview with ʿAbd al-Fattāḥ Ismāʿīl, February 1970.

59 ME/2636/A/1–2; Little, *South Arabia*, pp. 181–2; *Keesings Contemporary Archives*, 16–23 December 1967, p. 22414.

60 *UN General Assembly, 22nd Session Official Records 1630th Plenary Meeting*, 14 December 1967, p. 8.

61 ME/2636/A/1, 1 December 1967.

62 Closing Statement in ME/2636/A/1; Political Declaration as *Bayyān Siyyāsī min al-Ḳiāda al-ʿĀma lil D̲j̲abḥa al-Ḳawmiyya al-Munbat̲h̲iḳa min al-Muʿtamar al-Rābiḥ*, in Ḥawātma, *Azmat*, pp. 239–49.

63 *Barnāmad̲j̲ al-Taḥarrur al-Waṭanī al-Dīmuḳrāti al-S̲h̲aʿabī*, in Ḥawātma, *Azmat*, pp. 133–66.

64 Ḥawātma, *Azmat*, p. 135.

65 *Ibid.*, p. 217.

66 *Bayyān*, in Ḥawātma, *Azmat*, pp. 240–5.

67 *Ibid.*, pp. 242–3.

68 *Ibid.*, p. 253.

69 *Ibid.*, p. 245.

70 ME/2719/A/1–2, 13 March 1968.

71 General Command Statement of 14 May 1968, in *Orient* (Paris), vol. 14 (1970), pp. 43–8.

72 ME/2722/A/1, 16 March 1968; ME/2733/A/1, 29 March 1968.

73 ME/2773/A/1–3, 18 May 1968.

74 ME/3107/i, 24 June 1969; *Le Monde*, 24 June 1968 and 25 June 1968.

75 ME/3108/A/6, 25 June 1969; *Le Monde*, 24 June 1969.

76 ME/3108/A/6.

77 *Le Monde*, 24 June 1969.
78 ME/3213/i, 27 October 1969.
79 *Le Monde*, 27 November 1969; People's Republic of Southern Yemen, *Law No. 37 of 1969, The Economic Corporation for the Public Sector and National Planning*, text in author's possession.
80 *Le Monde*, 12 November 1970; text of 1970 Constitution in *al-Djabḥa al-Ḳawmiyya, al-Thawra al-Waṭaniyya al-Dīmuḳrāṭiyya fī al-Yaman*, Beirut, 1972, pp. 151–84.
81 ME/3661/A/12, 19 April 1971.
82 ME/3267/A/2, 1 January 1970; *Le Monde*, 1 January 1970.
83 PDRY, Ministry of Information and Culture, Information Office, Address of the Political Organisation and State delivered by Sālim Rubiyyaʿ ʿAlī, 30 November 1970, p. 7.
84 ME/3753/A/3, 5 August 1971; *Le Monde*, 4 August 1971.
85 ME/3932/A/8–9, 6 March 1972; *Le Monde*, 27 May 1972.
86 *al-Thawra al-Waṭaniyya*, pp. 105–20.
87 *Barnāmadj al-Tanẓīm al-Sīāsī al-Djabha al-Ḳawmiyya*, in *al-Thawra al-Waṭaniyya*, pp. 65–81.
88 *Ibid.*, pp. 69–71.
89 *Ibid.*, p. 101.
90 *Ibid.*, p. 102.
91 *Ibid.*
92 *Ibid.*, p. 103.
93 *Ibid.*, p. 104.
94 *Ibid.*
95 *Ibid.*, p. 101.
96 *Ibid.*, p. 102.
97 Fred Halliday, 'Yemen's Unfinished Revolution', *MERIP Reports*, no. 81 (October 1979), pp. 16–19.
98 *Le Monde*, 28–29 May 1972.
99 ME/4062/A/5–6, 9 August 1972.
100 ME/4674/A/15, 10 August 1974; ME/4683/A/1, 21 August 1974; *Documents of the National Struggle in Oman and the Arabian Gulf*, translated and published by the Gulf Committee, London, 1974, pp. 87–104.
101 *Financial Times*, 25 March 1976.
102 *Al-Djabḥa al-Ḳawmiyya, Al-Tanẓim al-Sīāsī al-Mawḥid, Al-Muʾtamar Al-Tawḥīdī, Oktobr 1975*, Beirut, 1976.
103 *Ibid.*, pp. 29, 217.
104 *Ibid.*, p. 135.
105 *Ibid.*, p. 218.
106 *Ibid.*
107 *Ibid.*, pp. 219–20.
108 *Ibid.*, p. 220.
109 Further details of this in Halliday, 'Yemen's Unfinished Revolution'.
110 Interview with Muḥammad Hādī ʿAwwaḍ, PDRY Ambassador to London, 10 September 1978, and with other PDRY officials at later dates.
111 Author's observation, Aden, November 1977.

112 *The Guardian*, 29 August 1978.
113 ME/5850/A/6–7, 28 June 1978.
114 ME/5850/A/8, 28 June 1978.
115 ME/5854/A/2, 3 July 1978.
116 ME/6604/A/1, 30 December 1971.
117 ME/5959/A/5–6, 3 November 1978.
118 Author's observation during attendance of President's speech, Aden, 30 November 1977; text as 'Address by Brother Sālim Rubiyyaᶜ ᶜAlī, Assistant Secretary-General of the Central Committee of the Unified NFPO and Chairman of the Presidential Council on the occasion of the Tenth Anniversary of National Independence, Aden, December 1977'.
119 Interview with Muḥammad Hādī ᶜAwwaḍ.
120 The reaction of the Saudi newspaper *Ūkāz* in ME/5850/A/5, 28 June 1978, and that of the Egyptian paper *al-Aḥrām* in ME/5853/i, 1 July 1978.
121 *Peking Review*, no. 27 (1978), p. 41.
122 For example, Donald Zagoria, 'Into the Breach: New Soviet Alliances in the Third World', *Foreign Affairs*, Spring 1979.
123 Henry Kissinger, 'Communist coups in Afghanistan and South Yemen', in July 1979 testimony to the Committee on Foreign Relations of the US Senate, in Henry Kissinger, *For the Record, Selected Statements 1977–1980*, Boston, 1981, p. 217. Few would doubt that there *had* been a 'Communist coup' in Afghanistan.
124 ME/5855/A/5–6, 4 July 1978.
125 *International Herald Tribune*, 7 August 1978.
126 ME/5855/A/9, 4 July 1978.
127 ME/5862/A/1, 12 July 1978.
128 ME/5941/A/1, 13 October 1978; ME/5943/A/3, 16 October 1978.
129 *Barnāmadj al-Ḥizb al-Ishtirākī al-Yamanī*, n.p. n.d., p. 82.
130 *Ibid.*
131 *Ibid.*, p. 83.
132 *Barnāmadj*, pp. 82, 86, 87.
133 *Ibid.*, pp. 82–3.
134 *Ibid.*, p. 89.
135 *Ibid.*
136 *Ibid.*, p. 88.
137 *Ibid.*, pp. 17–24.
138 *Ibid.*, p. 14.

2 The Yemeni Socialist Party

1 ME/6224/A/5–7, 20 September 1979.
2 ME/6264/A/8, 6 November 1979.
3 ME/6191/A/3, 11 August 1979; ME/6193/A/7–9, 14 August 1979.
4 Interview with Yemeni informant, 15 June 1981.
5 ME/6402/A/1–2, 23 April 1980, for the official statement.

6 *Al-Muʾtamar al-Istithnāī lil-Ḥizb al-Ishtirākī al-Yamanī*, Beirut, 1980, p. 452; *Le Monde*, 22 October 1980.
7 *Al-Muʾtamar*, p. 450.
8 *Ibid.*, pp. 453–4.
9 ME/6818/A/1–3, 3 September 1981.
10 Interview with Yemeni informant, June 1981.
11 ME/6666/A/11, 6 March 1981.
12 *The Observer*, 22 August 1982.
13 Author's observation, Moscow, July 1984.
14 See chapter 5, pp. 198–9ff for details.
15 ME/7933/i, 24 April 1985; ME/8128/A/5, 7 December 1985.
16 See my 'The Yemens in War', *The World Today*, August–September 1984.
17 ME/7876/A/1–2, 15 February 1985; *Le Monde*, 16 February 1985.
18 This analysis of the antecedents to the 1986 crisis draws heavily on the reportage by Jean Gueyras in *Le Monde* and on subsequent discussions with him.
19 ME/8085/A/5, 18 October 1985, and corrections in ME/8088/A/8, 22 October 1985.
20 Report on Secretary-General ʿAlī Nāṣir in *Arbatʿashara Oktobr*, 14 October 1985.
21 ME/8249/i, 3 May 1986; *Le Monde*, 22 January 1988.
22 SWB/8178/A/4, 8 February 1986.
23 ME/8167/A/1–7, 27 January 1986.
24 For the foreign policy positions of the 1987 Conference see report of ʿAlī al-Bīḍ, Appendix 7, pp. 250ff., and chapters 5 and 6 of the main discussion document circulated prior to the conference, *al-Wathika al-Naḳdiyya al-Taḥlīliyya li-Tadjriba al-Thawra fī al-Yaman al-Dimuḳrāṭiyya (1978–1987)*, Aden, 1987. Final statement of the conference in *al-Thawri*, 27 June 1987.
25 ME/8210/A/8, 18 March 1986.
26 Fuad Khuri, *Tribe and State in Bahrain*, Chicago, 1980, provides an excellent account of the evolution of tribalism in a context of state formation, with considerable relevance to South Yemen.
27 ME/8166/A/10–11, 25 January 1986.
28 On the new Central Committee see ME/8371/A/13, 23 September 1986.
29 ME/8173/A/2, 3 February 1986; ME/8174/A/6, 4 February 1986. The final judgement of the court makes no specific mention of foreign connections on the part of ʿAlī Nāṣir's followers.
30 ME/8184/A/1, 15 February 1986.
31 *al-Wathika al-Nakdiyya*, p. 98.
32 Fred Halliday 'Self-Reliance in the 1980s', *Monthly Review*, no. 3 (1988).
33 *Le Monde*, 22 January 1988.
34 As one South Yemeni diplomat put it: 'When they see how hard we fight our own brothers, no outsider would ever dare to intervene in our internal affairs'.
35 Vitali Naumkin, 'Southern Yemen: The Road to Progress', *International Affairs*, no. 1 (1978), p. 14.
36 *Al-Muʾtamar al-Tawḥīdī*, Beirut, 1976, p. 154.

37 ME/2636/A/2, 2 December 1967.
38 *Keesings Contemporary Archives*, 12–19 July 1969, p. 23452.
39 ME/3108/A/7, 25 June 1969.
40 ME/3599/A/13, 2 February 1971.
41 ME/3758/A/8, 11 August 1971.
42 ME/4229/i, 24 February 1973.
43 ME/6193/A/9, 14 August 1979.
44 ME/7029/A/4; *Le Monde*, 3 September 1982.
45 *Al-Muʾtamar al-Tawḥīdī*, p. 154.
46 Thus articles 97 and 104 of the 1978 Constitution, *Constitution of the People's Democratic Republic of Yemen*, n.p. n.d., pp. 45, 48–9.
47 See chapter 3, *passim*.
48 Author's observation, Aden, October–November 1977.
49 E.g. ʿAbd al-Fattāḥ Ismāʿīl, Muḥammad Saʿīd ʿAbd Allāh, ʿAbd al-ʿAzīz ʿAbd al-Walī.
50 ME/7177/i, 8 November 1982.
51 Interview with Muḥammad Salmān Hasan, London, August 1975.
52 Author's observation, Aden, October 1977.
53 ʿAlī Nāṣir Muḥammad, ʿAbd Allāh al-Khāmrī, Ṣāliḥ Muṣliḥ, ʿAlī ʿAntar, ʿAlī al-Bīḍ.
54 World Bank, *3–570 YDR PDRY – Economic Memorandum*, 29 January 1982, pp. 1–5.
55 World Bank, *People's Democratic Republic of Yemen, A Review of Economic and Social Development*, Washington, 1979, pp. 27–9.
56 World Bank, *Memorandum*, 1982, p. 5.
57 *Middle East Economic Digest*, 20 April 1984. See also Appendix 8, below, p. 260.
58 World Bank, *Memorandum*, 1982, p. 4. Figures for remittances in World Bank, *World Development Report*, annual.
59 Sylvia Edgington, '"The State of Socialist Orientation" as Soviet Development Politics', *Soviet Union/Union Soviétique*, Autumn 1981; Jerry Hough, *The Struggle for the Third World*, Washington, 1985.

3 The advanced capitalist countries

1 *UN General Assembly, 22nd Session, Official Records 1630th Plenary Meeting*, 14 December 1967, pp. 1–9.
2 An Amnesty mission visited Aden in 1975, but following the publication of a critical report in 1977 the PDRY refused to have any further contact with the organisation until the trial of ʿAlī Nāṣir supporters in 1987. In October 1987 Amnesty observers visited this trial, and Amnesty was later to condemn the death sentences passed. Coverage of the PDRY is found in the annual *Reports* of Amnesty International.
3 *Le Monde*, 11 December 1976.
4 Interview with Minister of Finance and Planning, ʿAbd al-ʿAzīz ʿAbd al-Walī, Aden, 4 November 1977.

5 For example, Ḳaḥṭān al-Shaʿabī's favourable remarks on the French stand on 'Israeli aggression' in the 1967 Arab–Israeli war, ME/2680/A/12, 27 January 1968.
6 Trevelyan, *Middle East*, p. 263.
7 *UN General Assembly*, p. 8.
8 The opening of the trial in ME/2703/A/8, 22, February 1968.
9 Trial sentences in ME/2736/A/10, 2 April 1968, and *Keesings Contemporary Archives*, 12–19 July 1969, p. 23452.
10 McCarthy interview, 16 July 1983.
11 *The Times*, 28 February 1968.
12 *The Times*, 29 February 1968.
13 Me/2708/A/5, 29 February 1968; *The Times*, 28 February 1968.
14 *The Times*, 29 February 1968.
15 *Ibid.*
16 ME/2710/A/2, 2 March 1968.
17 South Yemeni statement in ME/2768/A/3, 13 May 1968; Ḳaḥṭān al-Shaʿabī, criticism of the UK in ME/2761/A/3, 4 May 1968.
18 *The Times*, 12 June 1968; ME/2794/A/1–2, 13 June 1968.
19 Interview with Patrick Bannerman, FCO, 5 February 1981.
20 *Keesings Contemporary Archives*, 29 November–6 December 1969, p. 23690.
21 783 HC Deb., 12 May 1969, cols. 954–6.
22 Interview with ʿAbd Allāh al-Khāmrī, Aden, February 1970.
23 337 HL Deb., 21 December 1972, col. 1218.
24 964 HC Deb., 21 March 1979, col. 595.
25 Information from PDRY Foreign Ministry, 1982.
26 Interview, 1981.
27 798 HC Written Answers, 19 March 1970, cols. 208–9.
28 *Ibid.*
29 338 HL Deb., 6 February 1973, cols. 988–94.
30 855 HC Deb., 18 April 1973, cols. 620–1. Later figures 943 HoC Written Answers, 31 January 1978, cols. 145–6. Figures for the 1980s in FCO communication to author, 30 April 1985.
31 Address by Brother Sālim Rubiyyaʿ ʿAlī, 30 November 1970, p. 5.
32 PDRY, *Official Gazette*, 18 June 1970, Law no. 17 of 1970, section 4.
33 PDRY, Central Statistical Office, *Statistical Yearbook 1980*, Table I/XI, p. 159.
34 ME/5482/A/1, 6 April 1977, on the transfer of the BP refinery; ME/5773/A/11, 28 March 1978, on the transfer of Cable and Wireless installations.
35 Author's interviews with Muḥammad Miḍḥī, Minister of Trade, Aden, December 1977, and with Aḥmad Ḳutayb, Birmingham, May 1976.
36 Author's visit to Maʿala Technical Institute, 2 December 1977.
37 Information gathered during author's research in Yemeni communities of Manchester, Liverpool and Birmingham, 1976–8.
38 *Ibid.*
39 See chapter 1, *passim*.
40 E.g. ME/6686/A/4, 30 March 1981; ME/6764/A/1, 30 June 1981.

41 PFLOAG and NDLFOAG statement of 1971, 'The British-Backed Plan for a Union of the Six Amirates', in *Documents of the National Struggle in Oman and the Arabian Gulf*, translated and published by the Gulf Committee, London, 1974.
42 ME/3837/A/1, 12 November 1971, where ʿAbd Allāh al-Khāmrī talks of the 'extreme panic' of Britain and the local rulers.
43 For example, the speech of Sālim Rubiyyaʿ ʿAlī of 23 December 1971 in ME/3873/A/12, 28 December 1971.
44 ME/3859/E/5, 8 December 1971.
45 Bannerman interview, 1981.
46 Interview with Muḥammad Hādī ʿAwwaḍ, PDRY Ambassador, London, June 1972.
47 Robert Saint-Véran, *A Djibouti, avec les Afars et les Issas*, Cagnes-sur-Mer, 1977.
48 *International Herald Tribune*, 15 September 1981.
49 Muṭiyyaʿ interview, 1977.
50 Interview with Jibuti opposition politician, Daʿan Muḥammad, Aden, 7 May 1973.
51 Supplies of medicine, ambulances and an aircraft reported in ME/4955/A/3, 1 September 1975, for July 1975; May 1977 Agreement on Cultural and Technical Co-operation, in *Maghreb-Mashrek*, July–September 1978, p. 80.
52 ME/3944/A/10, 20 March 1972.
53 *Le Monde*, 11 December 1976.
54 *Le Monde*, 7 January 1982.
55 Interview with ʿAbd Allāh Muhayrīz, Director Yemeni Research Centre, Aden, February 1984.
56 *Le Monde*, 11 December 1976.
57 ME/4955/A/3, 1 September 1975; interview with French Ambassador to the PDRY, Jacques Ardebert, Aden, 10 February 1984.
58 *Keesings Contemporary Archives*, 12–19 July 1969, p. 23452.
59 Interview with Matthias Weiter, Ministry of Economic Cooperation, Bonn, 8 June 1982.
60 PDRY, *Statistical Yearbook 1980*, Table I/XI.
61 Texts provided by Foreign Ministry, Federal Republic of Germany, Department 311, June 1982.
62 Interview with Reinhard Schlagintweit, FRG Foreign Ministry, June 1982.
63 Weiter interview, 1982.
64 Interview PDRY Foreign Minister Muḥammad Ṣāliḥ Muṭiyyaʿ, Aden, 4 December 1977.
65 Schlagintweit interview, 1982.
66 ME/5643/i, 18 October 1977.
67 Schlagintweit interview, 1982; for example, see the interview with the former urban guerrilla Jürgen Block in *Der Spiegel*, no. 9 (1981), p. 117.
68 Weiter interview, 1982.
69 Text supplied by FRG Foreign Ministry.
70 Schlagintweit interview, 1982.

71 US Congress, House of Representatives, *New Perspectives on the Persian Gulf*, Hearings Before the Committee on the Near East and South Asia of the Committee on Foreign Affairs, Washington, 1973, p. 16.
72 *Keesings Contemporary Archives*, 25 August 1978, p. 29163.
73 E.g., ME/4757/A/3, 16 November 1974.
74 John Duke Anthony, 'Relations between the United States and the People's Democratic Republic of Yemen (PDRY): Problems and Progress', in US Congress, House of Representatives, *Diego Garcia, 1975: The Debate Over the Base and the Island's Former Inhabitants*, Hearings Before the Special Subcommittee on Investigations of the Committee on International Relations, Washington, 1975, pp. 85–92.
75 ME/2643/A/4, 11 December 1967.
76 John Badeau, *An American Approach to the Arab World*, chapter 7, especially pp. 151–2.
77 ME/2835/A/1, 31 July 1968, and Paul Findley, *Rescue in Aden, Report of Representative Paul Findley (R-Ill) on his trip to the People's Democratic Republic of Yemen April 29–May 6, 1974*, p. 8, and *They Dare to Speak Out*, Washington, 1984, pp. 1–11.
78 John Duke Anthony, 'Relations', p. 86.
79 Interview with ʿAbd Allāh al-Khāmrī, Aden, February 1970.
80 Interview with ʿAbd Allāh al-Ashtal, Aden, 27 February 1970.
81 ME/3213/i, 27 October 1969; *Department of State Bulletin*, 17 November 1969.
82 ME/4624/A/3, 13 June 1974.
83 US Department of State, Bureau of Public Affairs, *Background Notes North Yemen*, December, 1980, p. 6.
84 *New Perspectives*, pp. 2–4.
85 Representative Lee Hamilton, in *New Perspectives*, p. v.
86 US Congress, House of Representatives, *Proposed Expansion of US Military Facilities in the Indian Ocean*, hearings Before the Sub-committee on the Near East and South Asia of the Committee on Foreign Affairs, Washington, 1974, pp. 156–7.
87 ME/4443/A/7, 6 November 1973; ME/4466/i, 3 December 1973; ME/4520/A/6, 7 February 1974; Findley quotes ʿAbd Allāh al-Khāmrī as stating that 'three months earlier five vessels of the U.S. seventh fleet came within the twelve-mile territorial limits of Socotra' ('Rescue', p. 8).
88 *Proposed Expansion*, p. 156.
89 *Proposed Expansion*, p. 171.
90 *Proposed Expansion*, p. 177.
91 Interview with Representative Paul Findley, Washington, 2 March 1979.
92 Findley, 'Rescue', pp. 4–5.
93 *Ibid.*, p. 5.
94 *Ibid.*, pp. 14–15.
95 *Ibid.*, p. 20.
96 ME/4757/A/4, 16 November 1974.
97 ME/4772/A/4, 4 December 1974; ME/4971/A/8, 2 August 1975.
98 US Congress, House of Representatives, *United States Arms Policies in the*

Persian Gulf and Red Sea Areas: Past, Present, and Future, Report of a Staff Survey Mission to Ethiopia, Iran and the Arabian Peninsula, Washington 1977, p. 76.

99 Interview with Muḥammad Ṣāliḥ Muṭiyyaʿ, December 1977.

100 Address by Brother Sālim Rubiyyaʿ ʿAlī, 30 November 1977, pp. 34–5.

101 *International Herald Tribune*, 13 June 1977.

102 Findley interview, 1970; Paul Findley, *They Dare to Speak Out*, p. 10.

103 ME/5862/A/1, 12 July 1978.

104 *International Herald Tribune*, 6 August 1978.

105 *Ibid.*

106 Interview with Robert Pelletreau, US Department of State, Washington, 27 January 1982.

107 Henry Kissinger, *For the Record*, p. 217; Jimmy Carter, *Keeping Faith, Memoirs of a President*, London, 1982, p. 384.

108 *Presidential Directive 79–6, Memorandum for Secretary of State and Secretary of Defense*, 7 March 1979, obtained through Freedom of Information Act; *International Herald Tribune*, 13 March 1979.

109 Lt.-Col. John Ruszkiewicz, 'How the US Lost Its Footing in the Shifting Sands of the Persian Gulf – A Case History in the Yemen Arab Republic', *Armed Forces Journal International*, September 1980.

110 Interview with Gary Sick, former National Security Council official, London, 18 September 1985; US Congress, House of Representatives, *Proposed Arms Transfers to the Yemen Arab Republic*, Hearing Before the Subcommittee on Europe and the Middle East, Washington, 1979, p. 11; *New York Times*, 13 March 1979. An overview of US policy-making, and policy differences, during the Yemen crisis in Raymond Garthoff, *Detente and Confrontation*, Washington, 1985, pp. 653–60.

111 *The Guardian*, 5 December 1986.

112 *Proposed Arms Transfers*, p. 8.

113 US Congress, House of Representatives, *US Interests In, And Policies Toward, The Persian Gulf, 1980*, Hearings Before the Subcommittee on Europe and the Middle East of the Committee on Foreign Affairs, Washington, 1980, pp. 418–20.

114 *International Herald Tribune*, 10 May 1977.

115 Findley interview; *International Herald Tribune*, 5 March 1982.

116 Central Intelligence Agency, National Foreign Assessment Center, *Patterns of International Terrorism, 1980*, PA81–10163U, p. 9.

117 *Proposed Arms Transfers*, pp. 17–18.

118 Interview with State Department Yemens Desk Officer, Michael Arrietti, 6 March 1981.

119 *Ibid.*

120 Pelletreau interview, 1982.

121 *International Herald Tribune*, 24 August 1981.

122 Edward Luttwak, 'Cubans in Arabia?', *Commentary*, December 1979.

123 Reagan on South Yemen in *Miami Herald*, 8 February 1980.

124 *International Herald Tribune*, 5 March 1982.

125 Interview with President ʿAlī Nāṣir Muḥammad, 11 March 1983 see appendix 6, p. 247. For details see US Congress, House of Representatives, *US Security Interests in the Persian Gulf*, Report of a Staff Study Mission to the Persian Gulf, Middle East, and Horn of Africa, to the Committee on Foreign Affairs, Washington, 1981, pp. 15–20.
126 ME/6646/A/1, 11 February 1981.
127 Michael Klare, *Beyond the 'Vietnam Syndrome'*, Washington, 1981, p. 40.
128 ME/720A1, 9 December 1982; ME/7205/A/4, 10 December 1982; ME/7208/A/1–2, 14 December 1982; ME/7210/A/i, 16 December 1982; ME/7211/A/10, 17 December 1982.
129 ME/6956/A/1–2, 17 February 1982; ME/6963/A/11, 1982, ME/7010/1, 24 April 1982; ME/7031/A/8, 20 May 1982. For subsequent additional information, see n.132. In the March 1983 interview published as appendix 6, President ʿAlī Nāṣir cited the CIA sabotage campaign as the reason why his government had no intention of re-establishing diplomatic relations with the USA.
130 Luttwak, 'Cubans' *Proposed Arms Transfers*, pp. 3–4.
131 E.g. *al-Muʿtamar al-Istiṯhnāʾī*, Beirut, 1980, pp. 449–50.
132 Bob Woodward, *Veil, The Secret Wars of the CIA*, London, 1987, p. 215; *The Guardian*, 5 December 1986.
133 'Flirting with the West; South Yemen loosens its ties to the Soviet bloc', *Newsweek*, 28 January 1985.
134 *International Herald Tribune*, 9 July 1985; State Department comment, *International Herald Tribune*, 13–14 July 1985.
135 *International Herald Tribune*, 23 January 1986.
136 *New York Times*, 24 January 1986.
137 *Los Angeles Times*, 18 January 1986.
138 'Remarks of William J. Casey, Director of Central Intelligence at the Harry J. Sievers Lecture Series, Center for the Study of the Presidency, Fordham University, Lincoln Center Campus, New York City, Tuesday 25 February 1986', transcript.
139 Under Secretary Armacost, 'Dealing with Gorbachev's Soviet Union', *Current Policy*, no. 825, United States Department of State, Bureau of Public Affairs, Washington, 1986.
140 United States Department of Defence, *Soviet Military Power, 1987*, Washington, March 1987, pp. 140–1.
141 *New York Times*, 25 May 1986.
142 *Ibid.*
143 SWB ME/8167/A/9, 27 January 1986; *The Guardian*, 6 February 1986.

4 The enigmas of Yemeni unity

1 A comprehensive overview of the Free Yemeni movement can be found in Leigh Douglas, *The Free Yemeni Movement*, Beirut, 1987; p. 212 summarises views on the South.
2 *Mīṯhāḳ*, pp. 6–7.

3 *Bayyān Siyyāsī*, in Ḥawātma, *Azmat*, p. 245.
4 *Constitution of People's Democratic Republic of Yemen*, Aden, 1971, p. 3; Arabic version in al-Djabḥa al-Ḳawmiyya, *Al-Thawra al-Waṭaniyya*, pp. 153–4.
5 *Barnāmadj*, in *al-Thawra al-Waṭaniyya*, p. 69.
6 *Dustūr*, in *al-Thawra al-Waṭaniyya*, p. 69.
7 *al-Muʾtamar al-Tawḥīdī*, p. 225.
8 *Barnāmadj al-Ḥizb al-Ishtirākī al-Yamanī*, pp. 18–23.
9 *Constitution of the People's Democratic Republic of Yemen*, pp. 3–4; Arabic text, as *Dustūr*, Aden, 1978.
10 *al-Muʾtamar al-ʾIstithnāʾī*, pp. 453–4.
11 *The Encyclopaedia of Islam*, London, 1934, vol, IV (part 2) T–Z, p. 1155.
12 *Mīthāḳ*, p. 64, has the name of the NLF as *al-Djabḥa al-Ḳawmiyya li-Taḥrīr Djanūb al-Yaman al-Muḥtall*, while on p. 109 the name is given as *al-Djabḥa al-Ḳawmiyya li-Taḥr-ř al-Djanūb al-Yamanī al-Muḥtall.*
13 On the origins of the nationalist movement in the Yemens see: Douglas, *Free Yemeni Movement*; Sultan Naji, 'The Genesis of the Call for Yemeni Unity', and Leigh Douglas, n.1 above and the summary in 'The Free Yemeni Movement: 1935–62', both in B.R. Pridham (ed.), *Contemporary Yemen: Politics and Historical Background*, London, 1984; and J.E. Peterson, *Yemen, The Search for a Modern State*, London, 1982, chapter 3.
14 *Mīthāḳ*, p. 100.
15 *Ibid.*, p. 96.
16 *Ibid.*, p. 102.
17 *Ibid.*, pp. 103–4.
18 *Ibid.*, p. 56.
19 Clause 2 in *al-Thawra al-Waṭaniyya*, p. 155.
20 *Ibid.*
21 *al-Dustūr al-Dāʾim lil-Djumhūriyya al-ʿArabīyya al-Yamaniyya*, in Aḥmad Djābir ʿAfīf, *al-Ḥarakat al-Waṭaniyya fī al-Yaman*, Damascus, 1982, pp. 399–448.
22 Clause 1, *al-Dustūr al-Dāʾim*, in *al-Ḥarakat*, p. 402.
23 Clause 3, *al-Dustūr al-Daʾim*, in *al-Ḥarakat*, p. 402.
24 PDRY, *Dustūr*, 1978, p. 1.
25 *Barnāmadj al-Hizb* of 1978 talks both of al-Taḥarrur al-Waṭani al-ʿArabī (p. 9) and al-Harakat al-Waṭaniyya al-Yamaniyya (p. 12).
26 *Quṭr* can mean 'zone', 'region', 'section', 'country' or 'land'. For Baʿthist usage see Bahgat Korany and Ali Dessouki (eds.) *The Foreign Policies of Arab States*, London, 1984, p. 318, n.15.
27 On the early history see references in n.13 above.
28 See references in n.13 above.
29 Interview with former YAR President ʿAbd Allāh al-Sallāl, Sanaʿa, February 1984.
30 Interviews with Sulṭan Aḥmad ʿUmar, Aden, May 1973, and former YAR Premier Muḥsin al-ʿAynī, Exeter, July 1983.
31 ME/2994/A/9, 7 February 1969.

32 ME/3000/A/2, 14 February 1969.
33 ME/4130/A/3, 28 October 1972, for PDRY rejection of the 1934 agreement.
34 After the exchange of diplomatic recognition in 1982 a PDRY–Omani boundary commission was established (Omani Foreign Minister Yusūf ʿAlawī, Chatham House lecture, 26 September 1983).
35 On the nineteenth-century background see Bidwell, *The Yemens*, pp. 48–53.
36 ME/2642/A/3, 9 December 1967.
37 ME/2701/A/3, 21 February 1968.
38 Peterson, *Yemen*, p. 107; Halliday, *Arabia*, p. 118.
39 Interview with Sulṭān Aḥmad ʿUmar, Aden, April 1973, and ʿUmar's *Naẓra fī Taṭawwur al-Mudjtamaʿa al-Yamanī*, Beirut, 1970, pp. 188ff.
40 ME/3438/A/1, 24 July 1970.
41 *Official Gazette*, Aden, 16 April 1968.
42 ME/2761/A/3, 4 May 1968.
43 ME/2804/A/1, 25 June 1968.
44 ME/2837/A/5, 2 August 1968.
45 ME/2991/A/1, 4 February 1969.
46 ME/2992/A/2, 5 February 1969.
47 ME/2994/A/10, 7 February 1969.
48 *Ibid.*
49 ME/3002/A/6, 17 February 1969.
50 ME/3605/A/7, 9 February 1971.
51 ME/3544/A/14, 26 November 1970.
52 ME/3576/A/12, 6 January 1971.
53 ME/3338/E/2–3, 27 May 1970.
54 ME/3435/A/3, 21 July 1970.
55 PDRY, Ministry of Information and Culture, Address of the Political Organisation and State, 30 November 1970, pp. 17–19.
56 1970 Constitution, Arabic, in *al-Thawra al-Waṭaniyya*, p. 155.
57 ME/3550/i, 1 December 1970.
58 *al-Dustūr al-Dāʾim*, in ʿAfīf, *Harakat*, pp. 409ff.
59 Bidwell, *The Yemens*, p. 259; Halliday, *Arabia*, p. 133.
60 ME/3754/A/1, 6 August 1971.
61 Sulṭān Aḥmad ʿUmar interview, Aden, April 1973.
62 The Yemeni Revolutionary Resisters' Organisation – Yemeni Arab Republic, Central Leadership Statement, 25 January 1973, document in author's possession.
63 *Keesings Contemporary Archives*, 1–7 January 1973, p. 25654.
64 Bidwell, *The Yemens*, p. 259.
65 ME/3939/A/7–9, 14 March 1972.
66 ME/3941/A/2–4, 16 March 1972.
67 International Institute for Strategic Studies, *Strategic Survey 1972*, p. 29; *The Times*, 25 October 1972.
68 *The Times*, 25 October 1972; *Afrique-Asie*, 2 October 1972; *The Guardian*, 6 October 1972.
69 E.g. ME/4056, 2 August 1972; ME/4057, 3 August 1972; ME/4063, 10

August 1972; ME/4069, 17 August 1972; ME/4079, 30 August 1972; ME/4082, 2 September 1972.
70 ME/4095/A/8–10, 18 September 1972.
71 ME/4105/A/1, 29 September 1972.
72 ME/4124/i, 21 October 1972; *Financial Times*, 20 October 1972.
73 *The Times*, 3 October 1973; *Strategic Survey 1972*, pp. 29–30.
74 ME/4115/A/9–11, 11 October 1972; *The Times*, 9 October 1972.
75 *The Times*, 4 October 1972.
76 ME/4133/A/10, 1 November 1972; *The Times*, 30 October 1972.
77 ME/4133/A/10–13, 1 November 1972, see appendix 1, p. 233.
78 ME/4158/A/7, 30 November 1972.
79 ME/4158/A/9.
80 ME/4158/A/8.
81 SU/4156/A4/2, 29 November 1972.
82 ME/4143/i, 13 November 1972.
83 *Le Monde*, 5 December 1972.
84 E.g. the economic and financial affairs committee in February, ME/4230/A/7; the foreign affairs committee in March, ME/4240/A/9, 9 March 1973; the military affairs committee in April, ME/4276/A/7, 20 April 1973.
85 *Le Monde*, 29 December 1972.
86 Bidwell, *The Yemens*, p. 263; Peterson, *Yemen*, p. 111.
87 Interview with Sulṭān Aḥmad ʿUmar, May 1973.
88 Thus ʿAbd Allāh al-K͟hāmrī in ME/4250/A/i, 21 March 1973, and Ḳaḍī al-Īryānī in ME/4322/A/3–4, 16 June 1973.
89 Bidwell, *The Yemens*, p. 107; Wenner, *Modern Yemen*, pp. 146–7; translated text as 'Treaty of Islamic Friendship and Arab Fraternity between the Kingdom of Saʿūdi Arabia and the Kingdom of the Yaman, May 20, 1934', in Royal Institute of International Affairs, *Documents on International Affairs 1934*, Oxford, 1935, pp. 458–64. Article 22 gives the duration of the treaty as twenty lunar years.
90 E.g. ME/4130/A/3, 28 October 1972.
91 Joint YAR–Saudi Communiqué on the frontier in ME/4258/A/8.
92 ME/4399/A/5–6, 15 September 1973.
93 ME/4449/i, 13 November 1973; Joint Communiqué ME/4451/A/12, 15 November 1973.
94 Official statements on unity after the coup in ME/4626/A/5, 15 June 1974, for the YAR, and ME/4627/A/3, 17 June 1974, for the PDRY.
95 Bidwell, *The Yemens*, pp. 316–17.
96 Bidwell, *The Yemens*, pp. 274–6; Peterson, *Yemen*, pp. 117–21.
97 Bidwell, *The Yemens*, p. 295.
98 *Ibid.*, p. 275; Peterson, *Yemens*, pp. 119–20.
99 Interview with Sulṭān Aḥmad ʿUmar, 2 November 1977.
100 Interview with representative of *Ḥizb al-ʿAmal*, Aden, 30 October 1977.
101 *al-D͟jabḥa al-Dīmuḳrāṭiyya al-Waṭaniyya fī D͟jumhūriyya al-ʿArabiyya al-Yamaniyya*, in *Barnāmad͟j al-ʿAmal*, n.p. n.d.
102 *Ibid.*

103 ME/5442/A/2, 18 February 1977.
104 ME/5472/A/5–6, 25 March 1977.
105 ME/5589/i, 15 August 1977.
106 ME/5626/A/1–2, 28 September 1977.
107 ME/5639/A/5–6, 13 October 1977. Bidwell, *The Yemens*, p. 275; Peterson, *Yemens*, p. 121.
108 ME/5640/A/6, 14 October 1977; ME/5654/A/3, 31 October 1977.
109 ME/5646/i, 21 October 1977.
110 Peterson, *Yemen*, p. 122.
111 Initial statement in ME/5848/A/3–4, 26 June 1978; later detailed report in ME/5833/A/3–6, 8 June 1978.
112 Interview with PDRY Ambassador in London, Muḥammad Ḥādī ʿAwwaḍ, 6 August 1978.
113 Interview with Yemeni People's Unity Party representative, 'al-Ḥamdānī', Aden, 10 February 1984, in *MERIP Reports*, February 1985; Peterson, *Yemen*, February 1985, p. 122; *Le Monde*, 9 May 1979.
114 ME/5944/A/7–9, 17 October 1978; Peterson, *Yemen*, p. 133, n.37.
115 Al-Ḥamdānī interview; ME/6010/A/1, 8 January 1979.
116 ME/5944/A/9–10, 17 October 1978.
117 ME/5951/A/7–8, 25 October 1978; ME/5952/A/1–2, 26 October 1978.
118 Al-Ḥamdānī interview; *Le Monde*, 9 May 1979.
119 ME/6052/i, 26 February 1979; ME/6053/i, 27 February 1979; *The Guardian*, 23 February 1979.
120 ME/6054/A/5, 28 February 1979.
121 ME/6082/A/3, 2 April 1979.
122 Al-Ḥamdānī interview.
123 ME/6055/A/8, 1 March 1979; *The Guardian*, 13 March 1979, and 23 March 1979.
124 *International Herald Tribune*, 14 March 1979; *The Guardian*, 12 April 1979.
125 Statement of Deputy Assistant Secretary of State William R. Crawford, 12 March 1979, in *Proposed Arms Transfers to the Yemeni Arab Republic*, Washington, 1979, pp. 6–11; William Safire in *New York Times*, 15 March 1979.
126 *The Observer*, 25 March 1979.
127 Bidwell, *The Yemens*, p. 281; Peterson, *Yemen*, p. 124.
128 ME/6082/A/4, 2 April 1979.
129 *The Guardian*, 23 March 1979.
130 *The Economist*, 23 February 1980; *International Herald Tribune*, 19 March 1980 and 6 June 1980.
131 *Ḥizb al-Wahda al-Shaʿabiyya al-Yamaniyya*, al-Barnāmadj al-Siyyāsī (Political Programme), 1979. For an excellent overview of the changing balance of forces in the YAR after 1979 see Robert Burrowes, 'The Yemen Arab Republic and the Ali Abdallah Salih Regime: 1978–1984', *The Middle East Journal*, vol. 39 no. 3 (summer 1985).
132 *Washington Post*, 20 February 1980; *International Herald Tribune*, 19 March 1980.

133 *Le Monde*, 23 April 1980; *International Herald Tribune*, 23 April 1980.
134 Information gathered on visit to Aden, February 1984.
135 ME/6414/A/9–10, 8 May 1980; Communiqué in ME/6415/A/1–3, 9 May 1980.
136 ME/6446/A/1–4, 16 June 1980.
137 *Le Monde*, 22 February 1980; *International Herald Tribune*, 19 February 1980; *The Economist*, 23 February 1980.
138 ME/6439/A/3, 7 June 1980.
139 Al-Ḥamdānī interview; for further background see: *International Herald Tribune*, 7–8 June 1980; *The Economist*, 4 April 1981; *Sunday Times*, 6 September 1981; *Le Monde*, 18 November 1981; *Le Monde*, 7 June 1982.
140 *The Times*, 17 December 1981.
141 Text of 1981 YAR–PDRY agreement in ME/6898/A/1–5, 5 December 1981; announcement of constitution in ME/6917/A/8, 1 January 1982.
142 ME/7022/A/1, 10 May 1982.
143 Author's interview with ʿAlī Nāṣir Muḥammad, 11 March 1983, appendix 6. On the CIA campaign in 1982–3 see note 132, p. 273.
144 ME/7859/A/5, 26 January 1985; on oil production in the YAR see *Le Monde*, 23 October 1985, and special supplement on North Yemen in *International Herald Tribune*, 20–1 December 1986.
145 *Le Monde*, 6 May 1986, and 3 December 1986.
146 ME/8632/A/11, 29 July 1987.
147 *Le Monde*, 17 November 1987.
148 *Le Monde*, 14 October 1987. The South Yemeni view is given by Foreign Minister al-Dālī in *Al-Yawm al-Sābiḥ* (Beirut), 28 September 1987.
149 Thus the official PDRY statement on the death of al-Ḥamdī stressed that his life was 'marked by his rejection of all foreign interference in the affairs of the Yemen and Yemeni sovereignty', ME/5640/A/6, 14 October 1977.
150 Thus ʿAbd al-Fattāḥ Ismāʿīl in October 1978 spoke of the YAR leader as having sold the land of Yemen to foreigners (ME/5952/A/1–2), while YAR criticism of the PDRY in June 1978 took analogous forms (ME/5849/A/4, 27 June 1978).
151 *Le Monde*, 20 December 1980.

5 Regional orientations

1 *Mīthāḳ*, pp. 104–5.
2 In Ḥawāṭma, *Azmat*, p. 217.
3 ME/3065/A/8, 5 May 1969.
4 ME/3932/A/10, 6 March 1972.
5 ME/3836/A/6, 11 November 1971.
6 E.H. Carr, *The Bolshevik Revolution*, vol. 3, 1951.
7 On the war in Dhofar see John Akehurst, *We Won A War*, Salisbury, 1982; Fred Halliday, *Arabia*, chapters 10 and 11; John Townsend, *Oman*, London, 1977, chapters 5 and 6.
8 ME/6761/A/3, 29 June 1981.

9 Bertram Thomas, *Four Strange Tongues from South Arabia*, London, 1937.
10 Tom Hickinbotham (*Aden*, pp. 196–7) reports that Oman was sometimes mentioned as Yemeni territory. *Mīthāķ* (pp. 78–9) claims only the Kuria Muria Islands and the Eastern Protectorates, not any of the territory of Oman. In the immediate aftermath of independence, one left leader in Hadramaut, ʿAbd Allāh al-Ashtal, did assert a claim to Dhofar but he was reprimanded by Aden for doing so and after the March 1986 crisis he was expelled from the NF by Ķaḥṭān al-Shaʿabī, for this and other views he expressed (Interview with al-Ashtal, February 1970).
11 Author's observation, February 1970, May 1973, in the South Yemen–Oman frontier area.
12 Author's interviews with PFLOAG leaders, Dhofar, February 1970; Hashim Behbehani, *China's Foreign Policy in the Arab World 1955–75*, London, 1981, chapter 6.
13 'Declaration on the Launching of Armed Struggle, June 1965', in *Documents of the National Struggle in Oman and the Arabian Gulf*, translated and published by the Gulf Committee, London, 1974, pp. 7–9.
14 Julian Paget, *Last Post: Aden 1964–1967*, London, 1968, p. 174.
15 Author's interviews in Dhofar, February 1970.
16 Behbehani, *China's Foreign Policy*, pp. 139–43; Halliday, *Arabia*, pp. 305–18.
17 *Documents*, pp. 9–11.
18 Behbehani, *China's Foreign Policy*, pp. 175–88. Chinese coverage of the Dhofar war in *Peking Review*, no. 49 (1969), and no. 4 (1970). Chinese support for PFLOAG was affirmed in the earlier joint statements with visiting South Yemeni delegations; see chapter 5.
19 *Documents*, p. 10.
20 *Documents*, pp. 20–4; Behbehani, *China's Foreign Policy*, pp. 155–6.
21 *Documents*, pp. 20–30.
22 Political Statement in ME/4674/A/1–4, 10 August 1974, and *Documents*, pp. 87–94.
23 Author's interview with PFLO representatives, Aden, February 1984.
24 ME/7058/A/14–15, 22 June 1982; ME/7060/A/13, 24 June 1982.
25 Ranulph Fiennes, *Where Angels Fear to Tread*, London, 1975, chapters 4–6; Captain N.G.R. Hepworth, 'The Unknown War', *The White Horse and Fleur de Lys*, Journal of the King's Regiment, vol. 6 no. 6 (winter 1970).
26 Akehurst, *War*, p. 15; author's observation, Dhofar, February 1970.
27 Townsend, *Oman*, pp. 77–8.
28 Akehurst, *War*, p. 82.
29 *Ibid.*, p. 169.
30 Author's observation, Dhofar, 1970, 1973.
31 *Ibid.*
32 ME/3797/A/4, 27 September 1971, reports the start of a radio entitled 'Voice of the Masses, Voice of the PFLOAG' on 24 September 1971; ME/7177/i, 8 November 1982, reports the ending of the 'Voice of the Oman Revolution' on 6 November 1982.

33 PDRY statement in ME/3789/A/9–10, 17 September 1971; PFLOAG–NDFLOAG Joint Statement of July 1971 in *Documents*, pp. 34–6.
34 *The Times*, 13 February 1968.
35 'On Continued Violations by British Aircrafts on Democratic Yemen's Air Space', Official Statement by the Council of Ministers of the PDRY, issued by the PDRY Embassy, London, 10 May 1972.
36 *Ibid.*
37 Townsend, *Oman*, p. 104.
38 Author's observation, Hauf, May 1973.
39 Akehurst, *War*, p. 159.
40 Author's interview with PFLOAG leaders, Dhofar, May 1973.
41 ME/3981/A/5–6, 5 May 1972; ME/4172/A/3, 16 December 1972; ME/4173/A/7, 18 December 1972; ME/4196/A/1, 17 January 1973.
42 ME/4456/A/7, 21 November 1973.
43 Akehurst, *War*, pp. 159–60; Colonel Tony Jeapes, *SAS Operation Oman*, London, 1980.
44 Jeapes, *SAS*, p. 228.
45 *Financial Times*, 25 March 1976.
46 Interview with ʿAbd Allāh al-Ashtal, PDRY representative at the UN, 20 October 1976.
47 Author's observation, Aden, October–November 1977.
48 Akehurst, *War*, p. 29; Embassy of the Sultanate of Oman, London, press release, 23 December 1975. Small numbers of fighters from other countries also fought for some periods of the war, with the Dhofar guerrillas: these included around 150 North Yemenis and some Iranians.
49 ME/5046/A/2, 30 October 1975.
50 *Daily Telegraph*, 7 February 1974.
51 ME/5375/A/1–2, 27 November 1976.
52 *Financial Times*, 25 March 1976.
53 E.g. the YSP statement on the 9 June 1980 anniversary in ME/6442/A/1, 11 June 1980.
54 *al-Muʾtamar al-Istithnāʾī*, pp. 373–6.
55 ME/4564/A/4, 30 March 1974; *Le Monde*, 24 May 1974.
56 *Keesings Contemporary Archives*, 17–23 June 1974, p. 26579; ME/4667/i, 2 August 1974.
57 ME/4567/A/3, 3 April 1974; ME/4572/A/1, 9 April 1974; ME/4581/A/1, 23 April 1974; ME/4599/A/1–3, 14 May 1974.
58 *Documents*, pp. 40–6.
59 ME/4567/A/3, 3 April 1974.
60 ME/4845/A/6, 4 March 1975.
61 ME/4778/A/1, 11 December 1974.
62 *al-Muʾtamar al-Tawḥīdī*, p. 218.
63 ME/5534/A/35, 11 June 1977.
64 Interview with official of PDRY Embassy, London, 1979.
65 ME/6439/A/10, 7 June 1980.

66 ME/6462/A/7, July 1980.
67 Gary Sick, 'The Evolution of US Strategy Toward the Indian Ocean and the Persian Gulf Regions', in Alvin Z. Rubinstein (ed.) *The Great Game*, New York, 1983.
68 Raphael Iungerich, 'US Rapid Deployment Forces – USCENTCOM – What Is It? Can It Do the Job?', *Armed Forces Journal International*, 18 November 1984.
69 On March, see ME/6676/A/1, 18 March 1981; ME/6684/A/4, 27 March 1981; ME/6753/A/1, 19 June 1981; ME/6898/A/1, 5 December 1981.
70 ME/6752/A/1, 18 June 1981.
71 ME/6764/A/1, 2 July 1981.
72 ME/7045/A/1, 7 June 1982; ME/7046/A/1, 8 June 1982.
73 ME/7074/A/1, 10 July 1982; ME/7078/A/2, 15 July 1982.
74 ME/7169/A/1, 29 October 1982.
75 ME/7177/i, 8 November 1982.
76 ME/7168/A/1, 28 October 1982.
77 ME/7171/A/1, 1 November 1982.
78 *Ibid.*
79 PDRY officials consistently denied that any cease-fire had been agreed upon, stating, in part, that there could be no cease-fire since there had never been a war in the first place between Oman and the PDRY: see interview with Foreign Minister Mutiyyaʿ, appendix 3.
80 Yusuf Alawi, Lecture at Royal Institute of International Relations, 26 September 1983.
81 *Le Monde*, 16 October 1987; *The Observer*, 25 October 1987.
82 Interview with ʿAbd Allāh al-K̲h̲āmrī, February 1970.
83 Author's interviews with PDRY officials, *passim*.
84 This is evident from the tone of the 1968 official texts, in *Documents*; in 1970 guerrillas inside Dhofar wore Mao badges, studied his *Thoughts*, and denounced an unspecified 'tahrifiyya' ('revisionism') in their slogans (author's observation).
85 ME/3789/A/12, 17 September 1971; ME/3801/A/7, 1 October 1971. On Soviet policy towards Dhofar see Katz, *Russia*, pp. 113ff. The first Soviet delegation, comprising a reporter and a military expert, visited Dhofar in May 1969: a PFLOAG delegation had already made an unannounced visit to Moscow and some arms had been sent early in 1969.
86 E.g. ʿAlī Nāṣir Muḥammad on the need to resist financial pressure from the Gulf states, ME/4062/A/6, 9 August 1972.
87 ME/4162/A/3, 5 December 1972.
88 Interview with representatives of the People's Democratic Party in the Arabian Peninsula, Aden, May 1973. During this period the PDP published the journal *al-D̲j̲azīra al-D̲j̲adida*.
89 Four South Yemenis as well as ten Egyptians were amongst those on the list of people executed by the Saudi authorities after the Mecca incident, in January 1980, ME/6316/A/2–3, 11 January 1980.

90 David Holden and Richard Jones, *The House of Saud*, London, 1981, pp. 272, 303–4; William Quandt, *Saudi Arabia in the 1980s*, Washington, 1981, pp. 25–8, 68, 82.
91 ME/5850/A/5–6, 28 June 1978. For general discussion of South Yemeni–Saudi strategic relations see Nadav Safran, *Saudi Arabia*, London, 1985, chapters 11 and 15, and Anthony Cordesman *The Gulf and the Search for Strategic Security*, London, 1984, chapters 12 and 16. This 'Strategic' literature (e.g. Cordesman, p. 784) talks easily of a PDRY 'threat' to Saudi Arabia, but this is an exaggeration: at no time was Aden militarily strong enough to threaten the Saudis.
92 Harold Wilson, *The Labour Government 1964–1970*, London, 1971, p. 396.
93 ME/2641/A/10, 8 December 1967.
94 ME/2835/A/1, 31 July 1968.
95 ME/2838/A/2, 3 August 1968.
96 Quandt, *Saudi Arabia*, p. 82; author's interview with James Akins, former US ambassador in Saudi Arabia, London, 1 October 1980.
97 Holden and Johns, *House*, p. 272.
98 *Ibid.*, pp. 303–4.
99 *Ibid.*, p. 272.
100 *Ibid.*, pp. 281–2; ME/3244/A/1, 2 December 1969; *The Times*, 27 November 1969 and 28 November 1969; *Le Monde*, 28 November 1969.
101 Katz, *Russia*, p. 76, sees al-Wadiah as a Saudi invasion attempt. ME/3248/A/1, 6 December 1969; *The Times*, 18 December 1969.
102 Information Division of the Foreign Ministry of Southern Yemen, 'Facts on Saudi Arabian Aggression Against Southern Yemen', statement of 22 December 1969.
103 *New Perspectives*, pp. 4, 10–11.
104 Interview with ʿAbd Allāh al-Ashtal, New York, 20 October 1976.
105 FCO letter to author, 7 January 1982.
106 *Le Monde*, 1 December 1972.
107 *Ibid.*
108 ME/4253/A/i, 24 March 1973.
109 ME/4707/A/1, 19 September 1974.
110 ME/4771/A/4, 3 December 1974.
111 ME/5156/A/8–9, 11 March 1976.
112 ME/5421/A/5, 23 June 1976, in which, in June 1976, Sālim Rubiyyaʿ ʿAlī reaffirms support for the PFLO.
113 ME/5156/A/8–9, 11 March 1976.
114 ME/W934/A1/3, 21 June 1977. PDRY sources later stated that this Saudi aid was to be for the construction of 2,000 flats in Aden, and for rural roads.
115 ME/5240/A/5, 22 June 1976.
116 Saudi statistics for 1979 give the total for PDRY pilgrims on the *hajj* as 14,201.
117 V. Naumkin, 'Southern Yemen: The Road to Progress', *International Affairs*, no. 1 (1978), p. 68.

118 ME/7178/i, 9 November 1982, on the holding of direct talks about the border.
119 Author's interview with Muṭiyyaᶜ, see appendix 3.
120 ME/5580/A/1, 4 August 1977.
121 ME/5654/A/3, 31 October 1977.
122 ME/5852/A/4, 30 June 1978; ME/5855/A/9, 4 July 1978.
123 ME/5851/A/5–6, 29 June 1978.
124 ME/5855/A/5–6, 4 July 1978.
125 ME/6082/A/6–7, 2 April 1979.
126 For PDRY denunciation of the US role in the Peninsula, see ME/6064/A/2.
127 ME/6956/A/1, 17 February 1982; ME/6963/A/11, 25 February 1982.
128 ME/6458/i, 30 June 1980.
129 ME/7096/A/1, 5 August 1982.
130 *Le Monde*, 6 May 1986.
131 Townsend, *Oman*, p. 186; *Financial Times*, 4 February 1972.
132 ME/2913/A/2, 31 October 1968.
133 World Bank, *PDRY Economic Memorandum, 3–570 YDR*, Washington, 29 January 1982.
134 Author's observation, Aden, 1973 and 1977.
135 ME/6640/A/3–4, 4 February 1981.
136 ME/3758/A/8, 11 August 1971.
137 ME/3740/A/21, 21 July 1971.
138 ME/3779/A/9, 6 September 1971; ME/3789/A/9, 17 September 1971.
139 ME/3786/A/3–4, 14 September 1971; see also interview with Muṭiyyaᶜ, Appendix 3.
140 ME/3789/A/9–10, 17 September 1971.
141 ME/3753/A/3, 5 August 1971.
142 Behbehani, *China's Foreign Policy*, p. 156.
143 ME/3859/E/5, 8 December 1971.
144 In the General Assembly vote of 21 September 1971 on the admission of Bahrain and Qatar, no state was recorded as voting against Bahrain, and only the PDRY against Qatar (*UN General Assembly, 26th Session, Official Records, 1934th Plenary Meeting*, 21 September 1971, p. 8). In the vote on Oman of 7 October 1971 the PDRY voted against, while Cuba and Saudi Arabia abstained (*Official Records, 1937th Plenary Meeting*, 7 October 1971, p. 20). In the vote on the admission of the Amirates, only the PDRY voted against, and there were no abstentions (*Official Records, 2007th Plenary Meeting*, 9 December 1971, p. 2).
145 On each occasion, a representative of the Soviet bloc was amongst those making speeches of welcome to the new members. It is perhaps fitting that it fell to the Czech delegate, himself representing a country under foreign occupation, to welcome Oman (*1937th Plenary Meeting*, p. 21).
146 ME/4062/A/5–6, 9 August 1972.
147 *al-Thawra al-Waṭaniyya*, p. 102.
148 E.g. ME/4173/A/7, 18 December 1972.

149 ME/4771/A/3, 3 December 1974.
150 PFLO Congress, in *Documents*, pp. 87–94, and ME/4674/A/1–5, 10 August 1974.
151 Interview with representative of the PFB, London, December 1978. *The Political Programme of the Popular Front in Bahrain*, 5 March Publications, 1st edition 1984, includes amongst its tasks 'To support Democratic Yemen and its progressive regime, confronting the imperialist-reactionary plots and the full support to the Yemeni masses struggling for Yemeni unity' (p. 66). See also *Khamsa Mārs*, monthly organ of the PFB, *passim*.
152 ME/4857/A/5, 18 March 1975.
153 ME/5466/i, 18 March 1977.
154 See Muṭiyyaᶜ interview, appendix 3.
155 Information from PDRY Embassy, London, 1982.
156 On Abu Dhabi, see Townsend, *Oman*, p. 189.
157 See Rubinstein (ed.), *The Great Game*, and Quandt, *Saudi Arabia*.
158 ME/6704/A/1–2, 22 April 1981.
159 ᶜAbd Allāh Bishāra, GCC Secretary General, at Oxford Energy Institute Symposium, Oxford, 6 April 1984.
160 ME/6829/i, 16 September 1981; ME/6836/A/8, 24 September 1981.
161 ME/5232/A/3, 12 June 1976.
162 ME/6133/A/3, 5 June 1979; ME/6142/A/5–6, 15 June 1979.
163 Interview with Othmān Ṣāliḥ Sabbih, Aden, February 1970.
164 On ties to Somalia see, for example, ME/4943/A/1, 1 July 1975.
165 ME/5731/i, 4 February 1978.
166 Author's observation, Aden, October–November 1977.
167 Such charges can be found in Claire Sterling, *The Terror Network*, London, 1981, p. 117. For one German's account of his stay in the PDRY see Peter Jürgen Brock, *Der Spiegel*, no. 9 (1981). In an interview with *Der Spiegel*, no. 49 (1978), ᶜAlī Nāṣir Muḥammad denied (a) that the PDRY supported hijacking and (b) that it trained West German urban guerrillas in camps in the PDRY. It seems that those Palestinians training such foreigners linked to Sālim Rubiyyaᶜ ᶜAlī and that the PDRY tightened control on the Palestinians after June 1978.
168 At the Fifth Congress, of 1972, ᶜAbd al-Fattāḥ Ismāᶜīl reported that one of the first acts of the government that came to power in June 1969 was to recognise the provisional governments of Vietnam and Cambodia.
169 *The Guardian*, 6 October 1972; *The Times*, 23 October 1972.
170 ME/4930/A/3, 16 June 1975; ME/4933/A/4, 19 June 1975.
171 ME/5686/i, 7 December 1977.
172 Interviews with the Aden representatives of the ELF and EPLF, November 1977; their offices were not public at that time, and they were closed entirely in 1978.
173 ME/6203/ii, 25 August 1979.
174 ME/6289/A/2, 6 December 1979.
175 ME/6818/A/1–3, 3 September 1981.
176 ME/6823/A/9, quoting the Cairo paper, *al-Aḥrām*.

177 ME/5375/A/1, 27 November 1976.
178 ME/5835/A/9, 10 June 1978.
179 ME/6403/i, 24 April 1981; ME/7056/A/13, 19 June 1982.
180 *al-Muʾtamar al-Istithnāʾī*, p. 450.
181 ME/7116/i, 28 August 1982.
182 *Mīthāḳ*, pp. 104–5.
183 Author's observation, Aden, 1970, where both the PFLP and the PDFLP had offices, but not al-Fatḥ or the PLO.
184 *Le Monde*, 15 June 1971.
185 ME/4473/i, 11 December 1983; in his *Der Spiegel* interview of 4 December 1978, ʿAlī Nāṣir stated, in response to questions about Israeli shipping, that the PDRY, 'supports the freedom of international shipping routes'.
186 E.g. *Financial Times*, 9 October 1974; Mohamed Heykal, *Sphinx and Commissar*, London, 1978, p. 33.
187 ME/5441/i, 17 February 1977.
188 Interviews with PDRY Foreign Ministry officials, Aden, February 1984.
189 *al-Muʾtamar al-Istithnāʿī*, p. 449.
190 ME/6224/A/7, 20 September 1979.
191 See appendix 7, pp. 257–8.

6 In search of allies

1 *Soviet News*, 11 February 1987, see pp. 212–3.
2 Stephen Page, *The USSR and Arabia*, London, 1971, pp. 111–12. Interview with al-Khāmrī, Aden, February 1970. No credit need be given to the claims of a former Soviet official in the YAR that the USSR had 'controlled' FLOSY (Vladimir Sakharov, *High Treason*, New York, 1980, pp. 140, 157–9). For further background see *The Soviet Attitude Towards the NLF and FLOSY*, US Foreign Broadcast Information Service, Background Brief, no. 83, 1968.
3 On the leftward evolution of the MAN see Walid Kazziha, *Revolutionary Transformation in the Arab World*, London, 1975.
4 Page, *The USSR and Arabia*, pp. 75–6, 89; Behbehani, *China's Foreign Policy*, p. 358.
5 *Current Digest of the Soviet Press* (henceforward CDSP), vol. 19, no. 48 (1967).
6 N. Malayan, 'Struggle of the South Arabian People for Independence', *International Affairs* (Moscow), no. 12 (1967), pp. 136–7.
7 *CDSP*, vol. 19, no. 48 (1967).
8 ME/2701/A/7, 21 February 1978.
9 ME/2944/A/16, 6 December 1968.
10 Author's observation, Aden, February 1970.
11 ME/W55/A1/5, 30 January 1970; SU/2690/A4/1, SU/2964/A4/2.
12 ME/2737/i, 3 April 1968.
13 ME/2863/A/11, 2 September 1968.
14 Page, *The USSR and Arabia*, p. 113.
15 ME/2776/A/5, 22 May 1968.

16 Michael MccGwire, 'The Pattern of Soviet Naval Deployment in the Indian Ocean, 1968–71', in Michael MccGwire (ed.), *Soviet Naval Developments*, New York, 1973, pp. 425–6.
17 Page, *The USSR and Arabia*, p. 113.
18 *Ibid.*
19 *New Times*, no. 7 (1969), p. 4; Page, *The USSR and Arabia*, p. 113.
20 World Bank, *PDRY, A Review of Economic and Social Development*, Table 12.9, p. 162.
21 D. Volsky, 'The Two Yemeni Republics', *New Times*, no. 12 (1968), p. 14.
22 V. Davydov, 'Politics of South Yemen', *New Times*, no. 5 (1969), p. 17.
23 O. Gerasimov, 'Southern Yemen: Toiling Young Republic', *International Affairs*, no. 2–3 (1970), pp. 107–8.
24 A. Vasilyev, 'Visiting Southern Yemen', *New Times*, no. 3 (1970), p. 29.
25 *Pravda*, 25 April 1970, in *CDSP*, vol. 22 no. 16 (1970), p. 2.
26 ME/3396/A/11, 5 June 1970.
27 ME/4165/A/4, 8 December 1972.
28 ME/4162/A/4, 5 December 1972.
29 O. Orestov, 'Dawn over the Desert', *Pravda*, 26 December 1970, in *CDSP*, vol. 22 no. 52.
30 *Ibid.*
31 *Pravda*, 1 August 1971, in *CDSP*, vol. 23 no. 31, see also p. 281 n.85.
32 G. Drambyantz, 'The Persian Gulf: Twixt the Past and the Future', *International Affairs*, no. 10 (1970), pp. 66–71.
33 G. Drambyantz, 'Persian Gulf States', *International Affairs*, no. 1 (1972), p. 100; on Soviet bloc voting in favour of the entry of Bahrain, Qatar, the Amirates and Oman into the UN in 1971, see p. 283, nn.144 and 145.
34 *Pravda*, 26 November 1972, in *CDSP*, vol. 24 no. 47.
35 *Pravda*, 1 August 1971, in *CDSP*, vol. 23 no. 31, pp. 15–16.
36 ME/3789/A/12, 17 September 1971; ME/3801/A/7, 1 October 1971.
37 *Krasnaya Svezda*, 14 April 1971; in *CDSP*, vol. 23 no. 15.
38 *Pravda*, 1 October 1971, in *CDSP*, vol. 23 no. 40, pp. 13–14.
39 *Ibid.*, p. 14; ME/3810/A/10, 12 October 1971.
40 ME/W660/A1/6, 15 February 1972.
41 *Pravda*, 25 November 1972, in *CDSP*, vol. 24 no. 47.
42 *Pravda*, 26 November 1972, in *CDSP*, vol. 24 no. 47.
43 Author's information, Aden, May 1973.
44 Yitzhak Shichor, *The Middle East in China's Foreign Policy 1949–1977*, Cambridge, 1979; and Behbehani, *China's Foreign Policy*, especially chapter 5, for background.
45 *Pravda*, 11 July 1969, in *CDSP*, vol. 21 no. 28 (1969).
46 SU/4104/A4/4, 27 September 1972.
47 *Izvestia*, 22 August 1972, in *CDSP*, vol. 24 no. 34.
48 SU/4104/A4/3, SU/4107/A4/1, Su/4152/A4/1.
49 *Pravda*, 26 November 1972, in *CDSP*, vol. 24 no. 47.
50 *Ibid.*; and SU/4156/A4/2, 29 November 1972.
51 SU/4152/A4/1, 22 November 1972.

52 SU/4152/A4/6, 22 November 1972.
53 *CDSP*, vol. 23 no. 40, p. 14.
54 *CDSP*, vol. 24 no. 47.
55 ME/4062/A/6, 9 August 1972.
56 *CDSP*, vol. 23 no. 40, p. 13.
57 *Ibid.*, p. 14.
58 *CDSP*, vol. 24 no. 47.
59 *CDSP*, vol. 23 no. 40, p. 13.
60 *CDSP*, vol. 24 no. 52.
61 V. Grozdev, 'Changes in Democratic Yemen', *New Times*, no. 41 (1973).
62 Communication of PDRY Embassy in London to author, May 1972.
63 *CDSP*, vol. 25 no. 10, p. 26.
64 *CDSP*, vol. 25 no. 30.
65 *Ibid.*
66 *CDSP*, vol. 26 no. 39, p. 22.
67 *Ibid.*
68 Aryeh Yodfat, *The Soviet Union and the Arabian Peninsula*, Beckenham, 1983, pp. 14–15.
69 *Tass*, 9 August 1974, in Yodfat, *The Soviet Union*, p. 15.
70 Drambyantz, 'Persian Gulf States', p. 100.
71 Yodfat, *The Soviet Union*, p. 15.
72 *CDSP*, vol. 27 no. 43, p. 16.
73 *Krasnaya Svezda*, 2 November 1975, in Yodfat, *The Soviet Union*, p. 72, n. 30; *Financial Times*, 16 October 1975, reports the use of SAM-7s in Dhofar for the first time; Akehurst, *War*, p. 141, reports that the first SAM-7s were fired on 19 August 1975.
74 V. Naumkin, 'Southern Yemen: The Road to Progress', *International Affairs*, no. 1 (1978), p. 68.
75 *CDSP*, vol. 28 no. 31, p. 20.
76 *CDSP*, vol. 29 no. 19, p. 16.
77 Author's observation, Aden, October 1977.
78 *CDSP*, vol. 29 no. 15, p. 5.
79 *CDSP*, vol. 29 no. 19, p. 16.
80 *CDSP*, vol. 29 no. 49, p. 17.
81 *Pravda*, 5 February 1978, in *CDSP*, vol. 30 no. 5.
82 *Pravda*, 4 February 1978, in *CDSP*, vol. 30 no. 5.
83 A. Pravdivtsev, 'The USSR and the PDRY: On the basis of friendship and co-operation', *Selskaya Zhizn*, 15 February 1978, in *CDSP*, vol. 30 no. 7.
84 *CDSP*, vol. 30 no. 26.
85 *Pravda*, 30 June 1978, in *CDSP*, vol. 30 no. 26.
86 *Pravda*, 6 July 1978, in *CDSP*, vol. 30 no. 27.
87 *Pravda*, 25 October 1978, 'Relying on the Masses', in *CDSP*, vol. 30 no. 43.
88 V. Chirkin and Y. Yudin, *A Socialist-Oriented State*, Moscow, 1978.
89 *Pravda*, 28 February 1979, in *CDSP*, vol. 31 no. 9.
90 *Pravda*, 12 March 1979, in *CDSP*, vol. 31 no. 10.

91 For one rare mention of the NDF see reference in n.89 above.
92 *Pravda*, 30 June 1979, in *CDSP*, vol. 31 no. 26.
93 ME/6222/A/6–7, 18 September 1979; text of communiqué in ME/6224/A/5–7, 20 September 1979, and *Soviet News*, 25 September 1979; economic agreement ME/6223/A/4–5, 19 September 1979.
94 *CDSP*, vol. 31 no. 43.
95 *Ibid.*
96 Text in *Soviet News*, 13 November 1979, pp. 367–8, and appendix 4, pp. 241–5.
97 Zafar Imam, 'Soviet Treaties with Third World Countries', *Soviet Studies*, vol. 35 no. 1 (January 1983).
98 *Soviet News*, 13 November 1979, p. 367.
99 *Soviet News*, 23 January 1979, p. 15.
100 *Soviet News*, 14 October 1980.
101 Interview with Muṭiyyaʿ, December 1977; see appendix 3.
102 Discussions with author, 1980–1.
103 V. Kutuzov, 'SSSR–NDRI, Novii Realnosti i Perspektivi', *Vneshnyaya Torgolya*, April 1980.
104 ME/5818/A/5, 20 May 1978.
105 Yodfat, *The Soviet Union*, p. 111; Nimrod Novik, 'Between Two Yemens: Regional Dynamics and Superpower Conduct in Riyadh's "Backyard"', Center for Strategic Studies, Tel Aviv University, 1980, p. 20.
106 *Newsweek*, 26 November 1979.
107 Communications from Yemeni officials, July 1980.
108 *Pravda*, 27 May 1980.
109 *Soviet News*, 3 June 1980.
110 Discussions with Yemeni officials, 1980.
111 *Soviet News*, 3 June 1980.
112 *CDSP*, vol. 32 no. 14, p. 13.
113 Yodfat, *The Soviet Union*, pp. 97–9.
114 *New Times*, no. 44 (1981), and no. 45 (1981).
115 *CDSP*, vol. 33 no. 43, p. 8.
116 *CDSP*, vol. 34 no. 37, pp. 4–6.
117 *Ibid.*
118 A. Guskov, 'Southern Yemen on the Road of Progressive Change', *International Affairs*, no. 11 (1983), p. 28.
119 Anatoly Dinkevich, 'Principles and Problems of Socialist Orientation in the Countries of Africa and Asia', *Soviet News*, 16 October 1979.
120 A. Vasilyev, 'Visiting Southern Yemen', *New Times*, no. 3 (1970).
121 O. Gerasimov, 'Southern Yemen: Toiling Young Republic', *International Affairs*, no. 2–3 (1970).
122 Leonid Medvedko, 'Chain of Imperialist Conspiracies', *New Times*, no. 29 (1978); A. Usvatov, 'Provocation', *New Times*, no. 28 (1978).
123 A. Chistyakov, 'PDRY: Towards Consolidation of Economy', *Asia and Africa Today*, no. 1 (1980).
124 A. Guskov, 'Southern Yemen: Dynamics of Development', *New*

Times, no.49 (1982).

125 Vassily Ozoling and Reuben Andreasyan, 'Some Problems Arising in the Process of the Non-Capitalist Development of the PDRY', paper presented to Exeter University Conference on the Yemens, July 1983, in B. Pridham (ed.), *Economy, Society and Culture in Contemporary Yemen*, Beckenham, 1984.

126 Ozoling and Andreasyan, in Pridham (ed.), *Economy*.

127 V. Naumkin, 'Democratic Yemen: Concerning the Appraisal of the Results of Development', paper presented to Exeter University Conference on the Yemens, July 1983, in Pridham (ed.), *Economy*, pp. 1–5.

128 *Ibid.*, p. 17.

129 On Soviet economic aid as a whole, see V. Naumkin, *Narodnaya Demokraticheskaya Respublika Yemen*, Moscow, 1982, pp. 51–5.

130 Chistyakov, 'PDRY', p. 47.

131 Guskov, *New Times*, no. 49 (1982).

132 World Bank Data, see appendix 8.

133 'Soviet, East European and Western Development Aid 1976–82', Foreign Policy Document no. 85 (1983), tables 2 and 3, Foreign and Commonwealth Office, London.

134 World Bank, *PDRY Review*, 1977, table 3.8, p. 97.

135 World Bank, *PDRY Review*, 1977, table 3.6, p. 95.

136 Chistyakov, 'PDRY', p. 47.

137 CPSU General Secretary Yuri Andropov, in *Soviet News*, 16 June 1983.

138 Ozoling and Naumkin, Exeter papers, as above nn.125 and 127.

139 Author's observation, Moscow, 1982.

140 Author's observation, Aden, 1984.

141 ME/2955/A/6, 19 December 1968.

142 Page, *The USSR*, p. 114.

143 See e.g. Stockholm International Peace Research Institute, *Arms Trade Registers*, 1975, which give details of UK, Canadian and Soviet supplies of aircraft, naval craft and armoured fighting vehicles in the period 1967–73; updated in Michael Brzoska and Thomas Ohlson, *Armed Transfers to the Third World, 1971–1985*, SIPRI, 1987, pp. 275–6.

144 Stockholm International Peace Research Institute, *SIPRI Yearbook 1981, World Armaments and Disarmament*, London, 1981, p. 198; International Institute for Strategic Studies, *The Military Balance 1983–4*, London, 1983, p. 65, gives details of PDRY armaments at 1981. The 1967–85 figures in Norman Cigar, 'South Yemen and the USSR', *Middle East Journal*, (autumn 1985).

145 Interview with ʿAlī Nāṣir Muḥammad, New Delhi, 11 March 1983: appendix 6.

146 Anne M. Kelly, 'Port Visits and the "International Mission" of the Soviet Navy', in Michael MccGwire and John McDonnell (eds.), *Soviet Naval Influence, Domestic and Foreign Dimensions*, London, 1977.

147 Author's observation, Aden, November–December 1977.

148 Sick, *Evolution*, in Rubinstein (ed.), *The Great Game*, p. 68, says that Soviet

Il-38 reconnaissance planes began operating regularly from Aden in 1975; see also Novik, 'The Two Yemens', p. 20, and *Newsweek*, 22 February 1982.

149 For the PDRY statement of January 1980 see ME/6315/i. Naumkin, in *Narodnaya*, pp. 57–8, makes special mention of PDRY endorsement, at the October 1980 Congress of the YSP, of the 'internationalist character of the Soviet Union's assistance to Afghanistan'. Diplomatic relations between Aden and Kabul were not actually established until 1984.

150 ʿAbd al-Fattāḥ Ismāʿīl, in *al-Thawra al-Waṭaniyya*, p. 61.

151 ME/5731/i, 4 February 1978.

152 Author's observation, Moscow, July 1982.

153 Mark Katz, 'Sanaa and the Soviets', *Problems of Communism*, January–February 1984; interview with representative of the Yemeni People's Unity Party, 'Al-Hamdānī', Aden, 10 February 1984.

154 For an early Soviet account of the Dhofar war see A. Vasilyev, 'Rebels Against Slavery', *New Times*, no. 38 (1971).

155 *Le Monde*, 22 October 1981.

156 *CDSP*, vol. 33 no. 37.

157 *Soviet News*, 25 September 1979, p. 310.

158 In September 1987 an Israeli Journalist, Amnon Kapeliuk, visited the PDRY and reported on his visit in the paper *Yediod Ahanarot* (9–10 October 1987): but he did so on a French passport and did not discuss his Israeli affiliation. (Communication to the author from Kapeliuk.)

159 *International Affairs*, no. 11 (1983), pp. 27–8.

160 Author's observation, 1973, interview with Ḥusayn Ḳumāṭā, commander-in-chief of the militia, November 1977.

161 ME/4168/A/16, 12 December 1972.

162 Interview with ʿAlī al-Bīḍ, Minister of Local Government, Aden, October 1977.

163 Author's observation, Aden, February 1984.

164 *International Affairs*, no. 11 (1983), p. 28; Text of DDR–PDRY treaty in *Neues Deutschland*, 19 November 1979.

165 Accounts of Soviet policy during the 1986 crisis in: *Le Monde passim*; Mark Katz, 'Civil Conflict in South Yemen', *Middle East Review*, vol. 8 (Fall 1986); David Pollock, 'Moscow and South Yemen', *Problems of Communism*, May–June 1986; Manfred Wenner, 'The 1986 Civil War in South Yemen', in Brian Pridham (ed.), *The Arab Gulf and the Arab World*, Bakenham, 1988. Soviet accounts in: V. Naumkin, 'South Yemen After the January Tragedy', *New Times*, no. 48 (1986); Y. Glukhov, 'A Difficult Examination – Notes on the People's Democratic Republic of Yemen', *Pravda*, 8 September 1986, in *CDSP*, vol. 38 no. 36.

166 Martin Walker, *The Guardian*, 30 January 1986.

167 E.g. Department of Defense, *Soviet Military Power*, 1987, pp. 140–1.

168 On Afghanistan, see Fred Halliday, 'The War and Revolution in Afghanistan', *New Left Review*, no. 119 (January–February 1980).

169 In the 1967–87 period, the Soviet ambassadors to Aden were: Vladimir Ivanovich Startsev (1968–72); Vladimir Porfirevich Poliakov (1972–4);

Alexander Semenovich Semioshkin (1974–5); Vladimir Federovich Kaboshkin (1975–8); Feliks Nikolaevich Fedotov (1978–82); Vladislav Petrovich Zhukov (1982–6); Albert Ivanovich Rachkov (1986–). Poliakov, Fedotov and Zhukov had served as ambassadors in the Sudan, while Startsev had been a diplomat in Turkey and Syria, and Semioshkin in Egypt (Boris Lewytzkyj, *Who's Who in the USSR*, Munich, 1984). On Ethiopia, see Christopher Clapham, *Tranformation and Continuity in Revolutionary Ethiopia*, Cambridge, 1988 p. 232.

170 In *CDSP*, vol. 38 no. 3.

171 Quoted by Pollock, 'Moscow and South Yemen', p. 57, n.32.

172 *Soviet News*, 29 January 1986.

173 *CDSP*, vol. 38 no. 3.

174 *Pravda*, 11 February 1987, quoted in *The Soviet Union and the Middle East*, Jerusalem, February 1987.

175 ME/8678/A/11, 21 September 1987.

176 *Le Monde*, 17 April 1987.

177 *Soviet News*, 29 January 1986.

178 *Le Monde*, 18 January 1986; *International Herald Tribune*, 24 January 1986.

179 Thus Naumkin, 'South Yemen After the January Tragedy'.

180 *Soviet News*, 11 February 1987.

181 Glukov, 'A Difficult Examination'.

182 ME/0015/A/7, 2 December 1987.

183 *Peking Review* (henceforth *PR*), no. 50 (1967), p. 36; *New China News Agency*, no. 3602 6 December 1967.

184 On the establishment of diplomatic relations, *PR*, no. 6 (1968), pp. 14–15; on the nomination of Ambassador Li, Schichor, *The Middle East*, pp. 151–2.

185 Schichor, *The Middle East*, p. 152; *PR*, no. 39 (1968), pp. 28–30.

186 Schichor, *The Middle East*, p. 152; *PR*, no. 32 (1970).

187 Hashim Behbehani, *China and the People's Democratic Republic of Yemen*, KPI, London, 1985, p. 19.

188 *Ibid.*, p. 157.

189 Behbehani, *China's Foreign Policy*, p. 355; *PR*, no. 28 (1972), and no. 29 (1972).

190 *PR*, no. 46 (1974) and no. 48 (1974).

191 *PR*, no. 18 (1978); *New China News Agency*, no. 480 (27 April 1978), and no. 481 (4 May 1978).

192 World Bank, *Economic Memorandum 1982*, p. 30. See appendix 8, p. 260.

193 E.g. *PR*, no. 45 (1972), no. 49 (1972), no. 10 (1979), no. 43 (1982).

194 ME/4364/A/5, 4 August 1973.

195 *PR*, no. 39 (1968).

196 *PR*, no. 32 (1970), pp. 14–15.

197 *PR*, no. 28 (1972).

198 ME/4062/A/5–6, 9 August 1972.

199 On China's relations with the Eritreans, interview with ELF Secretary-General, Othmān Sāliḥ Sabbih, Aden, February 1970.

200 On China and Israel, see Schichor, *The Middle East*, pp. 114–16, and Behbehani, *China's Foreign Policy*, chapters 2–4, especially p. 88.

201 Schichor, *The Middle East*, p. 173; Behbehani, *China's Foreign Policy*, pp. 216–17.
202 Behbehani, *China's Foreign Policy*, p. 221.
203 *PR*, no. 50 (1967), p. 36.
204 *PR*, no. 39 (1968), pp. 14–16.
205 *PR*, no. 46 (1974).
206 ME/3795/A/6, 24 September 1971.
207 *PR*, no. 39 (1968), pp. 28–30.
208 *PR*, no. 40 (1968), p. 41.
209 *PR*, no. 34 (1970), pp. 6–7.
210 Speech of ʿAbd al-Malik Ismāʿīl, Permanent Representative of the PDRY at the UN, *PR*, no. 49 (1971), p. 33.
211 *PR*, no. 29 (1972), with the communiqué of 17 July 1972.
212 *PR*, no. 34 (1970), pp. 6–7.
213 ME/3707/A/10.
214 *PR*, no. 28 (1972), p. 10.
215 Schichor, *The Middle East*, p. 182.
216 *PR*, no. 46 (1974).
217 Chou En-lai in Schichor, *The Middle East*, p. 170.
218 *PR*, no. 28 (1976), p. 22.
219 On Saudi–PDRY relations, see *PR*, no. 12 (1976).
220 'Events in the two Yemens', *PR*, no. 27 (1978), p. 41; see also *New China News Agency*, Daily Bulletin no. 7381 (30 June 1978), p. 5.
221 *PR*, no. 10 (1979), p. 28.
222 *PR*, no. 19 (1979), pp. 22–3.
223 *Ibid.*
224 Author's observation, Aden, 1977.
225 *PR*, no. 43 (1982), p. 16.
226 *PR*, no. 12 (1987), p. 9; SWB FE/8576/A4/1, 14 March 1987; FE/8524/A4/1, 24 March 1987.

Conclusions: revolution and foreign policy

1 At a symposium on the 'experience' of the revolution in the PDRY held in Aden in February 1984 representatives of 28 organisations sympathetic to the regime were present: seven were from ruling communist or communist-related parties (Soviet Union, Hungary, the GDR, Czechoslovakia, Vietnam, Cuba, Ethiopia); fourteen were from non-ruling communist parties (Sudan, Iraq, Syria, Palestine, Jordan, Lebanon, Saudi Arabia, Bahrain, Italy, France, India, Greece, Morocco, Algeria); seven were Arab organisations descended from, or incorporating, former sections of the Movement of Arab Nationalists (PFLO, PFLP, PDFLP, Popular Front in Bahrain, NDF/YPUP, Labour Party in Saudi Arabia, Organisation of Communist Action of Lebanon).

Bibliography

Unpublished materials

Belkheiri, A, 'US–Algerian Relations, 1954–1980, – Balance Between Interest and Principle', PhD dissertation, University of Exeter, 1986.

Fagen, Richard, 'The Politics of Transition in the Peripheral Socialist Economy', paper, Stanford University, August 1983.

Findley, Paul, 'Rescue in Aden, Report of Representative Paul Findley (R-Ill) on his trip to the People's Democratic Republic of Yemen, April 29–May 6, 1974'.

World Bank, *PDRY Economic Memorandum, 3 570-YDR*, Washington, 29 January 1982.

Government publications

PDRY

Party documents (in chronological order)

al-Mīthāḳ al-Waṭanī, wa wufiḳa ʿalayhu fī al-muʾtamar al-ʾawwal lil-djabḥa al-ḳawmiyya li-taḥrīr djanūb al-yaman al-muḥtall al-munʿaḳad fī al-fitra bayn 22–25 yūniyyū 1965, Aden, n.d.

al-Djabḥa al-Ḳawmiyya, *Barnāmadj al-Taḥrīr al-Waṭanī wa Tarīḳ al-Lāra's-mālī*, and *Bayyān wa Ḳirārāt al-Muʾtamar al-Rābiʿ*, Nāyyif Ḥawātmah, *ʾAzmat al-Thawra fī Al-Djanūb al-Yamanī*, Beirut, 1968.

al-Thawra al-Waṭaniyya al-Dīmuḳrātiyya fī al-Yaman, Beirut, 1972.

al-Djabḥa al-Ḳawmiyya – al-Tanẓīm al-Siyyāsī al-Mawḥid, *al-Muʾtamar al-Tawḥīdī* (October 1975), Beirut, 1976.

The Closing Statement, Final Resolutions and Recommendations of the Unification Congress of the Three National Democratic Organisations (11–13 October 1975), Nottingham, 1977.

ʿAshara Sanawāt min al-Istiḳlāl al-Waṭanī fī al-Yaman al-Dīmuḳrātiyya, 1967–1977, Aden, 1977.

al-Ḥizb al-Ishtirākī al-Yamanī, *Barnāmadj al-Ḥizb al-Ishtirākī al-Yamanī* (11–13 October 1978), n.p. n.d.

Yemeni Socialist Party, *Proceedings of the First Congress of the Yemeni Socialist Party* (Aden, 11–13 October 1978), Moscow, 1979.

al-Ḥizb al-Ishtirākī al-Yamanī, *al-Muʾtamar al-ʾIstithnāʾī lil-Ḥizb al-Ishtirākī al-Yamanī* (October 1980), Beirut, n.d.

Taḳrir al-Ladjna al-Markazī lil-Ḥizb al-Ishtirākī al-Yamani ila al-Muʾtamar al-Ām al-Thālith lil-Hizb, Arbatʿashara Oktobr, 14 October 1985.

Report of the Central Committee of the Yemeni Socialist Party Submitted to The Party General Conference, Aden, June 20–21 1987.

State publications

Anon., *Aspects of Economic and Social Development in Democratic Yemen*, n.p., n.d.

PDRY, *Constitution of People's Democratic Republic of Yemen, 1970*, Aden, 1971. Arabic in al-Djabha al-Ḳawmiyya, al-Thawra al-Waṭaniyya, 1972, pp. 151–84.

Dustūr Djumhūriyya al-Yaman al-Dīmuḳrātiyya al-Shaʿabiyya 1978, Aden, 1978.

Constitution of the People's Democratic Republic of Yemen, Aden, 1978.

Central Statistical Organisation, *Statistical Yearbook 1980*, Aden, n.d.

Embassy to the United Kingdom, Collection of PRSY/PDRY London Embassy press releases and information sheets issued 1969–1988, incomplete, in author's possession.

Ministry of Economy, Commerce and Planning, *Economic Legislations*, Aden, 1968.

Ministry of Information, *Democratic Yemen in the United Nations*, Aden, 1977.

UNITED KINGDOM

Hansard, *Parliamentary Debates.*

HMSO, *Aden, Perim, and Kuria Muria Islands Act 1967*, London, 1967.

Foreign Office, *Memorandum of Agreed Points relating to Independence for South Arabia (the People's Republic of Southern Yemen)* (with financial note and final communiqué), Cmnd. 3504, London, 1968.

Soviet, East European and Western Development Aid 1976–82, Foreign Policy Document no. 85, London, 1983.

UNITED STATES

United States Congress, House of Representatives, Committee on Foreign Affairs, *US Security Interests in the Persian Gulf*, Washington, 1981.

United States Congress, House of Representatives, Committee on Foreign Affairs, Subcommittee on Europe and the Middle East, *Proposed Arms Transfers to the Yemen Arab Republic*, Washington, 1979.

Saudi Arabia and the United States, The New Context in an Evolving 'Special Relationship', Washington, 1981.

United States Congress, House of Representatives, Committee on Foreign Affairs, Subcommittee on the Near East and South Asia, *New Perspectives on the Persian Gulf*, Washington, 1973.

Proposed Expansion of US Military Facilities in the Indian Ocean, Washington, 1974.

United States Congress, House of Representatives, Committee on International Relations, *Oil Fields as Military Objectives, A Feasibility Study*, Washington, 1975.

Proposed Aircraft Sales to Israel, Egypt, and Saudi Arabia, Washington, 1978.

United States Arms Policies in the Persian Gulf and Red Sea Areas: Past, Present and Future, Washington, 1977.
United States Congress, Senate, Committee on Foreign Relations, *Persian Gulf Situation*, Washington, 1981.
United States Foreign Policy Objectives and Overseas Military Installations, Washington, 1979.
United States Congress, Senate, Committee on Governmental Affairs, *An Act to Combat International Terrorism*, Washington, 1980.
United States Government, Central Intelligence Agency, National Foreign Assessment Center, *Patterns of International Terrorism: 1980*, A Research Paper, PA81-10163U, June 1981.
United States Government, Department of State, Bureau of Public Affairs, *North Yemen*, Background Notes, December 1980.
South Yemen, Background Notes, December 1980.
US Policy Toward the Persian Gulf, Current Policy no. 390, 10 May 1982.
Yemen Arab Republic: US Policy, gist, April 1979.
United States Government, Department of State, *Soviet and East European Aid to the Third World, 1981*, Washington, February 1983.

Books and pamphlets

ʿAbd al-Fattāḥ, Fatḥī, *Tadjribat al-Thawra fī al-Yaman al-Dīmuḳratiyya*, Beirut, 1974.
Abir, Mordechai, *Oil, Power and Politics, Conflict in Arabia, the Red Sea and the Gulf*, London, 1974.
Sharm al-Sheikh – Bab al-Mandeb: The Strategic Balance and Israel's Southern Approaches, Hebrew University of Jerusalem, The Leonard Davis Institute for International Relations, Jerusalem Papers on Peace Problems, March 1974.
ʿAfif, Aḥmad Djābir, *al-Ḥaraka al-Waṭaniyya fī al-Yaman*, Damascus, 1982.
Akehurst, John, *We Won A War, The Campaign in Oman 1965–1975*, Salisbury, 1982.
Amnesty International, *People's Democratic Republic of Yemen*, London, 1976.
Amirie, Abbas (ed.), *The Persian Gulf and Indian Ocean in International Politics*, Tehran, 1975.
Anthony, John Duke, *The Red Sea: Control of the Southern approach*, Middle East Problem Paper 13, Middle East Institute, Washington, 1975.
el-Attar, Mohamed Said, *Le Sous-Dévéloppement économique et social du Yemen*, Algiers, 1964.
Behbehani, Hashim S.H., *China and the People's Democratic Republic of Yemen, A Report*, London, 1985.
China's Foreign Policy in the Arab World, 1955–1975, London, 1981.
Bell, J. Bowyer, *South Arabia: Violence and Revolt*, Conflict Studies no. 40, London, 1973.
Bidwell, Robin, *The Two Yemens*, London, 1983.
Birks, J.S. and Sinclair, C.A., *Arab Manpower*, London, 1980.

Braun, Ursula, *Nord- und Südjemen im Spannungsfeld interner, regionaler und globaler Gegensätze*, Forschungsinstitut der Deutschen Gesellschaft für Auswäritge Politik e.V., Arbeitspapiere zur Internationalen Politik, Bonn, 1981.

Bujra, Abdalla S., *The Politics of Stratification, A Study of Political Change in a South Arabian Town*, Oxford, 1971.

Burmistrov, V.N., *Narodnaya Demokraticheskaya Respublika Yemen, Ekonomika i torgovo-ekonomichskiye otnosheniya*, Moscow, 1981.

Burrell, R.M. and Cottrell, Alvin J., *Iran, The Arabian Peninsula, and the Indian Ocean*, National Strategy Information Center, New York, 1972.

Burrowes, Robert, *The Yemen Arab Republic, The Politics of Development, 1962–1986*, London, 1987.

Bray, Frank and Cottrell, Alvin, *Military Forces in the Persian Gulf*, Washington Papers no. 60, London, 1978.

Chelhod, Joseph *et. al.*, *L'Arabie du Sud, Histoire et Civilisation*, vol. 1, *Le Peuple yéménite et ses racines*, Paris, 1984.

Chirkin, V. and Yudin, Y., *A Socialist-Oriented State: Instrument of Revolutionary Change*, Moscow, 1978.

Chubin, Shahram, *Soviet Policy Towards Iran and the Gulf*, Adelphi Papers no. 157, London, 1980.

Chubin, Shahram and Zabih, Sepehr, *The Foreign Relations of Iran*, London, 1974.

Cooley, John, *Libyan Sandstorm*, London, 1982.

Cordesman, Anthony, *The Gulf and the Search for Strategic Stability*, London, 1984.

Darby, Phillip, *British Defence Policy East of Suez 1947–1968*, London, 1973.

Dawisha, Adeed and Dawisha, Karen, *The Soviet Union in the Middle East*, London, 1982.

al-Djabḥa al-Shaʿabiyya fī al-Baḥrayn, *al-Ṣiraʿ ʿalā al-Khalidj al-ʿArabī*, Beirut, 1978.

al-Djabḥa al-Shaʿabiyya li-Taḥrīr ʿUman, *Withaʾik al-Dhikrī al-Thāniyya ʿAshara lil-Thawra al-ʿUmāniyya*, Aden, 1977.

al-Djabḥa al-Shaʿabiyya li-Taḥrīr ʿUmān wa al-Khalīdj al-ʿArabī, *Withaʾik al-Niḍāl al-Waṭanī 1965–1974*, Beirut, 1974.

al-Djināhī, Saʿīd ʾAḥmad, *Kuntu fī al-Ẓufār*, Beirut, 1974.

Douglas, L. Leigh, *The Free Yemeni Movement 1935–1962*, Beirut, 1987.

Farid, Abdel Majid, *The Red Sea: Prospects for Stability*, London, 1984.

Fayein, Claudie, *Yémén*, Paris, 1975.

Fiennes, Ranulph, *Where Soldiers Fear to Tread*, London, 1975.

Findley, Paul, *They Dare to Speak Out*, Washington, 1985.

Gambke, H., Jacob, K. and Mätzig, K., *Sultanspaläste in Volkes Hand*, Berlin, 1974.

Garthoff, Raymond, *Detente and Confrontation*, Washington, 1985.

Gavin, R.J., *Aden Under British Rule 1839–1967*, London, 1975.

Gerasimov, O.G., *Yemenskaya Revolutsia 1962–1975*, Moscow, 1979.

Glushchenko, E.A., *Yuzhnaya Arabia bez Sultanov*, Moscow, 1971.

Goryanov, Mikhail, *Two Ways of Looking at the Indian Ocean*, Moscow, 1981.

Gulf Committee, *Documents of the National Struggle in Oman and the Arabian Gulf*, London, 1974.

Gusarov, V.I., *Aden*, Moscow, 1981.

Guskov, A.S., *Natsionalni Front Demokraticheskovo Yemena, 1963–1975*, Moscow, 1979.

al-Ḥadaf editions, *al-Thawra fī al-Yaman al-Dīmuḳrātiyya al-Shaʿabiyya*, Beirut, 1972.

el-Habashi, M.O., *Aden, L'Evolution politique, économique et sociale de l'Arabie du Sud*, Algiers, 1966.

Hādī, Nabīl, *18 Saʿāt Taʾrīkhiyya ʿand Bāb al-Mandeb*, Beirut, 1978.

Halliday, Fred, *Arabia without Sultans*, London, 1974.

Iran: Dictatorship and Development, London, 1978.

Mercenaries: 'Counter-Insurgency' in the Gulf, Nottingham, 1977.

Soviet Policy in the Arc of Crisis, Washington, 1981; issued in the UK as *Threat from the East?*, London, 1982.

and Molyneux, Maxine, *The Ethiopian Revolution*, London, 1982.

Hassan, Mohammad Salman, *Report to the People's Republic of Southern Yemen on Guidelines for Industrial Planning and Policy*, Aden, 1968.

Ḥawātmah, Nāyyif, *Azmat al-Thawra fī al Djanūb al-Yamanī*, Beirut, 1968.

Heikal, Mohamed, *Sphinx and Commissar*, London, 1978.

Holden, David, *Farewell to Arabia*, London, 1966.

Holden, David and Johns, Richard, *The House of Saud*, London, 1981.

Hopwood, Derek (ed.), *The Arabian Peninsula. Society and Politics*, London, 1972.

Ingrams, Harold, *The Yemen*, London, 1963.

Ismael, Tareq and Ismael, Jacqueline, *The People's Democratic Republic of Yemen, Politics, Economics and Society*, London, 1986.

Jeapes, Tony, *SAS: Operation Oman*, London, 1980.

Katz, Mark, *Russia and Arabia, Soviet Foreign Policy toward the Arabian Peninsula*, Baltimore, 1986.

Kazziha, Walid, *Revolutionary Transformation in the Arab World*, London, 1975.

Kelly, J.B., *Arabia, The Gulf and the West*, London, 1980.

King, Gillian, *Imperial Outpost – Aden*, London, 1964.

Klare, Michael, *Beyond the 'Vietnam Syndrome'*, Washington, 1981.

Kostiner, Joseph, *The Struggle for South Yemen*, Beckenham, 1984.

Koszinowski, Thomas, El-Menshaui Magdi and Meyer, Alois, *Zur politischen und wirtschaftlichen Situation des Jemen; Einführung und Dokumentation*, Hamburg, 1980.

Lackner, Helen, *A House Built on Sand, A Political Economy of Saudi Arabia*, London, 1978.

P.D.R.Y. Yemen, Outpost of Socialist Development in Arabia, London, 1985.

Lapidoth – Eschelbacher, Ruth, *The Red Sea and the Gulf of Aden*, London, 1982.

Lapping, Brian, *End of Empire*, London, 1985.

Ledger, David, *Shifting Sands, The British in South Arabia*, London, 1983.

Little, Tom, *South Arabia: Arena of Conflict*, London, 1968.

Luqman, Farouk, *Democratic Yemen Today*, Bombay, n.d.
McLane, Charles, *Soviet–Middle East Relations*, London, 1973.
Molyneux, Maxine, *State Policies and the Position of Women in the PDRY, 1967–77*, Geneva, 1982.
Mondesir, Simone, *A Select Bibliography of Yemen Arab Republic and People's Democratic Republic of Yemen*, Durham, 1977.
Mylroie, Laurie, *Politics and the Soviet Presence in the People's Democratic Republic of Yemen*, a RAND Note, N-2052-AF, December 1983.
Naumkin, Vitali, *al-Djabha al-Ḳawmiyya fī al-Kifāḥ min ajli Istiḳlāl al-Yaman al-Djanūbiyya, wa al-Dīmuḳrāṭiyya al-Waṭaniyya*, Moscow, 1984.
Narodnaya Demokraticheskaya Respublika Yemen, Moscow, 1982.
Novik, Nimrod, *Between Two Yemens: Regional Dynamics and Superpower Conflict in Riyadh's 'Backyard'*, Center for Strategic Studies, Tel Aviv University, 1980.
On the Shores of Bab al-Mandeb, Soviet Diplomacy and Regional Dynamics, Foreign Policy Research Institute, Philadelphia, 1979.
Nyrop, Richard, *Area Handbook for the Yemens*, Washington, 1977.
Page, Stephen, *The USSR and Arabia*, London, 1971.
The Soviet Union and the Yemens, New York, 1985.
Paget, Julian, *Last Post; Aden 1964–67*, London, 1969.
Peterson, John, *Conflict in the Yemens and Superpower Involvement*, Center for Contemporary Arab Studies, Occasional Papers Series, Washington, 1981.
Oman in the Twentieth Century, London, 1978.
Yemen. The Search for a Modern State, London, 1982.
Plass, J.B. and Gehrke, U., *Die Aden-Grenze in der Südarabienfrage*, Opladen, 1967.
Price, D.L., *Oman: Insurgency and Development*, Conflict Studies 53, London, 1975.
Pridham, B.R., (ed.) *Contemporary Yemen: Politics and Historical Background*, Beckenham, 1984.
Pridham, Brian (ed.), *Economy, Society and Culture in Contemporary Yemen*, Beckenham, 1985.
Quandt, William, *Saudi Arabia in the 1980s*, Washington, 1981.
al-Rayyis, Riyyāḍ Nadjīb, *Ẓufār, Ḳissa al-Ṣirāᶜ al-Siyyāsī wa al-ᶜAskarī fī al-Khalīdj al-ᶜArabī 1970–1976*, London, n.d.
Schichor, Yitzhak, *The Middle East in China's Foreign Policy 1949–1977*, Cambridge, 1979.
Sicherman, Harvey, *Aden and British Strategy, 1839–1968*, Foreign Policy Research Institute, Philadelphia, 1972.
Smiley, David, *Arabian Assignment*, London, 1975.
Stookey, Robert, *South Yemen, A Marxist Republic in Arabia*, London, 1982.
Swanson, Jon, *Emigration and Economic Development: The Case of the Yemen Arab Republic*, Boulder, Colorado, 1979.
Townsend, John, *Oman, The Making of a Modern State*, London, 1977.
Trevelyan, Humphrey, *The Middle East in Revolution*, London, 1970.
Trevaskis, John, *Oman, The Making of a Modern State*, London, 1977.

ʿUmar, Sulṭān ʾAḥmad, *Naẓra fī Taṭawwur al-Mudjtamaʿ al-Yamanī*, Beirut, 1970.
UNDP, *Democratic Yemen and the United Nations*, Aden, 1985.
Wehr, Hans, *A Dictionary of Modern Written Arabic*, Wiesbaden, 1966.
Wenner, Manfred, *Modern Yemen; 1918–1966*, Baltimore, 1967.
World Bank, *People's Democratic Republic of Yemen, A Review of Economic and Social Development*, Washington, 1979.
Yodfat, Aryeh, *The Soviet Union and the Arabian Peninsula*, Beckenham, 1983.
and Abir, Mordchai, *In the Direction of the Gulf. The Soviet Union and the Persian Gulf*, London, 1977.

Articles and chapters

al-Abdin, 'The Free Yemeni Movement (1940–48) and Its Ideas on Reform', *Middle Eastern Studies*, January 1979.
Anthony, John Duke, 'Relations between the United States and the People's Democratic Republic of Yemen (PDRY): Problems and Progress', in US Congress, House of Representatives, Committee on International Relations, Special Subcommittee on Investigations, *Diego Garcia, 1975: The Debate over the Base and the Island's Former Inhabitants*, Washington, 1975.
Asshab, Naim, 'The People's Will is Invincible: Impressions of a Trip to the PDRY', *World Marxist Review*, vol. 21 no. 11 (November 1978).
al-Ashtal, Abdullah, 'Politics in Command. A Case Study of the People's Democratic Republic of Yemen', *Monthly Review*, no. 9 (1976).
Bell, J.B., 'Bab el Mandeb: Strategic Troublespot', *Orbis*, no. 4 (1973).
Bernier, T., 'Naissance d'un nationalisme arabe à Aden', *L'Afrique et L'Asie*, no. 44 (1958).
Burrowes, Robert, 'The Yemen Arab Republic and the Ali Abdallah Salih Regime: 1978–1984', *Middle East Journal*, vol. 39 no. 3 (summer 1985).
Campbell, John C., 'Rumblings Along the Red Sea', *Foreign Affairs*, April 1970.
Chistyakov, Alexei, 'PDRY, Towards Consolidation of Economy', *Asia and Africa Today*, no. 1 (1980).
Cigar, Norman, 'South Yemen and the USSR: Prospects for the Relationship', *Middle East Journal*, vol. 39 no. 4 (autumn 1985).
'State and Society in South Yemen', *Problems of Communism*, May–June 1985.
Decornoy, Jacques, 'Le régime d'Aden poursuit dans la rigueur son expérience de "Socialisme scientifique"', *Le Monde*, 6 December 1977.
Deffarge, Claude, and Troeller, Gordian, 'Sud-Yémen: une Révolution menacée?', *Le Monde Diplomatique*, April 1972.
Efrat, Moshe, 'The People's Democratic Republic of Yemen: Scientific Socialism on Trial in an Arab Country', in Peter Wiles (ed.), *The New Communist Third World*, London, 1982.
Gerasimov, O., 'Southern Yemen: Toiling Young Republic', *International Affairs*, no. 2–3 (1970).

Gueyras, Jean, 'Le Yémen du Sud: un Cuba arabe', *Le Monde*, 27–28 February 1979.

'Yémen du Nord: les Difficultés de la Reconciliation avec le Sud', *Le Monde*, 20 December 1980.

Guskov, Alexander, 'South Yemen, Dynamics of Development', *New Times*, no. 49 (1982).

'The Sound Foundations of Soviet–Yemeni Friendship', *International Affairs*, no. 12 (1982).

Gvozdev, Y., 'Democratic Yemen Forges Ahead', *International Affairs*, no. 10 (1974).

Halliday, Fred, 'The Fighting in Eritrea', *New Left Review*, no. 67 (1971).

'The Yemens: Conflict and Coexistence', *The World Today*, August–September 1984.

'Yemen's Unfinished Revolution: Socialism in the South', *MERIP Reports*, no. 81 (October 1979).

Hirst, David, 'The Yemens', three articles, *The Guardian*, 29–31 August 1978.

Hoagland, Jim, 'Yemen War Tests a New Carter Policy', *Washington Post*, 13 March 1979.

Imam, Zafar, 'Soviet Treaties with Third World Countries', *Soviet Studies*, vol. 35 no. 1 (January 1983).

Ismael, Tareq, 'The People's Democratic Republic of Yemen', in B. Szajkowski (ed.), *Marxist Governments: A World Survey*, London, 1981, III.

Ismail, Abdul Fattah, 'Der Nicht-Kapitalistische Weg', in Bassam Tibi (ed.), *Die arabische Linke*, Frankfurt, 1969.

'A New Vanguard Party', *World Marxist Review*, vol. 22 no. 4 (January 1969).

Kapitonov, Konstantin and Tishkov, Serghei, 'PDRY, A Transformed Land', *Asia and Africa Today*, no. 5 (1982).

Katz, Mark, 'Sanaa and the Soviets', *Problems of Communism*, January–February 1984.

Kelly, Anne M., 'Port Visits and the "Internationalist Mission" of the Soviet Navy', in Michael MccGwire and John McDonnell (eds.), *Soviet Naval Influence, Domestic and Foreign Dimensions*, London, 1977.

Khaled, Seif Sael, 'Democratic Yemen: Revolution: Sources, Goals, Accomplishments', *Asia and Africa Today*, no. 1 (1984).

King-yuh Chang, 'The United Nations and Decolonization: The Case of Southern Yemen', *International Organisation*, vol. 26 no. 1 (Winter 1972).

Klieman, Aaron, S., 'Bab al-Mandeb: The Red Sea in Transition', *Orbis*, Fall 1967.

Koszinowski, Thomas, 'Die politischen Ziele Süd-Jemens auf der Arabischen Halbinsel', *Europa-Archiv*, vol. 34 no. 12.

Kutschera, Chris, 'Yémen du Sud, L'Étoile Rouge pâlit-elle à Aden?', *Le Monde Diplomatique*, October 1982.

Kutuzov, V., 'SSSR–NDRI, Novii Realnosti i Perspektivi', *Vneshnyaya Torgolya*, April 1980.

Lawson, Fred, 'South Yemen's Troubles', *Orient*, vol. 27 no. 3, September 1986

Léfort, René, 'Révolution au Sud-Yémen', *Le Monde Diplomatique*, February 1971.

Luttwak, Edward, 'Cubans in Arabia? Or the Meaning of Strategy', *Commentary*, December 1979.
McNaugher, Thomas, 'Arms and Allies on the Arabian Peninsula', *Orbis*, vol. 28 no. 3 (Fall 1984).
Media Analysis Center, Jerusalem, 'The So. Yemen–Soviet Connection', Report no. 117, 5 January 1982.
'The Soviet–So. Yemen Connection', Backgrounder no. 167, 11 August 1983, part 2.
Molyneux, Maxine, 'Legal Reform and Socialist Revolution in Democratic Yemen', *International Journal of the Sociology of Law*, 1985, vol. 13, pp. 147–172.
Naumkin, V., 'Southern Yemen, The Road to Progress', *International Affairs*, no. 1 (1978).
'South Yemen after the January Tragedy', *New Times*, no. 48 (1986).
Payton, Gary D., 'The Somali Coup of 1969: the Case for Soviet Complicity', *Journal of Modern African Studies*, vol. 18 no. 3 (September 1980).
Perlmutter, Amos, 'The Yemen Strategy', *New Republic*, 5 and 12 July 1980.
Pollock, David, 'Moscow and South Yemen', *Problems of Communism*, May–June 1986.
Price, David L., 'Moscow and the Persian Gulf', *Problems of Communism*, March–April 1979.
Rodolfo, Claudine, 'La République Démocratique Populaire du Yémen', *Maghreb-Machrek*, no. 81 (July–September 1978).
Rouleau, Eric, 'L'Étoile rouge sur le Yémen du Sud', *Le Monde*, 27–31 May 1972.
'Le Yémen écartelé', *Le Monde*, 8–9 June 1982.
Rondot, Philippe, 'Les responsables à Sana et à Aden', *Maghreb-Machrek*, no. 74 (October–December 1976).
Rubinstein, Alvin, 'The Soviet Presence in the Arab World', *Current History*, October 1981.
Ruszkiewicz, John J., 'How the US Lost its Footing in the Shifting Sands of the Persian Gulf – A Case History in the Yemen Arab Republic', *Armed Forces Journal International*, September 1980.
Seale, Patrick, 'Why Moscow's Grip on Aden is Slipping', *The Observer*, 22 August 1982.
Smolansky, Oles M., 'Soviet Entry into the Indian Ocean: An Analysis', in Michael MccGwire (ed.), *Soviet Naval Developments, Capability and Context*, London, 1973.
Stork, Joe, 'Socialist Revolution in Arabia: A Report from the People's Democratic Republic of Yemen', *MERIP Reports*, no. 15 (March 1973).
Tarasov, Nikolai, 'The Pentagon's Plans for the Red Sea', *Asia and Africa Today*, no. 4 (1983).
Vatikiotis, P.J., 'Aden: Who Can be Leader?', *New Society*, 20 April 1967.
Viennot, Jean-Pierre, 'Aden, de la lutte pour la libération à l'indépendence', *Orient*, vol. 14 (1970).
'L'Expérience révolutionnaire du Sud-Yémen', *Maghreb*, no. 59 (September–October 1973).
'Vers l'union des Yémenites?', *Maghreb-Machrek*, no. 74 (October–December 1976).

Watt, D.C., 'Labour Relations and Trades Unionism in Aden, 1952–60', *Middle East Journal*, no. 16 (1962).

Weidnitzer, Frank, 'Grundzüge der Entwicklung der politischstattlichen Verhaltnisse im revolutionären Prozess der VDR Jemen', *Asien, Afrika, Latein-Amerika* (Berlin), vol. 6 no. 8 (1980).

Wenner, Manfred, 'The Civil War in South Yemen', in B.R. Pridham (ed.), *The Arab Gulf and the Arab World*, London, 1988.

'People's Republic of Southern Yemen', in Tareq Ismael (ed.), *Government and Politics of the Contemporary Middle East*, Homewood IU, 1970.

Newspapers and Journals

Afrique-Asie (Paris)
Armed Forces Journal International (Washington)
Arab Report and Record (London)
ʿArbat ʿashara uktubr (Aden)
Asia and Africa Today (Moscow)
Asien, Afrika, Latein-Amerika (Berlin, GDR)
Current Digest of the Soviet Press (New York)
The Daily Telegraph (London)
Der Spiegel (Hamburg)
Economist Intelligence Unit, Quarterly Economic Review, *The Arabian Peninsula: Sheikhdoms and Republics* (London)
The Financial Times (London)
Foreign Affairs (Washington)
Foreign Policy (Washington)
The Guardian (London)
al-Ḥurriya (Beirut)
International Affairs (Moscow)
Journal of Modern African Studies (Cambridge)
Keesings Contemporary Archive (Bristol)
Maghreb-Machrek (Paris)
MERIP Reports (Washington)
Middle East Economic Digest (London)
Middle East Journal (Washington)
Middle East Studies (London)
Le Monde (Paris)
Le Monde Diplomatique (Paris)
Monthly Review (New York)
New Times (Moscow)
The New York Times
The Observer (London)
Orbis (Philadelphia)
Peking Review (from 1979, *Beijing Review*)
Problems of Communism (Washington)
Soviet News (London)

Soviet Studies (Glasgow)
The Soviet Union and the Middle East (Jerusalem)
BBC Summary of World Broadcasts (Caversham)
The Sunday Times (London)
al-Thawrī (Aden)
The Times (London)
Tricontinental (Havana)
The Washington Post
World Marxist Review (Prague)
The World Today (London)

Index

ʿAbd Allāh, Faḍl Muḥsin (Minister of Finance), 42–2, 47
ʿAbd Allāh, Muḥammad Saʿīd, 'Muḥsin', (Minister of State Security), 34–7, 40, 42–3, 46–7, origins, 99, 134
Aden Nationality Law, 112
Aden, Port of, 8, 16, 18, 22, 228
Afghanistan, 30, 37, 52, 73, 78, 86, 192, 193, 195, 196, 201, 204, 205, 208, 209, 210, 215, 216, 218, 224, 225, 226, 258
Agreement on Technical and Economic Cooperation – PDRY/USSR, 188
Agreement on Unity, Tripoli 1972, 110, 117–18, 120,126, 233–6, 250, 251
Aḥmad, Muḥammad ʿAlī (Governor of Abyan Province), 46; 47; and corruption, 49; shelling of USSR Embassy, 217
Aḥmad, Sāliḥ, ʿUbayd (Minister of Defense), 43; visit to USSR 1987, 212
ʿAkkūsh, Muḥammad Sālim (Minister of Fisheries): and USSR, 35
al-Alawi, Yusuf Abdullah (Minister of State for Foreign Affairs, Oman): and Oman/PDRY agreement, 1982, 245–6
Algeria, 5, 21, 36, 60, 88, 171, 173, 218, 220, 257 *see also* Boumedienne; al-Mazhudi; Nuwayrat
ʿAlī, Aḥmad (PFLOAG): death of, 144
ʿAlī, Sālim Rubiyyaʿ (President 1969–78), 23–4, 27, 29–31, 34–5, 46–7, 47, 54, 57–8; ʿAlī Nāṣir Muḥammad on, 250; and China, 179, 219–23; and colonialism, 69; attempted coup 1978, 128, 191; and Cuba, 163; death, 85, 163; visit to Egypt 1974, 161; and Gulf States, 168; and internal divisions, 120–1, 171, 210; and Oman, 222–3; and opposition to PDRY, 171; and Red Sea Crisis, 122; replacement of, 94, 129; and Saudi Arabia, 114, 161, 163; and unity/YAR, 99, 100, 114, 116–17, 120, 122–3, 126; and US, 84–85, 94, 161; and USSR, 161, 163, 183–6, 191, 198, 215
Aliev, Geider (CPSU, USSR): 1986 visits, 212
al-ʿAlim, ʿAbd Allāh ʿAbd (YAR): and revolt, 123
Amnesty International, 61, 241
al-ʿAmrī, (Prime Minister YAR): and PDRY opposition, 115; and Saudi Arabia and royalists, 111; and unity, 115
Angola, 30, 86, 178, 192, 193, 204, 218, 258
ʿAntar, ʿAlī Aḥmad (Minister of Defense), 12, 23, 39; and 1986 crisis, 213; death of, 42, 45; and internal divisions, 40; and NDF, 130; tribal origins, 47, 99
Arab–Israeli Conflict, 1, 10, 22, 25, 38, 64, 75, 80, 81, 83–5, 92, 151–4, 163, 170, 175–7, 190–1, 206, 233 *see also* Egypt, Front of Steadfastness & Rejection, Israel, Palestine, Liberation of, Lebanon, PDFLP, PFLP, PLO
Arabian Gulf, 1, 16, 21, 25, 26, 28, 32, 35, 36, 37, 53, 62, 70–2, 73, 75, 79–80, 98, 122, 165–70 *see also* Arabian Peninsular, Bahrain, Kuwait, Qatar, United Arab Amirates
Arabian Peninsula, 1, 16, 22, 23, 25–9, 32, 39, 46, 50, 59, 61–2, 63, 71–3, 108, 210; and PDRY committment to revolution in 140–65, 169–72, 177, 232, 247; and USA in 79–81, 164, 180; and USSR, 179, 180, 185, 186, 188–9, 203, 205, 208, 213–15 *see also* Arabian Gulf and individual countries
Arab League, 6, 30, 86, 117, 124, 125, 145, 148, 149, 150, 153, 163, 166, 167, 175, 257 *see also* al-Majid; al-Mazhudi; Riad, al-Yafi
ʿArafāt, Yāsir 19, 38, 176, 213
Armacost, Michael (US Under Secretary for Political Affairs): on inclusion of PDRY with USSR-influenced states in crisis, 95, 97
al-Asnadj (FLOSY): in YAR government,

United States of America (*Cont.*)
and destabilisation, 80–1, 87, 90, 91, 255–6; and East-West conflict, 80, 85–7, 180, 196, 204, 208, 214, 217–18, 221, 226, 253, 255, 258; and Horn of Africa, 80, 86; and Indian Ocean, 180, 204; and interests in Arabian Peninsular and Gulf, 62, 79, 92, 180, 183, 203, 205, 221, 258; and Iran, 196; and military deployment, 195, 196, 204, 247; and Oman, 82, 85, 91, 189, 196, 247; and opposition to PDRY, 80–1, 96–7, 131, 125, 214, 218; and Saudi Arabia, 202; and 1979 war PDRY/YAR, 87–8, 125, 192, 196; and Red Sea blockade, 82–3; relations with PDRY, 23, 31, 38, 61, 62, 79–98, 179, 240; on terrorism and PDRY, 88; and unity PDRY/YAR, 249; and YAR, 85, 86–87, 126, 128, 137, 192, 196 *see also* Armacost, Michael; Atherton, A.; Brezezinski, Zbigniew; Bush, George; Carter, Jimmy; Carlucci, Frank; Casey, William; CIA; Crawford, William; Findley, Paul; Haig, Alexander; Javits, Jacob; Johnson, Lyndon; Kissinger, Henry; Kraft, Joseph; Perry, Dale; Reagan, Ronald; Sisco, Joseph; Twinam, Joseph; Vance, Cyrus

Ustinov, Dmitri, Marshal (Minister of Defence, USSR): and 1978 meeting with ʿAlī Nāṣir Muḥammad, 191

Vance, Cyrus (US): meetings with Muṭiyyaʿ, 85, 240

Vietnam, 23, 26, 28, 52, 192, 193, 200, 201, 204, 224, 225, 226, 258

al-Waḥḥāb, ʿAbd al-Raḳīb ʿAbd (opposition leader YAR): death, 112

al-Walī, ʿAbd al-ʿAzīz ʿAbd (Minister for Industry & Planning), 34–6; death of, 37, 45–6

Warsaw Treaty Organisation, 193–4, 207

West Germany *see* Federal Republic of

Wilton, John (PDRY Deputy High Commissioner, UK), 12

World Bank, 61

World Federation of Democratic Youth, 56

World Peace Council, 56

Yaḥyā, Anīs Ḥassan, 24; and internal divisions, 40

Yao Tilin (Vice Premier, China): and 1985 visit to Oman, 223

Yemen Arab Republic (YAR): and Arabian Peninsular, 108; arms sales to, 203; author's interview of officials in, 5; and China, 220, 223, 224, 225, 227; and 1970 civil war, 108; and 1967 coup, 17; and 1974 coup, 120, 189; and 1986 crisis, 7, 50, 52, 133–136, 173, 214, 215; and Egypt, 10–11, 17, 62, 108; and export of revolution, 3, 141, 230; and factionalism, 108, 120–4, 128, 163, 205; and FLOSY, 121; and FRG, 78; and historical links, 101, 104–5, 109; and independence, 9, 39, 179; and independence in South Yemen, 9; and MAN, 19; and NDF, 129, 130, 173; and NF, 18; and NLF, 119; and oil, 133; and opposition to PDRY, 35, 42, 47, 93, 116, 119, 120, 124, 127, 134–5, 186, 225, 249; and PDRY cooperation against royalists in, 111; and PDRY support for opposition to, 3, 6, 7, 22, 24, 32, 62, 110, 116, 120, 124, 127, 129, 186, 228, 230, 232; and diplomatic relations with PDRY, 27, 30, 36, 38, 53, 56, 59, 60, 111, 119, 120, 122, 123, 124, 129, 130, 131, 133, 134, 174, 186, 189, 197, 215, 223, 225, 247, 252; revolution in, 9, 62; and Saudi Arabia, 108, 109, 111, 114, 119, 120, 121, 122, 128, 135, 163, 165, 191; and Tripoli Agreement, 119; and unity PDRY/YAR, 3, 21, 22, 28, 32, 79, 91, 99–112, 116, 117, 119–128, 132, 135–139, 171, 173, 186, 196, 197, 223, 225, 233–236, 237–238, 248–249, 250–251, 252; and USA, 79, 85, 86–87, 128, 192, 196, 203; and USSR, 62, 128, 131, 174, 179, 185, 186, 192, 196, 201, 203, 205, 214, 220, 224, 227; and war with PDRY, 88, 110, 117, 124–126, 171, 192 *see also* Afif, Aḥmad Jabir; Agreement on Ceasefire; Agreement on Development Cooperation; Agreement Between the Governments . . ; Agreement of Principles . . ; Agreement on Unity; al-ʿAlim, Abd Allāh ʿAbd; al-ʿAmrī; al-ʿAynī, Muhsin; Constitution, 1970; al-Ghanī, ʿAbd al ʿAzīz ʿAbd; al-Ghashmī, Ahmad Husayn; al-Hadjrī, ʿAbd Allāh; al- Hamdī, Ibrạhīm; Imam; al-Iryānī, ʿAbd al-Karīm; Labour Party; Sālih, ʿAli ʿAbd Allāh; Sallāl; Supreme Yemeni Council; Twenty Year Treaty; Unification Congress; United Democratic Yemen; al-Wahhāb, ʿAbd al-Rakīb ʿAbd

Cambridge Middle East Library

24 JILL CRYSTAL
Rulers and merchants in the Gulf: oil and politics in Kuwait and Qatar

23 DONALD MALCOLM REID
Cairo University and the making of modern Egypt

22 EHUD R. TOLEDANO
State and society in mid-nineteenth-century Egypt

21 FRED HALLIDAY
Revolution and foreign policy: the case of South Yemen 1967–1987

20 GERSHON SHAFIR
Land, labor and the origins of the Israeli–Palestinian conflict 1882–1914

19 MAHFOUD BENNOUNE
The making of contemporary Algeria, 1830–1987
Colonial upheavals and post-independence development

18 DANIEL J. SCHROETER
Merchants of Essaouira
Urban society and imperialism in southwestern Morocco, 1844–1886

17 TIMOTHY MITCHELL
Colonising Egypt

16 NADIA HIJAB
Womanpower
The Arab debate on women at work

15 BENNY MORRIS
The birth of the Palestinian refugee problem, 1947–1949

14 MIRIAM COOKE
War's other voices
Women writers on the Lebanese civil war

13 MARY C. WILSON
King Abdullah, Britain and the making of Jordan

12 SEVKET PAMUK
The Ottoman empire and European capitalism 1820–1913
Trade, investment and production

11 JOHN C. WILKINSON
The Imamate tradition of Oman

10 SAMIR A. MUTAWI
Jordan in the 1967 war

9 NORMAN N. LEWIS
Nomads and settlers in Syria and Jordan, 1800–1980

8 OLIVIER ROY
Islam and resistance in Afghanistan

7 JUDITH E. TUCKER
Women in nineteenth-century Egypt

6 RAYMOND A. HINNEBUSCH JR
Egyptian politics under Sadat
The post-populist development of an authoritarian-modernizing state

5 HELENA COBBAN
The Palestinian Liberation Organisation
People, power and politics

Cambridge Middle East Library

4 AFAF LUTFI AL-SAYID MARSOT
Egypt in the reign of Muhammad Ali

3 PHILIP S. KHOURY
Urban notables and Arab nationalism
The politics of Damascus 1860–1920

2 NANCY ELIZABETH GALLAGHER
Medicine and power in Tunisia, 1780–1900

1 YORAM PERI
Between battles and ballots
Israeli military in politics

FRED HALLIDAY is Professor of International Relations at the London School of Economics and Political Science. He is the author of *Arabia without Sultans* (1974); *Iran: dictatorship and development* (1978); *Threat from the East?* (1981); *The making of the second cold war* (1983) and co-author of *The Ethiopian revolution* (1982).